ORGANIZATIONAL COMMUNICATION

SAGE ANNUAL REVIEWS OF COMMUNICATION RESEARCH

Other Books in This Series:

Volume 13

SAGE ANNUAL REVIEWS OF COMMUNICATION RESEARCH

Organizational Communication:
Traditional Themes and New Directions

ROBERT D. McPHEE
and
PHILLIP K. TOMPKINS
Editors

 SAGE PUBLICATIONS Beverly Hills London New Delhi

For information address:

SAGE Publications, Inc.
275 South Beverly Drive
Beverly Hills, California 90212

SAGE Publications India Pvt. Ltd.
M-32 Market
Greater Kailash I
New Delhi 110 048 India

SAGE Publications Ltd
28 Banner Street
London EC1Y 8QE
England

Printed in the United States of America

Library of Congress Cataloging in Publication Data

Main entry under title:

Organizational communication.

    (Sage annual reviews of communication research ; v. 13)
    Bibliography: p.
    1. Communication in organizations—Addresses, essays,
lectures. I. McPhee, Robert. II. Tompkins, Phillip K.
III. Series.
HM131.6695   1985   302.3′5   85-14488
ISBN 0-8039-2186-1
ISBN 0-8039-2187-X (pbk.)

FIRST PRINTING

CONTENTS

INTRODUCTION AND AFTERWORD

Phillip K. Tompkins and Robert D. McPhee

IN HER PREFACE to her translation of Derrida's *Of Grammatology* (1976), Gayatri Spivak recounts the perils or sins that are liabilities of an introductory or prefatory essay. She notes the derivation of "pre-face" from the Latin for "saying beforehand" (implicitly a lie, because a preface is commonly written after, not before, the text), and the danger that such a prior statement detracts from the dynamic argument of the main text, destroying that text in a "gesture of homage and parricide" (!; pp. x-xi). Similarly, one might worry that our introduction/afterword is an attempt to "take in" our readers, and to have the last word against our contributors. We will try to avoid these temptations, limiting ourselves to two tasks: explicating some unifying themes we have found in these essays, and explaining the special choices of topics and chapter content included in this book. The "afterword" in our title acknowledges that this was not written until the chapters were before us—luckily so, because the chapters have emerged in forms often differing substantially, and for the better, from plans outlined long ago in our original prospectus.

In our original plan, we asked the chapter authors to spend one third or so of their essays reviewing an important body of past literature related to organizational communication, and the rest of their space exploring new directions—recasting traditions, calling for future research or critique, theory building, even reporting study results. We thus expected to produce the result reflected in the subtitle "Traditional Themes and New Directions." But as we read the resulting papers, we were surprised at how well beyond our expections our authors exploited the dual focus on tradition and innovation.

We can place this theme of tradition and novelty in perspective by stressing the recent growth of interest in organizational communication and the sense of excitement attendant to that growth. The bare facts: In the past five years both the Academy of Management and the Speech Communication Association, following the earlier example of the International Communication Association, have created full-fledged divisions of organizational communication, which in turn have organized lively and well-attended programs at recent conventions. This volume itself, number 13 in the Sage Annual Reviews of Communication Research, is the first on organizational communication to take its place alongside previous volumes devoted to such research areas as interpersonal and mass communication. The annual conferences on Interpretive Approaches to Organizational Communication (sponsored by the Speech Communication Association and the International Communication Association), held high in the Wasatch Mountains at Alta, Utah, since 1981, have certainly helped to stimulate interest and creativity in the area. Oddly, the uncertain economy of the last eight to ten years has also added to the interest in a noneconomic approach to organizations. It is well known that new Ph.D.s in "org comm" from the few established programs can be selective about job offers from both the "real world" and the academic world, whether from business schools or communication departments. For all these reasons, the readers, researchers, and writers of organizational communication number more now than ever before. But before we go too far in acclaiming this growth, we should admit to the reader that the unquestioned dean, if not founder, of the field of organizational communication—W. Charles Redding—characterizes in the next chapter the short history of the field, including recent progress, as a "stumbling toward identity."

With this growth comes a tendency for academics to individuate (not to say distinguish) themselves by seeking new lands to conquer and plunder: In academic jargon, they (we) proclaim paradigm shifts, new object domains, new theories or perspectives. We support such efforts (and engage in them ourselves), but we regret their overblown self-description. When a social scientist thinks he or she has created something "new under the sun," usually he or she is merely self-centered, forgetful, or ignorant of precursors and roots in the past. And in neglecting precursors and roots, the social scientist often forgoes the most important evidence and persuasive support for the new position.

To enlarge on this claim, we turn to one of the wisest, if briefest, reflections on social science we know. Mancur Olson, responding positively to high-minded critics of his network theory of economics, was reminded of his reading of Einstein's popular book on the theory of relativity. He had been struck by the observation that Einstein's proudest moments were those in which his predictions and calculations were shown to be in perfect agreement with Newton's. Einstein, of course, was also pleased that his theory could explain a few things the prior theory could not, but, to repeat, his proudest moments were in showing that his new directions could conform with the established findings of tradition. Olson (1983: 29) then contrasted that case with the social sciences and humanities, where so many "seem to assume that intellectual advance requires first the refutation of existing orthodoxies and then putting wholly new concepts in their place—that advances occur on the intellectual battlefield and that every victory implies a defeat."

Organizational studies in general and organizational communication in particular have recently exhibited the tendencies decried by Olson. Yesterday's hard-won innovations in ideas and methods are now despised by some. But if Olson is correct in comparing such intellectual activity to the "world of fad and fashion," it is hard to "repress the thought that we will not have to wait very long before some of the current enthusiasms are belittled by a new cohort of scholars" (Olson, 1983: 29). It seems a wiser, less wasteful course to take pains to show congruence with a tradition before flashing the new ideas and phenomena that one's innovation highlights, labels, and/or accounts for.

In fact, the recent innovations in organizational communication are not so recent or new after all. Tompkins (1983) showed that the "interpretive" approach to organizational research can be traced back to Weber; indeed, Weber called his work "interpretive sociology" because it was based on the subjective understanding, *Verstehen*, of the organizational actors. Another presumed innovation, the "cultural approach," often justifies itself with a by-now familiar quotation from Clifford Geertz. Geertz's sentence is often edited in the process of quotation, giving the impression that the metaphor of culture as a spider's web is in sharp contrast with the past. The complete sentence, however, runs thus: "Believing, with Max Weber, that man is an animal suspended in webs of significance he himself has spun, I take culture to be those webs, and the analysis of it to be therefore not an experimental science in search of law but an interpretive one in search of meaning" (Geertz, 1973: 5). In short, both the interpretive and cultural approaches have a tradition reaching back as far as one of the founders of organizational social science. At least Geertz thinks so—and so do we. It is a strength of the contributions to this volume that the authors have grounded their new directions in the traditions of organizational communication, without uncritically accepting and applying the traditions.

Perhaps the clearest and most dramatic example is William Richards's chapter on network analysis. It was Richards's talent and rigor that propelled the tradition of network analytic studies in organizational communication studies at Michigan State University. Richards elaborated a system of rigorous definitions of network groups and roles as he devised the software now called NEGOPY. In his chapter, Richards shifts from the common tendency to treat networks as "real things," scientists' constructs of actual behaviors, to defend what we might label a "networks as subjectively construed by organization members" view. He uses insights from this constructivist perspective to cast doubt on research critical of subjective methods of gathering data about networks. The chapter by W. Charles Redding is made no less dramatic by his admission that our field began (and we emphasize that Redding was present at the creation of organizational communication) with uncritical acceptance of a narrow management bias and with methods designed according to the suggestions of logical positivism—"character traits" that we have not fully outgrown to this day. Some kind of bias is inevitable in any theorizing, but it is clear in retrospect that the positivistic currents of the 1950s and 1960s made invisible the proclivity to see problems from the top manager's desk alone. We think it would be equally erroneous, though, to abandon totally the ideas, findings, and methods that received initial justification from positivist philosophy. Instead, a correction is called for in which a variety of methods can bring forth evidence in support of and explained by theories not modeled or constrained by the principles and prejudices of traditional empiricism.

The other chapters work out similar shifts, in two main ways. Marshall Scott Poole's chapter on climate, Joseph Turow's chapter on resource dependency and mass media organizations, and Rebecca Blair, Karlene Roberts, and Pamela McKechnie's chapter on hierarchical communication (and we would include Richards's chapter here) all provide "new twists on traditional topics." These essays use a central generative insight to *transform* a traditional topic area and body of literature. Poole relies on the central structurational insight of the "duality of structure" to reorient climate research, arguing that a whole organization can have a single climate structure, which different subgroups interpret and enact in different ways, according to their unique experiences and powers. Turow illustrates how the products of mass media organizations may be explained anew by focusing on strategic responses by managers and creators to pressures from outside organizations. Blair et al. analyze the range of new phenomena and processes, spawned by information processing and artificial intelligence technologies, that will reconfigure the traditional subfields of vertical communication and communication networks. All four of the chapters have important new methodological implications: They point out, and illustrate to varying degrees, new ways of approaching and studying traditionally central topics of the field of organizational communication.

Our other chapters—Robert McPhee's on formal structure, Phillip Tompkins and George Cheney's on identification and control, Charles Conrad and Mary Ryan's on power, and Linda Putnam's on bargaining—proceed by *constructing* a new perspective, often from "parts" drawn from various fields and topical literatures. McPhee's chapter reinterprets the formal structure of an organization as a communication process, and argues that the communication process itself helps separate and give identity and varying powers to worker, support staff, and top management roles. Tompkins and Cheney articulate a new mode of control, unobtrusive concertive control, which operates via employee identification with the organization; they, too, interpret this mode of control as a process of communication of decision premises. Conrad and Ryan construct a perspective via contrast: They describe traditional and "symbological" (or, in some ways, interpretive-critical) models of power, then depart from both of these to concentrate on a "radical-critical" approach that avoids certain reifying assumptions of consensus and rationality that the other two approaches share. Putnam integrates the multidisciplinary literature on bargaining around three perspectives: traditional (game-theoretic or economic), process (cognitive and learning centered, interaction oriented), and context (centered on organizational structural impacts). She sketches a unifying framework that can draw on insights from all three approaches.

A second unifying thread, which we identify much more tentatively, is a general movement away from the focus on observable behaviors that has characterized most past writing on organizational communication. In these essays, concepts and propositions are not often cast at the level of behaviors. Nor do they primarily refer to *systems* of behaviors or events. In part, this is a movement away from positivism, as we have noted, and toward the "interpretive" approach (Putnam and Pacanowsky, 1983). But that description seems to us too gross—none of our authors advocates grounded research, phenomenology, or hermeneutic philosophy, the prototypical interpretive paradigms. Rather, we might better describe this movement as motion toward a "field view" of communication. The message contents, network patterns, and strategic uses of communication are discussed with special emphasis on their general organizational properties and significance. The organization is portrayed as a complex of meaning centers, interpretation centers, power centers, decision centers, and—most of all—communication centers, with interchange of messages among these centers overshadowed by the multiply understood relations among centers to which the messages contribute and within which they are interpreted. Thus Putnam argues that an interaction-process approach to particular negotiations must be modified by attention to the context of bargaining, which includes a history of many kinds of negotiation in various parts of the organization. For Poole, all climate-relevant messages have an obvious systemic significance, constrained to some extent by general climate while adapting it to the particular context of the communicators. Similar examples could be given for all the chapters. The main implication to be drawn here is that theories of organizational communication must describe the "field" of meaning and action generated by communicators. That field is not observable, so theory is not merely a collection of empirical propositions, and studies must be designed to help describe the fields in ingenious ways.

There is another perspective, the "critical," that is often treated as a variant or subcategory of the interpretive paradigm, and that surfaces in several chapters as a theme we might label "microhegemony." Hegemony is the societal process of control even of opposed groups through reality creation (ideology articulation, consensus-making, justification). Its typical treatment at a macroanalytic level can be joined by a more particular development of an analysis of microhegemony as a communicative process productive of "organizational common sense." Such a focus has already proven fruitful (Willis, 1977; Burawoy, 1979), and the chapters in this volume by Turow on socialization and control in mass media organizations, Tompkins and Cheney on the unobtrusive control processes of inculcating decisional premises and conscripting identification, Poole on "kernel" climates and their relation to subgroup "climates," McPhee on domination through the communication of formal structure, and Conrad on the relation of power to identity and rationality all add up to a specifically communicational analysis of microhegemony. Although stated in somewhat different terms, the notions of these chapters have much in common and provide valuable conceptual bases for the discovery and critique of the "false consciousness" present in organizations.

Having discussed the three common themes we detect in these essays, we move to our second task: explaining the topics and contents of chapters.

Considered positively, this is an easy task. We chose topics that were reasonable in "size," and about which there was a major tradition of communication-relevant studies and ideas available. (The first chapter was a partial exception: We felt that our exploding field needed a greater "sense of tradition" than was available from any accessible source we knew of.) For authors, we sought scholars who have made a significant and ongoing contribution to their topical areas, and we were very pleased that our present group chose to accept our request to write. Indeed, who could speak as authoritatively as W. Charles Redding on the entire tradition of organizational communication? Our objective in this case was not merely to obtain a historical narrative from Redding, valuable as that would be, but also to give him the opportunity to *profess* his firmest convictions while surveying the past and future potential of organizational communication. Similarly, we tried to give the other chapter authors space to develop the lines of thought they and others will follow in advancing our field.

One recent development is, however, conspicuous by its absence: the topic of organizational "culture." A recent popular vogue of the topic of "corporate cultures" (see Deal and Kennedy, 1982; Allen and Kraft, 1982) has accompanied a multitude of valuable theoretical, methodological, and empirical articles on the topic (Pacanowsky and O'Donnell-Trujillo, 1982a, 1982b; Administrative Science Quarterly, 1983; Pondy et al., 1983). Of course, as we have noted, only the faddishness and general consciousness of this topic is new—social scientists have for decades dealt insightfully with organizational culture. Indeed, the problem we perceived was that the domain of culture is vast, too vast and inchoate a topic to occupy a single chapter. Two papers delivered at the 1984 convention of the Speech Communication Association reinforced our belief. The first, by Conquergood (1984), advocated the application of Mary Douglas's (1982a, 1982b) grid/group schema, drawn from the larger field of cultural anthropology, to the study of organizational communication/culture. Nearly every chapter in this volume addresses either grid (formal control mechanisms, such as rules and hierarchy) or group (control through allegiance to community) concerns or both, and therefore comments on primary Conquergood uses to describe organizational culture. Although this schema, like all 2 × 2 tables, invites and even begs for the charge and criticisms of positivism, one is hard pressed to gainsay Conquergood's (1984: 9) diagnosis that the current approach to communication/culture is "piecemeal description" and in need of more systematic analysis.

The other SCA paper, by Sotirin (1984), was more ambitious in its attempt to use the cultural metaphor as synthesizing focus on current approaches to organizational communication. One such current approach was the structurational view of organizational climate initiated by Poole and McPhee (1983) and developed more fully and systematically by Poole in his chapter in this volume. Another current approach classified by Sotirin as "cultural" was an early version of this volume's chapter by Tompkins and Cheney. So, it seems clear, a number of different chapters can potentially be claimed by the climate domain/ perspective. But even Sotirin's analysis rests on a perception of rival orientations and paradigms, each of which claims that its own analysis of culture is the correct one; and she notes that "culture" is commonly regarded as an "amalgamation" or "constellation" concept, including almost everything in the domain of social science (except, notably, formal structure). Hence our decision to let cultural material be treated in several chapters, but be the private preserve of none.

We are proud of the contributions that follow, sad only that we can claim so little credit for their obvious quality. They do not deal with simple matters or develop in a simple way, but we do not doubt that, if you give the chapters the care and attention in reading that the authors did in writing, you will come to share our conviction that it is an exciting time to be a writer, researcher, or reader in the field of organizational communication—or even to be an editor.

Chapter 1

STUMBLING TOWARD IDENTITY
The Emergence of Organizational Communication as a Field of Study

W. Charles Redding

He who . . . considers things in their first growth and origin, whether a state or anything else, will obtain the clearest view of them.

—Aristotle, (*Politics*, 1252a; Jowett, trans.)

THE FRAME OF REFERENCE

First, a disclaimer. This chapter is not intended to be a comprehensive summary of the total history of organizational communication. One crucial limitation is that the primary concern is with a *field of study* rather than with "real-life" *practice*. Moreover, attention will be focused especially on a selected period, the decades of the 1940s and 1950s, because it was during this span of roughly twenty years that the academic field of organizational communication, albeit in a rather erratic and accidental manner, emerged as an identifiable entity. Hence relatively brief treatment will be accorded the events preceding and following these decades.

I have said that the concern here is with study rather than practice. But this is not meant to imply that I ignore the decisive impact that practice has had on study. It is common to observe that in almost every area of human inquiry, practice has preceded systematic conceptualization. Writing a history of the actual practice of organizational communication—even if it were limited to the twentieth century—would be both an attractive and a valuable endeavor. Such a history is yet unwritten—a fact much to be deplored.

AUTHOR'S NOTE: I wish to acknowledge the valuable suggestions of Dr. R. Wayne Pace, Professor of Communication, Brigham Young University, who kindly made available to me a copy of his unpublished seminar handout on the history of the field.

Addressing ourselves, then, to the academic field now known as organizational communication, we begin by acknowledging two overriding facts: (1) the subject matter associated with the field has been designated by a variety of labels, of which "organizational communication" is the most recent. Indeed, this label did not achieve general use until the late 1960s, or perhaps even the early 1970s; moreover, in the 1980s other labels frequently emerge. (2) Academic course work and research programs dealing with organizational communication always have been, and still are, offered in a bewildering diversity of departments or other administrative units. These include such entities as business administration, psychology, sociology, speech, speech communication—and, finally, communication. Thus if we were to define "field" in terms of a single departmental "home," we might be forced to conclude that no field of organizational communication exists. However, I shall adopt the position that, as of the 1980s, we can indeed identify the field in terms of its *literature* (regardless of source), rather than its academic affiliation. Having said as much, we must also acknowledge that, as of the mid-1980s, it has been in departments labeled "communication," "speech," or "speech communication" that the central core of the field has been most frequently articulated.

This chapter will not attempt to provide a literature review, much less a "state of the art" evaluation. I will, or course, identify important conceptual trends as they are reflected in publications or other events. But, with minor exceptions, the detailed contents of articles, books, or research reports will not be examined. Readers are urged to reflect upon the term "emergence." It is used here to mean that our main concern is with answering the question: *How did the field get started?* Who were the pioneers? Where were they located? What kinds of ideas and problems occupied their attention? "Emergence," then, is contrasted with "growth and development." Only a comprehensive history could deal usefully with all the twists and turns, over a period of several decades, that have characterized our concepts, hypotheses, methodologies, major findings, and philosophies. A brief chapter cannot accomplish this task.

I begin by considering a lexical matter: the label "organizational communication." This is a convenient way to obtain a quick overview of the field as a whole. Discussion follows of such topics as the early fixation on "business and industrial" as the modifier of "communication," names and events associated with the years of World War II (for example, "TWI"), influential publications of two periods ("the seminal years" and "the decade of crystallization"), the decisive impact of the "human relations" ideology, and the ways in which ideas were transmitted from place to place—with the result that strategically placed people arrived at a consensus: A field emerged.

A NOTE ABOUT "ROOTS"

Any book-length history of the field would assign a significant amount of space to such precursors as "business English," "business and professional speaking," "basic communication skills," and the like. In addition, the role of popularizers such as Dale Carnegie (whose courses have had an enormous impact upon managers in numerous companies), would require careful assessment. The business English, business speech, and Carnegie courses all drew, although in different ways, upon an established tradition of rhetorical principles: methods of adapting discourse to specific audiences of listeners and readers, stylistic devices, language usage, vocal delivery, and other principles. One of the most important "roots," then, of the field of organizational communication is unquestionably what we call today "rhetorical theory."

This is not the whole story, of course. Our hypothetical book would also have to deal with other roots, especially those classifiable under the rubrics of industrial psychology (roughly dating from World War I), traditional management theory (including "scientific management"), and "industrial journalism." It must be remembered that, beginning around the turn of the century and extending beyond the 1940s, the dominant form of organizational communication *practice* was the "house organ" (that is, the employee publication; see Peters, 1950: 46-54); and the field of study associated with employee publications was (and is) journalism.

Another root is what I would call "proto-human relations." By this term I refer to an identifiable, but unorganized, body of thought that was widespread during the period roughly between 1900 and 1940. This philosophy, closely allied to "welfare capitalism," advocated treating employees like human beings instead of machines, which in turn implied being approachable and friendly, using tact in giving orders, being patient in answering questions and giving instructions, and, in general, being a "nice person." Proto-human relations, despite its benevolent intentions, was flagrantly paternalistic and management-oriented. In fact, many of the famous prescriptions in Dale Carnegie's *How to Win Friends and Influence People* (1936)—in addition to those derived from rhetorical theory—could be categorized as advocating proto-human relations.

No doubt the reader could suggest other roots. However, within the limitations of this chapter, none of these extremely important historical forces can be accorded anything more than this passing reminder. To recapitulate: A complete history of the academic field of organizational communication would need to include significant discussions of at least the following "roots":

- business English
- business speech, including business and professional speaking
- basic communication skills (including applications of general semantics)
- Dale Carnegie courses
- industrial psychology (of the 1910-1940 era)
- traditional management theory
- industrial journalism
- "proto-human relations" (about 1900-1940)

Let us begin now by considering a linguistic phenomenon: the label "organizational communication."

"ORGANIZATIONAL COMMUNICATION": THE STORY OF A LABEL

Labels can be no more than lexical tags, or they can speak volumes about their referents. When "business and industrial" was generally dislodged by "organizational" as a modifier, this symbolized what I nominate as the most important conceptual shift in the history of our field: the final acceptance of the blatantly obvious fact that the world is full of many kinds of organizations in addition to just those we call businesses and industries.

Moreover, the noun term "communication" is also noteworthy. It gradually came to replace narrower labels denoting such specific skills (or processes) as "speaking" and "writing," not to mention even narrower ones like "public speaking," "report writing," and "corporate publications." Although we can find instances of "communication"—or its variants, "communicate" and "communications"—in the business literature as early as the late nineteenth century, the term appears to have become popular only after the United States entered World War II. I have identified a six-year period, 1942-1947, as "The Seminal Years" in the history of the field. It was during these years that "communication" emerges repeatedly in both academic and nonacademic publications. However, the cases in which "communication" was paired with "organizational" were extremely rare until the 1960s. We now get down to specifics about the phrase "organizational communication," in its literal lexical form.

Let it be said at once: The answer to the question, "Who first used the label 'organizational communication,' and when?" is that nobody knows. However, we can locate some early examples—very few before 1960. First we find that H. A. Simon, renowned authority on organization theory (and a Nobel laureate), used a phrase very similar to "organizational communication." In his classic treatise *Administrative Behavior* (1945) he discussed "organization communications" systems. Note the omission of the suffix *al*, and the plural *s*.

Simon left no doubt, in his separate chapter devoted entirely to "communication" (the generic term, no *s*), that the basic process of communication was of the highest importance in his theory of organizational behavior. Simon is famous for positing the "decisional premise" as the fundamental unit of organizational functioning. It was in this frame of reference that he offered a formal definition of communication as "any process whereby decisional premises are transmitted from one member of an organization to another" (Simon, 1945: 154).

However, despite his sophisticated theorizing, Simon was also able to slip into a less exalted view of communication in the organizational setting. Modern readers may be startled, for example, by such pronouncements as the following:

> The crucial point is whether the recipient of an order, or of any other kind of communication, is influenced by the communication in his actions or decisions, or whether he is not. The problem of securing employees' compliance with a safety rule is not *very different from the problem of securing a customer's acceptance of a particular brand of soap* [Simon, 1945: 164; emphasis added].

Indeed, Simon proposed that there are just two basic dimensions characterizing all organizational messages: "intelligibility" and "persuasiveness" (p. 171).

Those who are familiar with "Boulwarism," the labor relations philosophy espoused by Lemuel R. Boulware, vice president of General Electric in the 1940s and 1950s, may recall that Boulware also insisted that persuasion was the major objective of corporate (that is, managerial) communication. It is not enough, Boulware said repeatedly, for management to "do right." The company must also *persuade* its employees that it is indeed doing right. In one of his earliest published statements (1948), Boulware urged managers to *sell* their employees (see Baritz, 1960: 242; also Northrup, 1964: 25-36). Whether Boulware had read Simon (1945) is, of course, impossible to determine. What matters is that, at least in some limited respects, the views of the theoretician Simon and of the corporate manager Boulware overlapped. This can be said while at the same time honoring Simon for having made some of the most creative and sophisticated contributions to the theory of communication in this century.

In 1951 Bavelas and Barrett, two mathematically oriented experimenters, published a paper that has become one of the most influential publications in the history of the field—a paper with the precise lexical phrase "organizational communication" in its title: "An Experimental Approach to Organizational Communication." Like Simon, they postulated communication as a fundamental determinant of organization:

> *Simon (1945):* "Communication is absolutely essential to organization."

> *Bavelas and Barrett (1951):* It [communication] is the essence of organized activity and is the basic process out of which all other functions derive."

The authors went further to suggest a minimum of three basic dimensions of organizational communication: (1) message content, (2) technique (for example, rhetorical devices), and (3) channels. Then they proceeded to devote their research report entirely to the last of these: channels—or networks. The paper described experimental manipulations of communication channels in small (five-person) groups, operating in highly controlled laboratory settings. Results were couched largely in terms of effects upon speed and accuracy of problem solving, as compared with effects upon "morale."

Although conducted with small groups in restricted settings, and with highly artificial modes of transmitting messages, the Bavelas and Barrett (1951) study was a pioneer in the network tradition. If we were to select a single contribution as the starting point for the network approach to the study of organizational communication, the Bavelas and Barrett paper would probably qualify. However, it would have to share this particular "first" with another influential paper published the same year (1951) by Jacobson and Seashore. The difference between the two is important. Whereas Bavelas and Barrett concerned themselves with a small laboratory group operating under artificial, controlled circumstances, Jacobson and Seashore applied network analysis to a large real-life organization (n = 204), using a descriptive rather than experimental design. Also, Jacobson and Seashore spoke in terms of "communication practices in complex organizations" and especially of the "communication structure of organization"; at no time did they use the label "organizational communication."

Five years after the Bavelas and Barrett article had appeared, the journal *Advanced Management* printed an essay by Professor Harold Zelko of Pennsylvania State University. A widely known professor of speech and consultant to corporations and government agencies, Zelko addressed himself to the problem of determining the overall effectiveness of a business firm's total communication efforts: "How effective are your company communications?" (Zelko, 1956). What concerns us here is that the label "organizational communication" was a prominent feature of the Zelko article. More important, the article itself was a preview and summary of major topics discussed in a college-level textbook, written by Zelko and a coauthor, the following year: *Management-Employee Communication in Action* (Zelko and O'Brien, 1957).

Both in the article and in the textbook, the phrase "organizational communication" was used in a less-than-comprehensive sense. First, two broad divisions of the total subject were delineated, under the labels "internal communication" and "external communication." No label was offered that would embrace both these divisions: Obviously, the title of the book, *Management-Employee Communication in Action*, could not logically subsume the heading "external." One might imagine that "organizational" would have been reserved to provide a single, comprehensive designator—at least for all "internal" communication phenomena. But such was not the case. The authors, rather surprisingly (as it appears from the vantage point of the 1980s), chose to subdivide "internal communication" into two areas, one of which was called "organizational"; the other, "interpersonal communication." In fact, they went so far as to declare, "It is a *long jump* from organizational to interpersonal communication," adding that "the close, personal relation between supervisor and worker and between employees themselves is the *key* to the communication system" (Zelko and O'Brien, 1957: 21; emphasis added).

One can justifiably regard the Zelko and O'Brien (1957) book as the first comprehensive, college-level *textbook* taking a broad view of *communication* in the organizational setting—as contrasted to earlier titles that consistently dealt only with restricted aspects of communication, such as speaking or writing. Adapting principles taught in speaking and writing courses (especially group discussion), rather than findings from "scientific" research, Zelko and O'Brien set out to provide a general-purpose guide to practical application. Considerably more than half their book was devoted to specific, detailed instructions for improving communication skills—with heaviest emphasis upon the oral situations of public speaking, conversation, interview, and small-group conference. As the authors pointed out in the preface:

> The principles and suggestions in this book are the result of years of experience in organizing and conducting training programs in communication. We have found our proving ground for testing our theories and methods in many consultative activities with groups and industries [Zelko and O'Brien: xiii].

Whereas Zelko and O'Brien (1957) were offering a practical textbook and singing the praises of communication as a humanizing elixir in organizational life, another book came out in the same year that could almost be regarded as a point-by-point rebuttal of Zelko and O'Brien. Chris Argyris—who has since become one of the most famous authorities on organizational behavior—published *Personality and Organization*. Ostensibly a painstaking, scholarly review of the theoretical and research literature (and, in fact, a very good one), the book is much more. It is a well-documented polemic, attacking the typical modern organization as an engine of destruction, frustrating any "mature" needs its members might harbor. It is included in the present discussion because: (a) it singles out "organizational communication" (see p. 142) for special attention, and (b) it brings its heaviest artillery to bear against the then-popular precepts of "human relations," with particular reference to corporate communication programs. Argyris directly challenges many of the most widely touted communication "rules," arguing that most organizational communication practices are based upon such assumptions as "management knows best," and employees "are inherently lazy" or stupid. Communication programs, he charges, are filled with mindless gimmicks derived from the "human relations fad" (Argyris, 1957: 139-174). Although much of the research cited by Argyris is now outdated, contemporary students of organizational communication would do well to go back and read his book, for much of what he says still poses a cogent critique of important concepts and premises in the field.

THE FIXATION UPON "BUSINESS AND INDUSTRIAL" AS THE MODIFIER OF "COMMUNICATION"

Looking at publications that appeared until the end of the 1950s, we find no important documents other than the few already cited that featured "organizational communication" as a title or chapter heading. What terminology, then, was in fashion during those early years? The fact is that no single label earned unanimous support. However, as the years passed, the terms "business," "industrial," and especially "business and industrial" appear to have been used more often than any others. When one adds such adjectives as "administrative," "managerial," "corporate," "employee," or "management-employee," about ninety percent of all the modifiers paired with "communication" are accounted for.

One key development, however, must be noted: the rapid increase—after 1940—in the frequency with which "communication" (or one of its variants) was used. Two psychologists, Sexton and Staudt (1959) published an exhaustive review of the literature, using the overall label "business communication." This is the earliest systematic and comprehensive literature review to be completed in the history of the field. The authors listed a total of 178 titles, the great majority of which had appeared between 1945 and 1958. Of these 178 entries, the only one displaying "organizational communication" in the title was the piece discussed earlier by Bavelas and Barrett (1951). But a quick count indicates that about one hundred, or almost 60 percent of the whole list, contained "communication," "communications," or "communicate" in their titles. Before 1940, any derivative of the verb "communicate" was a rare occurrence in publications dealing with subject matter relevant to this chapter.

However, while "communication" was steadily gaining ground throughout the 1940s, "organization" did not fare nearly so well. Of the 178 items in the Sexton and Staudt (1959) review, only three revealed in their titles any variant of the term "organization." This is a highly significant fact, for it reflects the astounding reluctance, on the part of both scholars and practitioners, to conceptualize "organization" as a genre in its own right. Everyone was preoccupied with one or more particular types of organization: business, industry, the military, government, and the like. But it was not until 1958 that March and Simon published their groundbreaking book *Organizations*. And when the pioneering anthology *Modern Organization Theory* appeared the following year, the editor remarked, "Even ten years ago, it would not have been possible to bring together such a group of papers," considering that "the term 'organization theory' itself would have seemed out of place" (Haire, 1959: 1). Reflecting upon this state of affairs, then, we can hardly be surprised that several years were to pass before the phrase "organizational communication" achieved a semblance of general currency.

The fact is, the label "organizational communication" did not resurface with significant frequency until the late 1960s. A convenient landmark event is the "Conference on Organizational Communication," which took place at the Marshall Space Flight Center, in Huntsville, Alabama, August 8-11, 1967 (Richetto, 1967). Under the direction of Walter Wiesman, internal communication coordinator for the Marshall Center (NASA), the four-day conference brought together management representatives from government agencies and MSFC contractors, as well as academic specialists from four universities. The major address, delivered by Phillip K. Tompkins (then of Wayne State University, and a consultant to the Center) consisted of a comprehensive review of *empirical research* that had been completed in the field up to that time. It was a pioneering "state-of-the-art" effort, and the earliest (to my knowledge) to be published explicitly under the title "organizational communication" (Tompkins, 1967). This 1967 conference at Huntsville was also, so far as can be determined, the first conference specifically devoted to theory and research (along with implications for practice) ever held under the label "organizational communication."

Coincidentally, the earliest known bibliography of the field to be published under the "organizational communication" label also made its appearance in 1967: Voos (1967). Like the NASA conference at Huntsville, this project was also underwritten by a government agency, the Office of Naval Research. Thus, with these two events occurring in the same year, I would nominate 1967 as *"The Year of Official Acceptance"* in our history. (An important literature review and bibliography had, indeed, appeared in 1965, under the authorship of Harold Guetzkow; but its title was "Communications in Organizations" [Guetzkow, 1965]. More about this later.)

With "official acceptance" of the label accomplished in 1967, our attention should now be directed to salient events occuring in the 1940s and 1950s. It was during these decades that the field as we know it today—under whatever label—emerged as a recognizable entity. It is no exaggeration to say that the basic contours of "organizational communication" were determined by around 1950, with no drastic changes for the next fifteen to twenty years. I have suggested that the most influential events of the 1940s and 1950s can be marked off in terms of two periods:

- 1942-1947: The Seminal Years
- 1948-1958: The Decade of Crystallization

The boundary events for the Seminal Years, arbitrarily selected, are as follows: for 1942, the publication of Alexander Heron's pioneering book *Sharing Information with Employees*; and for 1947, the first NTL (National Training Laboratory) conference to be held in Bethel, Maine. The boundary events, again arbitrarily chosen, for the Decade of Crystallization are, for 1948, a cluster of research studies, publications, and other activities (in other words, so much was happening in 1948 that no single event could be isolated); and for 1958, the publication of Janis's *Business Communication Reader*.

THE SEMINAL YEARS: 1942-1947

This period obviously corresponds with the participation of the United States in World War II, supplemented by the immediate postwar years of 1946 and 1947. In my judgment, it was during this period that fundamental concepts were germinating, later to emerge as guiding forces containing an impact that is still exerted today. It was at this time that the notion of "communication," taken as an overarching process beyond speaking and writing, took hold. It was also at this time that "business and industrial" (as we have already mentioned) became entrenched as the accepted view of communication in our field. And it was then that "human relations" (sometimes combined with "proto-human relations") began to assume the position of dominant paradigm for "industrial communication." We now examine these developments in more detail.

ALEXANDER R. HERON: NEGLECTED PIONEER

Suppose the question were asked: "Who wrote the first comprehensive, book-length exposition of our field?" My answer would be Alexander R. Heron, author of *Sharing Information with Employees*, published by Stanford University Press in 1942. The date indicates that Heron had to be writing about practices in American industry during the late 1930s, surely no later than at the time of the Pearl Harbor attack. It is ironic that this ground-breaking volume was not only the first of its kind but that, despite its supply of ideas far in advance of the times, it rather quickly faded into the shadows. I have no hypothesis to explain this unfortunate fact, except that perhaps the book was not "jazzy" enough to serve the suddenly exploding needs of industries scrambling to meet the fantastic goals imposed by the war.

Admittedly, like virtually all other writers in the field during the next twenty years, Heron was unabashedly prescriptive. But at least his prescriptions were based on acute observation of real-life events, viewed through a remarkably humanistic prism. Like a large proportion of the authors writing about this field throughout the 1950s, he devoted much space to written media: employee publications, annual reports, handbooks, and direct mail. However, unlike many of the other writers, Heron left no doubt that oral, face-to-face communication was the most crucial form of human interaction.

THE INFLUENCE OF THE
WARTIME COMMUNICATION COURSES

A powerful stimulus behind the rapid ascendancy of "communication" in the 1940s was the explosive growth of "basic communication(s) skills" courses taught in colleges and universities. When the United States entered the war in late 1941, the country was faced with the formidable problem of converting millions of untrained civilians into either industrial workers or military trainees. Both students and male faculty members were drafted in droves, college enrollments plummeted, and industries sprang up overnight. The spirit of the times was rush, rush, rush. So the conditions were right for encouraging curricular experiments and for discovering new instructional techniques.

Out of all this ferment, one of the major experiments to emerge was the creation of "integrated" courses, in which students were expected to improve their performance in two or more communication skills, taught in a single course rather than separately as "English" or "Speech." Two major reasons appear to have supported this move; one was from expediency, the other from theory. A member of the committee charged with recommending general education courses for the armed services has testified that the committee "decided that the teaching of communication should be integrated into one course" (Davidson, 1945: 143). The governing rationale here seems to have been one of expediency: time for instruction was limited, the supply of competent instructors was short, and "hurry up" was the watchword of the day.

Whether the concept of the basic communication(s) skills course had its beginnings in academe or in the military is a question that need not detain us. Two facts are beyond dispute: (1) The academic and the military streams of thought converged at about the same time. (2) The result of this convergence was to lend massive support to practitioners who were becoming concerned with communication problems in the war industries.

THE TRIPLE ALLIANCE:
ACADEME, THE MILITARY, AND INDUSTRY

What happened during the war years was that the "communication" idea seemed to take hold, almost overnight, on all sides. One reason can be found in the fact that many college faculty members from English and Speech departments served as instructors—whether in uniform or civvies—in the communication skills courses offered in officer training programs (many of these programs were conducted on college campuses). In turn, interaction occurred between these instructors and those who were struggling to establish supervisory training courses, on a crash basis, in industry.

Industry was as much a part of mobilization as the military services themselves. And industry employed numerous academics as trainers and personnel experts. Hence the passage of ideas among people in the military, in academe, and in industry was both rapid and easy during the war. With the military a continuing presence in both colleges and industries, the "military-industrial" complex was more accurately termed the "military-industrial-academic" complex. Both the university and the factory were, for all intents and purposes, subdivisions of the military establishment.

Instructors and trainers in the three environments frequently conversed and read one another's journals. It can be argued that the earliest publications in the *academic* field, as we know it today, were wartime articles advocating the transfer of concepts and pedagogical techniques from military and industrial settings to the campus. Typical examples of such articles include the following titles, all from the *Quarterly Journal of Speech* (similar pieces were appearing in journals for English teachers):

- "Speech Training of Army and Naval Officers" (April 1943)
- "Public Speaking in the Army Training Program" (April 1943)
- "Speaking Instruction in College Military Units" (December 1943)
- "Toward Better Communication in 1944, and After" (April 1944)
- "What Can We Learn from Military Speech Courses?" (April 1945)
- "Discussion Methods in War Industry" (April 1945)

Of particular interest is the last-named article. Its author was Milton Dickens, who had been employed during the war at Douglas Aircraft, on leave from his faculty position at Syracuse University. Dickens (1945) made a strong case for reciprocal learning between college speech professors and industrial trainers, specifically in the area of small-group discussion skills. As a direct result of his experience in war industry, Dickens was instrumental in encouraging work in "industrial communication" when he moved from Syracuse to the University of Southern California—especially when he became head of the Department of Speech there (in 1950).

A Personal Note

My own experience—not really atypical—provides some illumination on the workings of the triple alliance. At the urging (highly persuasive) of my California draft board, I found myself instructing future naval officers in a basic communication course at the University of Washington (Seattle). When the war ended, I returned to Los Angeles, to resume my doctoral studies (in speech) at the University of Southern California. Dickens became one of my major advisers, in addition to supervising my work as an instructor in the basic course. In both the campus classes and "adult extension" workshops, I found it helpful to apply much of what I had learned as an instructor for the U.S. Navy.

During 1946 and 1947, my experience in the military setting and Dickens's observations in a war industry were cited in numerous dialogues that occurred in the department. One important outcome was that the possibilities of a serious program of advanced study and research in "industrial communication" began to be acknowledged. At USC, as at a number of other universities, the triple alliance was providing the cocoon from which organizational communication, as an academic field of study, eventually emerged. (I shall have more to say about all this in a later section of the chapter.)

THE IMPACT OF TWI

TWI stands for "*Training Within Industry*," a label designating a massive crash program sponsored by the War Manpower Commission. Its objective was to design easily disseminated methods for teaching millions of workers in war industries the skills required to boost productivity and efficiency. In order to accomplish this, TWI found it necessary to train the trainers, that is, to train *supervisors* in techniques they would need if they were to be effective with their workers. Thus a gigantic program of supervisory training was born.

Not surprisingly, the core content of these supervisory training courses turned out to be a cluster of oral and written communication skills. The total TWI program actually embraced three subdivisions, each corresponding to a major communication task facing all foremen:

- JIT (Job Instruction Training): dealing with teaching workers how to perform their jobs
- JMT (Job Methods Training): dealing more specifically with work simplification, adapted from traditional time and motion studies ("scientific management")
- JRT (Job Relations Training): dealing with the "human" problems of employees, such as absenteeism, complaints, drunkenness, and motivation

The third item, Job Relations Training, is especially noteworthy, for it was a close analogue of what we know today as "human relations." Another boost for human relations-communication doctrine was provided when "Labor-Management Productions Committees" were introduced as a device to increase productivity. These committees represented an early—and rudimentary—version of participative management.[2]

TWI is an especially good example of the reciprocal influence that "study" and "practice" have on each other. During the war, numerous publications—with the number of copies of some titles running into the millions—were issued by both governmental and industrial sources. Typically, these were concise, highly prescriptive, how-to manuals, designed especially for untutored supervisors. However, despite their preoccupation with immediate application on the shop floor, the TWI publications constituted a boiled-down version of the state of the art in communication at the time.

Most important, the TWI programs (1) reinforced the disposition to perceive communication strictly in the industrial setting, (2) lent support to the view that communication is primarily a matter of teachable skills, rather than a subject for study and research, and (3) helped to identify communication with "human relations" (1940s version).

INTIMATIONS OF THE
BIRTH OF A NEW FIELD

For the United States the war ended with V-J Day in August of 1945. But even before the guns had been silenced, writings were beginning to appear purporting to draw lessons from the war experience, with special attention devoted to those lessons believed to cast light upon the perennial problem of achieving higher and higher levels of productivity at lower and lower costs. What had been widely promulgated in practice—through the basic communication courses, TWI, the Labor-Management Production Committees—now became an increasingly popular subject for study. The components of the Triple Alliance gradually mingled with "human relations" (derived chiefly from the Harvard Business School), so that a coalescing of the concepts "human relations" and "communication" took place. But important differences also remained, as we shall see.

As early as 1945, for example, a manager published an article in *Supervision* in which he announced that the foreman's job is essentially a "selling" job: in order to "win the cooperation of his workers" (Pigors, 1949: 80). In the following year Corson's (1946) much celebrated article posed the provocative question, "Management—Tongue-Tied, Deaf and Blind?" In 1947, Keith Powlison, a vice president of Armstrong Cork, published two highly influential articles, the first in the prestigious *Harvard Business Review*: "Explaining the Facts to Employees" (Powlison, 1947). He was also the author of a two-part exposition with the significant title, "How Can We Help Workers Grasp the Truth About Profits" (Pigors, 1949: 84).

The reader is invited to take special note of the phrases "the facts" and "the truth," along with the explicit statement that the facts and the truth are to be explained not to managers, but to employees. The hidden assumption—not really too well-hidden—was clear: Management was in possession of "the facts," of "the truth"; employees, by and large, were not. The corollary was that employees, when they learned the facts, would come to understand managers' problems, would "cooperate" as "loyal" members of the team, and would therefore work harder and be more productive. The informed worker would be the productive worker. Given this ideology, it is no surprise to discover a steady outpouring of publications in the 1940s (and continuing through the 1950s) advising management on ways of writing clear prose, on using a variety of media to disseminate its messages, and on techniques for winning assent.

Occasional exceptions notwithstanding, the following items are a fair representation of themes dominant during the period of 1945-1947. *Keep in mind that we are looking at the very foundations of the literature in our field.*

- The American Management Association (1947): "Does management get its message across to employees?"
- *Personnel Journal* (1946): "How to communicate with employees"
- *Mill and Factory* (1947): "Basic economic facts for supervisors"—a description of methods one company used to "educate its employees by teaching them the economics of free enterprise" (Pigors, 1949: 82)
- University of Illinois, Institute of Labor Relations (1947): "Selling company policy to employees"

A plausible case could be made that this body of literature constituted a giant leap backwards from many of the positions that Heron had advanced in 1942.

The ideology of rational, omniscient management versus nonrational, uninformed employees. In the opinion of David W. Ewing, a professor in both the business and law schools of Harvard University, this ideology was alive and well in the 1970s. He calls it "the philosophy of 'management knows best' " (Ewing, 1977: 72). And sociologist Charles Perrow, also writing in the 1970s, has written what I would regard as probably the most incisive critique of the entire "human relations" rationale in print (Perrow, 1979). Focusing his attack primarily on early theorists and researchers from two universities—Harvard and Michigan—he describes the assumption, running through all their work, "that management behavior is mainly rational and workers' behavior nonrational" (Perrow, 1979: 83; see pp. 82-95).

It is not difficult to document these charges. In addition to the "popular" advice-to-management articles that were appearing in a steadily swelling stream from 1945 onward, Fritz Roethlisberger himself published two carefully reasoned expositions in the *Harvard Business Review*. Both articles were to become famous as concise statements of human relations doctrine. The first, "The Foreman: Master and Victim of Double Talk," appeared in 1945; the second, "Human Relations: Rare, Medium, or Well-Done?" in 1948 (at the beginning of what I have called the Decade of Crystallization). As coauthor of *Management and the Worker* (Roethlisberger and Dickson, 1939) and as professor of human relations in the Harvard Business School, Roethlisberger's views were indeed authoritative. We shall therefore examine—all too briefly—certain salient themes in these two articles.

Roethlisberger (1945: 287) first established the premise that "the relation between a subordinate and his immediate superior" is the source of most "breakdowns of coordination and communication" in the entire "industrial structure." Next he reiterated what so many practicing managers had been insisting, that a major responsibility of any supervisor is to secure "spontaneity of cooperation at the work level" (p. 291). Then, addressing himself explicitly to communicating and persuasion, he made this recommendation for all who aspire to become the new style of manager:

> The "new" administrator will have to understand better the problem of communication—and not only the aspect of communication *which by persuasion attempts to sell one's own point of view*, but that *which tries to understand and has*

respect for another's point of view . . . as the first step in *obtaining that person's cooperation* [Roethlisberger, 1945: 296-297; emphasis added].

Attention is called especially to the italicized phrases. Although we are urged to listen carefully to the other fellow (that is, the employee), and to understand his [*sic*] "point of view," the focal objective remains: the manager is to secure—by communicating, combining persuasion and empathic listening—the employee's cooperation.

Now we come to one of the core propositions of the human relations ideology, referred to earlier as "management knows best": In any business (or other) organization, explained Roethlisberger, there are two basic "social processes going on." The first, concerned with achieving the main purposes of the organization, results in the "formal organization." The second, concerned with "spontaneous social processes," results in the "informal organization." And the clincher: The formal organization involves behavior that is "essentially *logical* in character"; the second involves such things as "folkway, tradition, social norms, and ideals," which are "*not logical* in character" (Roethlisberger, 1945: 290-291; emphasis added).

Roethlisberger carried the argument one important step further. Informal organization, contrary to what many managers believe, is actually valuable, since it "binds people together," "gives people a feeling of belonging," and facilitates the "fulfillment of human satisfaction." But managers, Roethlisberger warned, seldom perceive this truth. And they often try to "break up" informal groups in their plants. This task, which is actually impossible to accomplish, results in frustration for the workers. "There develops a feeling of being 'pushed around' . . . which often provokes the reaction of trying to push the pusher with equal intensity in the opposite direction" (Roethlisberger, 1945: 291). More basically, the workers' "desire to belong" and to enjoy "intimate association at work with other human beings," when frustrated, induces in the worker behavior that is "*essentially nonlogical and at times irrational.*" Thus a worker does things "to cut off his nose to spite his face"—something "management should know only too well" (p. 293; emphasis added).

From this conclusion it is but a small step to infer that employees' "resistance to change" is typically "nonlogical and at times irrational." And, indeed, when we take note later of the famous Coch and French (1948) field experiment (appropriately titled "Overcoming Resistance to Change"), we shall have before us just one example of how subtly but decisively the rational-management/non-rational-employees premise can shape the design of "scientific" research.

A cautionary note on "human relations" and Dale Carnegie. Roethlisberger took pains to warn us that human relations should not be identified with two counterfeits that frequently circulate under the "human relations" label: (1) the verbal "expression of humane sentiments," and (2) popular compendiums of "rules for 'success,' on how to get other people to do what you want them to, on how to make friends, and on how to be 'happy' and 'human' at the same time" (Roethlisberger, 1948: 106). Writing several years later, William Foote Whyte of Cornell, himself a recognized authority on human relations, made the same points even more vividly:

> The term "human relations" has been used to apply to everything from sex education to race relations. When we tack the phrase "in industry" onto it . . . [to] some it seems to mean "how to win friends and influence people" in an organization. To others it means how to be nice to people [Whyte, 1961: 5].

Obviously, without mentioning his name, both Roethlisberger and Whyte had Dale Carnegie in mind. A comparison of many of Carnegie's prescriptions in *How to Win Friends and Influence People* (1936) and those appearing in the managerial communication literature of the 1940s and 1950s (including several textbooks) reveals unmistakable similarities.

This is not the place to engage in a disquisition on the alleged merits and faults of the Carnegie approach (see Redding, "The Third Sophistic," an unpublished lecture presented to audiences in the 1960s). However, the organizational psychologist Harold Leavitt makes an astute observation:

> Although social scientists have tended to reject it out of hand, current research on influence processes . . . suggests that the Carnegie model is not technically foolish at all. . . . Moreover, much of the early work on "overcoming resistance to change" [Leavitt cites Coch and French, (1948), explicitly] was still responsive to the same manipulative question [Leavitt, 1965, p. 1152].

A bit later we will return to the issue Leavitt has raised. Meanwhile, whether the Carnegie version of human relations is the same as, or different from, that of the academicians, there can be little doubt that the "conventional" literature of industrial communication in the 1940s and 1950s reflected various (sometimes puzzling) combinations of Dale Carnegie, Harvard, and traditional public speaking concepts—a sort of mushy melange, if you will. For better or for worse, neither the Carnegie nor the Harvard versions of human relations can be excluded from the history of our field.

Same theme, but with variations. While Roethlisberger and his Harvard associates were talking about two-way communication between superiors and subordinates (frequently the term "interaction" was used instead of "communication"), managers and popular writers were beginning to jump on the band-wagon. By the late 1940s "two-way" had become almost an automatic modifier of "communication." *Factory Management and Maintenance* (1946) assured its readers that "Two-way information flow pays off"; the *Conference Board Management Record* (1947) argued the merits of "tapping employee thinking"; and a writer in *Modern Management* (1947) urged managers to "recognize the importance of the individual," describing a good corporate program as one that "allows the employee to be heard" (note the word "allows") (Pigors, 1949: 84). The Silver Bay Industrial Conference, sponsored by the YMCA in 1947, chose as its theme "Better Relations through Better Understanding." Several papers dealt with methods of improving communication, within management ranks as well as between management and employees; for example, Mussman (1947) on "Two-Way Communication Within Management" (Pigors, 1949: 68, 83).

Also in 1947 two prominent organizations, each with a reputation for encouraging interaction between business practitioners and academic researchers, published monographs noted for their relatively broad vision of managerial communication:

- The American Management Association, *Checking the Effectiveness of Employee Communication* (Personnel Series, No. 108), containing chapters on what employees want to know and on methods for conducting employee polls
- The National Industrial Conference Board, *Communication Within the Management Group* (Studies in Personnel Policy, No. 80), with chapters on such topics as "informal communications," conferences, and newsletters

The burgeoning popularity of regarding communication as a two-way process should not blind one to the fact that the basic orientation was still downward-directed communication, from management to workers. The benefits of "tapping employee thinking" were primarily to be found in providing information about the employee audience, which in turn would enhance the probability that *management's messages* would be more effective. Hence it is understandable that a large proportion of the early efforts to produce "scientific" findings about industrial communication took one or both of two forms: (a) surveys, or polls, of employee audiences (especially "readership surveys," focusing on such publications as handbooks and house organs); and (b) content analyses of corporate publications, usually linked to surveys. These research efforts were indeed manifestations, albeit highly formalized, of "upward" communication. But even if their rationale was still a downward-directed one, they undoubtedly constituted real progress toward establishing a respected research enterprise.

A bibliographic search suggests that very few titles published before 1948 or 1949 reflected any significant application of the best scientific techniques available at the time. Surveys were usually ad hoc affairs, guided by seat-of-the-pants empiricism; and experiments were almost nonexistent (the Hawthorne studies, completed between 1927 and 1932, are an obvious and dramatic exception).

GROPING TOWARD A "SCIENCE" OF ORGANIZATIONAL COMMUNICATION

With very few exceptions truly scientific work in our field—until well after 1950—was completed by researchers identified with various "*non*communication" areas of interest. These include such academic fiefdoms as social psychology, industrial (later "organizational") psychology, sociology, applied anthropology, "human relations" (an amalgam of several social sciences), business administration, management, economics, and industrial (or labor) relations. The fact is that the typical *scholarly* study of industrial communication in the 1940s and early 1950s treated "communication" not as a focal object of inquiry, but as a *by-product* of investigating some other topic. Indeed, this statement can still be made of a substantial portion of our literature in the 1980s.

It has become commonplace, for example, to trace the underpinnings of our field to such early sources as *The Functions of the Executive* (Barnard, 1938/1968), "Patterns of Aggressive Behavior in Experimentally Created 'Social Climates'" (postulating "autocratic," "democratic," and "laissez-faire" styles of supervision; Lewin et al., 1939), *Management and the Worker* (Roethlisberger and Dickson, 1939), and *Administrative Behavior* (Simon, 1945). When we add to this list other names (such as Carl Rogers, Abraham Maslow, Rensis Likert, Edwin A. Fleishman, James G. March, and Douglas McGregor), a persuasive case can be made to defend the following general proposition: *Most* of the concepts, *most* of the variables, and at least *many* of the hypotheses constituting the stock-in-trade of the typical "industrial communication" researcher of the 1950s and 1960s were lifted from noncommunication sources. It is instructive to recall such topics or concepts as: autocratic versus democratic leadership, information channels, communication nets, serial transmission of messages, superior-subordinate interaction, "uncertainty absorption" (March and Simon, 1958), "initiation of structure" and "consideration" (Fleishman, 1951), directive versus nondirective interviewing, feedback, openness, "Theory X" and "Theory Y" (McGregor, 1960), upward versus downward versus lateral channels, participative decision making, and so on. As students in my seminars of the 1890s repeatedly discovered, even many questionnaire items used in studies conducted by specialists in our field were borrowed from instruments originally devised by social scientists—sometimes dating back as far as the early 1950s.

The purpose here is descriptive, not pejorative. After all, any emerging academic field can be defended for seeking out ideas, wherever they may be found, that promise to advance the cause. And so it is that during those early years in the 1940s contributions were being made toward establishing a corpus of "respectable" theory and research in organizational communication. The labels were typically "industrial," "managerial," "administrative," "employee," or similar terms. And the contributors associated with academic institutions represented a variety of departments. Table 1.1 displays, in chronological order, some of the more significant *academic* writers and publications responsible for creating the conceptual foundations of our field. (Remember that the *non*academic writers frequently—perhaps most of the time—were the original sources for ideas that the academics appropriated for research purposes.)

The entries in Table 1.1 speak for themselves. Clearly, they presage many of the most pervasive currents of thought running throughout the history of our field. When combined with such nonacademic sources as Heron and Corson, discussed earlier, they provide the contemporary reader with a balanced perspective toward the topics and issues that have for years engaged organizational communication scholars.

COLLABORATION:
EARLY STAGES OF CRYSTALLIZATION

We have been considering, in Table 1.1. and in our earlier discussion of the Harvard human relations "ideology," the scattered efforts being made by social

TABLE 1.1
Chronology of Seminal "Academic" Publications: 1942-1947

Prefatory Note: 1940 and 1941
- Likert & Willits, *Morale and Agency Management* (1940; first issued as a series of pamphlets in 1939): summarizing field research program, directed by Rensis Likert for the Life Insurance Sales Research Bureau. Described by Likert himself as "the first study where I used quantitative methods to measure the leadership style of managers and other factors [including communication–WCR] as they affect morale, motivation, productivity, and performance" (ISR Newsletter, 1971, p. 3). The genesis of "System 4" concepts?
- Industrial Relations Section (Dept. of Economics and Social Institutions), Princeton University: brief pamphlet, "Methods of Transmitting Information to Employees" (1941; see Pigors, 1949: 84), believed to be *earliest university-sponsored publication specifically dealing with industrial communication* as such.
- Roethlisberger, *Management and Morale* (1941): contains a discussion of "the problem of communication." Employee morale was a popular topic as U.S. defense industries were cranking up.
  [December 1941–Pearl Harbor–U.S. at war]

1941
- (Heron–nonacademic–has already been noted: some influence on academe.)
- Arensberg and McGregor, "Determination of Morale in an Industrial Company"; one of McGregor's earliest publications; another morale study (communication behaviors involved). Intimations of "Theory X" versus "Theory Y"?

1943
- Kurt Lewin, "Forces Behind Food Habits and Methods of Change": description of government-sponsored field studies using "group-decision" methods to induce housewives to change food-buying habits. Early research allegedly demonstrating superiority of "participative" group discussion over "persuasive" lectures as a means of obtaining behavioral changes.
- Two M.A. theses (Speech Department), University of Denver, directed by Elwood Murray: believed to be *earliest postbaccalaureate degrees awarded by any U.S. university on topics specifically addressed to communication in business or industry.* Data derived from case study and survey: John L. Jacobs, "A History of the Communication in the Bauers Stores of Denver, Colorado"; Antha E. Mallander, "A Survey of Speaking Situations in Business Enterprises of Denver."

1944
- Mayo and Lombard, *Teamwork and Labor Turnover in the Aircraft Industry of Southern California:* human relations study by Harvard Business School researchers, forerunner of series of such studies in the 1950s.
- McGregor, "Conditions of Effective Leadership in the Industrial Organization": further gestation of "Theory Y"?

1945
- (Dickens–already discussed in an earlier context.)
- Gardner and W. F. Whyte, "The Man in the Middle: Position and Problems of the Foreman": early classic; William Foote Whyte, who later became famous after he moved from Chicago to Cornell (1948); Burleigh Gardner, University of Chicago human relations program, author of early and influential book, *Human Relations in*

(continued)

TABLE 1.1 Continued

Industry (1945), with prominent treatment of "the lines of authority and communication." (Whyte has described his theoretical position as "interactionism," with heavy emphasis upon "symbols"; see W. F. Whyte, 1961: 14-37.)

- Marrow and French, "Changing a Stereotype in Industry": pioneering industrial study, under general direction of Kurt Lewin, conducted at famous Harwood Mfg. Co. (about which, more later); same methods and rationale that were used in Lewin's food habits studies *(supra)*.
- Mayo, *The Social Problems of an Industrial Civilization:* essentially a philosophical essay, developing implications of Harvard-Hawthorne human relations model; much consulted in later years by communication people.
- Roethlisberger, "The Foreman: Master and Victim of Double Talk": already discussed in an earlier context; one of two Roethlisberger *HBR* articles expounding basic principles of "human relations" theory (the other, Roethlisberger, 1948).
- Simon, *Administrative Behavior* (1st ed.): already discussed (1945a).
- Simon, "The Fine Art of Issuing Orders" (1945b): a practical-advice piece, similar to dozens of others that appear in managerial journals starting in the 1940s and continuing to the present. Interestingly, that author later was renowned as theorist, and as Nobel Laureate. (So far as I know, this is the only publication in which Simon dealt *exclusively* with industrial communication.)

1946

- Estes, "Speech and Human Relations": although modest in scope, a landmark essay (originally delivered to a speech convention in 1945); author: an officer of U.S. Conciliation Service. I have called Major Estes a traveling "agitator" (see later section of chapter)—he visited campuses from coast to coast urging *speech* professors that they were the best situated to establish a new field of study: industrial communication.
- Survey Research Center, University of Michigan (about which, more later), "A Program of Research on the Fundamental Problems of Organizing Human Behavior" (cited in Likert, 1961b: 341): the first publication issued by the organization that later became famous as the Institute for Social Research (ISR); a prospectus outlining what has since become one of the largest social science research programs anywhere. As an extremely important influence upon organizational communication, ISR will be discussed in more detail later.
- Industrial Relations Section, Princeton University (see Prefatory Note, *supra),* "Channels of Communication in Industrial Organization" (cited by Pigors, 1949: 84): a brief pamphlet, symbolizing continuing attention of this agency upon "industrial communication."

1947

- Selekman, Benjamin M., *Labor Relations and Human Relations:* early classic, one of the first to attempt extension of Harvard-type human relations principles to management-union relations (rather than just to management, the dominant focus of human relations writings). Important implications for later students of organizational communication.
- Warner and Low, *The Social System of the Modern Factory:* an early classic, pioneering in the application of social-anthropological concepts; part of the famous "Yankee City" series, directed by W. Lloyd Warner, University of Chicago.

scientists to lay the foundations of what is now recognized as a respectable academic field. Note the word "scattered." In very few places, before the late 1940s, did there exist organized structures to encourage active *collaboration* among scholars who, although isolated in physical or intellectual space, shared common interests.

The primacy of the "human relations" program in the Harvard Business School is well known. As early as the 1920s, with the active collaboration of Western Electric executives, the team of Harvard researchers, led by Elton Mayo, was interdisciplinary in the full sense of that term. Practicing managers, industrial engineers, sociologists, psychologists, and others coordinated their efforts at the famous Western Electric plant located in Hawthorne (a subdivision of Chicago). The "human relations" phase of the research program (arising from unexpected or "serendipitous" circumstances) began in 1927; because of the impact of the Great Depression, the program was terminated in 1932. Although partial reports and discussions of the Hawthorne findings were issued from time to time (see especially, Mayo, 1933), the first complete, book-length account did not appear until 1939: *Management and the Worker* (Roethlisberger and Dickson, 1939).[3] Interestingly enough, the Harvard people never formally labeled their work as "human relations" until Roethlisberger (1948: 90), in a *Harvard Business Review* article, explicitly "christened" it as such:

> I feel that the time has come to christen this combination [of studies]. . . . For want of a better name I shall hereafter refer to it as *human relations* [emphasis in original].

Excepting only the Mayo and Lombard (1944) study—see Table 1.1—no other major empirical work emerged from the Harvard group until the early 1950s (see Ronken and Lawrence, 1952). (Readers will no doubt recall that 1939 witnessed more than the publication of *Management and the Worker*; there was also the distraction of Hitler's uninvited visit to Poland.) Nevertheless, out of the collaborative, interdisciplinary effort at Hawthorne evolved the crystallization known as "human relations." Also contributing to this were the innumerable pamphlets, lectures, training workshops, and pep talks associated with TWI—especially the diluted version of human relations doctrine promulgated in the JRT (Job Relations Training) programs and the Labor-Management Production Committees (discussed earlier).

Sanborn (1964: 6) was conservative when he characterized the Hawthorne studies as "the first serious scientific attack upon the problems of employee communication." Not only were these studies a scientific effort; they generated concepts, premises, and hypotheses—about such matters as "superior-subordinate communication," "participation," and "informal group processes"—that informed a countless number of organizational communication studies for decades. Despite philosophical and methodological attacks upon the Harvard/Hawthorne approach (see our earlier discussion; also the devastating summary in Perrow, 1979: 90-98), the pervasive influence of Harvard-style human relations doctrine upon both teaching and research in our field is incontestable.[4]

The other human relations bastion: the Institute for Social Research (ISR) at Michigan. There was more—much more—to human relations than Harvard and Hawthorne. Under the direction of Rensis Likert, the Institute undertook what is unquestionably the most ambitious and far-ranging program of social science research anywhere. It is of *overwhelming* importance to everyone associated with organizational communication in particular, because (according to my count) nearly one half of all Ph.D. dissertations in our field, completed by around 1970, made significant use of concepts and data-gathering instruments generated by ISR researchers.

The Michigan/ISR version of human relations is a direct descendant of concepts developed by the renowned social psychologist Kurt Lewin, combined with ideas about supervisory styles and employee morale that Likert had studied in his work for the life insurance industry (see Table 1.1, Likert and Willits, 1940). Although it has an academic ancestry different from Harvard's, the ISR program is built upon premises about human relations—and communication— that are almost indistinguishable from those identified with Harvard. So obvious is this fact that an authority like Perrow has justifiably combined the Harvard and ISR frmes of reference under a single "human relations model" (Perrow, 1979: 90-138).

There were, of course, other social science centers in addition to those at Harvard and Michigan that made contributions to the conceptual foundations of our field. Space does not permit detailed descriptions of these, but Table 1.2 contains a list of them—including Harvard and Michigan—in a chronological format, extending from 1927 to 1948.

A NEW FIELD TAKES SHAPE:
THE DECADE OF CRYSTALLIZATION,
1948-1958

What had been a few freshets of pioneering publications during the Seminal Years became a flood in the decade of 1948-1958. As previously mentioned, Sexton and Staudt (1959) listed 178 titles in their bibliography; of these, approximately 95 percent appeared during the Decade of Crystallization. However, the reviewers, according to my records, omitted about 50 items. Thus in all probability at least 225 titles directly relevant to "industrial communication" were published during this period. (It must be said that most of the topics they dealt with had been suggested, in one form or another, during the Seminal Years.)

CONSCIOUSNESS-RAISING PUBLICATIONS: 1948-1953

The most significant development of the crystallization years is that—in a faltering, almost accidental way—a number of writers, investigators, and

TABLE 1.2
Social Science Programs in Operation by 1948
Making Significant Contributions (in the 1940s or Later)
to the Field of Organizational Communication

Year Program Was Begun	Location	Formal Title or Academic Administrative Unit	Some Well-Known Scholars Associated with Program
1927	Harvard	Business School (informally: "Hawthorne studies"; "human relations")	Elton Mayo (earliest research supervisor); F. J. Roethlisberger, successor; P. Lawrence; G. Lombard; Harriet Ronken
1941	Princeton	Industrial Relations Section (Dept. of Economics and Social Institutions), established 1922	Helen Baker (senior researcher) [See Baker, 1948; Baker, Ballantine & True, 1949]
1943	University of Chicago	Committee on Human Relations in Industry	W. Lloyd Warner (chair); B. Gardner; H. Thelen; Wm. Foote Whyte
1944	Yale	Labor and Management Center	E. Wight Bakke (director); Chris Argyris; F. L. W. Richardson; C. R. Walker
1945	MIT	Research Center for Group Dynamics (moved to Michigan, 1947); later: Sloan School of Industrial Management	Kurt Lewin (founder and director, died 1947); A. Bavelas; D. Cartwright; J. French, R. Lippitt, A. Zander [later: D. McGregor]
1946 1947 1948	University of Michigan	(a) Survey Research Center, 1946; (b) Research Center for Group Dynamics, 1947; (c) Institute for Social Research (ISR), 1948	Rensis Likert (founder and director until retirement, 1970); Angus Campbell (director, 1970—). In addition to Cartwright, French, Lippitt, Zander [see MIT]: R. Kahn; D. Pelz; S. Seashore
[1947]	Bethel, Maine[a]	[National Training Laboratory for Group Development (NTL)]	
ca. 1946?	University of Minnesota	Industrial Relations Center	Dale Yoder (director) [see Paterson & Jenkins, 1948]
1948	Cornell	N. Y. State School of Industrial and Labor Relations	Wm. Foote Whyte [see W. F. Whyte, 1948; 1949; 1961]

a. Bethel, famous headquarters for "sensitivity-training," "T-groups," and the "human potential" movement, is a special case, combining both academic social science and nonacademic training activity.

program directors, residing in scattered locations, seemed to be converging upon one central idea: Here was an identifiable entity, a new field with real research potential. Some examples follow.

- The Industrial Relations Section at Princeton published what is probably the earliest academic research monograph explicitly addressed to an industrial communication topic: Helen Baker (1948), *Company-Wide Understanding of Industrial Relations Policies: A Study in Communication.* This was quickly followed up the next year by Baker et al.'s (1949) *Transmitting Information Through Management and Union Channels.*These were both survey studies, but many of the conclusions and recommendations reflect problems still being investigated in the 1980s.

- The Industrial Relations Center at the University of Minnesota showed a lively interest in the field when two of its staff members, Paterson and Jenkins (1948), published a readability study of corporate informational documents. The authors—both psychologists—made the significant observation that the time had arrived to recognize "the problem of communication between management and workers" as a topic for organized research (Paterson and Jenkins, 1948: 73). The Minnesota group produced quite a few research studies during the next several years, two of which introduced statistical analyses of employee information and morale that have become minor classics in the field: Funk and Becker (1952) and Perry and Mahoney (1955). (It should be noted, however, that neither the Princeton nor the Minnesota program ever developed into a sustained, organized research enterprise specifically centered upon industrial communication.)

- Two books came out in 1949 that set the tone of the field for many years thereafter. One of them—*Effective Communication Within Industry* (Pigors, 1949)—only 88 pages in length, was really just an extended essay, but it was full of wisdom, utilizing the semantics of Ogden and Richards as well as current Harvard-type human relations concepts. It was a combination of prescriptive and philosophical content, in many ways ahead of its time. The other— *Communication Within Industry* (Peters, 1949)—was more down-to-earth, being essentially the interpretive report of an extensive survey of current corporate communication practices; its underlying rationale could again be described as "Harvard human relations." The first author, Pigors, was a professor of industrial relations in the Department of Economics and Social Science at MIT; the second, Peters, was head of employee relations research at Esso Standard Oil.

- Another book appeared a few years later: *Communication in Management* (Redfield, 1953). I regard this as the first truly comprehensive "treatise" in the field, covering the full range of topics represented in the literature, and including extensive documentation to both nonacademic and academic sources. The author had (and has) held a variety of positions in universities as well as the business world. The book, however, was intended as a practical guide for managers, not as an academic text. (It was issued in a revised edition in 1958—somewhat enlarged and much more sophisticated.)

- When something is worthy of responsible attack, we know it has attained a degree of status. So it was with industrial communication, which by the early 1950s was being called a fad. *Fortune* magazine began publishing a series of articles in 1950, then brought them together into a book edited by W. H. Whyte, Jr. (1952) called *Is Anybody Listening?* The book constitutes, even today, one of the most devastating, yet thoughtful, assaults ever launched upon the whole rationale of corporate communication. The writers leveled their heaviest artillery upon such targets as the "plain talk" (or "shirt-sleeve English") movement, hard-sell free-enterprise campaigns, manipulation disguised as group decision making, and especially the worship of "teamwork" (introducing, twenty years in advance, the term "groupthink," made famous in the 1970s by Irving Janis). Regrettably, the perversions identified by *Fortune* in the 1950s have not entirely vacated the corporate scene in the 1980s.

Thus by 1953 the articles and books described above, from authors representing different viewpoints and working in different locales, had produced, by accident, a convergence of perceptions. Each in his or her own way was acknowledging the emergence of a new field, worthy of serious investigation. By 1953 (the year of Redfield's book), the process of crystallization was clearly evident. Meanwhile, between 1948 and 1953, the most decisive development in the history of the field was unfolding: the inauguration of graduate work (especially in speech departments).

GRADUATE PROGRAMS GET STARTED, WITH THE CENTER OF GRAVITY IN THE FIELD OF SPEECH

The role of the wartime communication-skills courses, the triple alliance, and the TWI programs has been noted, as has the "business speech" tradition, dating from the early years of the century. Many speech professors, therefore, were strategically situated to observe at least a limited range of communication problems in the organizational setting—problems stemming from inadequacies in oral discourse. Moreover, speech teachers, typically trained in the Aristotelian model of audience analysis and conciliatory persuasion, found it easy to assimilate many of the concepts being promulgated by social scientists under the rubric of "group dynamics." (To be sure, speech teachers were also among the sharpest critics of group dynamics, articulating some of the same objections voiced by W. H. Whyte and the editors of *Fortune*.)

In any event, a concatenation of circumstances—including the rapid expansion of graduate curricula in speech departments after World War II— resulted in a fact of the first magnitude:

> *It was in speech, rather than in any of the social sciences, that separately identified, sustained graduate programs in industrial communication evolved.*

This state of affairs came into being despite the unchallenged fact that most of the published research of the 1950s originated with social scientists, particularly those affiliated with human relations or industrial relations programs. (I shall have more to say about this later.)

Here are some of the things that were happening between 1948 and 1953:

• The first formally organized graduate program (as far as I can determine) was publicly announced by P. E. Lull, professor of speech at Purdue University, in 1948. (In 1952 an official title was added with the formation of the "Industrial Communication Research Center.")

• Graduate seminars and master's theses were being authorized by speech departments in at least the following institutions (listed alphabetically):

Denver (apparently the earliest—two master's theses, 1943; a seminar, 1945)

Kansas (a master's thesis, 1949)

Northwestern (a master's thesis, 1949)

Ohio State (a survey, 1949)

Penn State (a survey, 1949; a seminar, 1950)

Purdue (see above; seminar, 1948; master's thesis, 1950)

Redlands (a master's thesis, 1949)

Wayne [now Wayne State] (two master's theses, 1948)

Whittier College (a master's thesis, 1950)

Very likely there are others that have eluded my searches (see Zelko, 1951; Murray, 1952; Hicks, 1955; Brownell, 1978). Consistently, the topics addressed in these master's studies emphasized "speech training" (usually in public speaking or group discussion) for supervisors, and the typical methodology featured the survey. The focus was practical and pedagogical, not conceptual or theoretical.

• The first Ph.D. degrees, conferred by *speech* departments for work done *explicitly* in "industrial communication," were recorded in the year 1953: at Northwestern and Ohio State (for more details on the doctorate, see a later section).

• Conferences, sponsored by speech departments, served the network function of bringing together representatives from both the academic and business worlds, thus providing a forum where those with overlapping interests but different perceptions could exchange views.

In 1950: Under the direction of Harold Zelko, Pennsylvania State College (now Penn State University) offered its first "Workshop in Industrial and Business Speech Communications." The goal was to help industrial trainers become more competent "speech instructors" (Zelko, 1951: 62).

In 1951: With Irving J. Lee as the guiding force, the "Northwestern Centennial Conference on Communications" involved such figures as Carl Rogers and Fritz Roethlisberger (Rogers and Roethlisberger, 1952). The conference symbolized the reciprocal influence between Harvard-style human relations and general semantics, including the impact of Lee's semester-long visit to the Harvard Business School in the spring of 1951 (for a thorough discussion of this reciprocity, see Tompkins, 1965; for direct testimony, Roethlisberger, 1948; Lombard, 1955).

In 1952: Two conferences, both held in the state of Ohio, had their first annual meetings. One was at Kent State University, the "Annual Conference on Communication in Business and Industry," organized by James N. Holm; the other, at Ohio State University, the "Annual Conference on Communications Research and Training in Business and Industry," organized and directed by

Franklin H. Knower. Also, Purdue University formally announced its "Industrial Communication Research Center."

The very special case of the National Society for the Study of Communication (NSSC). Spurred by their experience with basic communication courses during the war (see the earlier discussion of the triple alliance), a group of dissidents within the speech profession met at the annual speech convention, in December of 1949, in Chicago. The leading spirit was Elwood Murray (University of Denver), who may rightly be called the "founder" of the National Society for the Study of Communication (NSSC; after 1968, the International Communication Association, or ICA). Others who served with Murray on the ad hoc committee established by SAA to investigate the issue, or who were closely involved in the organizing process, were: Paul Bagwell (Michigan State), W. Norwood Brigance (Wabash College), Ralph Nichols (Minnesota, St. Paul campus), W. C. Redding (Southern California), and Wesley Wiksell (Louisiana State). Wiksell and Redding wrote the original constitution; Bagwell was designated the first president; and the Society began operations in January of 1950 (see Nichols, 1951; Weaver, 1977; Brownell, 1978, 1983).

What concerns us here is that NSSC, from the start, focused its efforts primarily upon two areas: (a) teaching the basic communication course, and (b) investigating communication in business and industry. Since NSSC was a unit (until 1967) within the Speech Association of America, it was an important and unique instrument in our history; it created a structural arrangement encouraging people from speech departments to exchange ideas and to share a growing realization that a new "communication" area was taking shape *within* the traditional, rhetoric-oriented field of speech.

Although Society members were inordinately preoccupied in the first few years with pedagogical (especially training) concerns, a significant innovation was the appointment of no fewer than fifteen "Study and Research" committees, with the stipulation that theory and research were matters of top priority (Weaver, 1977: 610). One of the most active of these committees was the one designated "Communication in Industry," with its members representing both academe and the business community. When the Society began publishing its *Journal of Communication* (in 1951), it thereby provided a major outlet for articles dealing with industrial communication. Most of its authors were affiliated either with business firms or speech departments. So crucial, then, was the role of NSSC in the history of organizational communication that I have no hesitation in affirming this proposition: *Without NSSC, our field—including especially its close association with speech—could never have developed into what it is today.*

THE ARRIVAL OF ORGANIZED PH.D. PROGRAMS, PRIMARILY IN SPEECH

Although occasional doctoral dissertations in various social science departments or institutes dealt with topics directly related to industrial communication throughout the decade, speech departments took the initiative in introducing *separately identified, organized and sustained* Ph.D. programs in our field. Typically, researchers identified with the social sciences regarded communication as one of numerous variables within larger areas (such as organization theory or management). However, even when investigators associated with the human relations programs at Harvard or Michigan (ISR) elevated communication to a high-priority explanatory concept (see Ronken and Lawrence, 1952; Lombard, 1955; Cartwright and Zander, 1953; Mellinger, 1956), they took no steps to establish formally organized *programs* dedicated explicitly to research in communication.

Interestingly enough, the Ph.D. dissertation that I consider the very first in our field (entitled "Channels of Personnel Communication Within the Management Group") was earned not in speech, but in personnel administration—a part of the business school. The year was 1952, the author was Keith Davis, and the university was Ohio State. Using a quasi-experimental design featuring his famous "ECCO" technique, Davis traced the flow of "grapevine" messages within the management group of a real-life company. Based upon his statistical analyses, he suggested implications that are still being studied in the 1980s (Davis, 1952, 1953). Davis has told me that, as a graduate student, he learned his communication concepts from course work in psychology and that he had no contact with the new program in industrial communication then getting under way in the speech department (under the direction of F. H. Knower; see below).

The charter members—1953 and 1954. Speech departments (or schools) in four universities granted Ph.D.s in industrial communication during the Decade of Crystallization: starting in 1953 at Northwestern and Ohio State; in 1954, at Purdue and Southern California. The deaths of two directors, both occurring in 1955, caused disruptions in the programs at Northwestern and Purdue. Irving Lee died (as a young man) in May; P. E. Lull (not much older), in August. The Northwestern program never fully recovered. I had just moved to Purdue in September of 1955 from Southern California; but it took two or three years to reestablish continuity. And, since Southern California produced only the single Lewis (1954) dissertation during the decade, we can say that only at Ohio State did an uninterrupted flow of Ph.D. graduates continue.

In charge of the Ohio State program was Franklin H. Knower. As one of the three or four most prolific behavioral-scientific researchers in the history of the speech profession (his Ph.D. was in psychology), Knower occupied himself with a broad range of topics. Industrial communication was only one of his interests, but the doctoral studies he directed during the 1950s still stand as landmarks.

The list below identifies seven of the eight earliest Ph.D. dissertations in the field we call today "organizational communication" (the eighth was actually the first, chronologically: Davis, 1952, discussed above). I have included the titles, since they provide the modern reader with a reasonably good picture of the kinds of topics regarded as "researchable" at the time. It will be seen that only the two years 1953 and 1954 are represented; the reason for this is that the first Ph.D. granted by each of the four universities falls in one or the other of these two years. (Space will permit only brief mention of selected doctoral studies completed after 1954.)

1953

- Angrist: Ohio State; Knower, director. "A study of the communications of executives in business and industry."
- Nilsen: Northwestern; Lee, director. "The communication survey: A study of communication problems in three office and factory units."

1954

- Dahle: Purdue; Lull, director. "An objective and comparative study of five methods of transmitting information to business and industrial employees."
- Goetzinger: Purdue; Lull, director. "An analysis of irritating factors in initial employment interviews of male college graduates."
- Lewis: Southern California; Dickens and Redding, codirectors. "A survey of management's attitudes regarding oral communication needs and practices in large industries of Los Angeles County."
- Ross: Purdue; Lull, director. "A case study of communication breakdowns in the General Telephone Company of Indiana, Inc."
- Tatum: Northwestern; Lee, director. "Communication in the sales training program of IBM corporation."

According to my records, speech departments awarded a total of about sixteen or seventeen Ph.Ds in industrial communication between the years 1953 and 1958, inclusive (because of borderline cases and the possibility of omissions, no definitive count is available). Interestingly, the school that had produced the earliest master's degrees and offered the earliest graduate seminar—Denver—did not offer a doctoral program in industrial communication until some years later, even though Murray encouraged the idea (see Murray, 1952). The well-known Mellinger (1956) dissertation, "Interpersonal Trust as a Factor in Communication," completed at ISR/Michigan, could certainly be listed as a bona fide industrial communication study (with the word "communication" in its title). But, as in the case of Keith Davis, Mellinger cast his study in a social science frame of reference.

Among the remaining speech Ph.Ds still frequently cited in our literature are the following: Freshley (1955, Ohio State; a psychometric study of management attitudes toward communication); Piersol (1955, Purdue: a micro-observational study of oral communication acts on the job); Funk (1956, Purdue; a statistical comparison of communication attitudes of high versus low-rated foremen); Dee (1957, Ohio State; an analysis of communication in a labor union local); and Weaver (1957, Ohio State; a semantic-differential analysis of union leaders' versus managers'"frames of reference"[see Weaver, 1958]). Productivity tended to taper off at Ohio State after 1958, but the Purdue program got back into stride with the Level (1959) dissertation. It was not until the mid- to late sixties that more than three or four speech departments were turning out doctoral candidates on a continuing, annual basis. (For a brief account of post-1958 events, see the Postscript.)

A note on speech research—exclusive of dissertations. Notwithstanding the doctoral programs described above, the anomaly remains that, aside from dissertations, very little empirical research directly concerned with "industrial communication" originated in speech departments during the decade. Most publications written by speech professionals fell under one of two headings: (a) prescriptive articles or textbooks concerned with the improvement of speech skills (Lee, 1952; Phillips, 1955), or (b) hortatory pieces urging speech teachers to apply their expertise to the training of supervisors and managers (Hinds, 1954, 1955). (During the sixties, it must be said, this state of affairs underwent a dramatic change.)

We can, however, point to two influential survey studies produced by speech researchers: (1) Zelko (1951) canvassed several hundred respondents (representing both academic and nonacademic affiliations). He was investigating perceived needs for skills-training in such areas as human relations, public speaking, and conference leadership. The title of his article is worth noting: "Adult Speech Training: Challenge to the Speech Profession." (2) The Industrial Communication Research Center at Purdue issued a widely distributed monograph, *Business and Industrial Communication from the Viewpoint of the Corporation President* (Lull, et al., 1954). Approximately seventy executives of "Fortune 500" companies responded to a set of ten questions covering written as well as oral modes.

I am deliberately excluding a substantial body of well-designed research produced in the 1950s by the speech profession, namely the work in group discussion (sometimes called "conference participation and leadership"). Many of the findings were clearly relevant to the organizational setting; and, indeed, conference skills were a major topic in the business speech textbooks of the time (see Zelko and O'Brien, 1957, for example). However, the researchers themselves conducted their studies typically in the Dewey problem-solving frame of reference, most of the time with student subjects in classroom or laboratory settings. Almost never did they design their investigations with the organizational context in mind; and only rarely did they suggest applicability of findings to the business or industrial situation (an exception was Barnlund, 1955).

A PROFILE OF THE LITERATURE:
1948-1958

As I have mentioned earlier, my estimate is that a total of approximately 225 "serious" titles, properly subsumable under the rubric of organizational communication, appeared during the Decade of Crystallization. If we were to add fifteen or so doctoral dissertations, the number could reach somewhere in the neighborhood of 240. According to my records, approximately eighty or ninety of these entries could reasonably be considered examples of acceptable scholarship (judged by the standards of the time) and they would fall under two main categories: case studies and critical essays, as well as "quantitative" or "scientific" investigations. A cursory scanning of the Sexton and Staudt (1959) bibliography suffices to substantiate the conclusion that, even when we add the empirical research reports to the rest, no less than 95 percent of the literature during these years was clearly prescriptive.

Not only was the literature prescriptive, *virtually every title was addressed, either directly or indirectly, to helping management solve managerial problems.* This applies to the work of the social scientists as well as to the torrent of books and articles advising managers how they could use this or that communication technique to become better managers. Usually of course, though not always, the academic writers framed their contributions in terms of concepts, constructs, variables, hypotheses, or (occasionally) theories. The following titles (all verbatim) are a fair sample of the kinds of concerns that captured the attention of both professors and managers during the decade:

- "Employee Magazines Build Morale" (1950)
- "Selling the Plant Newspaper to Employees" (1949)
- "How to Talk to Joe Doakes" (1950)
- "How to Make Employee Publications Pay Off" (1956)
- "A Formula for Good Communication" (1954)
- "How Supervisors Can Communicate Better" (1953)
- "You Know—But Do They?" (1955)
- "Effective Communications—One Road to Productivity" (1950)
- "Influence of 'Plain Talk' on AMC Communications" (1951)
- "The Reading Ability of Industrial Supervisors" (1950)
- "How House Magazines Improve Industrial Relations" (1953)
- "The Communication of Merit Ratings" (1953)
- "Tell It to the Boss!" (1957)

(All these articles appeared in respected journals, some of them written by and for social scientists—none of them came from the "Sunday supplement.")

Even conceptually sophisticated, in-depth case studies (most of the famous ones came from Harvard) arrived at conclusions explicitly formulated in terms meaningful to management. Sometimes "scientific" experimenters announced their problems in unadorned managerial language. A case in point is the classic study of "participative" decision making, conducted in the famous Harwood pajama factory by Michigan/ISR researchers: Coch and French (1948), "Overcoming Resistance to Change." (For a recent critique of this experiment see Bartlem and Locke, 1981.)

As was explained at the beginning, this chapter is not a literature review. Hence, neither description nor evaluation will be applied to any of the titles listed below. Moreover, the purpose will be merely to provide an overview of the most salient features of the publications landscape (in the process, identifying some of the best-known landmarks). Our concern, with a few exceptions, will be focused here upon that segment of the literature considered to be *academically relevant*: either (a) empirical research, or (b) conceptual/critical position statements. The items listed are a sampling; no attempt is made to offer an exhaustive inventory of 80 to 100 "scholarly" titles! The "topical clusters" identified below are admittedly arbitrary devices, intended to promote our making sense of what would otherwise be an amorphous conglomerate.

SALIENT FEATURES OF THE RESEARCH AND CONCEPTUAL LITERATURE, 1948-1958

Under each subtopic appears a sampling of the most influential—that is, most frequently cited—titles (arranged chronologically and, for multiple titles in a single year, alphabetically; no rank ordering by merit is implied).

Topical cluster 1: "Managerial pragmatics." This heading includes such matters as the following (not a complete list):

- diffusion of information; transmission and receipt of corporate policy statements, job information, rules, safety regulations, and so on; relationship between employee knowledge or "understanding" and such criteria as morale and productivity (for example, see Baker, 1948; Baker et al., 1949; Browne and Neitzel, 1952; Funk and Becker, 1952; Habbe, 1952; Dahle, 1954; Perry and Mahoney, 1955). *Note:* includes the "semantics" of industrial relations (Whyte, 1949; Exton, 1950; Weaver, 1958)

- "readability" of company documents, employee handbooks, house organs, union contracts, and the like (see Paterson and Jenkins, 1948; Carlucci and Crissy, 1951; Lawshe et al., 1951)

- upward communication (taken separately from participative decision making) (see Kelley, 1951; Planty and Machaver, 1952; Cohen, 1958)

- channels of "message flow"; networks and network roles; feedback loops, giving and receiving feedback; relationships to morale and productivity (see Bavelas and Barrett, 1951; Jacobson and Seashore, 1951; Leavitt and Mueller, 1951; Davis, 1953; Burns, 1954; Weiss and Jacobson, 1955; Weiss, 1956)

- evaluations of overall communication policies and practices, in terms of corporate efficiency and the like, including "communications audit" (a term introduced by Odiorne, 1954) (see Cook, 1951; Whyte, 1952; Redfield, 1953, 1958; Odiorne, 1954; Zelko, 1956)

Topical cluster 2: Techniques for improving basic communication skills. Under this cluster belong the innumerable articles and books giving advice (occasionally citing research findings) intended to help the reader become a better speaker, listener, reader, writer (and "evaluator"/"symbol-user" in the General Semantics approach [see especially the books by Irving J. Lee, 1952, 1954]). Space permits citing only a few titles from a potentially enormous assembly. This cluster includes, for example, the entire "business speech" *corpus*—which in turn encompasses public speaking, conference participation, and interviewing (Zelko, 1951; Lee, 1952; Sanford and Yeager, 1952; Angrist, 1953; Lee, 1954; Zelko, 1954; Hinds, 1955; Sexton and Staudt, 1957).

Topical cluster 3: "Human relations" and its derivatives. So pervasive was the influence upon our field of "human relations" doctrine that an entire book could be written on the subject. This is not surprising in view of two facts: (a) Many of the concepts taught by business-speech instructors, inherited from the Aristotelian rhetorical tradition, bore a striking resemblance to a number of human relations principles. These include particularly an emphasis upon audience analysis and adaptation, the need to treat people considerately if one is to persuade them, and a recognition of the "emotional" springs of human behavior. Speech professionals also, as we have mentioned, had devoted much attention to the merits of group discussion as a decision-making mode. (b) Typically, the social scientists working in one version or another of what Perrow (1979) calls "the human relations model" featured communication as at least an important "variable" among—it is true—other important variables.

Illustrative of this second point are such instances as the following: Ronken and Lawrence (1952), from the Harvard group, entitled the concluding chapter of their case study "Communication and Change" and identified communication as the manager's most basic skill. Lombard (1955), also from Harvard, explicitly credited Irving Lee (School of Speech, Northwestern) as his source for the communication/General Semantics paradigm used to interpret his case study data (see pp. xii and xiv). Another Harvard researcher, Lawrence (1958), examined, on a minute-by-minute basis, the communication acts occurring between members of superior-subordinate dyads. Similarly, at the University of Michigan (ISR), Pelz (1952) conducted his famous study of supervisors' "upward influence" upon their own bosses (as perceived by their subordinates)—one of the most important concepts in the history of organizational communication (see Jablin, 1980). Other ISR investigators, in one of their numerous field experiments on "participative decision making," emphasized participation as a "form of communication" (French et al., 1958).

To grasp how deeply human relations concepts had penetrated our field, one need only rehearse such well-worn terms as the following: informal groups, reciprocal trust, "supportive" supervision (Likert's group at ISR/Michigan), participative decision making, two-way communication, group dynamics, "openness" of communication, self-disclosure, and the like. Notions such as these entered the communication field primarily from three sources: (a) The Harvard Business School group (Roethlisberger and his associates; (b) the Institute for Social Research (ISR) at the University of Michigan (Likert and his colleagues), closely associated with the NTL conferences at Bethel (T-groups and the like); and (c) the Ohio State group working in the areas of personnel and educational research (Hemphill, Fleishman, and others).

Harvard Business School. We have already mentioned the cross-fertilization of ideas between the Harvard human relationists and General Semanticists, with Irving Lee as the central liaison in 1951 (his visit to Harvard, and the Northwestern conference, with Roethlisberger participating: Rogers and Roethlisberger, 1952; Lombard, 1955; Tompkins, 1965). For some it may come as a surprise to discover that, back in 1948, Roethlisberger reported he had not yet found an adequate "integration" of human relations theory and practice, but he suspected "the field of general semantics seems to offer a fruitful lead" in the right direction (1948: 105-106). Then, in 1953, Roethlisberger delivered the Alfred Korzybski Memorial Lecture in General Semantics, published later in the *Harvard Business Review* under the title "The Administrator's Skill: Communication" (Roethlisberger, 1953).

From the Harvard researchers came several famous book-length case studies so saturated with communication concepts that they are now regarded as "belonging" to the literature of organizational communication. We should recall especially, in chronological sequence: Ronken and Lawrence (1952), Walker and Guest (1952), Lombard (1955), Walker et al. (1956), and Lawrence (1958).

ISR at Michigan. Little needs to be added to what has already been said about this great fountainhead of quantitative and experimental research in the human relations tradition. Most of the ISR studies focused upon such communication-involving topics as "supportive" supervision, "employee-center-ed" versus "job-centered" leadership, and "participation" via group dynamics methods (imported, as we have seen, from Bethel). The following represents a minimal list of works that have had a lasting impact upon subsequent research in organizational communication: Coch and French (1948), Katz et al. (1950, 1951), Mann and Baumgartel (1952), Pelz (1952), Cartwright and Zander (1953), Mellinger (1956), Morse and Reimer (1956), French et al. (1958), and Likert (1958). (These human relations titles are in addition to the "network" studies, cited earlier: Weiss and Jacobson, 1955, Weiss, 1956.)

Ohio State: Personnel Research. This group—with Fleishman's name probably the most familiar to communication specialists—generated the renowned (and controversial) two-factor model of supervisory leadership: "initiation of structure" and "consideration" (see Fleishman, 1951, 1953; Fleishman et al., 1955). Organizational communication specialists would do well to keep in mind that the formal definitions of these factors identified communication behaviors as central components. In fact, I am convinced that both could profitably be studied as *rhetorical* concepts.

Some other contributors. Many names could be added here. But I shall be content to mention only four titles that have wielded unusual influence upon communication specialists: (1) Whyte, *Human Relations in the Restaurant Industry* (1948); (2) Bakke, *Bonds of Organization* (1950), a combined case study and theoretical treatise; (3) Levine and Butler, "Lecture Versus Group Discussion in Changing Behavior" (1952), purporting to demonstrate the superiority of group discussion over persuasive speeches (see Lewin, 1943: Marrow and French, 1945); and (4) Tannenbaum and Schmidt, "How to Choose a Leadership Pattern" (1958), proposing their famous seven-step continuum of managerial communication behavior, from autocratic to participative.

In summary, we can confidently assert that, in terms of sheer quantity of research, the work published by human relationists (of various persuasions) represents the largest single source of both empirical and conceptual data—published during the period 1948-1958—for the field of organizational communication.[5] Having made this assertion, we must now confront the question that has been lying below the surface all along: How did it come about that departments of speech, rather than any of the social sciences, became the major sponsors of identifiable, sustained programs at the postgraduate level?

WHY SPEECH?

My response to this question will take the form of three hypotheses: the first two are recapitulations of (or at least inferences from) facts already presented. The third will introduce a factor not specifically mentioned before, but easily deducible from much of what has been said.

Hypothesis 1: The social scientists, in effect, abdicated. Communication, even when it was accorded a prominent place, was typically regarded as one of many variables, and specifically as less "basic" than some of the other variables in explaining organizational behavior. This widely held view is neatly epitomized in the words of none other than Douglas McGregor (of "Theory X—Theory Y" fame):

> It is a fairly safe generalization that difficulties in communication within an organization are more often than not *mere symptoms* of underlying difficulties in relationship between the parties involved [McGregor, 1967: 151, emphasis added].

Hypothesis 2: The speech profession was strategically positioned to fill the void left by the social scientists. In earlier pages we have seen the importance of: (a) the rhetorical tradition in speech, including business speech; (b) basic communication and the triple alliance; (c) experience in industrial training, including the area of group discussion (conference); and (d) the National Society for the Study of Communication (NSSC). Moreover, since the late thirties, speech professionals had been conducting social-scientific research of their own; and speech departments all over the country, during the 1940s and 1950s, were developing impressive postgraduate programs. Many of the topics investigated by speech researchers, as we have noted, bore a marked resemblance to topics investigated by social scientists.

Hypothesis 3: The individual persuasive efforts of a small group of "speech pioneers" were decisive forces in inducing speech departments to establish sustained graduate programs in "industrial communication." I have no hesitation about declaring that, without the effective advocacy of a few pioneering individuals, our field could never have evolved as it has—especially as an area dominated (until recent years) by the speech profession.

Proposing names for a special group of pioneers is admittedly a risky, subjective business. But I shall take the plunge and suggest nine individuals. Three criteria governed the selection process: (1) The individual must have been an active, forceful advocate urging the recognition of an identifiable field (regardless of labels). (2) The individual must have gained some measure of national recognition in this advocacy role. (3) The individual must have been involved in persuasive efforts for much of the time between 1948 and 1955, inclusive. The year 1955 is, of course, an arbitrary cut-off. It was chosen mainly because in that year, two of the fields's pioneers died within a few weeks of each other: Lee in May, and Lull in August. By definition, then, if an individual's activity took place primarily after 1955—*and I include myself in this category*—that fact is enough to disqualify the individual.

Arranged alphabetically, the names are listed below. Space limitations will permit no more than brief identification of each person (in an article under preparation I include more biographical information).

(1) *Major Charles T. Estes*, special assistant to the director, U. S. Conciliation Service (after Taft-Hartley, 1947, the independent Federal Mediation and Conciliation Service)

(2) *George L. Hinds*, Speech Department, Wayne (now Wayne State) University

(3) *James N. Holm*, School of Speech, Kent State University

(4) *Franklin H. Knower*, Speech Department, Ohio State University

(5) *Irving J. Lee*, School of Speech, Northwestern University

(6) *Paul Emerson (P. E.) Lull*, Speech Department, Purdue University

(7) *Elwood Murray*, head, Department (later School) of Speech, Denver University

(8) *Wesley Wiksell*, Speech Department, Louisiana State University

(9) *Harold P. Zelko*, Speech Department, Penn State College (later University)

If, backed into a corner, I were compelled to nominate a single individual as the founder of organizational communication—at least in the context of the speech profession of the 1950s—that person would be Charles Estes. Although technically a nonacademic and unattached to any speech department, he took upon himself—starting in the mid-1940s—a one-man campaign to convince speech professors, from coast to coast, that (a) An important new field for both teaching and research was about to emerge, and (b) Speech professionals were the most appropriate ones to define and develop the field of industrial communication. Estes was repeatedly popping up at speech conventions, NSSC meetings, and regional conferences; he delivered a "breakthrough" paper at the 1945 speech convention (see Estes, 1946), and became a cochairman of the NSSC committee on Communication in Industry (see Estes, 1951). If the demand is for a founder, he is the one. (I speak from several years of personal experience with the man.)

CRYSTALLIZATION

One of the signs that an academic field of study is emerging takes the form of summaries—summaries of principles, concepts, and findings. These summaries generally appear as textbooks or anthologies, sometimes as conceptual essays or even as treatises. I have already noted early exemplars: Peters (1949), Pigors (1949), W. H. Whyte (1952), and Redfield (1953). The tabulation shown below indicates the quickening pace of development during the five-year span from 1954 through 1958:

- 1954:   Lee, *Customs and Crises in Communication*
- 1955:   Phillips, *Oral Communication in Business*
- 1956:   (a) Dooher and Marquis, *Effective Communication on the Job*
           (b) Lee and Lee, *Handling Barriers in Communication*
- 1957:   Zelko and O'Brien, *Management-Employee Communication in Action*
- 1958:   (a) Janis, *Business Communication Reader*
           (b) Maier, *The Appraisal Interview*
           (c) Redfield, *Communication in Management*

    NOTE: The classic theoretical treatise, *Organizations* (March and Simon) also appeared in 1958; it contributed concepts and hypotheses of enormous import for organizational communication.

Of the eight books, only Dooher and Marquis (1956), published by the American Management Association, was unequivocally nonacademic. It consisted of a collection of prescriptive articles recommending techniques for solving managerial communication problems. Significantly, the kinds of communication receiving the lion's share of space were *oral*. Four of the titles were written by speech professionals (Lee, 1954; Phillips, 1955; Lee and Lee, 1956; Zelko and O'Brien, 1957); and the pioneering anthology (Janis, 1958), by a professor of business English (New York University). Maier was a faculty member affiliated with ISR/Michigan; Redfield (1958) by this time was a professor of administrative communication and management at the University of Pittsburgh. Taken as a whole, the eight books gave predominance to oral communication, further substantiating the pivotal role being played by the speech profession.

Thus by 1958, the field—under various labels—had clearly crystallized. Redfield, in the preface to his revised edition, declared that in 1953 "administrative communication was a novelty," whereas by 1958 it had become established as one of "the most popular subjects in the United States" (1958: ix). Teachers, writers, and researchers, representing a broad spectrum of orientations, had *stumbled* into identifying a new field (the only ones who should not be described as stumblers were the speech pioneers). And, so far as organized, sustained graduate programs are concerned, the field found its center of gravity in speech departments—rather than in the social sciences.

At the end of the 1950s (and into the 1960s), the field was appropriately known as business and industrial (or managerial, or administrative) communication. We have seen that even the scientific work was designed with prescriptive, or at least normative, purposes in mind. Management problems determined the basic agenda for the field. These problems, in turn, reflected the pervasive premise that, by and large, managers are well-informed and rational; employees, not very well informed and generally nonrational (even irrational when "resisting change").

As corollaries, such themes as the following can be found woven throughout the literature of the 1940s and 1950s (and they were not absent in the 1960s and 1970s): (a) Employees, if supplied with "the facts" and treated decently, will respond by working harder and being more productive. (b) "Correct" communication techniques can be identified for obtaining "cooperation" and "teamwork," cooperation being defined in terms of cooperating with management's goals and policies. (c) Downward-directed communication, with particular attention to the print media (house organs, and the like), is the foundation of all corporate communication programs. Upward-directed communication, although something to be encouraged, is useful chiefly for purposes of improving management's messages to employees. (d) "Morale" is defined in terms of employees' identification with management-determined goals; and an important means of building morale is skillful use of persuasive communication. (e) "Participation" is desirable, primarily because it softens resistance to change, creates a sense of teamwork, and builds morale—all of which will increase productivity. (f) Changes in both attitudes and behavior can frequently (perhaps always) be more effectively accomplished through "group dynamics" than through conventional lectures. (This list is not complete.)

Generally speaking, the field at the end of the 1950s had made very little use of "systems" approaches (Ronken and Lawrence [1952], drawing upon Barnard [1938/1968], is an exception), despite the popularity of Lewin's field-theory concepts. As a consequence, the almost universal tendency, even in the best research, was to examine communication or human relations phenomena in a closed system, without regard for environmental forces. And "contingency" thinking was rare (an exception: Pelz, 1952).

The study of organizatonal communication in the 1980s exhibits dramatic changes of focus, expansions of horizons, and inventions of new models (the Putnam and Pacanowsky 1983 volume will serve as an impressive example). However, the field has not yet cut itself off from its roots of the 1940s and 1950s. Morever, the newest approaches—for example, those derived from cultural anthropology, phenomenology, and Critical Theory—are best understood when viewed as figures against the ground of what happened in the forties and fifties. Even the attention to management-oriented problems has its place: as Bakke (1959: 28-29) warned years ago, whenever organizational researchers get to the point where the topics they investigate make no sense to managers in the "real world," the research is in trouble.

A few years ago one of the editors of this volume was bold enough to declare in an open meeting: "I shall assert that organizational communication has arrived. By that I mean that there have been signs of legitimation bestowed on the field by cognate disciplines" (Tompkins, 1978: 1). My instincts are to second this optimistic pronouncement, but I lack the confidence to make an irrevocable commitment. After all, only a year before Tompkins uttered his benediction, a textbook—with the title *Organizational Communication: The Keystone to Managerial Effectiveness*—came out that contained the following statement in the preface: "The emerging discipline of organizational communication is not fully identified in previous books" (Wofford et al., 1977: xiii). So one never knows. With the development of major graduate programs in several business schools (those directed by Keith Davis at Arizona State and by Karlene Roberts at California-Berkeley are examples), the dominance of speech/communication departments is no longer what it was in the 1960s. The field has stumbled into its present identity. Nothing guarantees that it will not some day stumble out of that identity, or into a totally different identity.

POSTSCRIPT:
AFTER 1958, STEP-BY-STEP ACCEPTANCE

●1959: Sexton and Staudt (1959), first comprehensive, academic literature review; *Communication in Organizations* (Foundation for Research on Human Behavior, 1959), a collection of research reports.

●1960: Haney (1960), *Communication: Patterns and Incidents*; applications of general semantics by professor of management (student of Irving Lee); Wiksell (1960), *Do They Understand You?* textbook (oral communication); Schutte and Steinberg (1960), *Communication in Business and Industry,* textbook (despite title, main emphasis on written communication).
NOTE: McGregor (1960), *The Human Side of Enterprise.*

●1961: Thayer (1961), *Administrative Communication,* pioneering effort to build elements of a theoretical base for the field; Maier et al., (1961), *Superior-Subordinate Communication in Management,* research from ISR/Michigan.
NOTE: Likert (1961), *New Patterns of Management.*

●1963: *Journal of Business Communication* inaugurated, published by American Business Communication Association (formerly American Business Writing Association).

●1964: Redding and Sanborn (1964), *Business and Industrial Communication,* advanced-level text/anthology.[6]

●1965: Guetzkow (1965), "Communication in Organizations," literature review published in *Handbook of Organizations* (March, 1965).

●1967: "The Year of Official Acceptance" (see early section of the chapter): Tompkins (1967), state-of-the-art review; Voos (1967), bibliography, both using "organizational communication" in the titles.[7]
NOTE: Likert (1967), *The Human Organization.*

●1968: Thayer (1968), *Communication and Communication Systems,* broad-ranging treatise, theory building; new major graduate program at Michigan State (Department of Communication) under way, directed by R. V. Farace—first dissertation, Schwartz (1968); new Division IV, Organizational Communication Association, established in NSSC (later ICA, International Communication Association, starting in 1970).

●1972: Redding (1972), *Communication Within the Organization,* review of theory and research, published jointly by Industrial Relations Council, New York, and Purdue Research Foundation.

●1973: New divison of Academy of Management, Organizational Communication, authorized at Boston convention.

●1975: First annual *Organizational Communication Abstracts* (for 1974) (Greenbaum and Falcione, 1975), published jointly by American Business Communication Association and International Communication Association.

NOTES

1. For an overview, see Paul et al. (1946), as well as the initial issue of the *Journal of Communication* (May 1951).

2. For the official report, see War Manpower Commission (1945). For popular accounts, see Chase (1945, 1948). For contemporary testimony on the close link between military and academic communication courses, note McKelvey: (1952: 11) "The Communications Course idea, as it exists today, stems largely from an impetus received during World War II. It was a war baby."

3. There are, of course, other publications besides Roethlisberger and Dickson (1939) featuring descriptions of the Hawthorne studies. For a superb modern summary, see Appendix C in Cass and Zimmer (1975).

4. A history of how the human relations "ideology" developed lies beyond the scope of this chapter. Interested readers may refer to such sources as: Mayo (1933), Heyel (1939), Roethlisberger and Dickson (1939), Roethlisberger (1941), Gardner (1945), Mayo (1945), Marrow (1969), and Bartell (1976). See especially Cass and Zimmer (1975), published for the 50th Anniversary celebration, for a valuable collection of articles responding to the implications of Hawthorne as perceived in the 1970s. Readers are warned that, starting in the 1960s, critics have made an important distinction between old-style "human relations" and modern "*human resources*" models: see especially the seminal article by Miles (1965); also Redding (1984), Chapter 8.

5. Influential contemporary books, summarizing theory and research in human relations and putting communication in a prominent position, include: Maier (1952), Cartwright and Zander (1953), and Keith Davis (1957). Important critiques were provided by W. H. Whyte, Jr. (1952), Argyris (1957), and the revised edition of Redfield (1958). The report of the Robert Wood Johnson Commission—a large *ad hoc* group of industrialists, educators, and religious leaders—was issued in booklet form under the title *Human Relations in Modern Business* in 1949. Commonly referred to as the "Magna Carta of Human Relations," it represents probably the nearest thing to a consensus summary of human relations doctrine for the 1950s.

6. The title of our book was the subject of frequent debates with the publishing company of Harper & Row, who felt that "organizational communication" was too "esoteric" and that we had no assurance it would really "catch on" in the field. As a concession, Sanborn and I were permitted to use "Organizational Communication" as the heading for Part II in the book.

7. Symbolic of the vagaries attendant upon determining a satisfactory label for the field is a chronicle of the titles attached to the research seminar at Purdue University. P. E. Lull inaugurated the seminar, but under a catch-all "Research Topics" label, in 1948. Starting in 1955 (immediately preceding Lull's death), the seminar bore the title "Oral Communication in Business and Industry." With no change in title, the catalogue description included the phrase "organizational communication" for the first time in 1964. Then the name was changed in 1966 to "Interpersonal Communication in Business and Industry." Although the Department of Speech became the Department of Communication in the fall of 1969, it was not until 1974 that I was able to gain approval for the catalogue listing, "Organizational Communication."

Chapter 2

VERTICAL AND NETWORK
COMMUNICATION IN ORGANIZATIONS
The Present and the Future

**Rebecca Blair, Karlene H. Roberts,
and Pamela McKechnie**

WE HAVE LONG ARGUED (Porter and Roberts, 1976; Roberts and Callaway, in press) that communication is the social glue that ties organizations together. If this is indeed the case, as organizations grow increasingly complex we can expect that understanding more about how communication affects various aspects of them will become more important. Most students of organizations write as though they believe tomorrow's organizations will be fairly similar to today's (see, for example, Mitchell, 1983; Steers, 1984; Gibson et al., 1982). We believe that by the year 2000 many organizations will probably be mirror images of existing organizations. However, some organizations, particularly those that take full advantage of the information revolution, will necessarily be designed and operated differently.

It appears to us that three major issues will be affected by, and have major implications for, communication in organizations: sheer complexity of information, participant power, and managerial decision making. If organizational communication is the glue that keeps organizations together, it is also a central construct in examining complexity, decision making, and power. The purposes of this chapter are to review what the structural branch of the organizational literature tells us about these constructs and to predict what organizations of the future might look like in these terms. We focus on the structural communication literature because it addresses issues of how organizations are tied together and, consequently, is most central to our concerns.

The first half of the chapter brings us up to date on superior-subordinate and network communication research. The superior-subordinate section focuses on the issues of power and status and decision making. The network literature is discussed in terms of its implications for complexity, power, and decision making. (Complexity is not discussed in the superior-subordinate section because it is not addressed in the superior-subordinate empirical literature.)

These areas are summarized in terms of an information-processing approach to their further articulation.

The second half of the chapter outlines some future technological developments and suggests their probable impacts on superior-subordinate and network communication. Advanced telecommunications, computerization, and artificial intelligence are discussed. Technological developments affect not only the quantity of information available, but also what information is available and the speed with which it can be used. This, in turn, has implications for complexity, power, and decision making.

THE PRESENT

SUPERIOR-SUBORDINATE COMMUNICATION

Our review of superior-subordinate communication research will center on three topics: power, status, and decision making using vertically communicated information.

Power, Status, and Communication

The amount of information sent appears to be affected by perceived power and status differences among interactants. Early studies (Dubin and Spray, 1964; Kelly, 1964; Lawler et al.,1968) report that approximately two-thirds of a manager's communication time is spent communicating with superiors and subordinates, and the remaining one-third of the time is spent on lateral communication. A later study (Mintzberg, 1975) found that managers spend about 78 percent of their time communicating by verbal means alone. Whereas Dubin and Spray (1964) found that as one goes higher in the hierarchy, the ratio of superior to subordinate interaction increases, Burns (1954) and Dubin (1962) found the opposite relationship, and Martin (1959) found no relationship at all.

More detailed studies attempted to separate the effects of power and status and found that the combined presence of these two variables restricts upward communication considerably more than does status alone (Cohen, 1958). A recent study (Bradley, 1978) found that high-power and high-status people receive more upward communication than high-power but low-status people. High status, devoid of power, is not sufficient to cause subordinates to increase their friendliness or supportive behavior toward superiors. In other research focusing solely on status (Barnlund and Horland, 1963; Allen and Cohen, 1969), high-status people have been shown to communicate more with one another than with low-status individuals, and low-status individuals have been shown to be more likely to attempt to communicate with high-status persons than with other low-status persons.

Organizational structure and status (a supposed reflection of power) are intimately connected. When leaders attempt to dominate leader-subordinate relationships, subordinates respond by deferring. Slobin et al. (1968) found that in a business organization, individuals in middle-level positions are much more willing to communicate self-disclosure information upward than to divulge it downward. This has been interpreted as an attempt to establish greater "intimacy" with high-status, high-power individuals in order to achieve more equality between the two levels, while at the same time avoiding downward self-disclosure that would signify personal relationships with those at lower levels (Porter and Roberts, 1976).

Regardless of type (peer-peer or superior-subordinate), dyads are more willing to talk about task than nontask topics (Baird, 1973). Willingness to talk appears to be a function of the individual's perception of the other's willingness to listen. Redding (1972) asserts that communication openness involves both sender and receiver behavior, and that in open communication relationships between superiors and subordinates, both parties (a) perceive the other as a willing and receptive listener, and (b) refrain from responses that might be perceived as nonaccepting.

These findings have implications for the formal performance appraisal or review and the subsequent administration of rewards and punishments based on those reviews. The requirements for a good performance appraisal interview have been examined extensively (Cederblom, 1982; Ivancevich, 1982; Wexley, 1982). They include participation, support, goal setting, focused discussions, minimal criticism, and splitting of administrative from developmental feedback. Training managers in giving feedback has also proved effective and appears to result in a more positive perception of the process (Ivancevich, 1982). A good feedback interview may also affect performance (DeNisi et al., 1982; Ivancevich and McMahon, 1982).

Thus the performance evaluation process, which includes both the observation evaluation process and a communication process, is a central mechanism, or a management tool designed to improve an organization's efficiency. During the performance evaluation process, three primary functions of communication exist: to inform, to instruct, and to motivate.

Much of the early research contained the implicit assumption that those in higher positions have more power. It is clear that high-ranking positions tend to have considerable access and control over information and thus they certainly do have power. However, several researchers argue that this assumption may be too narrow, and that power also exists at lower organizational levels. In essence, power may be derived from formal organizational structure and hierarchical communication paths. However, much communication within an organization circumvents these paths. Access to, and control over, this informal communication also results in power.

One of the earliest authors to discuss this phenomenon was Mechanic (1962), who argued that the power of lower-order participants results from (1) individual access to information, persons, and organization instrumentalities; (2) the unique expertise of the individual; and (3) the individual's effort. Mechanic argued further that a person's location in physical and social space are important factors influencing access to persons, information, and instrumentalities. The more central a person is within an organization, the greater his or her access. Thus a lower-level person, such as an executive's secretary, may have little formal authority but considerable control over the information the executive receives and, therefore, considerable power.

A more recent article (Blackburn, 1981) integrates many of Mechanic's concepts with the strategic contingency theory of organization power (Hickson et al., 1971). Hickson et al. argue that to the extent that an individual is in a position that provides for increased visibility and interaction with those at the upper levels in the organization, that individual's power is increased. However, mere access to those with power does not improve one's power position unless one is willing to cultivate such opportunities. To the extent that lower-level employees cultivate access, and enhance control, over important organization resources, they can achieve a position central to either the core technology of the organization or the major organizational network.

Again, drawing on Mechanic's concepts of lower participant power, Farrell and Peterson (1982) argue that individual political behavior in organizations has been inadequately studied. Three key dimensions on which communication and political influence can be examined are internal (within company) or external, vertical or lateral, and legitimate or illegitimate. Porter et al. (1981) also emphasize the informational aspects of subordinate power and political influence. These authors classify upward political influence as control of either sanctions or information. Within the information category three methods are identified: persuasion (both the actor's objectives and influence attempts are open), manipulative persuasion (the objective is concealed but the attempt is open), and manipulation (both the objective and the attempt are concealed). They predict that persuasion will be used a low or moderate amount, but that both manipulative persuasion and manipulation will be used frequently. In manipulative persuasion the motive seems to be, "If I can convey my message in such a way that my own self-interests are disguised, I have a better chance at successful influence." The manipulation tactic, which involves withholding or distorting information as well as overwhelming the target person with too much information, was one of the three most commonly observed tactics mentioned in an empirical study of managers from thirty industrial firms (Allen et al., 1979).

Recent research suggests that the implications of power and status on communication may vary depending on certain structural elements. Structural aspects affect not only the quantity of information flow but also its type and accuracy. The findings vary and are far too few to warrant sound conclusions. In a study of organization size, Ingham (1970) found that workers in small firms (fewer than 100 employees) have significantly more nonwork communication with their foremen on a daily basis than workers in larger companies (over 30,000 employees).

Another study (Bacharach and Aiken, 1977) reports that the effects of organizational structure on communication frequency depend on which hierarchical level is examined. Structural variables, such as size and shape, tend to have greater impacts at subordinate organizational levels than at higher levels. In addition, these researchers found that organizational size is positively related to the amount of verbal upward, downward, lateral, and total communication by subordinates. Jablin (1982), on the other hand, found that subordinates in very large organizations perceive less superior-subordinate openness than do subordinates in smaller organizations (fewer than 1000 employees). Together these studies imply that as organization size increases, subordinates increasingly communicate with their superiors, but this large volume of communication is task related and is perceived by subordinates as increasingly closed rather than open.

Research on span of control, another structural aspect of organizations, indicates that (a) narrow span of control tends to increase the total amount of upward and downward communication between superiors and subordinates (Brewer, 1971); (b) span of control seems to have no effect on the means (written or oral) by which a superior communicates with his or her subordinates (Udell, 1967); and (c) subordinate perceptions of openness in superior-subordinate communication are not differentially affected by superior's span of control (Jablin, 1982). These findings suggest that it may not be the quantity of time spent interacting with one's superior but the quality of the interaction that most affects perceptions of superior-subordinate communication openness.

Decision Making and
Superior-Subordinate Communication

The standard pyramidal shape of most organizations suggests that the most important decisions are usually made by top management. Decision makers require information both to define problems and to generate lists of alternative solutions. Often this information is acquired through upward communication from subordinates. To the extent this is true, both quantity and accuracy of superior-subordinate communication influence managerial decision making.

Intuitively, it seems obvious that the possession of accurate and relevant information improves decision making. A large body of research on information and decision making (Connolly, 1977; Slovic et al., 1977; O'Reilly, 1977) substantiates this. Too much information, however, can be harmful (O'Reilly, 1978) and does not lead to improved decisions.

Information for decision making has to be edited as it passes through successive levels in the hierarchy if managers are to avoid becoming completely overloaded. Thus top management has to rely on the accuracy and summarization skills of subordinates who have access to, and control over, this information. Upward communication is often distorted and filtered (Jones et al., 1963; Watson, 1965; Watson and Bromberg, 1965). When a subordinate is providing information to a superior who has control over the subordinate's fate, he or she is likely to be more guarded than when communicating with other employees of similar status. Consequently, information that reflects favorably on the subordinate is passed upward and unfavorable information is suppressed. Trust between superior and subordinate is an important factor influencing information accuracy. O'Reilly (1978) demonstrated that when trust is low, subordinates are more likely to withhold unfavorable but relevant information, while passing favorable but irrelevant items. Research on source credibility also suggests that trustworthiness of the source may be more important than the source's expertise (O'Reilly and Roberts, 1976).

Another factor influencing the accuracy of information received by a decision maker is the mobility aspirations of the subordinate. Early research (Kelley, 1951; Cohen, 1958) confirms that when subordinates believe those in higher positions have the power to influence their upward mobility, they are more likely to attempt to create a favorable impression by becoming friendlier and more supportive of the higher-power person. High subordinate mobility aspirations can result in decreased accuracy of message to superiors that is manifested in filtering and the omission of negative information (Read, 1962; Roberts and O'Reilly, 1974).

A final factor influencing the accuracy of information received by a decision maker from his or her subordinates is group norms. As summarized by O'Reilly (1978), when group conformity is high, and when clear rewards and punishment accompany transmission of certain types of information, distortion is both possible and probable.

COMMUNICATION NETWORKS

Superior-subordinate communication is a limited dyadic relationship in the totality of organization communication. Rather than represent this totality simply in terms of a summation of such dyadic relationships, a more accurate picture of the organization emerges if we focus on networks of interaction at successive levels of aggregation, stopping at the organization's boundaries.

Networks are sets of relatively stable contacts among people through which information is generated and flows. Obviously networks are used for all sorts of things; not only are they the warp and woof of the fabric of organizational life, they also define authority, social, political, and other organizational systems, and are the funnels through which flows information used to make decisions through which the organization is warned of external dangers, and so on. The emerging picture is one of blooming, buzzing confusion, the unravelling of which is a real challenge for organizational communication research.

Early network studies used small (usually five-person) experimental problem-solving groups assigned simple or complex problems (Bavelas, 1950; Shaw, 1964). Only when high-speed computers were developed that could handle large data sets did network studies become more sophisticated and move into real organizations (see Burt, 1980; Roberts and O'Reilly, 1974). Today a number of data-analytic strategies are available (Fombrun, 1978) that enable increasingly sophisticated questions to be addressed in the network literature.

The earliest laboratory studies demonstrated that imposing communication networks on groups influenced their problem-solving efficiency, communication activity, organizational development, and member satisfaction. In the 1970s, communication research identified network properties and attempted to determine whether networks used for different purposes are the same or overlapping (see Roberts and O'Reilly, 1974; Schwartz and Jacobson, 1977). These studies found that organizational members are linked through several types of relationships—such as friendship or authority—and that these networks may vary considerably in structure.

A number of communication roles were identified in networks, such as participant, isolate, bridge, liaison, and tree node (Monge and Lindsey, 1973). Role research began with interests in diffusion of information in informal systems (Davis, 1953; Sutton and Porter, 1968) and diffusion of innovation (Coleman et al., 1966). It has come the full route to describing, with some care, the various kinds of communication roles seen in organizations (Roberts and O'Reilly, 1974; Schwartz and Jacobson, 1977; Tushman and Scanlon, 1981), and suggesting that some roles may act as magnets for such phenomena as power in organizations (Blau and Alba, 1982; Fombrun, 1983). This work is nicely summarized by Monge et al. (1978: 311-331).

Network research has also identified descriptive properties of group or intergroup relations in organizations. These properties include connectedness or cohesiveness (Roberts and O'Reilly, 1974), centrality or the degree to which relations are guided by the formal hierarchy (Tichy et al., 1979), vertical differentiation or the degree to which different organizational hierarchical levels are represented in work networks (O'Reilly and Roberts, 1977), horizontal differentiation or the degree to which different job areas exist in a network (Mohr, 1971), and coalitions or linkages among individuals that consolidate their power (Thibaut and Kelley, 1959).

Complexity and Networks

The network literature developed because of the increased recognition that organizations are complex systems. Complexity is assumed but not studied in the network literature. Here we define complexity as having to do with the number of different things that must be dealt with simultaneously (Scott, 1981). Generally, complexity refers to division of labor, job titles, multiple divisions, and hierarchical levels. Other kinds of complexity are bound to be identified as computerization and automation increase. The three most commonly discussed forms of complexity—horizontal differentiation, vertical (hierarchical) differentiation, and spatial dispersion—are good candidates for examination in network studies. They are undoubtedly influenced by, and influence, the ways networks develop. However, the network literature has given relatively little attention specifically to vertical differentiation.

Horizontal differentiation is concerned with the way tasks are assigned. There are basically two ways this occurs: (1) A worker completes many aspects of the job, or (2) the total work package is divided rather minutely and different workers do each task (Hage and Aiken, 1969). The early laboratory investigations of networks varied tasks along a dimension of problem complexity and in so doing left people with simple, repetitive, or more complicated tasks. Recent field studies, however, have been more concerned with how networks are structured and how outcome variables such as star status and satisfaction are related to these structures. Studying how tasks are hooked together seems an important extension of this because it expands our knowledge of how to design tasks from individual difference studies (see, for example, Hackman and Lawler, 1971; Roberts and Glick, 1981) to an extended knowledge base in which individuals are placed within the social fabric of their work groups. This kind of horizontal differentiation in which tasks are a focus could be combined with a kind of differentiation in which information and information flow are also key aspects.

Another aspect of horizontal differentiation is subunit breakdown. This includes both the number of jobs and the number of subunits. Organizations are considered to be complex to the extent that they have more subunits and more jobs than other organizations (Blau and Shoenherr, 1971). Network approaches to this kind of complexity highlight pockets of information and activity, and quickly identify magnets of power.

Spatial dispersion may be either horizontal or vertical. Except for the interorganizational network literature, which focuses primarily on issues such as interlocking directorships and the associated possibilities for organizational control, the network literature has not been concerned with impacts of organizational dispersion on any aspect of communication, such as accuracy or reliability, or on any other outcome such as decision making and power. In one respect this is logical, because it is self-evident that the key decision makers will not be at organizational peripheries or outside organizations altogether. But is it self-evident? Some organizational boundary people who have control of information and other resources are probably important contributors to major decisions. Outside regulatory agencies, interests groups, and the like (Mintzberg, 1983) make decisions that influence the kinds of decisions that can be made in organizations. It is important to study spatial dispersion issues because more dispersion is occurring.

Granovetter's (1973) interesting work on the strength of weak ties might be extended to issues of both complexity and power. This work claims that weak ties between two distinct but richly articulated networks, through people weakly tied to each, are important for purposes of adaptability.

Power and Networks

Power is a relation among social actors in which one social actor can get another to do something he or she otherwise would not do (Dahl, 1957). Most studies of power focus on hierarchical power, such as the power of bosses over subordinates, or the power of low-level employees, as previously discussed. A nice example of how interpersonal power is discussed relatively independently of organizational power is Manz and Giola's (1983) explication of the interrelationship of power and control. Until recently this preoccupation with interpersonal power led to the neglect of an obvious aspect of organizations

(Perrow, 1970). That is, in organizations tasks are divided among a few major departments or subunits, and all the subunits are not equally powerful. This recognizes that power is a structural as well as an interpersonal phenomenon, created by the division of labor and departmentalization that characterizes organizations (Pfeffer, 1981). This broader view of power is one that lends itself easily to a network approach. Fombrun (1983) demonstrates that attributions of power across a social network are much more dependent on structural than on member characteristics.

Power goes hand in hand with politics. Politics are the activities undertaken in organizations to acquire, develop, and use power and other resources to obtain preferred outcomes in a situation in which there is uncertainty or dissensus about choices (Pfeffer, 1981). Thus manifestations of power can be identified through examining political activities in organizations designed to obtain power.

According to a number of authors, power includes both authority and influence (Lawrence and Lorsch, 1967; Bacharach and Lawler, 1980). It is argued that power vested in authority is dichotomous (one either does or does not have it) and power vested in influence is continuous (one can have some, a little, or a lot of influence). Astley and Sachdeva (1984) explicate three sources of power: (1) hierarchical authority, (2) resource control, and (3) network centrality. A number of studies support the existence of these sources of power, but none is done from a strictly network tradition. According to the strategic contingencies theory (Hickson et al., 1971), power is derived from the ability to cope with uncertainty, centrality, and nonsubstitutability of the task. Pervasiveness of work-flow links among departments, and task criticalness, or the speed and severity with which the activities of a department affect the primary activities of the department, are additional aspects influencing power (Saunders, 1981).

Influence is more elusive than authority, and, consequently, formal organization structures do not always pick it up. One could assess, to some degree, formal organization structures as repositories of authority. Finding the links among key coalitions is critical to identifying influence, but a focus on influence networks provides a more complete view of organizations as political animals. Roos and Hall's (1980) development of influence diagrams may offer a way to uncover influence and its relation to decision making.

One of the few investigations of political processes in organizations that lends itself to a network paradigm is Riley's (1983) examination of three major structural features of institutions: signification, legitimation, and domination. Signification arises from the codes or modes of coding information. It reflects the symbolic orders or cultural components of an institution. Legitimation concerns the interplay between value standards and sectional interests, and does not necessarily imply collective agreement about values. Domination is developed through authorization and allocation. "Authorization" refers to the capability to have command over objects or material, and "allocation" refers to resources. Political themes were derived from analyzing interview content from two organizations. Three categories of symbols were examined: verbal symbols, or what the organization's repository of metaphors, myths, jokes, legends, and the like could tell; action symbols, or those expressions of rituals, strategies, and processes such as decision making and socialization; and material symbols.

Verbal symbols provided a rich insight into the political imagery of the organizations. In one organization signification was observed through the game and military metaphors that dominated discussion, and interviews were filled with images of cards and players, wars, teams, battles, armies, pugilists, and wounds. The game metaphor provides legitimation by providing the sanctions and generalizations of organizational political processes. The verbal symbols of authority and allocation illustrate the power of political images. (One interviewee talked of being the "sacrificial lamb.") Verbal themes had to do with how to use power and authority to engage in political action.

Action symbols that denote signification have to do with playing or not playing the game. One way to do this is to obtain control over information. Legitimation is gained through competition that legitimates actions that would otherwise provoke negative sanctions. Covert action is used to get things done. Internal competition that fosters these activities often produces a political culture in which employees are wary of each other. The power to allocate resources reproduces one's power. Material symbols act as signs, legitimate the status and behavior of these who have them, and serve as bases for power.

While this study was not done from a network perspective, its content fits well with that methodology. If one looks at the verbal, action, and material symbols of power from a network perspective, one might obtain a more complete understanding of the political culture of organizations.

Decision Making and Networks

Again, although network analysis offers a strong methodological tool for studying decision making, it has not been applied to this area. The first major issue that must be considered in organizational decision making is how problems are defined and who is allowed to make decisions (Beyer, 1982). The solutions to these two issues reflect the attitudes, values, and ideologies of people in organizations. Something about those ideologies might be fathomed by investigating network articulation and change as a problem is recognized. Often problems are not chosen or even recognized by organizations, but are thrust on them from outside. These kinds of problems will probably be the easiest to research in terms of identifying the networks into which they fall and the manner in which they are transmitted and messaged.

Several models of organizational decision making might best be subjected to empirical investigation using network approaches. Underlying all these models is the assumption that more than one actor is usually involved in the decision process. Some writers (Lindblom, 1959, 1979; Allison, 1971) view organizational decision making as an incremental process, in which only small changes from some previous course of action occur. One could examine over time how information flows with the decision process and how people come together to formulate decisions, taking network pictures of information flows and use of that information over time. One problem with this approach is that the observation of stable patterns of change over time does not necessarily prove incrementalism. It may reflect a rational choice model of decision making, the model favored by economists. This model suggests that decisions are made rationally, based on limited information, and with the goal of maximum or satisfactory benefit to the decision maker (March and Simon, 1958). Empirical observations of networks in which people are asked why they make the choices they do might help differentiate incrementalism from rational choice behavior.

Another approach to decision making is the garbage can model, in which organizations are conceptualized as contexts, or garbage cans, into which problems, solutions, participants, and choice opportunities are poured (Cohen et al., 1972). A key variable is the right to participate. Sometimes everyone in a situation has that right; at other times the right is limited. Cohen et al. conclude that in organizations, problems are rarely resolved. Decision makers and problems tend to follow each other through choice situations; important problems are more likely to be resolved than unimportant ones, but unimportant choices are more likely than important choices to resolve problems. These authors provide a simulation of the model. Again, one could test the model with sequential network observations of how problems move through organizations and choice situations. In fact, Roos and Hall's (1980) illustration of influence diagrams and organizational power is a primitive beginning in this direction.

A third approach to decision making emphasizes equivocality in organizations, and focuses specifically on interpretation of events (Weick, 1979). Weick focuses on how people make sense of their environments, noting that inputs are equivocal because they are devoid of meaning or have confusing meaning. As actors come into organizations, they select meanings and interpretations of them. Selection is guided by people's intentions to be rational, ethical, deliberate, and plausible. But intentions often fail (Salancik, 1977) and, because of this, organizational selection often exhibits a haphazard quality. Often, according to the model, the enacted environment occurs when people treat incoming input as known, rather than unknown. In this case, people may well do what they did before, and the environment appears stereotypic and routinized. What is done bears a close resemblance, then, to invoking standard operating procedures. Selection is conservative, and this suggests one reason organizations are slow to change. People try to fit novel interpretations and actions into what they knew all along. When something does not fit, it is discarded or misinterpreted. Again, one might begin to test the tenets of this complex model through sequential network observations. A set of observers could independently interpret information coming into an organization, attach meaning to it, and then observe how it is used and changed as it goes through organizations. The decision process would be uncovered using this strategy.

SUMMARY

Recent approaches to organizational communication research have used a conceptual framework based on information processing (Galbraith, 1973; Tushman, 1979; Tushman and Nadler, 1978). This model treats information as a change in knowledge that is the consequence of gathering, interpreting, and synthesizing data. An organization's effectiveness depends on its ability to match its information-processing requirements with the information-processing capacity of its units. Tushman and Nadler (1978) propose that as both the task and environmental uncertainty and complexity increase, there are greater demands for information processing (Duncan, 1972; Lawrence and Lorsch, 1967). This requirement for increased information processing may result from two factors. First, with greater uncertainty more information must be processed to obtain some degree of predictability. Second, increased environmental complexity causes more signals and stimuli to be received and processed (O'Reilly and Pondy, 1979).

Within this framework, information can be viewed as a valuable resource, and access to and control of channels of communication lead to power acquisition. As formulated in the strategic contingency model (Hickson et al., 1971) and echoed in Pfeffer's (1981) resource dependency theory, power stems from the ability to reduce the primary uncertainty that faces an organization; those who control information can reduce uncertainty and acquire power. More specifically, power varies according to (1) the criticalness of the uncertainty, (2) the effectiveness of a subunit in reducing uncertainty, and (3) how easily the uncertainty can be reduced by others. One's position in the organization structure affects the amount of information one possesses, as does one's centrality in the communication network. Both these factors affect the ability of a person to wield power and influence. And power has important ramifications for understanding the utilization of information. Research by Pfeffer and Salancik (1977, 1978) demonstrates that (1) power is directly related to the ability to obtain scarce and critical resources, and (2) power may be used to refine the criteria used in decision making. In addition, those in power are often able to institutionalize their positions and resist changes that might reduce their control.

Just as an information-processing view of organizations may elucidate complexity and power relationships, it may also clarify decision-making relationships. That too much information is detrimental to good decision making has already been shown (O'Reilly, 1980). Some heuristics are available for identifying the kind of information accepted and the kind ignored (Nisbett and Ross, 1980; Kahneman and Tversky, 1973). Relationships between an organizational subunit's needs and information attended to in decision making have begun to be uncovered, but are far from well understood.

Overall, it appears that applying an information-processing view of organizations to relationships among communication, complexity, power, and decision making might allow for the development of theoretical models to guide future research programs.

We contend that it is now time to draw network methodology and the themes of complexity, decision making, and power more tightly together, to deemphasize superior-subordinate communication in favor of broader sketches or organizational linkages, and perhaps to extend and integrate our knowledge by using an information-processing approach. It is also time to outline characteristics of future organizations that will influence communication and the relationships of communication to complexity, decision making, and power.

THE FUTURE

In addition to sophisticated research findings regarding superior-subordinate communication and observations of organizations as complicated networks, technological changes are taking place that in many ways may render these findings obsolete. Organizational communication is increasingly influenced by two major areas of technological advancement: (a) telecommunications, computers, and office automation hardware development, and (b) the development of artificial intelligence and "expert systems" to assist in various stages of a manager's decision-making process. Both these developments have immense consequences for organizational communication and communication structuring.

TECHNOLOGICAL CHANGES

Today, nearly 140 years after the creation of the telegraph, the first telecommunications device, we are on the verge of technological revolution that may reveal its greatest potential in the area of communication (Bell, 1979). Recent developments in microelectronics and telecommunications provide us with a new information technology to handle large amounts of information, transferred at greater speed and lower cost than ever before (Resnihoff, 1980).

The increased reliability, greater performance, and lower cost of integrated chips are based on their small physical size and increased "packing densities." Using telecommunications technology, these integrated chip-based information-processing devices can communicate with one another, leading to possibilities for transferring and utilizing knowledge that differ qualitatively and quantitatively from what existed before.

Communications technology provides the infrastructure to integrate such applications as electronic banking, network information systems, and teleconferencing. The interweaving of telecommunications, data base management, and office automation involves long lead times and significant organizational changes, and often meets with considerable resistance (Keen, 1981). Although much time is required to put such infrastructures into place, if they work, their exploitation may be rapid.

A number of technological developments on the horizon are expected to change the shape of organizational communication. The "smart" or "communicating" copiers, with an all-digital device capable of transmitting and receiving digital representations of pages, is under development. This machine will call up the image of a page from a computer's memory, direct it to an image transfer device, and then copy this "document that doesn't exist." This copier may also be equipped with editing capability and may have the ability to add or delete material passing through it. In addition, it could serve as a local printer for any kind of communication from a remote point: computer output, materials retrieved from archives, or telecommunication messages. Such a machine could be a central channel for the speedier, more accurate transfer of information, but, on the other hand, it could also be a tool for the creation of a new sort of organizational bedlam—unofficial "official documents."

A new generation of superphones known as "electronic voice messaging devices," "voice mailboxes," and "voice-store-forward" systems are being developed. Superphone users avoid time-wasting rounds of telephoning by recording and then sending phone messages digitally by computer to any number of recipients. In addition, they eliminate calls that require no immediate attention. For example, a sales manager may telephone a district office to ask for current sales figures that can be transmitted easily by automated voice messages.

Projections about other future telephone capacities abound. A vice president of General Telephone and Electronics (Schrage, 1983) predicts that before 1990 home phones with features now reserved for businesses, such as intercom and conference calling, will cost no more than today's basic telephone. Phone systems will also have capacities for call forwarding, automatic answering, voice responsive directory/dialing, and central dictation, and will also serve as simple terminals for retrieving information from public and private data bases.

Teleconferencing in organizations may well increase. The most common use of audio teleconferencing at present is for brainstorming sessions, business updates, and training programs. However, some companies are increasingly using it to conduct second-round interviews, and it is now legal in many states to conduct board meetings using teleconferencing. Early optimism regarding the demand for teleconferencing has abated somewhat, however, as executives encounter difficulties in presenting polished "TV" images. Some find that nonverbal communication (termed "body language") operates to its fullest only when both parties are physically present.

Other technological developments abound, including the following: electronic mail that allows reports, memos, and drafts to be transmitted simultaneously to a number of company employees, speeding up in-house communications, and resulting in faster decision making; computers that provide direct and timely access to accurate product, customer, and internal information; and systems that can turn reams of numbers into charts and colorful graphics that are easily digested and that result in faster action.

ARTIFICIAL INTELLIGENCE

A nontechnical description of artificial intelligence research, the development of thinking and intelligent machines, is sufficient to create visions of people dominated by their mechanistic progeny. While some may argue that the nature of this threat is reducible to a matter of definition, it is undeniable that computers and other "intelligent" machines have, and will continue to assume, many "uniquely human" characteristics. Herbert Simon (1977) addresses this problem by contrasting those capabilities people bring to the world of work with the potentials of intelligent machines. Beginning his comparison with the "dumb" machines of the earlier mechanization process, Simon concludes that the only remaining advantages of humans over machines at this stage are their general-purpose problem-solving capacity and the flexible use of sensory organs and fingers. Extending his investigation into the age of artificial intelligence, Simon finds humans with but one remaining comparative advantage: sensory capacity. With the introduction of artificial intelligence into the organization, we find that even the general problem-solving duties of top management may be challenged.

Current advances into the realm of "intelligence," however, are attributable less to breakthroughs in hardware technology than to advances in software technology. Although the speed of computers has increased many times over in recent years, the raw computing power can barely approximate the powers of the human brain (Alexander, 1982). Computers are intelligent when their programming duplicates the heuristic processes by which humans focus on sufficient information to make decisions and survive.

Some feel that even with these heuristic aids, computers as currently designed will never be more than pale copies of human intellect. The human brain is thought to be composed of neurons, each of which functions both as a memory unit and as a microprocessor (Sinclair, 1983). When engaged in a recognition task, the human brain operates in parallel, meaning that many bits of information may be processed simultaneously. Computers that have from one to a dozen processors operate serially with many times the memory capacity of the human brain. Hardware that can imitate the parallel processing of the brain is currently under development, but it is estimated that this technology will not be reliable for quite some time.

The juxtaposition of these two sources of "intelligence" in machines—guided information processing (heuristics), and parallel information processing—should suggest a final emphasis in our transposition of human qualities to machines. As Simon (1977:126) emphatically notes, "The first lesson of living in an information rich world [is] that a major task of an effective information system is to filter information, not to proliferate it." (1977: 126). The compression of vast amounts of information describes the functioning of a properly effective artificial intelligence system.

The software technology advancement relevant to the study of organizations is in codifying human problem-solving processes, ranging from day-to-day operational processes to lower-frequency expert decision processes. As an example of the former, interdepartmental scheduling, previously a guaranteed headache for middle managers due to the magnitude and complexity of the problem, has been transformed by means of operations research techniques into a well-understood, fairly automated process (Simon, 1977). Expert systems, such as Stanford Medical School's MYCIN, a system that helps doctors diagnose bacterial infections (see Rheingold, 1983), are created through a process of intensive multiple interviews with experts the systems will be programmed to imitate. These interviews reveal the unwritten rules or heuristics by which these human experts reach their decisions.

IMPLICATIONS OF FUTURE DEVELOPMENTS
FOR COMMUNICATION

While the effects of technological advancement and the development of artificial intelligence on communication in the workplace are unknown, some impacts and some areas of caution are fairly obvious. These impacts will have numerous implications for all forms of organizational communication. Here we limit ourselves to potential impacts on superior-subordinate and network communications.

Technological Change and Communication

Superior-subordinate communication. An important part of an organization's authority or influence system is the evaluation of performance and the administration of rewards or punishments based on that evaluation. If organizational rewards are important to participants, the right to evaluate provides power to the person possessing that right. Evaluations may be based on assessment of the process by which a job is done or of the outcomes of the process. Process evaluation is typically interpersonal in nature and difficult to do by computer. However, outcome evaluations are easily suited to information technology, facilitating a multitude of measures, their comparison, and their summarization. If one assumes that information used in evaluation is often the information that is most easily and quickly available (Pfeffer, 1978), then advances in information technology and computerization will lead to a greater focus on outcome measures. Outcome measures appear objective, require less direct supervision, and decrease the visibility of power in organizations (Pfeffer, 1978).

In addition, outcome measures become more important in a world in which spatial and physical constraints no longer determine organizational arrangements (Keen, 1981). With the advent of personal computers, the boundaries of organizations are expected to become even more abstract, once employees become "at-home contractors." It should be noted that outcome measures are generally difficult to employ when there is high interdependence among many positions or when connections between actions and outcomes are uncertain.

As discussed by Pfeffer (1978), information technology enhances the possibility of monitoring compliance with procedures. As a consequence, the implementation of formalized procedures is more possible. On the other hand, information technology also results in greater ability to obtain accurate and rapid feedback about organizational performance. As a result, the implementation of rules and procedures is less necessary because behavior does not need to be as directly and immediately controlled to ensure the same level of control. Pfeffer (1978: 77) concludes that "information technology . . . permits the use of fewer rules and procedures, as well as the delegation of decision making authority." As a precautionary note, superiors need to be aware that evaluation and feedback via computer is not equivalent to a person-to-person interaction. Computers rob us of body language and voice inflection, and it is likely that in many situations personal contact and control are needed to ensure accuracy and understanding, and to maintain harmony within the organization. Power will be held by those managers who can most aptly assess the organization's information needs and assure that data being fed into the new system are pertinent and accurate.

There are two opposing arguments concerning the influence of information technology and decision making in organizations (Pfeffer, 1978). The earliest argument stressed that because information technology enhances the capabilities of managers, recentralization of control and the movement of decision making to higher levels is inevitable. The counterargument maintains that information technology will increase decentralization of organizational decision making. Burlingame (1961) and Pfeffer and Leblebici (1977) note that with computers, feedback on performance and organizational processes will be more accurate and more rapidly available. Thus if the delegated decisions are not to a manager's liking, he or she can quickly determine the consequences of those decisions and take corrective action. A conceptual issue arises, however. If decision making is delegated because the decisions can be rapidly and accurately assessed, is there a real sharing of power or control? Pfeffer concludes that information technology can make possible the appearance of decentralization while maintaining centralized control over decision making. Since participation and decentralization are generally thought to be motivating, the organization benefits. It seems clear that some jobs will receive greater actual autonomy through computerization. Sales staffs, in particular, will consult their computers rather than their middle managers for pricing, inventory, and marketing information.

Another major impact of computerization and information technology is the huge quantity of information that becomes available, and the rapidity with which this is accomplished. Decision makers are likely to be inundated with information and, as noted earlier (O'Reilly, 1980), increased quantity of information does not necessarily correspond with improved decisions. It is unlikely that Simon's plea for distilling rather than expanding information will be heeded. Due to increased information flow, the manager's job will require many new skills in planning, controlling, reporting, and supervising (Keen,

1981). The main responsibility of managers may become the maintenance and improvement of decision systems and the training of subordinates (Simon, 1977). In addition, managers will spend more time and effort as members of task groups engaged in analyzing and designing policies and systems for implementing them. Middle managers will need to possess more general skills as companies demand solutions to interdisciplinary problems.

To evaluate and make decisions, superiors are likely to use information that is easily available (Pfeffer, 1978), just as they have always done. This may result in increased emphasis on computer-generated statistics and quantitative measures of organizational performance. It is not yet clear whether this information will replace personal face-to-face communication or merely supplement it. Simon (1977), however, predicts that as decision making is increasingly automated, the behavior of the system becomes more predictable and controllable, and hourly and daily decisions require less human intervention and more computer access. It is clear that personal contact requires greater effort than merely logging onto a terminal.

Communication networks. The kinds of technological changes discussed will probably have their greatest impact on communication structuring. The creation of documents that do not exist and the use of partially complete documents through image transfer devices, use of superphones, and further developments in teleconferencing predict far more complexity for organizations than we see today. Very complex systems lend themselves to the proliferation of a new kind of error. These are errors with low probabilities but that result in catastrophic outcomes (Perrow, 1984). An example is Three Mile Island, a system in which four relatively low-probability events, none with extreme negative consequences, happened simultaneously, very nearly resulting in extreme consequences.

Thus, in the future, complexity will be even more central than it is now, and one of the tasks of network researchers might be to assess whether complexity itself is a discontinuous variable. Whereas certain degrees of it are manageable, increasing it above some finite level results in a system that cannot be managed. Alternatively, it may be that highly complex systems can be managed if complexity is accompanied by tight structuring among essential tasks and managers. It must also be overlaid by a loose managerial structure that can be brought to bear as the configurations of the systems change due to internal changes in either the technology or the people operating it. Finally, complexity in such systems might be handled by designing tight coupling in some places and loose coupling in others (Weick, 1979).

Examples of highly complex systems of these kinds are increasing in number. What happens, for example, when a part from a nuclear power plant, designed to help cool one system while heating another, becomes dysfunctional due to metal fatigue? Or, what happens when the operators of the current U.S. air traffic control system take on the far more complex and integrated operations of our proposed new air traffic control system? In both cases the systems change.

Network approaches, from both methodological and content perspectives, seem ideally suited to addressing issues of complexity, as well as to using these issues to develop the network literature itself and move it from a purely descriptive to a prescriptive stance. For example, some research shows that task networks dominate authority and social networks in work organizations (Roberts and O'Reilly, 1974). If these findings became more pervasive, one could prescribe to managers the necessity of devoting more time to nurturing both social and authority networks in order to maintain healthy, fully operational organizations, particularly under conditions of growing complexity in which employees are unlikely to communicate sufficiently with others to have a good representation of the whole picture. Or, using strength of weak ties (Granovetter, 1973) and loose versus tight coupling notions as springboards, it may be possible to develop designed strategies organizations can follow in hooking tightly and loosely coupled parts of complex systems together. New information technologies may be used to ensure the kind of organizational design that can work in these highly complex systems. Alternatively, they may reduce complexity in that they make differentiation less necessary. Differentiation is used to cope with limits to cognitive abilities that are reduced by new information technologies.

Rapidity of information flow and integration of information exchange in organizations will have tremendous impacts on decision making. Network researchers might be able to assess whether rational, garbage can, or enacting environmental models of decision making seem to operate in technologically sophisticated systems to a different degree than they do elsewhere. It will be extremely important to know how decisions are made if errors are to be avoided and organizations are to operate smoothly. The operations of a garbage can model, for example, suggest managers search for different information sources from those of the operation of rational decision-making models.

It will probably be more important to manage power in complex systems of the future than it is in today's organizations. Superphones, smart copiers, and computers are tools of the powerful, if for no other reason than that they contribute to the aggregation of information in central locations. These aggregations can be identified through network procedures, and the methodology of networking allows power to predict other variables as well. For example, if one unit in a complex system situates itself so the vast majority of information comes and goes from it, this creates a condition whereby other units are dependent on it. When information and decisions move rapidly through the system, distortion, amplification and other effects can be created by the powerful unit. Similarly, restriction of information by the powerful unit can create technological and human breakdowns in other parts of the organization. Parts break, but the expertise to fix them exists only in the powerful unit; morale in other units falls, and other effects follow.

ARTIFICIAL INTELLIGENCE AND COMMUNICATIONS

The implications of artificial intelligence for organizational communication are different from those of advancing machine technologies. The main implication for organizational communication has to do with where and how decisions are made and implemented. However, there are also implications for organizational complexity.

Superior-subordinate communication. The major impact of artificial intelligence, or expert systems, on superior-subordinate communication will probably be its reduction. As superiors determine that they can obtain more "reliable and objective" information through these means, they may require less information from their subordinates. As mentioned earlier, access to, and control of, information leads to power. Thus those subordinates who have information available through expert systems will be better able to retain their power.

Artificial intelligence and expert systems are not yet frequently used in organizations, and it is likely that their initial use will be treated with caution or mistrust. Thus a superior may use an expert system to collect information and provide a recommended solution, in addition to soliciting recommendations from trusted staff and subordinates. When differences exist, it is not clear how a decision maker will decide. If earlier research is correct, the degree of trust between superior and subordinate will influence the importance the superior attaches to information from subordinates and the decisions he or she makes.

The decision to use manually collected data versus an expert system may also be influenced by type of decision and how tightly coupled the organization is. Analyses of human decision methods yield not hard-and-fast decision rules but soft-and-squishy heuristics and rules of thumb. Writing computer programs to function in tightly coupled systems on the basis of these heuristics presumes they are functional guides to responses in tightly coupled systems. Most systems and our attachments to them are not very tightly coupled. Squishy heuristics rather than the tight heuristics of computer programs are functional decision aids to human beings because we are most often only loosely coupled to our environments (Simons, 1977).

If it is borne out that the only comparative advantage humans retain over intelligent machines is their sensory capacity, care must be taken that human workers are not transformed into data-encoding slaves for these insensible machines. Lower organizational processes are usually the sort that lend themselves to information automation, and, of course, this may eliminate some lower-level jobs and superior-subordinate problems. Management training programs will have to emphasize openness and trust in superior-subordinate communication. Strategies will have to be developed to aid superiors and subordinates in their mutual interaction with decision-making routines in order to use these devices effectively and to avoid buildups of misunderstanding. Superior-subordinate communication research must move in the direction of developing communication pattern strategies that will reduce the dysfunctionalities of tightly coupled, rapidly moving systems.

Communication networks. If artificial intelligence is to assume any part of top management's decision-making duties, information must be transcribed from human-readable to a machine-readable format, a process too laborious for most firms to contemplate. Designing information networks that may or may not be similar to those discussed here may be one way to deal with this problem, spreading the cost of this labor-intensive, time-consuming transcription. Another solution currently under development is to design computer software that will accept human-readable format as input. If publications of the kind top executives use in their information search are produced by computer (as most are), little or no further data encoding is required. The only task remaining is to design and implement information networks. This is another reason it is important for network researchers to move beyond descriptive to prescriptive stages in their research.

Implicit in the previous discussion of information flow and automation is another implication of the use of artificial intelligence in organizations. A major difference exists between processes at lower and higher organizational levels; lower-level processes are usually fairly well understood (for exceptions, see Perrow, 1984), whereas higher processes are more often poorly understood, and hence unstructured (Simon, 1977). Even with its current low utilization, if information encoded into computers is to be used in decision making, these elusive decision rules or heuristics must be uncovered, dissected, and codified. This may be accomplished in a manner similar to that used to create expert systems.

The consequences of decision rule clarification for communication in organizations are twofold. First, so that organizational goals and decision criteria are not forced to take shape through the averaging process implicit in the construction of expert systems, organizations should undertake significant goal and criterion clarification efforts. Second, we may find that the format and wording of communication in organizations becomes increasingly rigid as the informational demands of automated decision systems are met. This will be so only to the extent, however, that intelligent computers do not possess flexible semantic capabilities to match those of humans. In any case, communication in organizations should generally increase in precision as employees become accustomed to the rigorous demands of automated decision systems.

The implications of increased use of artificial intelligence for power in organizations is unclear. A common science fiction fear is that the few who govern artificial intelligence systems will have all the power in a society. However, this would be true only to the extent that all necessary information could be provided via artificial intelligence systems. At this time, however, there is insufficient information even to extrapolate wildly about the impact on power and the relation of power to networking in networks in which some nodes are not human beings.

CONCLUSIONS

Here we have seen that the nature of superior-subordinate communication influences how subordinates respond to their jobs. Quantity of communication is important to job performance, and accuracy is increased when superiors are perceived to have influence and subordinates trust them, but not when subordinates have high mobility aspirations. The extent and nature of feedback are important in obtaining high-quality job performance.

When superior-subordinate communication is placed in the large framework of network interaction, the complexities of modern organizational life are highlighted. To date, the network literature has been more descriptive of network forms and roles and less predictive of work outcomes than the older area of superior-subordinate communication.

In the research literature these two areas are not integrated. Yet, particularly when combined with guesses about what organizations of the future may be like, it is apparent that further thinking is required to integrate superior-subordinate and network communication. Future research in organizational communication should embed superior-subordinate communication into the larger network fabric of organizations, and focus on the two themes that seem to emerge from the superior-subordinate literature and that can be addressed more specifically in the network literature: the relation of communication to (1) power and (2) decision making; and a third theme inherent in the network literature, the relation of communication and complexity.

All in all, we predict greater communication problems in organizations as they become more complex, particularly if vast efforts are not made to improving information flow, encouraging appropriate interpretation, and the like. The use of power will be determined to a great extent by how communication systems and decision effectiveness will result from the flow of information in those systems, how well managers and others can handle vast amounts of information, and whether they can be trained to retain and ignore information appropriately.

Those who design technical systems and those who implement the designs currently make no effort to anticipate their human effects (Walton, 1982). Artificial intelligence systems are designed with human consequences in mind, yet unintended consequences occur. Policymakers undoubtedly do not recognize the unintended consequences of implementing those complex systems in organizations. More to the point for organizational communication researchers, it is probable that current approaches to research in complex organizations are insufficient to model and integrate communication systems to come. Either new models must be developed or new notions of organizational form and shape, in which new kinds of hierarchical communication will occur, must be added to older models.

Existing complex systems are usually inefficient. Nuclear power plant managers have known this for some time. Of the large-scale systems currently in operation, the U.S. air traffic control system is a model of efficiency (La Porte et al., 1977). However, unlike modern weapons systems and nuclear power plants, and even multinational firms, it operates with seemingly fewer variables, and it is possible to unhook various parts of the system in emergencies. One might call this a more linear system than complex nuclear power plants, nuclear aircraft carriers, and the like.

In these systems, as emergencies begin it is often impossible to observe causal variables and to decouple parts of the system from each other to isolate malfunctioning parts (Perrow, 1984). We have numerous examples today of the design and building of complex systems that have never operated, such as the numerous nuclear power plants currently unfinished or inoperable. While it is costly to humankind to design and build complex systems that cannot work, this may be our only salvation. Until we develop the social engineering strategies to handle such systems, we are in danger of creating massive, irreversible problems in trying to operate them. Alternatively, until social scientists can pinpoint the negative consequences of operating such systems, they cannot offer constructive criticism about design features that might be changed to reduce the possibility of unacceptable errors. Since it is highly likely that engineering breakthroughs will continue to render larger numbers of complex systems operational, it is truly important that the organizational research most appropriate to them be given greater emphasis. Understanding the communication, information, complexity, power, and decision-making aspects of such systems is critical to our survival.

Chapter 3

COMMUNICATION AND ORGANIZATIONAL CLIMATES
Review, Critique, and a New Perspective

Marshall Scott Poole

Because of a certain atmosphere that had developed in my working at the White House, I was not as concerned about its illegality as I should have been.

(Jeb Magruder, testifying about
the Watergate incident)

The construct implied by the term "organizational climate" is important for organizational and communication theory, because it represents the linkage between the organizational situation and members' cognitions, feelings, and behaviors. The profound effects of situation or context on human behavior are widely acknowledged. Hardly a review of organizational behavior research omits the now standard lament that the characteristics of situations must be better understood and more clearly defined if we are to explain behavior in organizations. However, despite a great deal of attention to this problem, there has not been much progress in defining organizational contexts in a behaviorally relevant manner.

There is considerable agreement on key dimensions describing organizational context and structure (for example, size, technology, centralization, formalization), but these dimensions are meant to describe properties of organizations and are not designed to articulate with individual behavior. Typically, relationships between such structural variables and individual attitudes and behavior are small but significant, indicating a link, but an ill-defined or mediated one (Porter and Lawler, 1965). Attempts to define the situation in terms of more specific properties, such as characteristics of the workplace or coworkers, have also yielded discouraging results. Several detailed taxonomies of situations have been developed (Sells, 1963; Barker, 1963; Fredericksen et al., 1972), but they are so complex that it is difficult to trace exactly what features of the situation explain behavioral variation.

It seems, then, that attempts to define situations in terms of objective properties pose a dilemma for organizational researchers: We must either confine ourselves to useful, but global, dimensions that exhibit weak relationships to behavior or descend into a confusing particularity that sacrifices theoretical power and parsimony. The concept of organizational climate promises a way out of this dilemma, on the premise that only those aspects of the situation that are meaningful for members, *the experienced environment*, are really relevant to members' actions.

A look at some definitions of climate may help clarify the term. The classic definition of climate is Tagiuri's (1968: 25):

> Climate is the relatively enduring quality of the total environment that (a) is experienced by the occupants, (b) influences their behavior, and (c) can be described in terms of the values of a particular set of characteristics (or attributes) of the environment.

Campbell et al. (1970: 390) offer this definition:

> [We] might define climate as a set of attributes specific to a particular organization that may be induced from the way that organization deals with its members and its environment. For the individual member within the organization, climate takes the form of a set of attitudes and expectancies which describe the organization in terms of both static characteristics (such as degree of autonomy) and behavior-outcome and outcome-outcome contingencies.

Finally, Schneider (1975: 474) proposes the following definition:

> Climate perceptions are psychologically meaningful molar descriptions that people can agree characterize a system's practices and procedures. By its practices and procedures a system may create many climates. People perceive climates because the molar perceptions function as frames of reference for the attainment of some congruity between behavior and the system's practices and procedures. However, if the climate is one which rewards and supports the display of individual differences, people in the system will not behave similarly.

Although the similarities in these definitions are clear, each also touches on unique facets of climate. Together they illustrate the complexity of the construct and also point to several critical problems in defining climate. As the following discussion indicates, there is much validity in Guion's (1973: 121) observation that "the concept of organizational climate is undoubtedly important, but it also seems to be one of the fuzziest concepts to come along in some time."

This essay attempts to reduce the fuzziness of the climate construct. It is both a review of the status of climate research and an attempt at reconstruction. While much of this chapter focuses on issues relevant to the study on climate in general, its central concern is with communication climate. Communication relates to organizational climate in two ways. First, communication itself is an important organizational practice, and therefore organizations should have a communication climate distinct from other aspects of climate, such as motivational climate (Litwin and Stringer, 1968) or climate for innovation (Hage and Aiken, 1966). This is supported by the fact that factor-analytic studies of climate have consistently isolated independent dimensions directly related to communication processes. But second, communication is implicated in other aspects of climate, because it is the medium for accomplishing much of the organization's work. One indicator of an innovative climate, for example, is whether members talk about new ideas. In a real sense, the whole concept of climate is bound up with communication. This chapter will focus on both relations: It will attempt to build a theory for understanding communication climates and will also explore the role of communication and interaction in creating climates.

This essay is divided into three sections: The first presents a review of previous theoretical work on climate and raises current controversies and problems in climate theory. The second section gives a selective review of the literature relevant to these theoretical propositions. It covers findings relevant to the validity of the climate construct, descriptions of climate, determinants of climate, and the effects of climate in the organization. Empirical research permits the resolution of some, but not all, problems raised in the first section. Following this, the third section critiques theory and research on climate and offers a structurational theory of climate as one answer to current dilemmas. Methods for conducting research within this theoretical framework are also discussed.

CONCEPTUAL ANALYSIS: STATE OF THE ART

THEORETICAL DEVELOPMENTS

Organizational climate is a contested concept. As the definitions catalogued above suggest, there is general agreement on many of its attributes, but there are also important areas of disagreement. Current thinking on climate can best be summarized as a series of theoretical statements, some of which are non-problematic and some of which are still the object of debate.

(1) There is consensus that organizational climate is a molar construct characterizing properties of an entire system, either the whole organization or an organizational subunit. James and Jones (1974) distinguish "psychological climate" which denotes individual perceptions of the organization, from "organizational climate," which refers to global attributes of the organizational environment that are salient to members. The empirical evidence indicates that this distinction is indeed a meaningful one, and that organizational climate is a construct independent of individual members' perceptions of the organization (see below).

This distinction also has important implications for how climate is operationalized and assessed. To measure *psychological* climate researchers need only measure individual members' perceptions of the organization. In the study of psychological climate these perceptions are of interest in their own right, and to obtain unit scores all the researcher has to do is take a mean. On the other hand, because *organizational* climate is a molar attribute of a system, merely assessing subjects' perceptions or meanings is not sufficient; researchers must also show that these perceptions or meanings index an attribute of the organization rather than idiosyncratic reactions. Guion (1973) has suggested two ways of doing this: Either researchers can validate summary measures of climate against some objective measure or they can show consensus in members' perceptions.

(2) There is also agreement that climate is descriptive rather than affective or evaluative. Using facet analysis, Payne et al. (1976) distinguish "organizational climate," which is a consensual description of the organization, from "satisfaction," which refers to the individual's evaluation of the job or organization, and also from organizational "morale," which refers to "the consensus of satisfaction with the organization." That climate is descriptive does not imply that value statements are not part of climate. Insofar as value statements occur in the organization's belief system (for example, "commitment is critical to this organization"), they are an integral aspect of climate. Only evaluations and affective reactions based on these values are excluded from the domain of the climate construct.

(3) It is also generally accepted that climate arises from, and is sustained by, organizational *practices*, which may be defined as systematized and customary activities deemed important by the organization or its members. Given its molar nature, however, climate is not tied to particular, specific instances, but rather to the general impressions members form after repeated experience with the system. Climate extends across time and situations in that it represents members' generalizations about the organization.

(4) There is disagreement concerning how "general" climate is. Some researchers assume that an omnibus set of dimensions or descriptive statements can be used to characterize *the* climate of a system. Climate dimensions developed by Litwin and Stringer (1968) (such as structure, reward, support) and Halpin and Crofts (1963) are often used for this purpose. In opposition, Schneider (1975) argues that organizations may have numerous different climates, such as a climate for safety (Zohar, 1980) or a climate for customer service (Schneider et al., 1980). Schneider et al. base this assertion on the connection between climates and organizational practices discussed in the previous point: If practices create climate, then there should be a separate climate for each distinct set of practices in the organization. This suggests that an organization has a communication climate insofar as communication is seen as a distinct, salient practice by the organization.

This is more than a difference in semantics or level of analysis, because the two positions imply different connections between climate and organizational practices. The assumption of an omnibus set of climate dimensions implies that people have a generalizable scheme of concerns that they bring into work situations (for example, workers are assumed to be concerned with the degree of job structure, whether they are adequately rewarded, and other aspects of the organization). Their specific experiences in this situation influence their apprehension of climate, but only insofar as they lead to reinterpretation of the general scheme. The general dimensions of climate remain more or less the same regardless of the nature of the organization and what its members do. On the other hand, the assumption of numerous climates presumes that the content of climates stems from particular practices the organization exhibits. Only those practices that are emphasized (for example, safety or customer service) will give rise to climates, and the resulting climate dimensions or themes will reflect the nature of the practices. For example, Zohar's (1980) safety climate has dimensions specifically reflecting safety issues, such as "perceived status of safety committee" and "management attitudes toward safety."

(5) There is also debate on whether climate is an objective or subjective construct. At the "objective" level, climate would be measured by means of physically verifiable artifacts or reseacher-based interpretations of organizational properties and processes (Jablin, 1980). For example, objective measures of communication climate include physical artifacts such as telephone calls or number of contacts recorded by the researcher or researcher-based codings of interaction among organizational members. Clearly these measures are not objective in the classic sense, because they incorporate the researcher's interpretations of organizational meanings, but they are arrived at independently of organizational members. At the "subjective" level, measures of communication climate would tap organizational members' perceptions of communication practices, such as how open their supervisors are or how much disagreements are tolerated. The relation between the two views is unclear. Payne and Pugh (1976: 1142-1143) review both objective and subjective measures of climate and conclude: "There have been very few studies which have examined the convergent validity of climate measures by comparing objective and subjective measures."

Theoretical statements of climate researchers exhibit an abiding uncertainty as to whether climate should be defined at the subjective or objective levels. Tagiuri (1968: 25), for example, characterizes climate as "phenomenologically external" to the actor, yet "in the actor's or observer's head." Campbell et al. (1970) state that the critical elements of climate are individual perceptions, yet they view climate as an organizational variable. How do the subjective and objective articulate in these views? The answer seems to be "not very well."

The standard account is given by Indik (1965) and Campbell et al. (1970), who postulate the model portrayed in Figure 3.1. The effects of objective independent variables such as size and organizational structure on member behavior are mediated by organizational and psychological process variables that include several dimensions of climate, such as perceived openness of communication and perceptions of the degree of coordination in the organizations. Because these mediating variables are dependent on common objective variables and on organizational processes through which they are experienced (for example, the organization's control processes) individual perceptions are assumed to be shared, accounting for the convergent perceptions found in many climate studies. The problem with this model is that it still leaves unclear what the status of climate is.

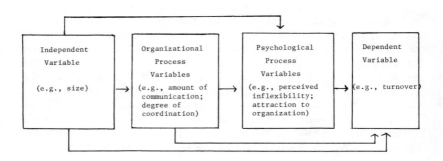

NOTE: The organizational process and psychological process variables include climate dimensions.

Figure 3.1 Prototype Paradigm for Influence of Organizational Structure on Outcomes (from Indik, 1965)

(6) It is widely assumed that organizational climates influence member behavior. Schneider (1975) argues that climates enable organizational members to apprehend order in the work environment and thus guide members' behavior as they attempt to adapt to the organization. Indik (1965) and Campbell et al. (1970) posit that climate mediates the effect of structural determinants on members' behavior. Evidence on the particular effects of climate will be summarized below.

(7) Climate also has affinities to the concept of organizational culture. Some authors claim that climate is an empiricist's substitute for the richer term, "culture," while others maintain that culture is vague and should be replaced by constructs with greater precision, of which climate is one. On the whole, climate seems to be a feature of, rather than a substitute for, culture. As a system of generalized beliefs, climate contributes to the coherency of a culture and guides its development. In terms of cultural analysis, the climate construct is closely akin to Bateson's (1958) concept of cultural *ethos*.

SUMMARY

Current views of climate agree on the following points: Climate is (1) a molar concept (2) that characterizes the practices and procedures of (3) an entire organization or subunit (4) in a descriptive rather than evaluative sense, and (5) influences the attitudes and behaviors of participants. There is still controversy or confusion over whether climate is subjective or objective, and over whether climates are generalized or distinct for distinct organizational practices. Empirical findings, discussed in the next section, shed some light on these issues.

EMPIRICAL EVIDENCE

The major findings of research on organizational climate can be organized into four categories, dealing with the validity, dimensions, causes, and effects of climate. This review is not intended to be exhaustive; it is limited to major studies and to studies that have important implications for the theoretical issues raised above.

The theoretical distinctions raised here and developed in the previous section eliminate some studies from consideration in this review. Since "climate" refers to an organizational construct, studies that define climate as individual members' perceptions of the organization will not be considered. In addition, this study omits reports using "climate" as a label or rubric for other variables, as when "leadership climate" is used to refer to variables that actually measure leader behavior (a large part of Redding's [1972] classic chapter on communication climate summarizes studies of this sort).

VALIDITY OF THE
ORGANIZATIONAL CLIMATE CONSTRUCT

Two kinds of evidence can be marshaled for the validity of the organizational climate construct. First, several studies support the contention that organizational climate is distinct from individual perceptions of the organization (psychological climate). Generally, variance in climate score is greater among organizations than within organizations, suggesting that climate is an organizational property (see Drexler, 1977; Zohar, 1980). In an explicit comparison, Paolillo (1982) investigated the relative strength of personal characteristics (sex, age, education level), situational variables (organization, size, number of levels of hierarchy, and specialization), and joint personal-situational variables (position tenure, hierarchical position, and percentage of time spent in supervisory activities) on climate in research units (as measured with Pelz and Andrews's 1976 instrument). He found that the four situational variables accounted for more than 60 percent of the variance in climate scores, lending support to the proposition that climate is a property of the unit and not of individual members. That organizational members consistently recognize climates and have little trouble reporting them also supports the sociological reality of the climate construct.

Second, studies support the discriminant validity of *descriptive* climate measures vis-à-vis measures of satisfaction and particular behavioral scales, such as leader consideration and initiating structure. Schneider and Snyder (1975) found relatively low correlations (.21 mean, with .55 to .00 range) between climate dimensions and two measures of job satisfaction, the Job Description Index (Smith et al., 1969) and Alderfer's (1972) measure of need satisfaction. Lafollette and Sims (1975) sampled 1161 employees of a major medical center and found that the correlation of climate with performance was markedly different than the relationship between satisfaction and performance, suggesting the independence of satisfaction and climate. These findings run counter to those of Johanneson (1973), whose study is often cited as evidence of the overlap between satisfaction and climate. Johanneson clustered climate measures with two measures of satisfaction (the Job Descriptive Index [JDI] and a measure developed by Science Research Associates, 1966) and found three clusters with both climate and satisfaction scores, leading him to conclude that climate and satisfaction measures were redundant. However, Payne et al. (1976) looked at the correlations between climate and satisfaction dimensions reported by Johanneson and noted that the median correlation between the two satisfaction measures and climate was .25 (maximum .67, minimum .05) and that between the satisfaction measures themselves was .33 (maximum .61, minimum .10). Correlations of this size suggest that satisfaction and climate are independent. House and Rizzo (1972) conducted a multitrait, multimethod validity study of a climate scale they developed vis-à-vis scales designed to tap behavioral descriptions (for example, role conflict, leader consideration, leader initiating structure). Despite the fact that their climate scales were considerably less general and more closely tied to behavior than most climate measures, they reported consistent findings of convergent and discriminant validity for six of eight climate dimensions.

These results bear out several theoretical conjectures from the previous section. They support the following assumptions: (a) Climate is an organizational as opposed to an individual property; (b) climate is distinct from evaluative reactions such as satisfaction; and (c) climate is a generalized description of organizational practices and can be distinguished from members' descriptions of particular persons or behaviors, such as supervisor consideration.

DESCRIPTIONS OF ORGANIZATIONAL CLIMATE

Strategies for the description of climates fall into two major classes: dimensional approaches and typological approaches. The *dimensional* strategy assumes climates are best described in terms of a set of distinct dimensions, each of which is regarded as a separate variable meaningful to organizational members on its own terms (for example, "supportiveness," "degree of structure"). Situational variation in climates is then reflected in different values on the various dimensions. In contrast, the *typological* strategy identifies types of climates, for example, democratic, authoritarian, or achievement-oriented climates. This approach characterizes climates as "wholes," integrated configurations of properties. These types can be rated on dimensions—for example, a democratic climate is high in supportiveness, low in structure, and emphasizes rewards rather than punishments—but they cannot be reduced to dimensions, because they are wholes. This strategy assumes members apprehend and react to their organizational situations as totalities and implies a smaller range of climates than does the dimensional approach, where there are potentially as many climates as there are combinations of values on the dimensions.

Dimensional descriptions. There are three distinct approaches to dimensional description of climate. Some researchers have attempted to specify dimensions that hold across organizations and describe climate in general. Litwin and Stringer's (1968) eight dimensions were originally designed to describe motivational climates, but they have been used as an omnibus measure. They include the following:

(1) structure—the degree to which the organization constrains member behavior;
(2) responsibility—the degree to which members are responsible for their work;
(3) reward—the degree to which the organization gives appropriate rewards for work;
(4) risk—the degree to which the organization is open to risks;
(5) warmth—the degree of interpersonal warmth in the organization;
(6) support—the degree to which members of the organization support one another in their work;
(7) standards—the degree to which the organization sets high standards for performance;
(8) conflict—the degree to which conflicts are acknowledged and worked out;
(9) identity—the degree of team spirit present in the organization.

Other researchers, including Halpin and Crofts (1963), House and Rizzo (1972), Pheysey and Payne (1970), Tagiuri (1968), Taylor and Bowers (1970), and Jones and James (1979), have also developed general measures of climate. In a review of climate studies, Campbell et al. described four dimensions they believed emerged consistently: (1) individual autonomy—the relative amount of freedom members have to make decisions and exercise initiative; (2) the degree of structure imposed on the position—the degree to which superiors established and communicated job objectives and the means of accomplishing them; (3) reward orientation—whether individuals felt rewarded for a job well done; and (4) consideration, warmth, and support given by managers and supervisors. Payne and Pugh (1976) suggest the addition of a factor for "orientation to development and progressiveness."

Communication, in particular, is encompassed in several of these dimensions, including warmth, conflict, and identity in the Litwin and Stringer scheme, and factors 2 and 4 in the Campbell et al. scheme. Taylor and Bowers have two factors directly related to communication in their schedule: "information flow" and "decision-making practices," and Pheysey and Payne found dimensions labeled "intimacy" and "participation" in their study.

For these dimensions to be useful in other than a heuristic sense, they must be applicable across a range of organizations; otherwise, they would not be general. Unfortunately, the evidence does not support the generality of climate dimensions. Sims and Lafollette (1975) and Muchinsky (1977) applied Litwin and Stringer's (1968) climate questionnaire to different organizations. Their factor analyses isolated considerably different dimensions from those found by Litwin and Stringer. (Interestingly, both studies isolated dimensions directly related to communication—"openness of upward communication" for Sims and Lafollette and "interpersonal mileu" for Muchinsky.) Other researchers report that standard climate questionnaires have to be modified considerably to work with different types of organizations (Newman, 1975; Wallace et al., 1975).

Problems with general schemes have given rise to the second dimensional approach, which identified climates for specific organizational practices, such as safety or communication. This approach assumes that organizations have a number of different climates, the contents of which are specific to particular practices. As Schneider (1975: 473) proposes:

> One way of thinking about these different climates is to consider the kind of outcome behavior(s) the climates would lead to (e.g., leadership, creativity, the display of individual differences). Another way is to think of the unit of analysis (work group, position, function, organization) of interest.

Thus different practices should give rise to different climates. Moreover, insofar as they occur differently in different organizations, subunits, or levels of the organization, they should give rise to different climates. Evidence of differences in climate across organizational subunits and levels lends support to the latter point (Powell and Butterfield, 1978; although see Drexler, 1977, for counter-evidence).

Dimensions found for practice-linked climates are unique and more particular than those generated by the first approach. For instance, Zohar (1980) identified eight dimensions of safety climate for twenty industrial organizations, including perceived importance of safety training programs and perceived management attitudes toward safety. Schneider et al. (1980) isolated dimensions of customer service climates for banks, including degree of enthusiastic orientation, degree of managerial support, and degree to which effort will be rewarded.

Communication is also an organizational practice. In terms of specific dimensions of communication climate, Roberts and O'Reilly (1974) have developed a suggestive measure of organizational communication. Although several variables in this measure refer to specific communication practices (such as modalities of communication, gatekeeping, summarization) or communication satisfaction, some tap what could be called general dimensions of communication climate, including trust, degree of influence, desire for interaction, accuracy, and openness downward, upward, or laterally. The only problem with this measure is that it "deals more precisely with individual communication in organizations than with organizational communication" (Muchinsky, 1977: 188).

Generally, development of climate measures for specific practices seems defensible. It largely eliminates the problem of adaptation that faces generalized climate measures. This strategy also permits researchers to assess the structure of climate in greater detail, because it concretely specifies beliefs attached to the practices in question.

The third approach to dimensional analysis is yet more specific than the second. It is exemplified by Johnston (1976), and relies on interviews or observations to identify the dimensions of climate unique to the organization in question. Johnston interviewed 60 employees of a 180-person consulting firm and asked them to describe their company. He used content-analytic procedures to identify themes of concern and the affect (positive or negative) associated with them. Themes included commitment to the organization, organizational changes, sales orientation, pressure on the job, personal goals, and bad faith in the individual-organizational relationship. On the basis of the patterns of positive and negative responses, Johnston found differences between newer and older employees' interpretations of climate in several areas, including commitment, goals, and superior-subordinate relations.

This approach, though complex and time-consuming, is much more sensitive to the particular nuances of organizations than the other two. In particular, it picks up those aspects of climate that are most salient to members. The resulting themes can be grouped and related to more general dimensions or concepts, providing a very sensitive operationalization of these dimensions. Obviously, this technique could also be applied to the construction of more general dimensions; Schneider et al. (1980) employed it in the development of their customer service climate scale.

Typological descriptions. Some of the earliest and most famous climate descriptions were typological. Lewin et al. (1939) distinguished among demo-democratic, autocratic, and laissez fair social climates depending on the leader's style and leader-member relationships. McGregor (1960) posited "Theory X" and "Theory Y" managerial climates. Litwin and Stringer (1968) described motivational climates for achievement, affiliation, and power in terms of particular patterns of values on the nine dimensions described above. Jack Gibb (1961a) advanced the most famous classification of communication climates when he distinguished "supportive" and "defensive" climates. Finally, Johnston (1976), in the study discussed above, was able to divide his subjects into two camps, those who saw the climate as "organic-adaptive (the more experienced members) and those who saw a bureaucratic, stultifying climate (the less experienced members).

These typologies describe their climates in terms of lists of attributes. For example, Gibb described behavior producing supportive climates as descriptive, problem oriented, spontaneous, empathic, equal, and provisional and that producing defensive climates as evaluative, controlling, strategic, neutral, superior, and certain. Lewin et al. distinguished their three climates in terms of (1) how policies were set by the leader and members, (2) degree of leader control over activity, (3) who decided how labor was to be divided, the leader or members, and (4) how the leader gave praise or criticism, personally or objectively. These attributes can easily be "dimensionalized," and it is tempting to conclude that typologies can be reduced to dimensional analyses. However, this would be incorrect for at least the following two reasons.

Typological analyses imply that the social world is best described in terms of coherent "packages" of attributes rather than in terms of discrete variables. Whatever their merits, types are designed to reflect the social world as it is apprehended by the researcher (and, presumably, by the actors themselves). The limitations of the social world (and, perhaps, the limitations of actors' minds) are reflected in the fact that there are a relatively small number of types. By implication, there are also only a small number of configurations of attributes; the extremely large number of possible configurations that could be generated by taking all possible combinations of values on climate dimensions simply cannot exist within the inherently limited social world. For this reason, assuming that dimensions are the essence of climate is misleading; climates are totalities consisting of coherent configurations of attributes.[1] Breaking dimensions out of these wholes is a viable strategy for research—it aids in the discovery of new types and enables statistical comparisons among types. However, it does violence to the representation of climate, because there is more to a type than dimensional or attribute lists can encompass. A supportive climate implies more than Gibb's list of behavioral concomitants: It also has a central principle that holds it together—the meaning and experience of supportiveness. Reducing climates to dimensional description attenuates its meaning, and thus robs the type of its coherence.

A few research findings suggest the validity of the typological view of climates. Lewin et al. (1939) and Litwin and Stringer (1968) were able to create their climate types in the laboratory. Both studies produced powerful behavioral effects in the expected direction, suggesting that the types did have an impact on subjects. Gibb (1961b) and Deutsch (1973) found strong effects of supportive (cooperative) and defensive (competitive) climates on communicative and bargaining behavior, and Deutsch provides some confirmation that subjects perceived the climate in a manner consistent with typological descriptions.

More research relevant to typological descriptions is needed. Studies demonstrating the integrity of types vis-à-vis dimensional descriptions are particularly critical at this juncture. Discriminant analysis might be employed to determine whether different organizational climates are indeed characterized by particular configurations of dimensional values. If no clusters of discriminating dimensional values are found, then reduction to separate dimensions may be justified. Qualitative, observation-based studies of climates can also be employed to ascertain whether climates are coherent types, and whether these are meaningful to organizational members.

The typological approach seems more consistent with a conception of climate as a molar, generalized construct than the dimensional approach. However, in view of the lack of evidence regarding the validity of types, this question must be regarded as still open.

Consensus on climate descriptions. If climate is conceptualized as an organizational attribute, it is not sufficient to assess individual perceptions of climate. The researcher must also demonstrate that these perceptions index the organization and are not idiosyncratic reactions. In the previous section it was noted that Guion (1973) suggested two methods for doing this: (a) demonstrate convergence of members' perceptions based on the assumption that members would agree only if they oriented to a common organizational situation or (b) show that the climate measure is related to some objective criterion for climate.

The first method is probably the best because it is directly concerned with commonalities of meaning among members, and it is the most widely employed. Unfortunately, results have been mixed.

A number of studies report evidence supporting convergence on climate descriptions (Drexler, 1977; Howe, 1977; Paolillo, 1982; Pritchard and Karasick, 1973; Zohar, 1980), but others find low consensus on climate (Bass et al., 1975; Jones and James, 1979; Payne and Mansfield, 1973; Schneider, 1975). In part, these differences may be a function of analytical technique. Studies employing analysis of variance to compare within- and between-group variance in climate scores generally report convergence, while studies that use intraclass correlations or reliability coefficients to assess level of agreement among participants tend to find less convergence. However, even allowing for this, there seems to be evidence of both dissensus and consensus on climate perceptions.

What do these findings indicate about the integrity of the climate concept? Some researchers have advocated that climate should be attributed only to those units or organizations in which there is consensus on climate (Powell and Butterfield, 1978). However, dissensus among organizational members does not always imply the absence of a coherent climate. Members may all share a common belief, but have different reactions to that belief—reactions or interpretations that would result in different answers on a climate questionnaire. For example, consider an organization with an achievement-oriented climate. As Kanter's (1977) study showed, members on their way up may well describe this organization as supportive, reward-oriented, and fairly low in terms of activity structuring, and members who are not being promoted (yet who also see the emphasis on achievement) are likely to describe the organization as nonsupportive, nonrewarding, and highly structured. A shared, commonly experienced climate could give rise to highly divergent responses on a questionnaire. Further research is needed to determine whether this possibility does in fact happen.

DETERMINANTS OF CLIMATE

This section will concentrate, first, on factors that determine climate and, second, on the processes through which these factors have their effects. During this discussion it will be helpful to refer to Figure 3.2, which portrays the relationship of structural features, organizational practices, climate, and other organizational outcomes.

Determining factors. Numerous studies have focused on the relationship between organizational structure and organizational climate. These studies have generally viewed structure as a cause of climate rather than the other way around, because structure seems logically prior to climate, and also because current concepts of climate make it difficult to imagine how climate could determine structure. Climate, in turn, is viewed as a construct mediating the influence of organizational context and structure on member attitudes and behavior. Moreover, almost all this research describes climate in terms of

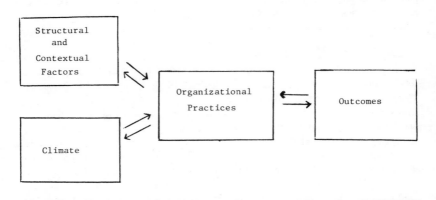

Figure 3.2 Model of the Relationship of Climate, Structure, and Organizational Practices

general dimensions, though the dimensions employed vary somewhat. Several structural and contextual factors have been shown to be related to climate, including size, centralization, and formalization.

Several studies have shown size to affect climate (Indik, 1965; Inkson et al., 1968; Child and Ellis, 1973; Payne and Mansfield, 1973; and Stern, 1970). Correlations with climate dimensions including innovativeness, interpersonal conflict, and communication openness have been moderate (.20 to .50), but consistently significant. One hypothesis for the effect of size on climate is that larger organizations tend to be more bureaucratic and therefore produce climates encouraging alienation, rule-boundedness, deference, and low commitment (March and Simon, 1958). However, relations of size to climate dimensions seem to be more complex than this. For example, Inkson et al. (1968) report that size had a positive correlation with innovative climate among British managers, while Inkson et al. (1971) report a negative correlation in a sample of Ohio managers. The particular structures and practices that size creates (which may vary depending on the organization's environment and technology) must be considered to explain the effects of size on climate.

Organizations perceived to have decentralized decision making are generally perceived to have warmer, more supportive, and more risk-encouraging climates than centralized organizations (Pheysey and Payne, 1970; Litwin and Stringer, 1968; George and Bishop, 1971). This relationship between measures of *perceived* structure and climate does not hold up as well when objective measures of structure are used. Inkson et al. (1968) found that centralization was largely unrelated to climate for a sample of British top managers; Inkson et al. (1971) reported that for a sample of Ohio top managers degree of centralization had a .46 correlation with perceived innovativeness (exactly the opposite of what was obtained with perceptual measures of structure) and a .43 correlation with perceptions of conflict (consistent with the results for perceptual measures). Child and Ellis (1973) found that objective measures of centralization were unrelated to perceptions of conflict, but positively related to perceived innovation. The relation between centralization and climate seems quite complex.

Degree of formalization—the extent to which the organization structures its members' activities—is also related to climate, but, again, in a complex manner. Pheysey and Payne (1970), summarizing several previous studies, report consistent negative correlations between structuring and potency. Litwin and Stringer (1968) report small positive correlations among perceived structuring and supportiveness, setting standards, and identity in their simulated organizations. Inkson et al. (1968, 1971) report clear differences in the effects of perceived structuring on climate for samples of top managers from Britain and Ohio: Role formalization relates positively to innovative expectations for British managers and negatively for Ohio managers; role routinization relates negatively to innovative expectations and innovativeness, and positively to conflict for British managers, but exactly the opposite relations hold for the Ohio managers. Child and Ellis (1973) found positive correlations for role formalization with innovation and conflict, and a negative correlation of role routinization with innovative behavior.

In general, inconsistent relationships seem to exist between structural variables and climate, and this poses a problem for any attempt to integrate the climate literature (for example, see Payne and Pugh, 1976). An interesting finding reveals that a high degree of structure is not necessarily related to a cold nonsupportive climate, as is commonly supposed. Litwin and Stringer (1968) and others find low positive correlations between structuring and climate dimensions such as warmth, risk taking, loyalty, and reward orientation, hardly what one is led to expect from the stereotypical accounts of cold, impersonal, rule-bound bureaucracy.

Processes. The inconsistent influence of macro-level structural and contextual variables on climate strongly suggests that mediating organizational practices play a key role in the definition and maintenance of climates. This conclusion is consistent with theoretical work emphasizing the link between climate and practices, and with Indik's (1965) prototype for the influence of structure on organizational behavior. There is also empirical evidence supporting the importance of practices. Child and Ellis (1973) employed path analysis to demonstrate how role routines and level of perceived authority (variables implicated directly in organizational practices) moderated the influence of centralization on perceived innovativeness. In a study of research and development organizations, Lawler et al. (1974) related climate to both macro-level structural variables (size, number of hierarchical levels, span of control, and centralization, which they termed "professional autonomy") and process variables, which described organizational practices (performance appraisal practices, assignment generality, collaboration). Among the structural variables, only one, centralization, related to one or more climate dimensions. Muchinsky

(1977) found sizable correlations between perceived characteristics of communication practices (trust, influence, accuracy, amount of lateral communication) and climate dimensions.

At least two models of the effect of practices on climate have been advanced. Zeitz (1983: 1089) has proposed what might be termed a "reverberation" model. In this view climate is an emergent collective trait that

> can also operate on the individual level, but becomes collective when possessed by multiple interacting members. For example, when individual behaviors and attitudes are reinforced and amplified through imitation, social rewards, or sanctions communicated by widespread interaction, they become pervasive, organization-wide characteristics.

There is much in this explanation, but it is vague about how and why this reverberation occurs.

Schneider and his associates (Schneider, 1975; Deiterly and Schneider, 1974; Schneider and Reichers, 1983) develop a more detailed account of how climates arise from organizational practices. Climates exist, Schneider (1975) argues, because people attempt to apprehend and create order in their work environment so they can effectively adapt their behavior to it. Climates are molar descriptions of practices and procedures that enable people to attain congruity between their behavior and the system's procedures and practices. They aid members in interpreting and making sense of others' behavior and in adapting their own behavior to various exigencies of the workplace. Climates provide a sense of continuity and predictability for members. In light of these functions, Schneider and Reichers (1983) advance an explanation for the etiology of climates grounded in symbolic interactionism. They argue that members develop and sustain their identity in the organization through interaction with colleagues, and that a key aspect of this identity is an orientation toward the organized activities in which the work group engages. As the members are socialized into the work group (a process that also continues throughout the worker's career), they adopt the attitudes and beliefs of coworkers, adjust their expectations to the work situation, and work out the meaning of the work situation. This understanding, which enables members to situate themselves in the organization, is the organizational climate.

> [The] same processes that act to socialize newcomers into the setting also give rise to climates. Specifically, social interactions in the workplace help newcomers to understand the meaning of various aspects of the work context. And it is through social interactions that individuals or the workplace come to have similar perceptions of that context [Schneider and Reichers, 1983: 31].

Schneider's approach represents a definite advance over previous work. As the previous section indicates, discussions of climate by Tagiuri (1968), Campbell et al. (1970), and others argued that it was an organizational attribute, and also subjective or perceptual in nature, but offered no explanation for how individual-level phenomena could constitute an organizational property. Schneider and his associates have attempted to specify this process, namely, work-group interaction that creates the collective convergence postulated by Zeitz.

EFFECTS OF CLIMATE

Climate has been shown to influence several other variables. A number of studies have shown strong relations between climate and job satisfaction (Hellriegel and Slocum, 1974: 263, Pritchard and Karasick, 1973; Woodman and King, 1978; Zeitz, 1983). Of direct interest to communication scholars, Muchinsky (1977) showed that communication climate dimensions such as trust, influence, accuracy, and desire for interaction are positively correlated to satisfaction. Wall (reported in Payne et al., 1976) found evidence that the importance of a given property may mediate the climate-satisfaction relationship. Wall asked students to rate their department on four descriptive climate dimensions and then had them rate their satisfaction with climate on each of the dimensions, as well as the importance of the dimension. Correlations between descriptive and effective measures ranged from .35 to .77 and the correlations were higher for those climate dimensions rated most important by students. Payne et al. (1976) report that this result was replicated for a sample of managers.

The relation between climate and performance is more complex. Hellriegel and Slocum (1974) report nine studies showing a significant relationship between organizational climate and job performance. The studies reported in Hellriegel and Slocum (1974) as well as other studies (Pelz and Andrews, 1976; Schneider et al., 1980) employed a wide range of climate dimensions and indicators of performance, so it is difficult to summarize or generalize. Instead, several patterns in the results will be noted.

First, a primary determinant of performance seems to be *compatibility* of climate with the person's needs, tendencies, or expectations, rather than any particular climate (Stern, 1970; Pelz and Andrews, 1976). For example, a person with a high need for achievement is likely to perform better in an achieving climate than will a person with high affiliation needs (Pelz and Andrews, 1976).

Second, there is some evidence that congruity among climate dimensions results in higher performance than inconsistency. In a laboratory study, Fredericksen manipulated climate along two dimensions, "encouragement of innovation" versus "reliance on standard procedures" and loose versus close supervision (reported in Campbell et al., 1970). He found task performance on an in-basket test to be more predictable for consistent climates (innovation + loose supervision or rules + close supervision) than for inconsistent climates (innovation + close supervision or rules + loose supervision). This result seems to support the typological view of climate. The consistent climates seem likely to exist as stable configurations (types), whereas the inconsistent climates seem likely to be unstable and generate pressure toward consistency, with the result that they are rarely encountered in practice (that is, they are not viable types). As a corollary, subjects are more likely to have worked in consistent than inconsistent climates. The greater predictability of performance in consistent climates may therefore be a function of subjects' having previously established routines for working in these climates, whereas they have little experience with and therefore no routines for inconsistent climates.

Third, climate and performance relations are often weak. Generally, they are higher when climate is measured for particular practices than when general climate scores are used. For example, using a dimensional measure of customer service climate, Schneider et al. (1980) found zero-order correlations ranging from .46 to .71 between climate dimensions and customer perceptions of quality. By contrast, Jones and James (1979) used sets of *general* climate variables and found multiple correlations with performance that were significantly smaller than the zero-order correlations reported by Schneider et al. (.37 and .36 for two samples of naval divisions).

In addition to influencing satisfaction and performance, climate may also have another important effect. Correlations between climate and structural variables have generally been interpreted to indicate the influence of structure on climate. However, practices mediate the relationship between climate and structure, and if climate shapes organizational practices, these correlations may also index a reciprocal effect of climate on organizational structure. Studies have shown how practices can change organizational structure (for example, Blau, 1963); through its influence on practices, climate may indirectly affect structure.

SUMMARY

Synthesis of theoretical and empirical research on climate yields this composite picture:

(1) Climate is a molar construct representing collective descriptions of an organization or subunit.

(2) Climate serves as a frame of reference for member activity and therefore shapes members' expectancies, attitudes, and behaviors; through these effects it influences organizational outcomes such as performance, satisfaction, and morale.

(3) Climates arise from and are sustained by organizational or unit practices. Structural and contextual factors influence climates, but their effects are mediated by organizational practices and processes.

(4) An organization may have several climates, corresponding to the major practices it exhibits. Because practices may vary from organization to organization, organizations are likely to have distinct and individualized climates. For this reason omnibus climate dimensions are not viable.

The relationships among climate, practices, structure, and outcomes are illustrated in Figure 3.2. In addition to these points, the jury is still out on several other issues in climate research:

(1) The status of the climate construct in terms of the objective-subjective distinction is still unclear.

(2) Whether climates are best described in terms of types or single dimensions is also not yet resolved.

(3) Despite a convincing theoretical argument that climate is an organization-level construct and evidence of differences in climate among organizations, the finding of low levels of agreement on climate within organizations casts doubt on the integrity of the construct.

The perspectives advanced by Schneider and his associates (Schneider, 1975; Schneider and Reichers, 1983) and by Poole and McPhee (1983) move toward a resolution of these issues. These positions argue that climates are created and maintained through interaction organized around common practices and attempt to analyze this generative process. This move has crucial implications for the conceptualization and study of climate, but they have not been developed in any full or systematic fashion. It is the purpose of the remainder of this essay to do so.

CONCEPTUAL ANALYSIS: STRUCTURATIONAL THEORY OF ORGANIZATIONAL CLIMATE

Schneider and Reichers's (1983) analysis of the etiology of climates is an important advance, but it is also incomplete and exhibits several problems. First, other than stating that socialization is a key focus for establishing climates, Schneider and Reichers provide little detail about *what* interaction processes generate climates and how these work. Their analysis remains at a very general level and "interaction" is used as an opaque, generic concept. If interaction is to be used as an explanation for climate, that explanation should be spelled out. Second, choice of the symbolic interactionist perspective has the advantage of focusing attention on micro-level interaction processes, but it also makes the role of structure and context unclear. Schneider and Reichers do not address the issue of how organizational structure could affect climate through symbolic interaction. Third, Schneider and Reichers's etiology is a weak one: they focus only on how climates come to be shared and implicitly assume the climate already exists. A stronger etiology would not only address this issue, but would also offer an explanation for how climates are generated and changed. Finally, Schneider and Reichers beg the objective-subjective issue. They still do not explain how climate becomes an organizational attribute through being shared.

The model developed in this section, which advances work by Poole and McPhee (1983), addresses these problems and attempts to resolve current controversies in climate research. The model assumes (a) that organizational climates are continually being structured through organizational practices and (b) that the key to understanding climate is to understand this process of structuration. This model moves in the same direction as Schneider and his associates, but has the advantage of achieving a more comprehensive and detailed account than a

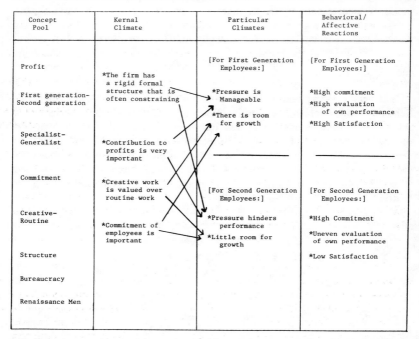

Concept Pool	Kernal Climate	Particular Climates	Behavioral/ Affective Reactions
Profit	*The firm has a rigid formal structure that is often constraining	[For First Generation Employees:]	[For First Generation Employees:]
First generation- Second generation		*Pressure is Manageable	*High commitment
		*There is room for growth	*High evaluation of own performance
Specialist- Generalist	*Contribution to profits is very important		*High Satisfaction
Commitment	*Creative work is valued over routine work	[For Second Generation Employees:]	[For Second Generation Employees:]
Creative- Routine		*Pressure hinders performance	*High Commitment
	*Commitment of employees is important	*Little room for growth	*Uneven evaluation of own performance
Structure			*Low Satisfaction
Bureaucracy			
Renaissance Men			

NOTE: Arrows indicate entailment of particular climate themes from kernel themes. The bases for entailment are explained in the text.

Figure 3.3   Schematic of Climate Structure

symbolic interactionist approach permits. Here we will elaborate the model in terms of its two components: the basic structure of climate and the processes through which climate is structured. Ideally, the model should provide a unified account of all relations depicted in Figure 3.2.

THE STRUCTURE OF CLIMATE

Climates are hierarchical structures of beliefs, expectations, and values. Figure 3.3 depicts one such hierarchy with a work climate and associated domains of concepts and member reactions. The hierarchy was derived from reanalysis of Johnston's (1976) study of a consulting firm and will be considered in more detail below.

The hierarchy consists of three layers. What we have referred to as climate forms the middle layers of this hierarchy. The most fundamental level is that of the organization's *concept* pool, the key terms and distinctions that enable members to define the organization. Included in this concept pool are unitary terms, such as "profit," "commitment" and "structure," and binary oppositions, such as "labor-management" or "specialist-generalist," along which organizational members range themselves and others. The unitary terms refer to basic features of the organization, the institutions, properties, and preoccupations members must deal with to work in the firm. Binary oppositions are fundamental to the social categorization process that enables members to position themselves and others in the organization (Tajfel and Turner, 1979; Doise, 1978). The concept pool defines the space of possible meaning for the organization; it is indispensable background knowledge for all organizational activities.

One important stucture that draws on the concept pool is the *kernel climate,* the basic structure of beliefs, values, and expectations collectively held by most or all organizational members. This structure consists of connections among concepts that constitute organization or unitwide climates. The kernel climate represents a common structure of beliefs that gives the organization its overall tone and forms the basis for subgroup differentiation. The propositions or elements of the kernel climate are linked in definite relations; although it will not be done here, a symbolic calculus of relations among climate terms could be derived.[2]

The differentiation of general terms into subgroup climates occurs in the development of *particularized climates,* structures of beliefs, values, and expectations held by subgroups within the organization or unit. *Particular climates* are qualifications and elaborations of kernel climates by subgroups. A particularized climate is based on the kernel climate and involves alterations and additions to the shared structure. The kernel climate provides the common backdrop without which climatic differences would not be possible or meaningful. Structural ambiguity in the premises of kernel climates permits different subgroups to reinterpret and elaborate them in a manner consonant with their own particular reality and goals. Although the subgroups that create particular climates may be formal subunits of the organization, many such groups are informal. Previous findings of differences in climate due to subunit, position, pay level, tenure, and level of authority index particular climates.

The final tier of the hierarchy refers to members' behavioral and affective reactions to the organization, and is in part determined by particular climates (other determinants include the reward structure, technology, and leadership). These reactions—such as strong feelings of commitment, a positive evaluation of one's performance, or a lack of attachment to the organization—lend a certain tone to members' participation in organizational practices. They "qualify" participants' actions in the sense discussed by Garfinkel (1967: 30) Members do not simply work or take orders; they work *furiously* or take orders *with resentment*—and this has crucial consequences for organizational performance.

Reanalysis of Johnston's study provides an excellent illustration of this structure. The firm in Johnston's study was about five years old and had grown from an original staff of 12 to 180 employees. Along with this growth came increased bureaucratization to facilitate coordination of the firm's many projects; the firm's hierarchy was elaborated, there was increasing task specialization, and the firm attempted to formalize roles, its information system, and its evaluation procedures. This bureaucratization presented a sharp contrast with procedures when the firm was young and small; in the beginning high involvement of all staff in decision making and planning and informal means of coordination were emphasized. As a result, Johnston found two "generations" of employees, one composed of employees from the early years of the firm, who were plugged into the old informal system and had helped evolve the bureaucratized structure, and one composed of newer employees, who were not tied into the informal system and had to accept the organization's structure.

From Johnston's account, the relevant portion of the conceptual pool is composed of several unitary terms—including profits, commitment, and structure—and three key oppositions—specialist-generalist, creative work-routine, and older employees-newer employees. (In the ideal case, these terms and oppositions would be drawn from the terminology of the interviewees themselves. However, Johnston substituted his own language for that of his subjects, so the basic concepts are drawn from his account.) These concepts appear in the kernel climate in beliefs such as "The firm has a rigid formal structure" and value statements such as "Creativity is the firm's cornerstone" and "Contributing to company profits is crucial."

At least two particular climates exist in Johnston's firm. One holds for first-generation employees, who can use their ties to the organization's informal network to bypass logjams in the formal structure, and who, by virtue of their position, have the opportunity to do creative work. For these members the organization does exert pressure, but the pressure is constructive; these members also believe supervisor-subordinate relations are good. There is a different climate for second-generation employees, who are not tied into the informal system and cannot get past routine procedures. They feel great pressure to produce and believe routine procedures hurt their performance; they also perceive bad superior-subordinate relationships because they do not have a well-developed informal friendship system. These particular climates lead to different affective and behavior reactions, as Figure 3.3 illustrates.

The scheme presented here gives a different picture of climate from that of Johnston. Johnston concludes that his firm has two separate climates that are a function of situational and personal factors. By this analysis, instead, the firm has a *single kernel climate* that is differentiated into *two particularized climates* by situational factors. The particular climates are important determinants of members' behaviors, but they are only possible in the context of the common kernel. This formulation offers an explanation for the finding of low member agreement on climate that also preserves the integrity of climate as an organizational construct (consistent with the finding of significant differences in climate between organizations). There is an underlying kernel climate common throughout the organization, but particularized climates result in differences on climate measures that produce low coefficients of agreement. In only two cases would high agreement coefficients be expected: (1) on measures that happen to tap the kernel (and these are likely to be few because the kernel is more abstract and less close to surface behavior than particular climates); or (2) where the sample is limited to a group with no particular climates. Low coefficients may have been obtained in previous research simply due to the fact that measures and designs have seldom met these conditions.

From this view, climates are not simply lists of beliefs and values; both kernel and their derivative particular climates have an internal cohesion that results from the structuring processes that create them (these processes will be discussed presently). Nor should climates be regarded as cognitive entities or logical maps. Rather, they are collective schemes of meaning established through interactions focused on organizational practices. Climate is not contained in any member's head; it is a cultural product and is properly regarded as neither objective nor subjective, but *intersubjective*. Individual responses to the question: "What is your organization's (or unit's) climate?" are therefore only indicators of an underlying intersubjective construct that is beyond any single individual and must be extrapolated from their answers and from experience with the organization (Poole and McPhee, 1983). As Poole and McPhee (1983) establish, the key to understanding an intersubjective construct such as climate is to grasp the processes by which its intersubjectivity is maintained, the processes that link numerous individuals' realities together.

THE STRUCTURATION OF CLIMATES

A number of social theorists and critics have studied structuration, which offers an alternative to the reification of structures common in social science and literary analysis (Barthes, 1971; Bordieu, 1977; Giddens, 1979; Poole and McPhee, 1983). Applied to social institutions, structuration refers to the production and reproduction of social systems via the application of generative rules and resources (Giddens, 1979: 64-76). Implicit in this definition is a distinction between system and structure. "System" refers to observable relations or beliefs, "regularized relations of interdependence between individuals and groups" (Giddens, 1979: 66). "Structures" are rules and resources used in the production and reproduction of systems. Structures, then, are both the medium and the outcome of action. Structures form the basis for action, but only through entering into action are they themselves produced and reproduced. System and structure form a duality, codetermining each other in a continuous process of structuration (Poole and McPhee, 1983).

From this perspective, a climate is a belief and value structure members employ as they act in the organization. Because it is a generative principle behind member action, the climate is involved in the production of organizational systems. Because it is a generalization applicable across settings and occasions, climate enters into the reproduction of the same systems (received knowledge is generally conservative). At the same time climate is a medium of action, it is also an outcome. As noted above, a climate is produced by organizational practices; it will persist only if some aspect of the activity system reproduces it. Sometimes the production and reproduction of structures is influenced by an indeterminant variation at the system level, a "random innovation" that reverberates throughout system and structure. More often, this process is conditioned by other structural features involved in the same practice and mediated by interaction (that is, the system). Climate, then, should be seen as a structure in process instead of the static, reified map of beliefs and values shown in the previous section.

The statement that one structure "conditions" another does not imply the iron determinism of causality implied by physical equations such as $F = ma$. Causality is involved, but it is of a different sort. Structures and systems exist in action, and so the effect of one structural feature on another is mediated by the whole complex of structures that bear on an activity system. When the president of a company institutes a structure of penalties for wastage, the effect of this policy on climate is not a direct determination, but is mediated, among other things, by the meanings of the penalties to members and the president's charisma or lack thereof (that is, by a structure of signification), by the availability of alternative channels of resistance, such as unions or work groups (that is, by power resources), by members' moral evaluations of work incentives (that is, by normative structures), and by the availability of distractions (joking, company parties) that might bleed off the resentment caused by the policy. This mediation is not a statistical mediation, but rather a qualification of the meaning or force of the penalty structure in interaction. Mediations influence the way actors "take" the penalties—how they regard them, react to them, use them, rebel against them, live with them. It is of the essence of action that the actor "could have done otherwise," so no "cold facts," direct determinism is possible. Mediations are inherently transformations, so causal analysis of structural effects must always deal with meaning. Therefore, it contains several grains of indeterminacy.

I will focus on three genres of elements that condition the structuration of climates: (1) structural properties of the organization, (2) apparatuses that directly produce and reproduce climates, and (3) members' knowledge and skills. These elements condition climate both through generating kernel climates and through setting up processes that differentiate kernel climates into particular climates. Throughout, this discussion focuses on climates arising from organizational practices, such as communication or work climates.

Structural properties. The organization itself sets fundamental constraints on climate. Organization structure determines the types of interaction processes possible within the organization, thus limiting the climates that can emerge. Structure also creates differential distributions of power and skills, setting the stage for differentiation of these climates into particular forms. The effects of structure in creating climates are clearly illustrated in the discussion of Johnston's firm. The results summarized in the section on determinants of climate also support this contention: "Structural" variables—centralization, formalization, and size—are related to climate, and their effects are mediated by organizational processes and practices. However, centralization, formalization, and size are not, in themselves, structures; rather, they are descriptors of system properties that result from underlying structural features. Centralization reflects the effects of structures of power and control, formalization is the way in which rules are employed, and size is an outcome of numerous interacting structures. To trace the influence of organizational features on climate it is necessary to focus on these underlying structural features and how they are mediated in interaction. For example, if an organization has a large body of written rules, these will undoubtedly influence climate. Their influence will be mediated by the meaning of rules in the organization (are rules to be followed to the letter or are rules made to be broken?), exactly what the rules regulate (rules on filling out paperwork may be constraining, while rules to facilitate problem solving may be liberating), and members' attitude toward rules (are they useful or a burden; are they neutral or a weapon?). Depending on these mediating processes, written rules will have different effects on climate. This is in line with results mentioned above, which showed no consistent relationship between formalization and climates. Rules could produce particular climates if they were enforced differently for different members or if, as in Johnston's firm, one group has a way of circumventing rules that the other does not.

Climate-producing apparatuses. One important feature of organization is the existence of institutional apparatuses for creating and maintaining climates, as well as symbols, attitudes, and ideologies (see Althusser, 1971). These apparatuses include socialization and training programs, work groups, sponsors, newsletters, internal publicity agencies, key managers, and figureheads. They are crucial because they represent foci of influence on climate. In some cases—training programs, sponsorship systems, and newsletters—the apparatus is consciously designed to control climate. Other apparatuses—work groups, key managers, figureheads—emerge as crucial "institutions" and control climate on their own terms. Apparatuses govern the communication and interaction systems that produce climates and, hence, not only introduce climate themes directly, but also mediate the effects of structural properties on climate. If they establish differentiations, particular climates will result. As recognized institutional components, apparatuses play a key role in reproducing and sustaining climates. An important phase in the study of climates is isolating an apparatus and clarifying how it structures and sustains generalized beliefs and values.

Member characteristics. Two aspects of members' skill and knowledge play an important role in the structuration of climates. First, members may have varying levels of penetration of their situation. On the one hand, they may accept the organization and its climate unreflectively; on the other, they may understand the attempts of apparatuses to create climates and the role of various structural properties in creating climate. In the latter case, members have greater control over climate. They can often take a role in shaping it themselves, or, at least, disregard or reinterpret prevailing beliefs and values. One well-known example of this is workers who sneer cynically at company efforts to motivate "open communication" when giving information may be grounds for punishment.

A second important aspect of members' knowledge is their mode of coorientation toward other workers' perceptions of climate (Scheff, 1967; Laing et al., 1966). Coorientation can be defined in terms of two concepts important for our purposes: agreement and accuracy. To the extent that two people's beliefs are similar, they are in *agreement*; independent of this, to the extent that one correctly knows the other's beliefs, he or she has accuracy about the other. The coorientation in a system can be described in terms of the agreement and accuracy members have. Scheff (1967) described a number of cases, including consensus (high agreement, high accuracy), dissensus (low agreement, high accuracy—people disagree and they know it), and "pluralistic ignorance"(high agreement, low accuracy—people agree, but they do not realize it). Poole and McPhee (1983) have noted the importance of coorientation in the structuration of climates. If members believe others share a climate (even if they do not), that climate will have a greater impact on their behavior because they assume others orient toward it and they are likely to adopt it as a guide for their own behavior. This results in the climate being reproduced as members use it. Conversely, if members believe others do not agree (even if they do), the climate is less likely to have force over their behavior; therefore its reproduction tends to be weakened, because members do not orient their behavior toward it.

Summary. A climate is a structure and (more important) a structurational process producing and reproducing the climate. Any description of climate that focuses only on a structural map (as do most previous studies) is seriously incomplete because it omits the generative principles that lend cohesion to the map. The explanation of climates, in particular, has to account for two levels of structuration, one that structures the kernel climate and another that differentiates it into particular climates. Factors that condition this two-tiered process include structural properties, climatic apparatuses, and member characteristics.

FURTHER IMPLICATIONS

Generality of climates. As noted in the second section, for some organizations a single, general climate exists, while for others there are subsystem climates. The theory just elaborated would explain this as a result of the reach of a practice within the organization. Only if a practice holds in the same form throughout the organization and if there are no differentiating forces in the structurational process will there be a uniform, organizationwide climate. Different climates or particular climates will result from different practices or differentiating forces. For this reason, larger, more complex organizations with no organizationwide climatic apparatuses will have more diverse climates. Indeed, some may have no systemwide kernel climate if there are no common practices or apparatuses to maintain it.

The status of the climate construct. Rather than being objective or subjective, climates are intersubjective constructs, collective constructs that bridge the perspectives of numerous subjects. The intersubjectivity of the climate is maintained through a continuous process of structuration that links members in systems of practice, and it can be explained by elucidating the mechanism driving this process.

Influence of climate on behavior and attitude. The degree to which climate affects member behavior depends on how well coupled it is with organizational practices. As Poole and McPhee (1983) observe, in some organizations apparatuses produce climates that are irrelevant to or uncoupled from the organization's work. For example, newsletters and interpersonal relationships may produce a sense of warm concern for others' feelings that does not transfer to work relationships. This climate is produced and reproduced by apparatuses unconnected with work practices, and therefore it does not strongly influence behavior and attitudes. Only those climates that are structured in a manner relevant to practices will influence behavior within them. In addition, climates may not influence attitudes or behavior when members have sufficent penetration to disregard or reinterpret them.

Recursive effects of climate on other structures. As a climate is structured it interpenetrates numerous other structures. Since climate also mediates interaction, it may influence other structures also being produced and reproduced in ongoing practices. These influences are too complex to explore further in this essay, but they are inherent in the nature of structuration.

Typological descriptions. The structurational perspective suggests that climates are likely to exist as types. As noted, structuring processes give climates internal cohesion. A corollary of this cohesiveness is the existence of constellations of properties that "go together," which implies the existence of a limited range of climate types for each practice rather than the very large number of combinations possible with independent dimensions.

METHODOLOGY FOR CLIMATE RESEARCH

The preceding discussion has important implications for methodology in climate research. For one thing, it implies the need to ground data-collecting systems—whether questionnaires, interviews, or direct observation—in the participants' perspectives. If climates have an impact because they shape the meaning of the organization for its members, and if the structuring of climates themselves depends on meaningful systems of action, then researchers are omitting the crux of the construct when they view climate only from their own remote perspective. As Payne and Pugh (1976: 1168) observe, referring to climate studies using researcher-concocted questionnaires:

> Future research can ignore most of these studies and utilize a completely different approach. We need deep involvement from the members of a complex system to gather meaningful data which accurately reflect these peoples' experiences.... The researcher needs to swap data interpretations with his subjects so that interpretations are more realistic.

Johnston's research design can serve as one model here. Albrecht (1979) uses multidimensional scaling, a quantitative technique with nonrestrictive response formats, to represent subjects' collective representation of climate (see Poole and Folger, 1981, for technical details on deriving collective representations via multidimensional scaling).

The preceding discussion also implies that the analysis of climate is a two-stage process. In the first stage, a structure of climatic beliefs and values is isolated. This involves identifying components of the climate structure portrayed in Figure 3.3—basic concepts, kernel beliefs and values, particular beliefs and values, and member reactions—and tracing linkages among them. Dimensions identified in previous research can be used as an analytic scheme to guide this search. Folger and Poole (1984: chap. 3), for example, propose a scheme of four categories of climate themes, related to authority relations, supportiveness, identity, and interdependence. Usually, key concepts, particular climates, and member reactions are identified first, and then kernel climates are deduced from these (although the sequence of discovery may vary). For example, in a study of climate in a small college conducted by Helmer et al. (1984), two divergent beliefs were located: (1) Achieving tenure is difficult, but straightforward (generally expressed by older, tenured faculty), and (2) achieving tenure is complex and difficult (generally expressed by younger faculty). Underlying these particular beliefs is a kernel belief (expressed by some and borne out by questionnaire responses and observation of the organization) that tenure criteria were unclear and subject to the whim of the tenure committee. Identification of particular beliefs and reactions for various subgroups via interviews and questionnaires allows triangulation to kernel premises.

Although systematic schemes and procedures for the discovery of climates can serve useful purposes, the particular set of themes and how they interlock is likely to vary from organization to organization. The outcome of climate analyses should be a structure unique to the organization in question (although, certainly, classes or types of structures may eventually be identified). In the ideal case, this climate structure would be returned to the organization to ascertain whether participants acknowledge its component beliefs and reactions.

The second stage focuses on discovery of the mechanisms producing and reproducing the climate structure. Rather than a static picture, the forces shaping this structurational process must be identified, including the structural properties, climatic apparatuses, and member characteristics mentioned above. The particular ensemble of forces will vary, depending on the content of the climate; in particular, climate-generating apparatuses are important, because they represent the center of the structuring process. Ideally, the second stage will identify a coherent mechanism (or mechanisms) to account for generation of the kernel climate and differentiation into particular climates. This mechanism should recast the stage-one structure into dynamic terms, and, as in Johnston's (1976) study should lead to a reinterpretation and fuller understanding of the initial map.

Since climates are produced and reproduced by more or less cohesive processes, typological descriptions will probably be more useful than dimensional schemes. A thoroughgoing structuring process should create a coherent ensemble of attributes and, given that there is a limited range of structuring processes, only certain configurations of properties are likely to occur. Hence descriptions of climates as supportive, defensive, and "organic-adaptive" are likely to be the ultimate product of structurational analysis.

CONCLUSION

The thrust of this chapter has been to show two connections between communication and climate. First, because communication is a key organizational practice, most organizations will have communication climates. A communication climate is a molar description of communication practices and procedures in an organization or subunit. It consists of collective beliefs, expectations, and values regarding communication, and is generated in interaction around organizational practices via a continuous process of structuration. The process of structuration produces and reproduces both a kernel climate common to members of the organization or subunit and related, particular climates for subgroups within the organization or unit. Through the process of structuration, the communication climate also influences member interaction and behavior and members' attitudes.

Second, at a more fundamental level, communication is the medium of all structurational processes and therefore a constitutive force for all climates. Structurational theory posits interaction systems as the locus of production and reproduction for climates and other intersubjective constructs. The forces that shape the structuration of climates operate through and are transformed by interaction processes.

The structurational theory of climate represents a synthesis of "objective" and "subjective" moments from previous climate theories, and points to the need for deep structural analysis of organizational processes. This analysis not only enables researchers to "see through" organizational practices to underlying forces, but also forms the basis for a systematic, unifying explanation of the simultaneous influence of structural factors, climate, and practices on member behavior and organizational outcomes. In addition, this perspective has the advantage of approaching participants as active, knowledgeable, symbol-using beings, which provides a fuller view of the human role in organizations than information-processing or behavioristic models support (Dandridge et al., 1980). The resulting picture of climate is considerably more complex than previous conceptions, but the investment in complexity will pay off in more useful, powerful theories.

NOTES

1. This argument parallels that made by Mintzberg (1979) with respect to organizational structure. After reviewing research on numerous independent structural parameters such as span of control and standardization, Mintzberg concludes that these parameters occur in particular configurations corresponding to types of organizations.

2. Techniques of semiotic analysis such as those employed by Barley (1983) have great promise in efforts to spell out the nature of connections and entailments among beliefs and concepts.

Chapter 4

DATA, MODELS, AND ASSUMPTIONS
IN NETWORK ANALYSIS

William D. Richards, Jr.

THE GOAL OF MOST NETWORK ANALYSIS TECHNIQUES is to produce a high-level description of the system under investigation. This description will usually include information about structural differentiation, often in terms of "cliques" or "groups"—clusters of individuals that work as subsystems within the larger whole. The description is based on specific kinds of patterns in the set of relationships among members of the system. The starting point for this type of analysis is thus a description of the pairwise relationships that exist between the individual members of the system. There are two important constraints on this description: First, it must accurately describe the relationships in the system. Second, it must be cast in a form that will be amenable to analysis with the tools that are available.

This essay examines the implications of these requirements, and shows that the process of getting data for network analysis is much more complex than is generally recognized. Along the way, a number of problems that have caused headaches for network researchers will be addressed. Some of these will have straightforward answers, while others turn out to be even more vexing than they may have originally seemed.

RELATIONSHIPS AND DESCRIPTIONS
OF RELATIONSHIPS

The "description" that is the starting point for network analysis, is, of course, the data that are collected and subjected to analysis. The data are *descriptions* of the pairwise *relationships* between members of the system. While the relationships among people who are members of systems exist or happen on a rather concrete level of reality, the data are necessarily abstract, and, to a degree, arbitrary. This distinction concerns not reliability (see Holland and Leinhardt, 1975) but validity: a set of descriptive categories cannot record all the facets and complexities of a relationship, and may well focus on unimportant or irrelevant dimensions, or code or scale dimensions in fruitless or inappropriate ways. Such invalidities generally pass through analysis to infect results.

What is this "relationship"? It is an ongoing, dynamic state of affairs, in which something happens between or among a certain number of people over a certain period of time. At any rate, "it" may be multidimensional, discontinuous, and apparently internally inconsistent. "It" may involve the simultaneous activities of a number of participants, or "it" may be made up of a sequence of asynchronous activities, like the moves of a board game. "It" may involve simultaneous symbolic or iconic encoding at several more or less discrete levels of abstraction, perhaps including "messages" (whatever they are), at some levels, that conflict with those at other levels. One significant aspect of "it" is that "it" may change from one moment to the next, so that, in a very real sense, it is only possible to describe a little bit of what "it" was at a moment in time, or to describe some kind of gross averaged summary of what it was over some interval of time. Referring to it as "a relationship" therefore makes it seem discrete, simple, and easily comparable to other "its" that happen between or among other people, when in reality it has none of these characteristics.

From the perspective of someone who is interested in what can be observed, relationships involve the behavior of a certain number of people, acting in ways that affect one another in some way. The behavior itself, or rather the externally visible parts of the behavior, may be observed directly; or the behavior may be observed by examining whatever evidence is left after the behavior occurs.

From the perspective of the participants in the relationship, while what was said in the last paragraph may be accurate, it may also be irrelevant, because it looks at relationships as bits of *behavior* that takes place over time (much like the individual frames of a motion picture), rather than as a gestalt, a more continuous, meaningful whole, in which the little bits are integrated into a socially significant process that is situated in a particular context. In this perspective, the specific behavior is more or less irrelevant, for it is the ongoing context, which provides meaning and allows the overt behavior to be interpreted and understood, that is critical.

In day-to-day life, there are few limitations on the kinds of relationships that may exist between and among people, other than those imposed by social custom. On the other hand, there are so many restrictions on the kinds of links that may be used in network analysis that it is much easier to say what is possible, rather than what is not. One key restriction that is not dealt with in the literature is that only *pairwise* relationships—those involving two people at a time—are considered. If there are three people involved, there must be at least three relationships for purposes of analysis: one between Floyd and Sharon, one between Floyd and Ellen, and one between Ellen and Sharon, even though this pairwise description cannot possibly capture the true nature of the triad. Furthermore, at the abstract level of description currently used with network data, the only qualities of relationships between people that survive are *symmetricality, transitivity,* and *strength.* Sometimes a form of "content" or "function" categorization is also permitted.

Symmetricality is related to direction or order. In a *symmetric* relation, if B is related to A, A must also be related to B. A symmetric relation has no direction—it is like a two-way street. In an *asymmetric* relation, the fact that B is related to A does not imply that A is related to B. In a *strictly asymmetric* relation, if A is related to B, B cannot be related to A. A one-way street is an asymmetric connection between points along its length—which can cause difficulty if you are at point A and are in a hurry to get to point B, which is in the wrong direction. If A is related to B in a *nonsymmetric* way, B may or may not be related to A. If I give you information, you might or might not give me information. With nonsymmetric relationships, there can be a mixture of one-way and two-way links in a network.

Symmetry should be distinguished from *confirmation* and *reciprocation*, although the ideas are closely related. Symmetry is a property both relationships and data may have, while confirmation and reciprocation are aspects of measurement. If I report a relationship with you (for example, I say I give you information) and you support my report of the relationship (for example, you agree that I give you information), the report is said to be "confirmed." If you do not report the relationship, my report is "unconfirmed." If I say I have a particular kind of relation with you (for example, I trust you), and you say you have the same kind of relation with me (for example, you trust me), then the me-to-you link is "reciprocated."

Symmetry also applies to data. The data matrix will be symmetric if the relationship is symmetric and there is 100 percent confirmation, or if the relationship is asymmetric and there is 100 percent reciprocation. If confirmation or reciprocation fall below 100 percent, the data matrix will not be completely symmetric.

Transitivity is a second aspect of relationships that is carried into the abstract level of descriptions. A relationship is *transitive* if, when A is related to B and B is related to C, A is also related to C in the same way. If I have authority over you, and you have authority over Floyd, then I have authority over Floyd. If I give you information, and you give information to Harry, Harry may be getting information indirectly (through you) from me. Note that this one is not as clean as symmetry. Some of the information I give to you may be passed on to Harry, but then it is quite possible that when you talk to Harry you do not say anything about what I told you.

It is common practice for network researchers to refer to the "distance" from one node in a network to another. There are at least two different meanings of the term "distance": many analytic techniques (factor analysis, and some other forms of multidimensional scaling) use the term to mean the opposite of "similarity," in which two nodes that have similar patterns of connection to other nodes in the network will be said to be similar or close to each other (in some usually unspecified multidimensional space). Also, there is the distance from one node to another, defined as the number of steps it takes to get from node X to node Y. The first sense of the word is not of interest here. The second is, because it raises issues related to the concept of transitivity. It makes little sense to speak of distance in terms of how many links must be passed through, unless the relationship that defines the links is transitive. If the relationship is intransitive, the fact that I am linked to you and you are linked to Margaret says nothing whatsoever about the nature of the relationship between Margaret and me.

The *content* or *function* of the relation creates some of the messiest problems in network analysis. The interaction between content and transitivity was briefly alluded to above. There is a notion that we want the same kind of thing happening in the A to B step as in the B to C step before we are willing to say that there is an implied or indirect relation between A and C. To do this, we might begin with some idea of the kinds of things that can happen in relationships. Many content category schemes have been used by network analysts (despite the BKS remark that "content has been universally avoided" [1978: 10]). Perhaps the best-known is Farace's Production-Innovation-Maintenance trichotomy, though more complex schemes have been used (see Lewis, 1984).

One problem is that there is no complete (that is, exhaustive and mutually exclusive) set of categories available for this purpose. Another difficulty is that the range of human behavior is not discrete—it does not easily fall apart into separate little boxes. Furthermore, those different categories come together in complex ways as managers manage and workers work. While there are reasons for looking at, say, the innovation network all by itself, this kind of isolation may be unfair to the processes going on in the organization, partly because what is innovation to one person is regular work to another, and partly because it is impossible to understand the innovation process outside the context provided by the work and social networks. These were some of the difficulties alluded to above, in the discussion of calling "it" a "relationship"—perhaps "it" is actually several relationships (in terms of symmetry, transitivity, strength, and content) all happening at once.

Finally, there is the issue of *strength*. One commonsense (and common in the literature) interpretation of the strength of the relationship between A and B is the "amount of interaction" between the two. This has been operationalized in many ways, including frequency of interaction, number of minutes of interaction per month or per week, or some combination of the frequency and importance of the interaction. Rarely is any clear argument given for why the proposed definition of strength is valid. This is one more example of the tenuous nature of the connection between what "it" is that happens between and among people in their day to day relationships and the abstract descriptions of relationships that are used in the analysis of those relationships.

FILTERS

So far, the focus of much of the discussion has been on the difference between reality—"it"—and the abstract characteristics of the analytic framework within which data (descriptions of bits of that reality) are collected and analyzed. Between the reality and final description resulting from the analysis of the data are two processes that can be thought of as acting like polarizing filters placed on the lens of a camera: They allow only a limited amount of what comes into them to pass through, and they shape what manages to pass through in their own peculiar way. These "filters" are the processes of measurement and analysis of the data. Both processes interact with the data in important ways.

MEASUREMENT

The bridging process by which data are obtained—measurement—plays a central role in determining how communication relationships are mapped onto abstract descriptions of those relationships. Measurement itself is really two processes: observation and coding. In the first, an observer "taps into" the situation somehow, perhaps by watching it happen, by examining something that is left as a result of it happening, or by "introspection." Coding involves the selection or abstraction of some aspect of what is seen, and the mapping of that aspect along some dimension or set of dimensions. In the process of coding, the simultaneous, continuous "stream" of reality that is observed is reduced to one or more arbitrary, discrete values (numbers), so that a digital representation may be constructed from the part of reality being "measured." Selection and abstraction are important activities in both processes, and they are activities in which the amount of information is dramatically reduced and altered—if not in content, at least in form.

I will describe here two approaches that are prevalent in the literature of communication network analysis: the self-report method and the outside observer method. In the former, people are simply asked who they communicate with, how often interaction takes place, and so on. The outside observer method uses data obtained either by direct observation of the interaction or by examination of some kind of trace naturally left by the interaction process.

The first approach might be called "subjective," as it relies on people's descriptions (and interpretations) of their own behavior, and as the information obtained is not directly verifiable, because the people themselves do the observing and encoding according to their own capabilities and understanding of the measurement situation. The second might be called "objective," because it relies on external observers who look at externally visible phenomena, and who encode their observations in a standard, reproducible way. Because they do not have access to the same range of "observables" as the participants in the self-report method, external observers cannot possibly construct the same kinds of descriptions of what happens in relationships.

The measurement method has a large impact on the resulting data: With the subjective self-report approach, there are many contradictions or inconsistencies in the data, because there are many "observers" who disagree with one another. Confirmation rates are rarely above 30 percent. When estimates of communication frequency or duration are collected with subjective data, it is possible to compare these estimates for participants in confirmed links. Exact agreement is rare. The disagreement is often so great that it is almost as if the respondents lived in different worlds.

With the objective method, in which there is a trained observer, confirmation is not an issue—the observer either did or did not see a pair of individuals interact, so there is no confusion about what did or did not happen. The subjective method allows information about the perceived importance of the interaction to be collected, while the objective method does not. The subjective method allows observers to consider a much wider range of kinds of information than does the objective method. In short, the objective world is much simpler than the subjective one.

With the subjective method, the analyst must decide what to do about unconfirmed links (Delete them unconditionally? Delete them if they are not stronger than a specified threshold? Add the missing halves? Ignore the fact that they are not confirmed?) and confirmed links in which the participants disagree about the strength or content (Delete them? Take the stronger of the two reports? Take the mean of the two strength reports?).

ANALYSIS METHODS

In the end, it might not matter which approach to measurement was taken, because analytic methods (almost always computer programs these days) turn out to be very strong "filters" indeed, sometimes requiring that major surgery be performed on the data, even before going into the operating room where things are done with and to matrices. Here are just a few of the major assumptions of some of the better-known programs (see Rice and Richards, 1985, for a far more detailed comparison of methods):

- All programs consider only pairwise relationships, so that relationships involving more than two people at a time must be "decomposed" into dyads, if this has not already been done in the measurement phase.

- Some programs can accept only *binary* data. This means that only the presence or absence of a link may be utilized in the analysis. In order to achieve this quality when links have strengths associated with them, a "cutting point" must be chosen, so that all links with strengths below this value are deleted from the analysis (notice how this alters the meaning of "strength"). Other programs allow *scalar* data, in which links have more or less continuously variable strengths.

- Some programs can accept only symmetrical data matrices. Something must be done with unreciprocated or unconfirmed links. One of two options are most frequently used: Delete them outright or add the missing halves. Since most researchers are uncomfortable with the idea of creating new data and adding it to the data that "really exist," the common choice is to delete the unreciprocated or unconfirmed links from the analysis. Note that directed or asymmetrical relations cannot legitimately be examined with these approaches. Other programs try to handle data that are less than 100 percent symmetrical, with varying degrees of success.

- Many programs implicitly assume relationships are transitive, so that if A is linked to B and B is linked to C, there is an implied relation between A and C. This assumption is made whenever the "distance" between nodes in terms of the number of steps from one to another is mentioned. This may be a problem when relationships are, in fact, not transitive.

• While a few programs try to handle multiplex links (in which there is more than one kind of relationship, in terms of content or function), none really does, because the ones that try simply add up all the data matrices, although the information about content or function may be carried throughout the analysis and made available in summary tables.

Note that neither the analytic nor the measurement filter adds anything to the data—information is lost, both in the process of measurement and in the process of preparation for analysis. Besides eliminating much of the richness of the data, the analytic process itself may make further changes that may or may not be consistent with the way the researcher understands the "reality" under investigation (see Rice and Richards, 1985).

NETWORK ANALYSIS:
TANGLED UP IN TWO PARADIGMS

While there has been no consideration given here to the way in which the researcher understands the relationship on which the network is based, it is clear that the choice of measurement method and analytic technique have a lot to say about what is or is not possible in the data describing that relationship—that these methods effectively impose a conceptual model of their own on the data. This is especially problematic when the implicitly imposed model conflicts with the one the researcher is working with explicitly.

Many of the differences among the different conceptual and operational approaches to describing and conceptualizing networks can be traced to connections with one of two basic epistemological positions or paradigms that have already been hinted at above. One position is called "objectivist," "positivist," or "functionalist" while the other is known as "subjectivist," "interpretivist," or "cognitive constructivist." The two positions are basically the same as those identified as "functionalist" and "interpretivist" by Putnam (1983).

The "objectivist" approach, based on a positivist orientation to science and research (Putnam, 1983: 34), resembles such approaches as structural-func-tionalism, behaviorism (Burrell and Morgan, 1979), and some versions of general systems theory as it is applied to social systems (Berlinski, 1976; Lillienfeld, 1978). This approach to networks wants a relatively "clean" kind of data, based on clear, verifiable, relatively concrete measurements. The best way to obtain these data is to use independent outside observers to do the measurement. An approach that is commonly used involves taking a kind of sample of the behavior of the members of networks.

In the case of nonmediated, face-to-face communication, all the observer has to go on is the fact that a pair of individuals are seen facing each other, opening and closing their mouths, and producing sounds. From this it is inferred that there is a communication relationship. While the observer may be able to indicate accurately how much time is spent in this kind of activity, he cannot tell who initiates the interaction, whether it is symmetric, how important it is, or what functions it plays for the individuals and anyone else who may be involved in any way. Without interviewing the people involved, all that can be said is that a conversation took place. The relationship is assumed to be symmetric. The perceptions, feelings, interpretations, beliefs, and other characteristics of the people involved are not considered. The adoption of this measurement strategy thus seems to imply the concurrent adoption of a fairly crude conceptual model of social interaction—one that says that it is possible to understand the patterns of social interaction by looking only at who talks with whom.

Watzlawick et al. (1967: 20) describe a situation in which the information obtained by "outside observers" was misleading, and because of the missing contextual information, led to a totally incorrect view of what "actually" happened:

> In the garden of a country house, in plain view of passers-by on the sidewalk outside, a bearded man can be observed dragging himself, crouching, round the meadow, in figures of eight, glancing constantly over his shoulder and quacking without interruption. This is how the ethologist Konrad Lorenz describes his necessary behavior during one of his imprinting experiments with ducklings, after he had substituted himself for their mother. "I was congratulating myself," he writes, "on the obedience and exactitude with which my ducklings came waddling after me when I suddenly looked up and saw the garden fence framed by a row of dead-white faces: a group of tourists was standing at the fence and staring horrified in my direction." The ducklings were hidden in tall grass, and all the tourists saw was totally unexplainable, indeed insane, behavior (1952: 43).

What is of interest with the outside observer approach to measurement is the actual behavioral sequences in which the participants engage. It is not necessary for there to be anything behind that behavior. Because internal events such as feelings, perceptions and the like are not considered in the processes of collecting, analyzing, or interpreting the data, this might be called the "external event" view.

Presumably, any competent observer would be able to verify the statements made by any other. It is for this reason that the description provided by outside observers, based upon external events, is considered to be "objective." This approach clearly has the ingredients of a traditional positivistic view of the world. This view holds that there is a true reality that can be accessed and known. Social reality exists "out there," and any recourse to unobservable internal events is nonscientific, since there can be no independent verification of the "truth" with these kinds of phenomena. Since there is a single true reality, it makes sense to speak of concepts like the accuracy of the data, and to measure this accuracy by comparison with a known standard, as Bernard, Killworth, and Sailor (hereafter referred to as BKS) attempted to do when they compared self-report data with their "standard"—outside observer data (see Bernard and Killworth, 1977, 1978; Bernard et al., 1980).

It is important to note, however, that observers must be trained to encode the same acts in the same way. Furthermore, only a small subset of the total range of behavior is significant, which means that most of what is observed is not recorded. The description produced by an observer is therefore not equivalent to the observed behavior, although it should at least be consistent with it. However, while consistency may be necessary, it may not be sufficient.

COMMUNICATION THEORY

Until sometime in the 1960s, a popular model of communication relationships held that communication involved a *source*, who sent a *message* through some *channel* to a *receiver*. Communication, in this model, is linear and directional. The message has an independent existence, apart from anything the sender or receiver does with it. Senders *encode* their ideas into messages, while receivers *decode* the messages to get the ideas back. If the model seems mechanistic, it is because it was based on Shannon and Weaver's *Mathematical Theory of Communication* (1949), which was designed to describe situations in which precisely quantifiable information was sent through a channel with known and limited capacity, such as a telephone wire or a microwave relay system.

It is easy to see how the Shannon-Weaver model fits into the abstract notion of relationships developed above. The relationship here is clearly directed, but, since it is possible for one person to talk back to a second person who earlier sent a message to the first, the data will be nonsymmetrical. That is, it will be possible to have both reciprocated and unreciprocated links in the network. The Shannon-Weaver model says nothing about strength of the link, although Shannon and Weaver did tell how to measure the amount of information in the message, as well as the carrying capacity of the channel, so one of these might be used as the measure of strength. The Shannon-Weaver model is silent on transitivity and content, because it says nothing about the characteristics of the sources and receivers—the people—and what they do with the messages, besides encoding and decoding, or about the messages themselves—how they are structured and what they might mean to people.

It is clear that an outside observer approach to measurement is appropriate with the Shannon-Weaver model of communication. There is no reason to talk to the participants, or to get any information from them about the interaction, because there is no way of using the information they can supply about what they thought or felt about the interaction, and because they can only introduce error into the data. However, while the model permits nonsymmetric data, the outside observer method will only give symmetric data, unless it is possible to determine unequivocally what was the direction of information flow. Few naturalistic situations will allow this to be done without the use of obtrusive observation techniques.

So the prior conceptual model of communication conflicts with the measurement method. The method filters out some of the variety permitted in the conceptual model, and, in effect, substitutes a different conceptual model—one in which little else can be said of the network beyond who is linked to whom.

Fortunately, the Shannon-Weaver model is no longer in popular use for the study of human communication. During the 1970s and early 1980s a new model of communication gained wide acceptance—a more subjective one that explicitly recognizes that individuals "construct" their own social realities:

Persons construct personally and socially meaningful understandings of events and persons in their world. . . . People do not live with understandings that reflect an external reality but rather with understandings that are construed in accordance with an internal system of personal concepts. Hence, the world in which persons live is in a very real way an invented abstraction. . . . it must be understood that the perceptual field constitutes reality for the person . . . the perceptual field is not, from the person's point of view, a construction of reality; *it is reality* [Swanson and Delia, 1976: 14-15; emphasis added].

This perspective, the "interpretive" view, differs from the positivist approach in a number of important ways. Unlike the positivist's world, in which there is one true knowable reality, the interpretivist's world is much more relativistic, incorporating an emphasis on context and an explicit understanding that personal knowledge and experience are parts of reality, and that the reality experienced by persons is based largely on individual interpretations of personal knowledge and experience. Where the positivist is interested in discovering universal laws of behavior that can be generalized and applied in a wide range of situations to enable both the prediction and the control of human behavior, the interpretivist's research is probably less likely to lead to the kind of knowledge that can be used in this way—for example, by managers who want to increase productivity by tighter control of workers' actions—and more likely to lead to a deeper understanding of the social aspects of the particular situation (Putnam, 1984: 36-39).

The interpretivist perspective, because of its emphasis on social reality as opposed to objective external reality, would favor the self-report method of measurement, in which respondents are asked to describe their own relationships to others. A careful examination of the measurement process from the interpretivist perspective, however, will show that there are problems with this method.

One of the most obvious problems is that it is possible for there to be a pair of individuals who, according to an outside observer, have an ongoing communication relationship although neither of them names the other as a social contact on a self-report form, or who, according to the observer, have no relationship although both say there is an important one. In other words, it is possible for the descriptions produced by an outside observer and those produced by the people themselves to be either highly correlated or totally independent. It is possible for the descriptions of the individuals themselves to be inconsistent with one another. These inconsistencies are not only possible, they occur frequently in self-report data. How is this problem to be resolved? What are the implications for measurement and analysis?

One approach would be to say that self-report data are useless and to use observers' reports instead. However, it has been argued that there is no reason to expect the reports of observers to be any more valid than self-reports, and that self-reports are more valid, since it is their beliefs and perceptions upon which people build their lives, and not what "actually" happens. A more careful response would be that what "actually" happens is valid, but that it is so difficult to establish what, in fact, did "actually" happen that self-report data can be accepted as the best approximation. This is largely because part of what "actually" happens is how people react to their perceptions: how they assign meaning, how they interpret them in a context. Outside observers can report on these activities only with great difficulty, to say the least. This is the case even when some sort of "natural trace" is left of each interaction, such as when a community of amateur radio operators is observed by monitoring tape recordings of all their broadcasts. Even if their radios were, in fact, their only means of communication, and the transcripts were available for analysis, it would still be impossible to describe the relevant cognitive activity. In other words, it would be impossible to say what "actually" happened, if what "actually" happened is to include descriptions of socially meaningful activity with enough detail to decide what is the social meaning.

The fact that the conceptual starting point for network analysis is the *relationship*, while the descriptions provided by observers are of *behavior*, provides a clue. Relationships are not the same as behavioral acts (although it may be argued that certain types of behavior are indicative of the existence of relationships). While it is clear that observers describe overt behavioral acts, the data obtained with self-report techniques are likely to be based on perceptions of *ongoing relationships*, rather than discrete decontextualized events. People see their interactions with other persons in terms of relationships, rather than in terms of discrete events. We speak and think of friends and acquaintances, rather than of people with whom we have moderately important interactions more than twice a week. While it is, in a sense, more precise to know that there were seven interactions between a pair of persons than to know that the persons involved claim to be friends, the latter, more abstract description is more meaningful both to the persons involved and to someone who wishes to gain a better understanding of a network of relationships.

But most self-report techniques are couched in terms of behavioral acts— "How often do you interact with this person?"—rather than in terms of relationships (friends, acquaintances and the like). In order to respond to this type of question, it is necessary to convert perceptions of relationships back into statements about behavior. Since the specific details of a behavioral event as it took place are probably less important than the social meaning of the event in a personal context, it is not likely that these details—such as the times at which interaction took place, or how long it lasted—will be reconstructed with any degree of accuracy. This is where "distortion" is likely to creep in. Since details are what is being asked for, and since people like to cooperate, they will obligingly supply some details that are, most likely, consistent with their understandings of and/or feelings about the relationship they are trying to describe. The result is thus a composition of actual recollections and cognitively constructed interpretations. Although it may be less precise than actual records of external events, it will tell more about the relationships that exist.

Where BKS (see the next section) argue that what people say about what they do is so inaccurate that it tells us nothing about social structure, they are really saying that what people say tells us nothing about what they do. If "what they do"—their behavior, taken out of context as it is by the use of outside observers—has pattern or structure, it seems this structure would be more properly called "behavioral structure." "Social structure" would include all the phenomena that make behavior socially meaningful, such as the kinds of cognitive activity that we like to think make us different from animals or machines.

BKS AND THE "ACCURACY" ISSUE: TANGLED PARADIGMS

Russ Bernard, Peter Killworth, and Lee Sailor (BKS) have an ongoing research program in which they attempt to address the issue of the accuracy of self-report data (see Bernard and Killworth, 1977, 1978; Bernard et al., 1980). They argue that, given that the self-report method is the one most commonly used by network researchers, and given that there are indications (such as confirmation rates below 30 percent) that there are inconsistencies with self-report data, it would be useful to have some indication of the amount of error, or, conversely, some indication of the level of accuracy in self-report data.

The basic method for the BKS tests was to collect two kinds of data from the same group of individuals: "cognitive" (self-report) data and "behavioral" (outside observer) data. BKS then compared the cognitive data with the behavioral data. Of course, if one is to assess the accuracy of a particular kind of measurement, it is necessary to have a standard of known accuracy against which to make the comparison. For BKS, the "standard" was the behavioral data. Why? Because such data were collected in an objective way, because they included only indisputable descriptions of concrete events, and because BKS take a strongly objectivist perspective toward social networks.

BKS (1980: 209) raise the issue of the difficulty of measuring "behavior such as communication." They say that the problem is "circumvented by shifting the object of study to something that can be observed, recorded, and measured: individuals' reports of their behavior, i.e., their cognition of recall. These reports are then taken as a proxy for behavior." They ask, "Is behavior recall a meaningful object of study in its own right?" and answer, "If cognition about a particular behavior does not relate to the behavior, it is unlikely to relate to anything else, either." So the idea is to see if, in fact, "cognition about a particular behavior" does relate to "the behavior." In other words, does what people say have any relation to what actually happens?

To help ensure the fairness of their test, BKS repeated their study in a number of different situations:

- In a college fraternity house in which the occupants had resided for at least three months ("frat"). The behavioral data were collected by observers who walked through the fraternity every 15 minutes, 21 hours a day, for 5 consecutive days, and recorded the occurrence of all conversations. "Any two persons in contact were scored. N-tuples were scored by counting each dyad" (BKS, 1978: 7). At the end of the period, "each member of the fraternity gave a rating, from 1 (no communication) to 5 (a great deal of communication) concerning his interaction with each of the other members."

- In a small research-oriented office ("office"). Behavioral data were collected here using the same methods used in the fraternity.

- In a group at a university associated with a graduate program in technology education ("techs"), including graduate students and secretaries. The same method was used for collecting behavioral data.

- With a group of amateur radio operators ("hams"). Behavioral data were collected semiautomically, be means of recordings made of all transmissions that used a common "repeater" station through which contacts were made.

"Cognitive" data were obtained from the office group by giving each participant a deck of cards containing the names of the other participants. They were asked to rank the cards

> from "most" to "least" on how often they talked to others in the office during a "normal working day." The question of frequency, amount, and importance of contact was raised often by the participants, but this was deliberately left vague. They were told to make up their own minds [BKS, 1978: 6].

This method produces what will be referred to here as "ranked" cognitive data. In a 35-member group, each person will assign one of the numbers from 1 to 34 to each of the other 34 members. Every number will be used exactly once by each respondent, even if he or she talks to only, say, 10 people. There can be no ties, unless mistakes are made in coding or keying-in the data.

For the "techs," the procedure was similar. Each person

> was handed a deck of cards containing the names of all other members of the group, and asked to rank the deck from "most to least communication that week." The question was purposely left rather vague; amount, frequency, or importance of communication was not specified [BKS, 1978: 7].

The "hams" were mailed a sheet with the FCC-assigned "calls" of the members of the group and asked "to scale them from 0 (no communication) to 9 (a great deal of communication)." Again, there was no elaboration on the coding system to be used. Applying this method to a 35-member group should result in 34 values for each of the 35 members. Each of those 34 values can be any from 0, 1, 2, . . . to 9. That is, all 34 values can be 0, all 34 can be 9, or there can be any combination. These are the *scaled* data. At the end of their description of the data collection procedures, the writers added this note:

> Note that in no case is content of communication part of the data. Obviously, content of communication may be an important factor in determining both interaction and people's perception of interaction. However, as far as we are aware,

content of communication is a topic universally avoided by researchers in social network theory [BKS, 1978: 10].

This note draws our attention to one of the most obvious problems with the BKS studies: By explicitly ignoring content, amount, frequency, and importance, and by refusing to elaborate on the intentionally vague scaling instructions, BKS virtually guaranteed that the cognitive data gathered with this method would contain an unpredictable mix of different kinds of data, representing different kinds of interactions, and scaled in different ways, when what was needed, if the comparison with the "standard" was to be fair, was some precision. But, since the behavioral data ignore content and importance as well, perhaps the looseness in the cognitive data is appropriate.

How did the comparison work? At the dyadic level, when cognitive links were compared one for one with behavioral links, BKS found a 50 percent error rate. At the triadic level the error rose to 76 percent. At the level of cliques, the error level was 160 percent (1978: 27). This is, BKS say, like representing a "behavioral clique" whose members are 1, 2, 3, 4, 5, and 6, by a "cognitive clique" whose members include 1, 7, 8, 9, and 10.

This section's subtitle is "Tangled Paradigms." The reason for this will now become clear. BKS inadvertently used conflicting methods or assumptions at just about every step in their studies: in the measurement and scaling of the data, in the operations they performed on the data to make them comparable, and in interpreting their results. Because of these conflicts, their final results are suspect. Since their very ingenious and at first straightforward-looking studies have so many problems, it will be instructive to do a quick review here.

It is not possible to make valid comparisons of the ranked cognitive data provided by any one person with those provided by any other person, even within any of the data sets. While this is due partly to the intentionally vague instructions respondents were given, it is also because these types of ordinal data allow comparisons only between one person's i^{th} and j^{th} ranks. There is no way of anchoring one person's ranks to those of any other person. One problem here is that the choice of scaling method (ranking with no ties) implied a concurrent assumption that people's communication patterns follow the kinds of distribution inherent in the scaling system, that is, that each person had the same amount of communication with the same number of people as did every other person. Although BKS probably did not believe this unlikely situation actually occurred, their method of scaling the data made that assumption for them. But this assumption was used only for the ranked cognitive data, because different methods were used for the rest of the data.

BKS moved from link-by-link comparisons to triadic and then clique-level comparisons because they thought some of the "noise" in the data might be filtered out at higher levels of description. I will skip directly to the clique-level comparison (BKS, 1978, 1980), because that is where the most interesting action happens. Here, BKS introduced more assumptions with which they probably wouldn't agree. First, they could offer no reason to choose any particular definition of what a "clique" was, or what method should be used to determine whether there were cliques in the data and who belonged to them. They stated that a "good clique finding algorithm should reduce the noise" and would produce clique structures from both the cognitive data and the behavioral data that are the same. In other words, the quality of a clique-finding algorithm depends on its ability to produce similar results, given different data (but not on any match between what the authors understand a "clique" to be and what the program "finds" or how it "finds" it). The poor quality of the cognitive data, on the other hand, is proven if the clique-finding algorithm cannot produce similar results when given different data. BKS mentioned that a number of researchers were invited to participate in the test, but that most did not respond. (They did not report that at least one refused because he felt his method could not produce valid results with ranked data.)

Second, the clique-finding algorithms BKS used required binary symmetric data, while none of the data were binary, and only the behavioral data were symmetric. In order to make asymmetric data symmetric, data must either be added or deleted. BKS chose to delete asymmetric data. In order to make ratio, interval, or ordinal data binary, it is necessary to dichotomize it somehow, so that continuous strength values become binary "present" or "absent." This is done by choosing a cutoff point and deleting all links that fall below this value. If there is some logical reason that would justify this kind of treatment, the result could possibly still be said to represent the network. If there is no such reason, it is not clear what relationship a dichotomized symmetricized matrix will have to the original situation.

An illustration of what happens in this process is provided by BKS's sketchy description of the "tech" group (1980). Cutoff points were chosen so that, for each person, K links would be retained in both the ranked and behavioral data. For the ranked data, this meant that for each person, links would be retained for those individuals ranked K and above. A similar operation was performed on the behavioral data "i.e., retaining the K people I communicated with most." Note that, although the cutoff was described as similar, it was, in fact, quite different. The ranked data were row-normalized, while the behavioral data were not. The ranked data were ordinal, while the behavioral data were cardinal. The operation described had different effects on the two kinds of data.

With the behavioral data there could be ties, which was impossible with the ranked data. BKS say that the cutoff was "adjusted" to account for this, and that it resulted in a reduction in the number of links. While they did not specify exactly how the procedure worked, inspection of their published results (1980: 198) allows the following reconstruction: Rank each person's behavioral data according to frequency of contact. For each person, count down eight links from the top. If you land in the middle of a string of links with equal strengths, drop the whole lot of them. If you land between two links of different strengths, drop all but the eight. This procedure has the drawback of giving some people more links than others, which does not happen with cognitive data.

The application of the cutoff in both cognitive and behavioral data resulted in the creation of asymmetric links, which had to be dropped from the analysis, because the clique detection routine wanted symmetric data. The net effect was to throw away 20 percent of the behavioral data in this case. (For the "office" data, 70 percent had to be dropped here.) It is impossible to tell how much real cognitive data were dropped, due to the problems with ranks described above, but 50 percent of the links were removed when they became asymmetric, due to the cutoff. It seems that moving to higher levels of analysis introduces more "noise" than it eliminates, mainly because of the basic incompatibility of the different kinds of data with one another and with the clique-detection routines.

Clearly there are problems with this research. Unwarranted assumptions were made by the method of collecting data, by the method of scaling the results, and by the method of detecting "cliques." While the whole process was an attempt to measure the accuracy of one type of data, massive amounts of those data did not have a chance to be tested, because they were thrown away before they even came close to the comparison. Most serious, though, is the use of the term "accuracy" to refer to what was being tested. This implies there is one true, objective reality, and that reality is adequately measured and described by the behavioral data, and, furthermore, that the cognitive data *should* correspond to the objective data. What happened, in short, is that a method of measurement that implied a peculiar subjective view of communication relationships was tested against a method of measurement that implied an objective view, and the test was done with methods that were not meant to imply anything in particular, but that nevertheless conflicted with the earlier assumptions.

BKS said that because cognitive data (of the sort they collected) were not accurate, that is, they did not agree (according to their definition of agree) with behavioral data (their peculiar operationalization of social reality), people's statements about what they do are of no use in understanding the social structure of communication. But no matter how accurate they are, when they are removed from the social context, descriptions of who talks with whom would not constitute a sufficient basis for an understanding of the *social structure* of communication, although they may be useful in examining some aspects of the *behavioral structure* of social interaction.

WHAT TO DO?

The suggestion is hereby made that the best way to achieve access to the social relationships among a set of persons in a network study is to ensure that the people perform the relevant transformations and integrations on their percep-tions, thereby encoding these perceptions in a socially meaningful way that is both available for study and useful in research. The way to do this is to ask them to describe their social relationships, which is what we have been doing all along when we use self-report data. The only difference is that by explicitly recognizing that this is being done, it is possible to develop the questions used in eliciting the responses so they take into consideration the more complex nature of the situation.

The two steps of the measurement process—observation and coding—are always present, whether the measurement is done "objectively" or "subjectively." In both cases, a clear specification must be made of what is to be observed and how it is to be coded. Both these steps should be chosen so they are compatible with whatever view of communication the researcher holds.

With the objective approach, conceptual or pragmatic considerations will make it fairly easy to determine what is being observed and how coding should be done. This approach would be appropriate, for example, if one wanted to determine patterns of communication so a more efficient mail delivery system or a better interoffice intercom could be designed. What is important here is knowing which points send messages to which other points. A straightforward count of messages would provide most of the needed data. What is observed is messages sent, and coding is done by counting them. Whatever method of analysis is used, it should not require major changes in the data that invalidate their representativeness.

With the subjective or interpretive approach, the situation is much more complex. Let us assume the goal is to understand networks of advice seeking and giving in a community of medical practitioners. This could be an approach that would be useful if one was interested in complementing or enhancing ongoing, continuing medical education programs. In one such study (Weinberg et al., 1980), the respondents were asked two questions: from whom did they seek advice and information, and to whom did they give advice and information. The relationship here was directed, but since reciprocated links were possible, that is, physician A could both give information to and receive information from physician B, it was nonsymmetric. Because the relation "gives information to" was directed, it was necessary to ask about the inverse of that relation (From whom do you get information?) in order to check for confirmation. Analysis of the data showed that confirmation rates were about 5 percent—only one physician in twenty who was listed by a recipient as a source of information said he was a source for that recipient.

An objectivist interpretation of this situation would state that if you receive information or advice from me, I must have given information or advice to you. Such a view would have some difficulty in understanding the results reported above. One possible interpretation that would be made is that people cannot remember where they received information, or that they forgot to whom they gave information. In any case, the objectivist would say such low rates of confirmation support the notion that self-report or "cognitive" data are unreliable and should not be used.

An interpretivist researcher would want to talk with the physicians and uncover how they interpreted both the question about giving or seeking information and the process of giving or seeking information. In this case, the interpretivist would discover that "giving advice or information" is not the inverse of "seeking advice or information." How could this be? It seems that many physicians go to conferences at which other physicians known as experts in their field give presentations. Many of those in the audience feel they are receiving advice or information from these speakers, but the speakers do not count the members of the audience as "coming to them for advice or information." Also, much advice and information is obtained informally, perhaps over a game of golf or handball. The conversation in which one physician receives information from another will often not be marked by statements such as "I need information from you" or "Here is the information you asked for." The result is that those who receive information may know they are doing so, while those giving information may feel they are simply having a friendly conversation. Keeping these points in mind, one would be more likely to focus the analysis on the answers to "From whom do you receive advice and information" than "To whom do you give advice and information."

What happened in this study is similar to what happens in many others: a more or less objectivist view is used to define the measurement instrument; data are collected and analyzed; the results contain so many inconsistencies that questions are raised about the nature of the situation; and it is realized that the way people understand and interpret their experiences and perceptions interacts with the measurement situation. A better approach to take would be to begin with an explicit recognition of the complex cognitive activities involved not only in day to day social interactions but also in the process of reporting who are one's contacts.

People do not walk around with descriptions of their social relationships clearly formulated, ready to be listed on request, the way a computer can list the contents of its files. The sociometric question is a complex stimulus that demands a significant amount of information processing as individuals attempt to construct from their memories, present feelings, moods, and so on (which are not stored as digital streams of linguistically-encoded symbolic information), which are highly structured, abstract, discrete representations of their social realities. The sociometric question can be seen as stimulating the encoding of memories, feelings, beliefs, and the like into a discrete symbolic format—either as a list of social contacts, in response to an open-ended question, or as a series of responses to a multiple-choice type roster. This encoding activity is complex, first in that tremendous amounts of emotional, iconic, and linguistic information must by mapped onto a coding system that is many orders of magnitude simpler (see Polanyi's *The Tacit Dimension*, 1966); and second, in that every individual has a unique way of going about the process. Simply asking respondents to indicate who their contacts are clearly ignores the complexity in this measurement process.

How might the interpretivist perspective be implemented in the study with the physicians? Perhaps a number of physicians would be interviewed and closely observed, so a better understanding of the kinds of relationships in which they participate could be developed. Tape recordings might be made of a number of "typical" conversations. Transcripts of these recordings might be subjected to content analysis, and a typology of kinds of interactions might be made. A sample of physicians would be asked to describe the kinds of relationships they have with other physicians, using specific examples to illustrate their descriptions. These descriptions would also be content analyzed and used to refine the typology of relationships developed above. The typology would be used to help specify the aspects of relationships that should be measured—observed and coded—and to determine how this "observation" and coding should be done. The result might be that a whole range of questions would be asked, rather than, "to whom do you go . . ." and "who comes to you. . . ."

The following multistage measurement process might be used (note that, given that none of the above activities were done, what follows is completely hypothetical):

- Have all respondents review an up-to-date list of physicians' names, specialties, and affiliations, and indicate the ones with which they are familiar.

- Have respondents rate the physicians they know on the basis of several criteria, such as how much they know, how up-to-date they are, their level of professional expertise, how well-respected they are by their colleagues, how available they are for consultation, how open they are with their information, how influential they are seen to be, and so forth.

- Have respondents indicate what personal contact they have or have had with each of the others. For each contact, include information about where the interaction took place, what communication channels or media were involved (face-to-face, telephone, or whatever), what kinds of interaction there were (discussion of social affairs, gossip, discussion of particular patients or cases, discussion of specific types of diagnosis or treatment, discussion of professional concerns such as Medicare or new legislation that affects the health professions, and so on), who initiated the contact and why, and so forth.

- Finally, have respondents describe the relationships they have with each of the others, using the typology developed above, along with a number of open-ended questions that would allow the typology to be refined further if necessary.

One additional set of decisions must be made. The issues all center on the choice of analytic methods. The measurement procedure outlined above will obviously result in more complex data that will require a wide range of analytic techniques and methods. If a traditional network analysis is to be done on part of the data, the particular method to be used should be chosen on the basis of that method's match with the goals and constraints of the research problem and all the relevant contingencies. In practice, it seems that methods are chosen more on the basis of availability than of suitability (as BKS clearly demonstrated). While limited distribution of many computer programs makes it difficult to select the most appropriate method, the current trend is toward increasing the availability of these packages, which should reduce the problem. This change should result in more studies capable of answering significant research questions, because they will not be constrained by the requirements and assumptions of particular research methods.

It is obvious that the interpretivist network approach outlined above is much more complex and labor intensive than the approaches commonly in use. This extra work and expense are not likely to be used if there is not a concomitant increase in the quality of the results. What improvements could be expected with this approach?

- greater validity at all levels
- more understandable and useful results
- much higher levels of confidence in the results and in any conclusions based on them
- easier interpretation of results
- much more meaningful results and conclusions

SUMMARY

The role of conceptual models in the collection of network analysis data was examined in light of research findings that indicate that data obtained by asking people to recall the others with whom they interact is inaccurate. The "problem" with these data was traced to the use of measurement and analytic procedures that implicitly make assumptions inconsistent with the ones explicitly made in the statement of the research problem. The interpretivist approach to communication was suggested both as a more appropriate way to view social interaction and as a basis from which to develop measurement techniques that should give more valid results. A number of suggestions were made for implementing this approach in specific research situations. While the adoption of this new approach entails considerably more effort than was needed with earlier approaches, the benefits, in terms of more valid and meaningful data, should be well worth the cost.

Chapter 5

BARGAINING AS ORGANIZATIONAL COMMUNICATION

Linda L. Putnam

EFFECTIVE CONFLICT MANAGEMENT is critical to organizational success. Interspersed with decision making and control, conflict management can lead to creative problem solving, improved worker-participation, and even increased organizational commitment. Negotiation represents a particular type of conflict management—one characterized by an exchange of proposals and counterproposals as a means of reaching a satisfactory settlement. Even though most researchers and practitioners examine negotiations through the lens of labor-management relations, the theories, contexts, and strategies of bargaining apply to a broad array of organizational events, including interdepartmental disputes, sales and marketing, superior-subordinate relations, and control-autonomy issues.

Moreover, the concepts prevalent in organizational communication under-gird bargaining proposals and relationships. Specifically, issues at the table frequently emerge from poor superior-subordinate communication, inappropriate power distribution, ineffective upward and downward communication, and struggles for autonomy and control. Thus negotiation is not only a form of conflict management, but a type of decision making and information processing that emanates from the daily routines, structural constraints, and organizational environment of participants.

This chapter critiques the theories that dominate traditional labor-management bargaining research. Then it explores two emerging themes on negotiation and communication, reviews relevant literature in each area, and concludes with a theoretical perspective that combines context, process, and interpretive models of collective bargaining. This chapter focuses on traditional labor-management negotiation because most communication research adopts this paradigm to study bargaining relationships. These relationships incorporate both the interpersonal and the intergroup levels of bargaining. Thus the topics covered in this chapter can apply to other contexts outside of formal collective bargaining. Specifically, the dimensions, processes, and outcomes discussed in this chapter also characterize legal transactions, international negotiations, and buyer-seller situations. Moreover, since bargaining is a form of conflict management, its processes resemble those discovered in marital conflicts and group decision-making (Gottman, 1979; Putnam and Jones, 1982a). Thus the research on bargaining reviewed in this chapter applies to negotiations in other contexts.

DOMINANT THEORIES
OF BARGAINING RESEARCH

From its inception economists, lawyers, and historians dominated theory development in collective bargaining. Economists relied on mathematical models that focused on clearly quantifiable measures. These models were tested at aggregate levels of analysis. Lawyers, in contrast, narrowed their focus to labor law, specifically to the legal ramifications of negotiated contracts. Historians rejected both the legal and the economic models as being too narrowly defined. They concentrated on transactions between groups, not simply as labor inputs to production, but as historical developments that shaped different economic forces in society. From these diverse orientations, three dominant theories emerged: game theory, bargaining theory, and institutional economics.

GAME THEORY

Game theory originated as a form of classical economics. Pure game theory, as espoused by von Neumann and Morgenstern (1944) in *Theory of Games and Economic Behavior* and as amplified by Rapoport (1964) in *Strategy and Conscience,* consisted of a set of assumptions for conceptualizing conflict. Through deductive analysis it aimed to develop a highly abstract logical structure for classifying conflict and identifying probable outcomes. Game theory assumed that (1) bargainers were rational and could calculate the best outcome from available information; (2) the rules of the game were known in advance and remained fixed throughout the game; (3) each player had perfect knowledge of alternative outcomes and values attached to these outcomes; (4) contextual and outside influences did not affect the model; and (5) perceptions and expectations remained fixed throughout the game (Gulliver, 1979: 44).

These assumptions, as Rapoport (1965) acknowledged, were admittedly false, intentionally divorced from real-life situations. The value of game theory stemmed from its ability to elicit questions beyond its capability. It served as a benchmark or as an ideal model for classifying and analyzing models of conflict. Pure models of game theory, then, were never intended for use in prescribing bargaining behavior. Despite these aims, social scientists borrowed liberally from game theory, especially from assumptions of rationality, perfect knowledge, and static variables. In game theory, rational players had complete skill to maximize their gains and minimize their losses.

Social science application of game theory split into two camps: laboratory gaming and bargaining theory (Strauss, 1982). Laboratory gaming became a psychological model of bargaining through the use of controlled dyadic experiments. Researchers developed complex matrix games, such as Prisoners' Dilemma, to predict the impact of personality and socioculture on bargaining behavior. Over time, theorists began to lift the restrictive assumptions of pure game theory by incorporating models that included risk taking, passage of time, constituent input, and use of persuasive tactics (Strauss, 1982). These theorists aimed to identify structural and strategic variables that impacted on negotiated settlements.

In the early laboratory gaming studies, negotiators were not allowed to communicate with one another. In the absence of explicit interaction, participants used moves in the game to interpret and give nonverbal messages (Gergen, 1969). These tacit maneuvers were ambiguous and confounded a bargainer's intentions with his or her actions. Deutsch and Krauss (1960) were two game theory researchers who allowed bargainers to communicate verbally before they made their choices. At first they concluded that increased communication led to increased cooperation (Smith, 1969; Greenwood, 1974; Steinfatt et al., 1974). But additional studies revealed distinct differences in competitive and cooperative interactions (Beisecker, 1970). In highly competitive bargaining, communication was distorted and manipulative, heightening the possibility of error and misinformation rather than promoting a settlement. Hence the opportunity to communicate did not automatically lead to increased cooperation. Other game theory studies incorporated assumptions of perfect knowledge to test effects of information exchange on negotiated settlements (Cummings and Harnett, 1969; Harnett and Cummings, 1971; Lamm and Rosch, 1972). Both lines of research operated from the assumption that players were competent individuals who, independent of systemic or external forces, aimed to maximize their gains.

As a model for studying the role of communication in bargaining, game theory was fraught with a number of shortcomings. First, it concentrated on fixed-sum dilemmas, characterized by clear-cut winners and losers. In real-choice situations communication often transformed win-lose situations into shared gains (Walton and McKersie, 1965). Second, communication frequently altered the goals, preferences, and expectations of bargainers. Game theory as a static model failed to account for these transformations, especially when the negotiation process clarified goals retrospectively. As Hawes and Smith (1973: 424) contended, "Our communicative behavior defines the nature of the conflict as we view it retrospectively. We do not know what the dimensions and implications of a conflict process are until we look back on it." In real-choice situations moves and strategies cannot be predetermined before the conflict begins. Third, game theory oversimplified the choices open to each party. With an emphasis on closure and logical structure, the variables included in the model were held constant and limited in number. In real-choice situations, alternatives for negotiated settlements often emerged from constructing new proposals or from packaging issues in unique ways. Such alternatives, often created jointly by both sides, were not envisioned by either side before the bargaining began. By operating from preconceived outcomes, game theorists limited and held constant the choices available to negotiators. These shortcomings indicated why the findings of laboratory gaming did not transfer readily to field settings (Kochan, 1980).

BARGAINING THEORY

Unlike laboratory gaming, bargaining theory centered on the conditions of bilateral monopoly that applied to real-life problems such as buyer-seller interactions and labor wage negotiations. Bargaining theorists adopted the assumption of rationality, but they focused on each party's moves, that is, on the offers and counteroffers that led to concessions and eventual compromises. When analyzed as a sequence of events, bargaining proposals depicted a negotiator's position and his or her ability to exert influence (Schelling, 1960). Although bargaining theorists incorporated dynamic features into their model, their analyses remained abstract and hypothetical.

In communication research, bargaining theory guided studies on the use of target and resistance points (Smith, 1971), initial offers (Chertkoff and Conley, 1967), reciprocal concessions (Komorita and Esser, 1975), and threats and promises (Bonoma and Tedeschi, 1974; Tedeschi, 1970). Experiments on initial offers and reciprocal concessions treated communication as a series of strategic moves rather than as a sequence of messages and meanings. This conceptualization heightened the artificiality of this work and obscured the meaning of any one move (Gergen, 1969). Moreover, researchers dichotomized the relationship between cooperation and competition by coding each move as either one or the other orientation. In actuality, any one move might contribute to both cooperation and competition, depending on its function in the structure of the game.

Even though bargaining theorists addressed real-life problems, their research designs did not parallel negotiation experiences (Gulliver, 1979). Their concepts were difficult to evaluate and they controlled for many naturally occurring variables. As Strauss (1977: 331) observed, "Bargaining theory made little allowance for such complexities as mixed-motive situations, past history, the socioeconomic environment, intraorganizational bargaining, or the institutional needs of the parties."

INSTITUTIONAL ECONOMICS AND HISTORICAL ANALYSIS

Institutional models of bargaining represented a dramatic departure from the traditional game theory paradigm. Reacting against the deductive methodology of classical economics, institutional theorists adopted a social reformist perspective by focusing on the structural barriers that separated labor from management. Institutionalists argued that labor-management relations consisted of groups engaged in collective action rather than individuals who served the instrumental needs of production. Three assumptions governed research on institutional economics (Kochan, 1980). First, labor should not be subjected to the same economic laws that governed production. Their welfare extended beyond their instrumental role. Second, the needs of workers for job security and the needs of management for profit and efficiency created an inherent conflict of interest between the two groups. This conflict was based on differences in structural, job-related goals rather than on economic class as argued by Marx. Third, both workers and employers had the right to assert their interests without destroying the capitalist economic system or the trade unions. Both sides could express their needs and compromise on their differences through collective bargaining, an activity that aimed to balance the goals of labor, management, and the public (Kochan, 1980).

Institutional economists distrusted the quantitative techniques that characterized game theory research. Instead, they "adopted the German tradition of historical, legal, and empirical analysis" (Kochan, 1980: 132). The historical approach concentrated on single cases by linking "thick descriptions" of particular bargaining events to negotiated outcomes. This orientation increased the relevance of research to actual negotiations, but it was often shortsighted and practical rather than theoretical. Hence institutional studies became entangled in unique cases and failed to contribute to theory development (Kochan, 1980; Bercovitch, 1983).

While focusing on the workers' needs as the foundation for unionization, institutional economists also overlooked the political, organizational, and power-related variables that shaped bargaining behavior (Kochan, 1980). Even though these theorists broadened the myopic lens of game theory, this perspective fell short of providing a model conducive to the study of negotiation and organizational communication. In fact, Gulliver (1979) indicted all three perspectives for excluding organizational rules, norms, and beliefs; distribution of power; and external-constituent influences on bargaining. Game and bargaining theories ignored the historical precedent of bargaining. By placing negotiations in a social vacuum, they treated power as being equally distributed between players. All three dominant theories failed to account for the multiple issues and interconnected organizational events that constituted bargaining agendas.

EMERGING PERSPECTIVES ON COMMUNICATION AND NEGOTIATION

Social scientists are moving away from economic models of bargaining. Since no alternative offers widespread appeal, researchers have typically complicated game theory models by altering rationality to include uncertainty, difficulties in processing information, and satisficing. But what is needed, according to Gulliver (1979), is a noneconomic model that analyzes processes of negotiation through social and organizational contexts.

Two themes—process and organizational context—are beginning to emerge. They center on the evolution of bargaining and on societal-organizational contexts that shape negotiations. The two are not mutually exclusive, but each emphasizes different components of communication in negotiations. These two are treated separately because the research tends to focus on one or the other, but typically not on both themes. An exception, however, is Strauss's model of negotiated order, which will be discussed later in this chapter. Both themes can and should be combined in research on communication and bargaining. The last section of this chapter outlines a model that combines process and context themes into a coherent perspective. This skeleton outline represents work toward a new theory. Space limitations, however, preclude a full development of this model. Before this combined perspective is presented, communication studies that fall into the two themes will be reviewed.

PROCESS THEMES

Process is a generic category that encompasses cyclical and phasic approaches to communication and bargaining. Cyclical patterns center on the sequences and cycles of strategies, information exchange, and arguments. Phase analysis focuses on the development of interaction from the beginning to the conclusion of a negotiation. Both approaches examine the moves and countermoves that bargainers employ and the way each party influences expectations, preferences, and behavioral assessments during the negotiation (Patchen, 1970).

Process themes differ from game theory models in that they emanate from the empirical study of real-life negotiations. Rather than purporting rationality as a key assumption, process research posits that bargainers have dissimilar abilities and limited skills in perceiving and reacting to their opponents' messages. For example, Donohue (1978) tests for negotiator competency and prenegotiation expectations. He observes that successful negotiators maintain their enthusiasm throughout the bargaining, rely on information gained in previous sessions, and use coercive strategies to restrict the freedom of their opponents. Thus successful bargainers exhibit skills that are different from those of their less successful counterparts. Given that knowledge is tested and altered as a result of the communication between negotiators, process approaches uncover circumstances in which maximization of gains may be an impossibility.

Two specific models undergird process themes. Cognitive models center on the way perceptions about future actions lead negotiators to readjust their expectations and interpretations of their opponents' behaviors (Gulliver, 1979). Learning models rely on past actions of the bargainers as a basis for the rules, norms, and behavioral patterns of future actions (Cross, 1977). Previous experience rather than anticipated action becomes the standard for choosing behaviors. Much of the current research on communication and bargaining employs a process analysis. These studies, for the most part, derive from learning models in that they rely on past actions to predict subsequent behaviors. Conversational and discourse approaches, however, adopt a more interpretive view by blending message analyses with cognitions of other actors. Three lines of research focus on cyclical patterns—conflict spirals, information exchange, and issue development. This review draws from two other extensive literature surveys on communication and bargaining (Putnam, 1984; Putnam and Jones, 1982b).

Cyclical Patterns

Conflict spirals. Studies of conflict spirals examine sequences of messages that escalate or deescalate conflicts. In his seminal work on conflict resolution, Deutsch (1973) contends that destructive conflict escalates through growth in the number of issues, motives, and costs that participants are willing to bear. This growth in issues and costs stems from an escalation in attack-defend patterns known as "conflict spirals."

Research on conflict spirals suggests that once interaction escalates to a point of redefining goals and matching attack-defend tactics, conflict cycles into an impasse or stalemate. Donohue's (1981a, 1981b) research tests for the rules that govern attack, defend, and regression tactics for successful and unsuccessful bargainers. His study demonstrates that successful negotiators maintain a strong position by demonstrating diversity in argument, giving more offers, denying faults more frequently, offering more rejections, and changing the topic more frequently than do unsuccessful negotiators. Analyses of the sequences of messages reveal an action-reaction pattern with extreme attacks (for example, threats, demands) balanced by regressive statements (for example, other-supporting comments, concessions). Thus the softer regression tactics offset the harder attack statements. Impasse dyads, however, use fewer action-reaction patterns than do agreement dyads.

In a similar study, Putnam and Jones (1982a) employ the Bargaining Process Analysis II to analyze the conflict spirals of labor and management negotiators. Their research shows that labor specializes in offensive statements (for example, attacking arguments, rejections, threats) and management monopolizes defensive remarks (for example, self-supporting arguments, retractions, commitments). For the most part, management and labor balance their bargaining styles with the use of specialized strategies that serve as buffers to prevent the escalation of conflict. If management moves into labor's domain and initiates an attacking remark, labor typically compensates with a concession or an other-supporting statement. Consistent with Donohue's (1981a, 1981b) work, impasse dyads demonstrate a tight, highly predictable interaction structure, characterized by reciprocating the other side's tactics. Labor follows management's defensive comments with a series of defensive moves; management follows labor's offensive tactics with offensive remarks. Thus a pattern of matching tactics depicts the growth of conflict spirals in these labor-management negotiations.

These studies, however, rely on student negotiators, dyadic designs, and simulations with short time limits. Donohue et al.'s (1984) work compares interaction sequences of a 2-day simulated teacher bargaining with 24 sessions of a private sector contract negotiation. Their comparison reveals that in the actual negotiation labor uses more attack sequences, presents more proposals, and offers more assertive responses than does management. Also, labor negotiators in the actual bargaining use more attack-oriented statements than do teachers in the simulated bargaining, but the pattern of specialization parallels findings of the Putnam and Jones (1982a) research. In effect, specialization and buffering through the use of offensive-defensive and action-reaction sequences tend to counterbalance the development of escalating conflict cycles. Matching the statements of one's opponent, however, leads to a tighter interaction structure that, in turn, escalates the conflict.

Information exchange. Another line of research, information exchange also espouses the assumptions that underlie learning models and process approaches. Information exchange in bargaining reveals preferences, intentions, and social perceptions of both teams. Negotiators use information to ascertain salient issues, to locate areas for trade-offs, and to assign meaning to their opponents' actions. Rubin and Brown (1975: 260) treat information exchange as the "fundamental strategic issue in bargaining."

Studies that adopt game theoretic models typically examine the properties of information, namely, amount and accuracy of information flow (Putnam and Jones, 1982b). A continual increase in information tends to proliferate the number of issues in a dispute, thus adding to the complexity of bargaining. Saine (1974) notes that increasing data beyond an optimal point leads to information overload, especially for bargainers with low cognitive complexity skills. Amount of information may overlap with distortion of messages and intentions. Initial proposals in bargaining typically exaggerate actual needs. In like manner, negotiators tend to accentuate the advantages and minimize the disadvantages of their positions. Hence both parties expect some degree of distortion and ambiguity in information flow, especially in the early stages when bargainers talk past each other, change topics arbitrarily, and test the water on issues (Putnam, 1984). In fact, neither information deception nor failure to disclose intentions have a marked effect on negotiated outcomes, unless these disclosures are scattered incrementally throughout the bargaining session (Johnson et al., 1976; Pruitt and Lewis, 1975; Putnam and Jones, 1982a).

Process studies, in contrast, focus on sequences of information exchange. Bargainers reshape their expectations and preferences by interpreting patterns of information received (Gulliver, 1979). Donohue and Diez (1983) use conversational analysis to investigate the use of questions and imperatives as two different syntactical forms of requesting information. Given that negotiators learn about their opponents' positions while revealing very little about their own stances, bargainers must control the way they access information. Donohue and Diez (1983) observe that questions are more successful than imperatives in gaining desired information because questions obligate the opponent to give a response. But as the opponents' responses are often short and abrupt, the questioner feels compelled to continue his or her quest for information. This information-expansion sequence controls the bargaining interaction through the use of inquiries and abrupt responses.

In addition to questions and answers, information exchange is managed through the use of arguments. Analyses of bargaining arguments reveal how negotiators disagree, how they delimit the content of their disagreement, and which rules govern the structure of arguments (Donohue et al., 1983). By tracking the types of claims and reasoning processes across a forty-hour teacher negotiation, Putnam and Geist (1985) analyze the reasoning processes of issues that are either dropped, retained, or modified in the final agreement. Their research suggests that issues become modified, not by adding more information, but by shifting types of claims and adding qualifiers. Teachers and administrators rely on evaluative and definitive claims with reasoning from analogy to substantiate their positions. For issues that become dropped from discussion, evaluative claims alter and shift the nature of the original proposal. Putnam and Geist also observe that the content of these issues grows out of superior-subordinate communication, specifically problems with performance appraisal. Thus, the process of argument in negotiations interacts with the content of information exchange to effect organizational decision making.

Issue development. Information exchange is directly related to the development of negotiation issues. Bargaining rarely consists of a single item. In fact, most contract negotiations center on multiple money-related and "language" items. Money-related issues entail salaries, insurance, and other fringe benefits while language items focus on policies and regulations that govern working conditions. For example, language issues might include stipulations for reduction in force, working hours, and performance evaluation. These items emanate from recurring problems between management and labor as well as from concerns of the international labor union. Hence, contract proposals contain multiple issues that arise from internal organizational events and environmental needs. Embedded in multiple issues are subissues that represent sections or segments of a major proposal. For example, the issue of reduction in force (RIF) might include such subissues as the conditions that necessitate RIFs, who gets laid off, and how and when layoffs are implemented. Issues are not only multiple and subdivided, they are complex in the way each party evaluates and prioritizes them. Hence negotiators are likely to disagree on the issues that merit discussion and the values linked to these issues (Gulliver, 1979). One critical function of the bargaining process is the sifting, reducing, and joint evaluation of multiple issues.

Issue development begins with proposals and counterproposals, couched in the language of demands, claims, and justifications that often represent extreme positions. Initially, each party concentrates on his or her own case rather than on the opponent's requests (Gulliver, 1979: 136). As negotiators begin to drop issues, simplify subissues, and build packages of items, interaction shifts from separateness and antagonism to coordination and cooperation. This transformation occurs when one party makes a "real" counteroffer rather than sticking with his or her "ideal" preference.

Strategies for narrowing, simplifying, and combining issues vary. Gulliver lists five of them: (1) taking issues one at a time in the order in which they appear, (2) dealing with the most important items first, (3) reducing issues to a common objective or attribute, (4) discovering the less difficult items and disposing of them first, and (5) trading issues. The packaging of issues, then, becomes a procedural as well as a substantive matter. These five evolve from the way interactions between bargainers and their team members lead to altering perceptions and interpretations of issues; thus issue development adheres to a cognitive model of process. Negotiators may withdraw issues, accent or sharpen others, transform them through redefinition, or add facts and interpretations that refocus them.

In an ethnographic study of bargainer role and issue development, Putnam and Bullis (1984) chart the communication patterns between bargainers and among team members to determine how issues evolve, how ordering takes place, and how items transform into a satisfactory settlement. Their study reports on a 12-hour negotiation of a 25-page contract. Both sides employ professional negotiators who engage in "private side-bar" meetings to facilitate translation of their needs. Data collection consists of written proposals and counterproposals; transcripts of the bargaining, caucus, and side-bar sessions; and 21 interviews with teachers and administrators. They examine the way participants add, drop, transform, and sharpen five central issues across each sequential session. Their results reveal that transforming negative to positive evaluations, dropping minor objections, and simplifying complex issues contributes to a settlement on language items. Settlements on salary, insurance, and other monetary items evolve from packaging these issues in creative ways. For instance, bargainers decide to cut 1 percent off the total monetary package by reducing salaries for extracurricular activities (ECA). Since the board operates from the perspective of total dollar costs and the teachers view "dollars in their pockets" as the essential criterion, both sides regard the 1 percent *decrease* as advantageous. The teachers feel it provides additional monies for other fringe benefits, namely, equalizing salaries for coaching men's and women's sports. The board feels it saves them from surpassing their salary guidelines. Both sides gain and both are satisfied with the way they package monetary items. Their satisfaction, however, stems from different reasons. By tracking the development of issues across sessions, researchers can determine how and why this creative packaging occurs and what it means to the participants.

Phase Analysis

Phase analysis, unlike research on cyclical patterns, focuses on contiguous sets of events and larger aggregates of communicative behavior. Researchers concentrate on how negotiations evolve over time rather than on how cycles and issues develop. This line of work originates with Douglas's (1957, 1962) classic field observations and audiotaped recordings of four private-sector negotiations. She identifies three phases: establishing the bargaining range, reconnoitering the range, and precipitating the decision-reaching crisis. Phase 1 consists of a series of lengthy public orations characterized by dogmatic pronouncements and vehement demands. In Phase 2 negotiators jockey for position by pressing the other side to capitulate while simultaneously showing signs of tacit agreement. Phase 3 entails reduction of alternatives in "yes-no" or "forced-choice" ways to reach a settlement. In effect, hard-hitting aggressive tactics typify the opening stage of negotiations whereas the closing phase resembles joint decision-making.

Gulliver (1979) breaks these three phases into eight stages: (1) search for an agenda, (2) formulation of an agenda, (3) statements of demands and offers, (4) narrowing of differences, (5) preliminaries to final bargaining, (6) final bargaining, (7) ritual confirmation of the final outcome, and (8) implementation. A crucial break between the aggressive hard-hitting tactics and joint decision-making is the narrowing of differences.

Douglas (1962) also notes that identification of party affiliation becomes more difficult in the second phase. Bargainers drop references to their constituents and work interpersonally in the middle rather than in the early stage of negotiation. Stephenson et al. (1977) replicate Douglas's study, but they employ the Conference Process Analysis as a special category system. Their findings parallel Douglas's for Phases 1 and 2 but show a gradual decrease in party affiliation for Phase 3. Bednar and Curington (1983), in their extension of Bednar and Glauser's (1981) work, note that Phase 1 differs from Phases 2 and 3 in the relational message exchanged between negotiators. Using a Markovian chain analysis and a relational coding scheme (Ellis, 1979), they conclude that Phase 1 reveals a higher degree of competitive symmetry between bargainers than do Phases 2 and 3. This competitive one-upmanship may explain why party affiliation is more prominent in the earlier than in the latter stages of bargaining. Phase analysis of negotiations seems limited in its unidimensional orientation. Not all bargaining sessions pass through a particular sequence of phases. Procedural restrictions and the evolution of issues over time may mitigate against a set pattern of phase development.

Process themes define the nature of bargaining, the strategies and tactics employed, and the negotiated outcomes through direct analysis of communication. The developmental nature of this research represents a radical departure from the static models of game theory. Moreover, process themes are grounded in empirical data and inductive analyses rather than in the abstract, deductive assumptions of game theory. Even though this work emanates from real-choice situations, it tends to limit bargaining to the formal, interpersonal dimensions. Process themes are well-suited for mixed-motive situations, but they must incorporate past history of bargaining, negotiator role, organizational context, and environmental effects into their analyses of the cycles and phases of negotiation.

ORGANIZATIONAL CONTEXT THEMES

Kochan (1980) presents a comprehensive model on the role of collective bargaining in the organizational context. His model consists of five major elements: (1) the environment—the impact of economic, technological, social and political forces on bargaining units; (2) bargaining structure—the scope of bargaining units, their history, and their inter- and intra-relationships; (3) union and management organizations—their internal power structures, leadership patterns, policies, and decision-making processes; (4) the negotiation process—the dynamics of bargainer behavior, interactions between negotiators and team members, and strategy and tactics of bargaining; and (5) negotiated outcomes—settlements, strikes, impasses, and third-party intervention. He posits that environmental factors impact on the internal structure of union and management organizations and on bargaining relationships. These factors, in turn, impinge on negotiation processes and outcomes. The model is cyclical in that outcomes influence the economy and the social environment.

In a similar vein but with less emphasis on organizational theory, Strauss (1978) presents a model of negotiated order. Negotiation, in Strauss's view, however, is not simply an event. Rather, it is the process of accomplishing organizational activities, a means of "getting things done." Negotiated outcomes are always in a state of flux because the product of bargaining modifies the existing order. Thus organizations continually produce goals, rules, and roles through explicit and implicit negotiations. Most negotiations, however, are implicit in that organizational members create new rules and goals through the management of ambiguity, the avoidance of open conflict, and the accomplishment of everyday tasks (McPhee, 1983). Individuals, in turn, legitimate the negotiated order by relying on the changed rules and goals to conduct organizational routines. Thus order is dynamic rather than static. In effect, order is negotiated as organizational members fluctuate their attention between existing structural concerns such as policies, procedures, and norms, and enacting everyday tasks such as conducting job duties, solving problems, and interacting with colleagues (McPhee, 1983).

Strauss contends that the larger context in which order is negotiated impacts on the meaning of the process. Therefore, to understand negotiations, researchers must examine their structural, bargaining, and awareness contexts. The structural context refers to the salient properties of the marketplace, that is, the economy and state laws, whereas the bargaining context focuses on relationships between the negotiators, history of the bargaining, visibility of transactions, and strategies and tactics. Awareness context centers on interpretations of the process, that is, on each person's theories of negotiation and on what he or she knows about the opponent's definitions and preferences. These contexts, however, are changing; hence both context and negotiated order are in states of flux.

Both models emphasize environmental and social contexts. Kochan's (1980) model adopts a stronger organizational focus than the negotiated order approach, but Strauss's theory includes the actors' interpretations as essential elements of the overall context. Both models treat communication as the strategies, tactics, and interactions between bargainers. But communication performs other functions crucial to the interface of bargaining with its environment, overall structures, and policies of labor-management organizations.

Socioeconomic Environment

Only a few studies examine the role of political and social environments on collective bargaining. In Kochan's (1975) investigation of negotiations between a city government and the International Association of Fire Fighters, environmental change and complexity have only a modicum of impact on the relationships between the union and the city council. However, the political and legal context of the negotiation directly influences the power bases of both sides. For the union the most important source of power is a state law that requires city governments to bargain with public employees (Kochan, 1975: 449). The extent to which union members can inflict political costs on elected officials affects the bargaining power of both groups. Although Kochan's (1975) study does not incorporate communication into its design, his findings have implications for communication researchers; namely, employee networks that pull the electoral strings of city officials impinge on the bargaining process. Tracking these communication contacts could show how politics contributes to bargaining settlements. Also, researchers could examine the way negotiation teams use interpretations of state laws to pressure their opponents, thus socially constructing the legal context through their bargaining strategies. Another investigation could focus on the processing of information about the political and economic climates of negotiation.

Bargaining Structure and Environmental Context

Boundary-spanning models. Adams (1976) presents another alternative to the study of collective bargaining and organizational environments. Given that bargaining manages interactions between the organization and its environment, it serves as a form of boundary-role spanning. Negotiators function as boundary-role persons (BRPs) by linking external agents, such as union headquarters, to internal hierarchically organized groups. Bargainers may feel trapped between internal and external forces and experience dual allegiances to both groups. Their latitude for reaching an "acceptable" settlement hinges on the visibility of the bargainers, their time pressures, and their prospects for future negotiations. Specifically, bargainers use conciliatory behaviors when their communicative climate is characterized by low visibility, few time pressures, and high expectations for future interactions.

Walton and McKersie (1965) also examine boundary-role communication between negotiators and their constituents. Their model, however, focuses on intraorganizational bargaining, the process of reaching consensus within each negotiation group. Bargainers influence their team's position through monitoring information disclosures, guiding expectations, and controlling emotional reactions. As they sift through information at the table and in caucus sessions, they draw inferences, ascertain preferences, and make the issues meaningful to their constituents. Negotiators, then, are not simply representatives of their respective groups; they shape outcomes by oscillating between their team's needs and their opponent's demands.

Putnam and Bullis (1984) investigate the impact of bargainer role on issue development in a twelve-hour teacher negotiation. Tracking the evolution of issues across side-bar and caucus sessions, they find that the teacher's bargainer functions primarily as a gatekeeper who manipulates information whereas the board's negotiator emerges as a facilitator who reports data and guides caucus deliberations accurately. In organizations a person can accrue power through his or her ability to filter, summarize, and analyze information as it is passed (Pfeffer, 1978). Because of his or her access to financial information, knowledge of the settlements in other districts, and ability to control information flow, the teachers' bargainer is recognized as the most powerful figure in the negotiation.

Coalitions and intergroup relations. Political-coalition approaches to organizational theory treat bargaining as a form of intergroup relations. Organizational groups vie with one another for resources, personnel, and policies (Cyert and March, 1963). In this perspective the organizational goal, as defined by management, "becomes a concept with little meaning" (Pfeffer, 1978: 5). Instead, coalition members disagree as to which goals and objectives should govern organizational policy. Withdrawal from the organization in the form of strikes and stalemates can occur if management fails to meet the needs of a particular interest group. Treating bargaining as a form of intergroup communication between coalitions differs from the boundary-spanning model in that the union becomes an internal coalition rather than an external organization. The coalition model places the local union in a more dominant role than the international affiliate. However, both the local and the international unions impact on the bargaining process.

Labor and management are not the only coalitions that emerge during negotiations. Each party may appear unified, but in prenegotiation meetings and caucus sessions, factions often develop. For example, Putnam and Bullis (1984) note that strong differences of opinion emerge between union officers and teachers and between administrators and board members. Thus, factions develop within each team, defining the boundaries of intraorganizational bargaining. Moreover, communication differentiates these factions into hierarchical levels, with the professional bargainers privy to more information and decision making than are team members and constituents. This access and control of information legitimates a climate of mystery and aura, one that makes settlements "behind closed doors" illusive and distant from constituents. But mystery ultimately facilitates the process because constituents are more concerned with the magnitude of their settlement than with the way it was reached (Adams, 1976). Communiques to constituents about the process are typically vague, unreliable, or irrelevant to the decision-making activities of the bargainers.

History of the bargaining process. One of the most neglected areas in research is the study of bargaining as a recurring event. Labor-management negotiations typically reconvene annually or at least every two years to bargain for wages and fringe benefits. In this sense bargaining is a ritualistic endeavor in that it observes certain ceremonial rites, initiations of newcomers, and celebrations of past successes. The composition of one or both teams may vary from year to year. Professional negotiators may come and go, but the ritual and the background that establishes bargaining history prevails.

This history is embodied in myths and stories about the early days of bargaining. These stories often exalt heroes, heroines, and villains of past bargaining relationships, but they signify more than tributes to the past. Putnam and Bullis (1983) note that stories of previous negotiations are enacted in current deliberations to pressure team members to adopt a particular proposal. For example, board members who want to give the teachers an additional 1 percent raise recall the years when unhappy teachers flocked to shopping centers, handed out leaflets, and aroused the community with their complaints. Putnam and Geist (1985) examine stories that are used to substantiate particular arguments—ones that recap efforts to build trusting relationships between the two teams.

History also functions to set the stage for future negotiations. Issues added to the settlement are open for scrutiny and grievances in future years. If the union fails to get an item accepted in the current contract, it can incorporate that proposal in next year's package. If the teams experience impasse or a strike, these outcomes color future negotiations as well as daily work routines of management and labor. Negotiators who meet annually to bargain contracts typically develop abbreviated codes that govern information management and relationship expectations. Few studies actually track negotiation behavior across subsequent years or over historical time periods. One exception is a case study of the 1969 and 1980 collective bargaining between the Teacher Assistants' Association and the University of Wisconsin—Madison. Keough (1983, 1984) analyzes interview data, arbitration transcripts, and historical documents to identify the structures and arguments used in the 1979 arbitration hearings. She reports differences between the university and the teacher assistants' reliance on past negotiations, prerogative arguments, and coalition appeals.

Unions and Organizational Structure

Labor unions as organizations. Unions exist as distinct organizations with their own leadership patterns, decision-making processes, and power struggles. Much of the current research in industrial relations centers on the growth and development of unions, union mergers, the structure of union bureaucracies, and the effects of strike activities on union members (Kochan, 1980). The bulk of these studies adopt econometric techniques or historical methods that contribute very little to our understanding of communication. Early research in organizational communication provides an exception to this indictment.

Since unions espouse a philosophy of democracy and voluntary participation, the effectiveness of their internal communication is critical to maintaining membership support. In a survey of members and shop stewards of a local United Steelworkers Union, Dee (1959, 1961, 1962a) reports that monthly meetings and contacts with the union stewards are the most effective channels of communication. Even though only 11 percent of the membership attends regular meetings, these sessions rank as an important source of information about local and international activities. Union stewards, by default, provide the major source of upward and downward communication between the membership and the officers, particularly as interpreters of the contract, as representatives in grievance disputes, and as sources of information about union events. Their effectiveness, though, is limited by their lack of training and the lack of clarity in defining their communication role (Dee, 1961).

Knapp and McCroskey (1968) and Dee (1962b) have surveyed AFL-CIO State Central Body Presidents, educational directors of unions, and directors of university-conducted institutes to ascertain communication problems, training programs in operation, and training needs. Communication skills emerge as vital for union officers and shop stewards, but less critical for union members. Union officers receive some training in public speaking, but more training is needed in the areas of discussion leadership, participation, and interpersonal communication. Knapp and McCroskey make a special plea for research on communication patterns and breakdowns between the international office and the local union, between the officers and the rank-and-file members, and between workers and other community groups.

Studies on perceptual differences between union members at different hierarchical levels begin to answer this plea. Tompkins (1962) employs the term "semantic information distance" to depict the perceptual gaps between management and employees and between union officers and their members. His case study reports significant semantic distance between the rank-and-file members and their international headquarters. In like manner, Weaver (1958) compares semantic judgments of such concepts as closed shop, arbitration, and union between union officers and their members. Perceptual differences suggest that semantic barriers exist between these two groups. Using semantic interpretations of nineteen concepts, Schwartz et al. (1970) sample two levels within both labor and management groups. Surprisingly, upper-level union officers resemble middle- and lower-level managers in their reactions to such terms as "seniority," "solidarity," "strike," and "management." In the general population, perceptual differences for the terms "union" and "management" begin as early as age twelve (Haire and Morrison, 1957). These disparities may influence differential attitudes in grievance handling (Lawshe and Guion, 1951) and empathic responses to supervisory problems (Miller and Remmers, 1950). As Tompkins (1962) notes, *perceived* semantic distance may be more salient than the *actual* distance. Through feedback and sensitivity, organizational members can reduce these semantic gaps.

Union impact on organizational structure. The presence of labor unions in a company has a marked effect on organizational structure. Specifically, unions lead to an increase in formalization of policies, redistribution of power, and coordination of decision making (Kochan, 1980). Since the union serves as a check and balance for managerial decisions, it contributes to environmental uncertainty and resistance to change. For example, the union might oppose management's decision to introduce new technology because this automation might displace workers. Unions also have influence on organizational structure through the development of new departments and realignment of specialized jobs. In particular, the growth of personnel and human resource departments is the achievement of union campaigns (Kochan, 1980). More recently, unions have initiated quality of work life (QOW) programs in many companies (Strauss, 1977, 1979). Communication researchers are beginning to examine quality circle groups, but these studies have not incorporated the union's role in these experiments (Savage, 1984; Savage and Romano, 1983; Stohl, 1984).

Administration of the negotiated contract is another avenue for communication research. Researchers need to study the formal and informal handling of work-related problems. In particular, how does communication in the grievance procedure relate to the handling of problems through other mechanisms? How do communication and problem solving between superior and subordinate emerge in a union-governed organization? To what extent do labor and management rely on "literal enforcement" of the contract in their daily activities? These queries demonstrate how communication research could yield insights about the union's role in organizations.

Negotiated Outcomes

Current negotiation literature is moving away from treating cooperation and competition and win-lose as the primary outcome variables. Cooperation and competition form a continuum that makes classification of negotiated outcomes rather arbitrary (Johnson, 1974). Strikes, impasses, and stalemates can emerge from negotiations that exhibit both cooperative and competitive behaviors. Similarly, winning and losing in real-choice situations confound perceived and actual measures. A labor team might receive fewer monetary or power-related gains than they wanted, but still feel they won important concessions from management. Hence satisfaction with the bargaining process may be inversely related to actual gains. Winning and losing are judgment calls, particularly in negotiations that involve multiple issues.

Recent studies focus on settlements, impasses, or stalemates as outcome measures. These occurrences forecast the probability of more severe outcomes, such as strikes or walkouts. Being able to predict a settlement or impasse seems less critical than understanding the factors that contribute to them. Case studies on the role of communication in satisfactory and unsatisfactory negotiations represent a starting point. Combined with findings of laboratory studies, researchers could assimilate composite pictures of negotiations that led to stalemates or to satisfactory settlements.

Research on third-party intervention, especially mediation, has grown in the past decade. The role of communication in mediation receives initial treatment in Landsberger's (1955) application of Bales Interaction Process Analysis to mediation and communication. His study reveals that the use of positive statements between bargainers increases as a result of a mediator intervention. Keltner (1965) distinguishes the communication patterns of mediators from those of arbitrators. Mediators aim to control the bargaining process while arbitrators act as judges who render decisions on proposals and final offers in a dispute. Mediators function as gatekeepers who simultaneously clarify and bias information flow between opposing parties (Wall, 1981). As facilitators, they can ask negotiators to paraphrase messages, to narrow topics of discussion, to avoid repetition, and to take the perspective of the other party (Douglas, 1962; Johnson, 1967; Pruitt, 1971). To structure the communication, mediators add interpretations and make estimates of the opponents' positions. Mediators must also establish an effective relationship between the disputants and him- or herself. Donohue et al. (1984) propose a model of mediation and communication competency. Their model identifies the mediator's process and content objectives for four different phases of interaction. The area of mediation and third-party intervention is wide open for communication research. Future studies could examine the impact of bargaining history, past mediation sessions, and sociopolitical activities on the mediation process.

Organizational context themes hold considerable promise for treating collective bargaining as both a process and an event. As a process, negotiation is an ongoing activity, fully integrated into the organizational environment in the form of relationships with affiliate unions and contractual arrangements that are legally binding. It consists of cycles and phases of interaction among bargainers, team members, and constituents. As an event, negotiations are recurring rituals with historical precedent, ceremonial activities, and evolving intergroup relations. Of central concern for collective bargaining research is the integration of these two. Communication researchers need to merge the negotiation process with political and social networks of bargaining teams, with coalitions and intergroup relationships in the larger organization, and with boundary-spanning roles of negotiators. Conclusions drawn from integrating process and context must be tempered by the union's role in the corporate structure and its uniqueness as a distinct organization.

TOWARD A NEW PERSPECTIVE ON BARGAINING AND COMMUNICATION

The models, perspectives, and different approaches presented in this chapter provide frameworks and building blocks for a noneconomic theory of communication and negotiation. These approaches offer taxonomies and structures for assembling concepts, but they do not account for the interrelationships among elements included in these models. Process and context researchers need to isolate the most critical constructs and integrate them in a way that accents communication and accounts for relationships among ingredients in the model. It would be difficult to integrate all the perspectives reviewed in this chapter. Moreover, some of them are inconsistent, if not mutually exclusive of one another. Thus, for the sake of brevity, this skeleton outline of a perspective concentrates on the key concepts and their interrelationships.

This interpretive approach to negotiation combines Gulliver's process theme with Kochan's (1980) context model. Communication represents the locus or starting point for theory development. Organizational reality in this theory is socially constituted; hence contextual features of bargaining are constructed through the messages and sense-making activities of organizational members. Negotiation is also a developmental process, governed by the way bargainers, team members, and constituents enact their environments over time. Organizations consist of multiple factions that coexist, but each has different opinions and priorities for organizational goals. Conflict exists in a temporary state of balance or in a standoff among factions—one that permits the organization to function through quasi-resolution of recurring disagreements, skirmishes, and upheavals. Coalitions separate on ideological grounds; they differ in their views of the values, goals, and overall foundation of organizational life. Factions may develop between hierarchical levels, within levels or units, and within lateral departments. Thus ideological rather than structural grounds form the basis for segmentation. For example, factions in a university might develop between undergraduate education and graduate research interests. These coalitions, however, do not have equal power. Groups who have greater access to resources, are located centrally in the information flow, and provide essential services emerge as dominant coalitions that exert both coercive and unobtrusive control over organizational decisions (Tompkins and Cheney, 1982). Bargaining must operate within this differential power base and knowledge of existing factions.

These assumptions undergird such key concepts as: contextual parameters, socially constructed meanings, cycles and stages of message development, historical evolution, and perceived and actual outcomes. Consistent with Kochan's (1980) model, contextual parameters include the social, political, economic, and technological environment, the union organization, and the structure of bargaining relationships. These factors influence negotiation primarily as social constructions that participants enact by making sense of their environment. Especially, a change in the economic and political climate might decrease monies in the public sector, but bargainers might attribute this shortage to upper managements' labor policies rather than to the political environment. Thus the contextual features that impinge on negotiation processes must be perceived, enacted, and interpreted in the bargaining cycles.

Negotiation processes, in turn, define bargainer roles, intergroup relationships, and boundary-spanning activities of participants. That is, the cycles and phases of interaction determine how bargaining roles emerge, how groups interrelate during the process, and the pressures that constituents place on negotiators. If information exchange and issue development lead to concessions and effective packaging of items, bargainers may engage in more filtering; constituents may become more unified on positions; and team members may grant bargainers more autonomy, trust, and power. In contrast, if conflict spirals develop, bargainers may function as tough representatives of their teams, constituents may become factionalized, and team members may monitor their negotiator very closely (Adams, 1976).

Historical development crystallizes as bargainers and team members relive their goals and relationships retrospectively. Participants reflect on the way negotiations have progressed and then construct social meanings for pivotal events. These shared meanings of past experiences shape the rituals and rites for current bargaining. Finally, negotiated outcomes are not simply the effects of bargaining structure and processes. They represent social constructions of the experience—forms of sense making and closure for participants (for example, "We signed an agreement.") and types of impression management for constituents and the public (for example, "We reached an impasse because management is unfair or workers are too demanding.").

This outline for an interpretive theory of bargaining is incomplete, but it constitutes a way of integrating process and contextual themes through interpretations that actors make of their experiences. Cyclical and phasic processes of communication embody the social constructions of bargaining reality when participants meta-talk about their own communication, form interpretations of their opponent's behaviors, reach consensus on the rationale for specific strategies and tactics, and invoke meanings attributed to the bargaining structure and the environmental context. The context of negotiation, then, forms the substance and parameters for negotiation processes.

Collective bargaining offers an ideal arena for the study of organizational communication concepts. Professional and trade unions, as fixtures of organizational life, impinge on the management of conflict, information processing, decision making, and power relationships. This review argues for a merger of traditional organizational communication with recent developments in negotiation and organizational theory.

Chapter 6

FORMAL STRUCTURE AND ORGANIZATIONAL COMMUNICATION

Robert D. McPhee

STUDENTS OF ORGANIZATIONS, and organizational communication, often seem to hate their work. Consider Chris Argyris (1964: 40), who considers organizational structures to be, by their very nature, unhealthy for human membership: "There is a lack of congruity between the needs of individuals aspiring for psychological success and the demands of the . . . formal organization." More recently, Rosabeth Moss Kanter (1983: 28) has argued that stagnation in American organizations is a result of segmentalism, which she links to "segmented structures: a large number of compartments walled off from one another—department from department, level above from level below, field office from headquarters, labor from management, or men from women." Of course, both these authors focus their criticism on current traditional or bureaucratic organizations, not on every possible organizational form, but the alternative would seem to be organizations that do not "act like organizations," in which the organization's *formal structure* is weakened, circumvented, subordinated to other processes, or eliminated.

The subject of this chapter is formal organizational structure and its relation to organizational communication. Since I will use the term "structure" over and over, in several different senses, it seems useful to create a special sign for formal organizational structure. I will simply capitalize it and call it "Structure."

What is Structure, exactly? Naturally, it would include things like official job titles, descriptions, and objectives for employees, along with their conditions of employment or "employment contracts"; the official differentiation of divisions, departments, and work units; the book or books of standard operating procedures; the "corporate charter" and other documents establishing the legal basis of the organization, and so on. Almost on a par with these are derivative descriptions such as the organizational chart, official work-flow diagrams, and the like. And I would include in Structure the various systems for decision support, management information, work evaluation and compensation, and financial control.

AUTHOR'S NOTE: I feel tremendous gratitude to Dale Kalika, Scott Poole, Phil Tompkins, and Art Van Lear for their suggestions for revisions of this article—wading through the first draft was no small task.

These various instances of Structure have certain defining features in common. First, they are explicitly stated and recorded, available for any authorized person (often, just anybody or any employee) to examine. Second, they are prescriptive, telling what the organization should be like, and these prescriptions have *authority*—the commonly recognized "weight of the organization" behind them. Third, they generally involve statements that apply to members of the organization, to employees' activities, roles, relationships, and rewards. A final characteristic is trickier. Formal Structure is generally thought of as analytically separate from the work processes or "technology" (Perrow, 1967) of an organization—more or less the same work could be done by the same people under various different choices about formal Structure.

I should clarify some possible misunderstandings here. First, organizations differ vastly in the extent and sort of Structures they possess. Some have annual reports or organizational charts or strategic planning systems; others do not. Second, organizations also differ as to where records of Structure are located, how accessible they are, and how widely they are understood. Third, as decades of research (discussed more fully below) have shown, the specific consequences of Structure vary. Structure is authoritative but not necessarily powerful or representationally accurate. Indeed, organizations never run like clockwork—whatever Structure is, it is not simply and mechanically "in control" of operations in organizations. Rules are broken or routinely ignored, employees take orders from people without authority and ignore orders from people with authority, work proceeds as employees do not even attempt to meet official goals. The paragraph above merely attempts to point out those elements in any organization that I will call Structure.

Nevertheless, I would say that Structure is a defining characteristic of an organization—*it* is what brings about or makes possible that quality of atmosphere, that sustained, routine purposiveness that distinquishes work in an organization from activities in a group, a mob, a society, and so forth. Of course, Structure alone is not enough—an organization is a collection of people doing work within a formal Structure. But Structure is probably what stands out about organizations, what makes them economically powerful and socially fearsome. And while Structured organizations are as old as war and religion, the prevalence and variety of Structures that have come into being over the past two centuries seem to make modern times unique, to make our social order an "organizational society" (Presthus, 1960). For all these reasons, I would argue that Structure is also a defining condition of specifically "organizational" communication: "We will define organizational communication as communication which is shaped by, and shapes, task processes and formal structure in the organization" (McPhee, 1983).

If Structure is not simply "in control" of things, what *is* its place in organizations? The rest of this chapter attempts to answer that question, first by reviewing a variety of themes in the literature about Structure, then by developing a distinctive view of Structure and organizational communication.

THEMES IN DISCUSSIONS
OF ORGANIZATIONAL STRUCTURE

Many times, when researchers look at organizational Structure, they fail to attend to the variety of its meanings and implications. It is easy to depict "span of control" in a textbook or measure it in an empirical study, but rarely is the multifaceted significance of such Structural dimensions fully developed in comments about the picture or explanations of the study's findings. To keep us alert to the breadth of implications of Structure, a survey of some of the themes most commonly developed about Structure in the social scientific literature is useful.

STRUCTURE AS AN EMPIRICAL OBJECT

Social scientists have long been fascinated with organizational Structures as simply raw objects of study, almost like the skeletons of biological individuals. Within this perspective, specific traits or dimensions describing organizational Structure are identified and their theoretical and empirical interrelations are assessed.

Indeed, some of the most distinquished founders of organizational theory fall, in part, within this tradition. Max Weber (1968) listed a number of features of bureaucracy—a hierarchy of authority, formal rules governing work, selection and promotion of employees on the basis of work qualifications, and the like—which he found in many real organizations. Although this list is a derivative part of his general position (see McPhee, 1981), the list has been highly influential in later organizational theory. For instance, Gouldner (1954) describes three alternative forms of bureaucratic structure that differ in source and nature from that identified by Weber. Again, perhaps resting on the keystone work of Burns and Stalker (1966), a debate developed in the 1960s and early 1970s over whether organizational structures varied unidimensionally between Weber's "mechanistic" bureaucracy and an opposite pole, the minimally formal "organic organization," or whether such Structures are multi-dimensional, with relatively independent dimensions such as formalization of work processes and centralization of authority (see Pugh et al., 1968).

More recent work has attempted to isolate multiple, distinctive types of organizational Structures. For instance, on empirical and theoretical grounds Mintzberg (1979) differentiates five (or six; 1983) prototypical "structural configurations" of organizations, each of which is internally coherent and consistent with particular contextual patterns. McKelvey (1982) goes even further by adopting biological taxonomic methods, likening particular organizations to individual organisms, and arguing for an "organizational species" concept. Species would be sets of organizations with similar competences and practices; McKelvey holds that general environmental forces condition the evolution of species and that they can be identified using quantitative methods of numerical taxonomy.

This theme, though rather abstract and macroscopic, is important to students of organizational communication for two main reasons. First, many of the traits or dimensions analyzed by these theorists specifically describe communication processes—for instance, Weber's stipulation of written messages and vertical consultation about exceptional problems. Second, underlying many of these discussions is an understanding of an organization as an information-processing entity. For instance. Mintzberg's five structural configurations rest, in part, on his distinction of five coordination mechanisms that the configurations embody and depend on. Each coordination mechanism is either a form of communication or a Structural substitute for communication. This perception of Structure as related to information processing leads to our next theme.

STRUCTURE AS AN INFORMATION PROCESSING/ COORDINATION MECHANISM OR TOOL

The utility of organizational Structure as a means of organizing the efforts of vast numbers of individuals has been recognized in writings about organizations from the very beginning. This idea is fully consistent with functionalism and the confluence of ideas in social theory described by Parsons (1937). But a very modern and influential formulation of the idea appears in James March and Herbert Simon's *Organizations* (1958).

March and Simon noted that human beings are characterized by "bounded rationality"—their capacities to gather and process information, to notice problems and solve them, are very limited. In particular, they are completely incapable of effectively adjusting their activities to those of hundreds of other unorganized individuals. So, March and Simon argued, organizational Structure, as well as a variety of other less formalized practices in organizations, are created to ease the decision-making tasks of individuals. Structural information tells the employee roughly what to do, whose commands to follow, and whom to inform about activities and results. It is designed to ensure that there is someone to do every task the organization requires, and that they are surrounded by an appropriate information environment to make proper decisions.

The clearest recent celebrants of this theme have been the "contingency theorists" (Perrow, 1967; Thompson, 1967; Lawrence and Lorsch, 1967; Galbraith, 1973), whose views I have considered in more detail elsewhere (McPhee, 1983). Their central argument is that organizational Structures vary because, as mechanisms for coordination or information processing, they should be and generally are adapted to the organization's needs for coordination/information processing. For instance, an organization is likely to be highly decentralized when matters requiring decisions are so turbulent or complex that high-level managers are too far removed from the action to make informed decisions. Generally, these theorists have gone further in analyzing organizational information processing needs, rooted in task complexity or environmental dynamism, than in describing the exact capacities of Structural elements or dimensions for information processing.

I have argued that contingency theory is one pole defining the domain of organizational communication studies (McPhee, 1983). For one thing, their conception of Structure makes communication central to the nature of organization. But beyond that, their theories have inspired an impressive number of studies of communication patterns in organizations (Van de Ven et al., 1976; Hage, 1974; the review in Tushman and Nadler, 1980).

STRUCTURE AS SYSTEM FORM

As we already noted, the theme of Structure as information processing or control mechanism involves a functional logic—Structure is purposefully and appropriately organized for its ends. This sort of logic is very tempting in the organizational arena since Structures are apparently purposeful human creations, belonging to social subsystems—organizations. So we should not be surprised at the pervasiveness of "systems" interpretations of structure, drawn from a long intellectual tradition of holism and vitalism (Phillips, 1976).

Systems theories of organizations have their immediate sources in the social systems views of Parsons (1937) and the general systems approach of Bertalanffy (1968), but the *locus classicus* of the theme is Katz and Kahn's *Social Psychology of Organizations* (1965, 1978). Katz and Kahn begin by theoretically describing general social systems, then account for Structure (and organizational processes) in terms of the components and requisites of the organization as social system. Organizational Structure separates and delimits the bounds of subunits; it also creates means for their integrative coordination. In short, it determines, to a large extent, the form or arrangement of subcomponents of the system. Systems theory serves both as a basis for integration of a wealth of other literature, and as an analytical instrument that stimulates attention to new organizational features.

Of course there are other and earlier systems-theoretic treatments of organizations—Simon's theory and sociotechnical systems theory (Emery and Trist, 1960) come immediately to mind. But in the field of communication, Katz and Kahn's chapter, "Communication: The Flow of Information," was required and inspiring reading: "Communication—the exchange of information and the transmission of meaning—is the very essence of a social system or an organization" (1966: 223). Much of the study of networks (see Rogers and Kincaid, 1982) and vertical communication (see Jablin, 1979) is inspired by the sense that important information flow processes are guided by Structure, or by a desire to discover the nonstructured, supplementary contributions of communication.

STRUCTURE AS NEGOTIATED

The other pole (in addition to contingency theory) for orienting communication studies in organizations is the set of theories that describes organizational regularity as negotiated. The "negotiated order theorists" (Strauss et al., 1964; Strauss, 1978; Maines, 1977; Day and Day, 1977), with strong affinity to symbolic interactionism, argue that order in at least some organizations has little to do with Structure. In looking at professional organizations, especially psychiatric hospitals, they note that professionals from a variety of disciplines must achieve a working consensus on duties, relationships, and influence despite their variant interests and world views. This "working consensus" is usually based on compromises achieved during work on specific concrete cases, where direct, intense involvement of low-status employees gives them disproportionate influence. It generally involves departures, both from the dictates of Structure, and from the disciplinary world views of the professions involved (for example, psychiatry, medicine, and nursing). And, in an important finding by theorists along these lines, the working consensus achieved in particular cases is often a basis for long-term, general Structural change. Negotiated order theorists have achieved influence in occupational sociology, where this theme has been extended to nonprofessionalized organizations (see Goldner, 1970).

Another line of research that develops this same theme is the recent work of James March (March and Olsen, 1976; Cohen and March, 1974). In particular, March and Olsen have demonstrated that organizational decision making often departs from the dictates of rationality. Organization members have limited resources of attention, and, in complex, ambiguous contexts, can pay attention to only part of the decisions and other matters that, by formal criteria, should concern them. In organizations where complexity and ambiguity are typical, problems, solutions, participants, and choice opportunities are thrown together in a random way that Cohen, March, and Olsen call a "garbage can model." Such organizations are called "organized anarchies." Although these often have Structures that look rational, the Structures are poor-quality, outdated pictures of the organizational processes.

STRUCTURE AS POWER OBJECT/RESOURCE

In viewing Structure as subject to negotiation, the writers just discussed have sometimes been accused of paying too little attention to power as a resource distributed in its own right. In a relatively recent development, organizational theorists have advanced power as an important topic of discussion in connection with Structure. Generally, even in traditionally Marxist literature mentioned below (and in Conrad and Ryan, this volume), intra-organizational power has been seen as derivative of Structure, which always confers power with authority and responsibility. But in this theme, the opposite occurs: Power is separated out as a discrete variable, something that organization members strive for, and a matter of popular concern.

A good example of this theme is Jeffrey Pfeffer's *Organizational Design* (1978). Pfeffer analyzes the various implications of Structure for power. He begins by noting bases of power—formal position, to be sure, but also such matters as assigned responsibility for critical and uncertain tasks, a structural location that results in information and access to decision makers, and control over important resources—all of which are at least partly determined by Structure. He also describes the power implications of Structural specialization, differentiation, formalization, and information systems. Correlatively, he describes major strategies employed by individuals and coalitions in the organization to control Structure so as to maximize their own power or minimize Structural effects on it.

Of course, this theme has been developed at a number of levels in recent popular and scholarly literature, with great appeal. For instance, in Korda's *Power* (1975), along with the various informal strategies mentioned are such Structural matters as control of the office files and the regular scheduling of meetings. At the more macro-economic end of the scale, John Kenneth Galbraith's *The New Industrial State* discusses the reallocation of power over large organizations, from their owners to the set of employees who "contribute information to group decisions," a set Galbraith calls the technostructure, the growth of which has been determined, of course, mainly by the growth of Structural complexity (1967: 82).

Like the preceding themes, this is one in which Structure is very intimately related to the communicative functions of information transmission and influence. Power is treated as an unseen force, ordering flows of information and influence attempts, at once their goal and the resource on which they depend.

STRUCTURE AS CARRIER OF
SOCIAL PSYCHOLOGICAL PROCESSES

In the next two themes, Structure is not exactly the central focus: It becomes instead a stimulus or backdrop to other phenomena. Here, our interest is in social-psychological processes that are transformed in organizations due to the presence of formal Structure. Many people would include organizational communication as such a process (I give it a broader status—see below, and McPhee, 1983), but numerous others have been examined.

One example, widely studied in organizational contexts, is role conflict—a person is torn as he or she tries to meet the incompatible expectations of various different role senders. Various researchers have noted that Structural features in organizations make certain persons or groups (for example, one's boss, one's subordinates) especially likely to "send" expectations that will result in role conflict (Kahn et al., 1964). Indeed, certain Structural forms—the matrix organization, in which the typical employee reports to two different superiors—are well-known for their tendency to engender role conflict.

Two more examples are the dual referents of the term "intergroup processes." The naive sense of this term includes what Doise (1977) calls "group differentiation"—any human group forms in contrast to some "foreign" entity, to which it often opposes itself. The formal differentiation of Structure sets groups of people apart, labels them in common as a work unit, relates them to contrasting groups on which they are dependent—differentiation, mis-understanding, and conflict are natural results. But the more common sense of "intergroup" involves racial or other minority groups. Here Kanter (1977) has made clear how formal structures can affect social psychological processes. Even where clear-cut prejudice is not present, majority perceptual processes such as attention, contrast, and assimilation, cued by the "token" status of minority individuals rising in organizations, can lead to a vicious cycle of real and perceived failure.

Other commonly studied social-psychological processes can be listed ad infinitum: alienation, conformity, motivation, status comparison, attribution, social perception of various sorts, and the like. One process emphasized by Simon, identification, has been dealt with in detail by Tompkins and Cheney (this volume). Another process that might belong here is formation of "climate" (but see the more complex interpretation of Poole, this volume).

STRUCTURE AS CARRIER OF SOCIAL PROCESSES

Structure is not merely a backdrop for relatively microscopic processes—more or less vast historic social movements have also found a worthy medium in organizational Structures, according to many social theorists. Indeed, the progressive *rationalization* of society was the Weberian theme within which the articulation of the bureaucratic model discussed above took place. Weber argued that modern history was distinguished by rationalization in many respects—the growth of modern science and the corresponding "disenchantment of the world" in the evolution of religion, for instance. Bureaucracy can exist only because of the general change in world view that makes "rational-legal authority," the motivational basis of bureaucracy, understandable and con-vincing. But it also contributes to rationalization, by making the actions of organizations efficient and predictable.

Organizational Structure has also been linked to the division of modern societies into social *classes*. Beginning at least with Marx, social theorists have argued that class divisions have been mirrored in the distinction between owners of organizational resources and laborers in organizations, who can only sell control over their labor power. The dynamics of capitalist production "re-produce" class distinctions by supplying a capital return to upgrade, replace, and expand factories and machinery, while furnishing workers with enough money to live and raise children—the next generation of workers—but not enough to let them accumulate capital and escape their class. Alternately, it has been argued that organizational Structuring has allowed the emergence of a "middle class" of professionals and managers (Walker, 1979; Giddens, 1971).

Beyond these major social processes, some writers have found relatively transient social trends to be reflected in Structures. For instance, Mintzberg has argued that *fashion* can be a determinant of Structure, as organizations adopt fads such as long-range planning, management by objectives, organizational development, matrix Structure, and so forth, in response to "pitches" by business periodicals and business schools (1979: 295; see Meyer and Rowan, 1977).

STRUCTURE AS A CONTROL/DOMINATION MECHANISM

Theorists who see the organization as reproducing societal divisions also often see Structure as a tool for one side in such conflict: generally, as a tool of those in charge of an organization in attempts to manipulate other organizational members against their interests. The most notable elaborations of this analysis have come from recent theorists in the Marxian tradition (Braverman, 1965; Edwards, 1979; Friedman, 1977; Clegg and Dunkerley, 1979; Salaman, 1982, 1983; Storey, 1983), who portray the evolution of Structural forms as part of a series of attempts by owners and their managerial stooges to bribe, bludgeon, or brainwash labor into cooperation. Current corporate Structures are seen as forms of organization that maximize, not general output or social utility, but profitability for the few.

This theme focuses consistently on a number of Structural features. For instance, the development of the modern managerial hierarchy and technical staff served to "deskill" or proletarianize formerly skilled work, by separating "conception" (planning, design, and coordination) from "execution" (the actual labor) and assigning them to different ranks of employees, in order to make laborer's work less valuable, less highly paid, and more easily substituted for if the worker quits or disobeys and is fired. The consequent possession by managers of crucial information and functions serves to conceal the inequity of organizational control by giving managers special claims to legitimacy and authority. Structure can also increase control by rewarding workers with autonomy—room to act freely, set up comfortable group cultures (Katz, 1968), work on technically interesting projects, or wield organizational power—in exchange for compliance; and, for loyalty and long tenure, with increasing salaries and eventual promotion. This sort of bribery, in conjunction with the specialized division of labor, also can weaken the position of the working class by dividing it against itself, rewarding some occupations and thereby leading them to resist the claims of less favored groups. Indeed, managers might be seen as simply workers who have been recruited by this tactic.

An interesting twist of this theme is the argument that top management groups, via Structural elaborations, have gained power over owners and important environmental elements (Galbraith, 1967; Pfeffer and Salancik, 1978). In a number of respects, this theme is a complement to the view of Structure as an information-processing mechanism: Structure is again viewed as communicatively significant, but here as a form of or substitute for compliance-gaining strategies.

STRUCTURE AS COUNTERPRODUCTIVE/DYSFUNCTIONAL

The views quoted in the beginning of this chapter exemplify the line of argument that organizational Structure often has unintended and unfortunate consequences. This theme is very old, and early attached the connotation of rigidity and red tape to the term "bureaucracy" (Albrow, 1970). It is popular with students of communication, who prefer the flexibility and humaneness of interaction to the formality of Structure.

One variant development of this theme is the argument that these unfortunate consequences are the result of a self-reinforcing cycle started by Structure: Its consequences stimulate further reliance on Structure, which eventually produces extremes of the consequences (March and Simon, 1958; Crozier, 1964). Such consequences include: rigid rule-following due to a sense that behavior must be defensible; goal displacement of organizational goals by subunit goals; and increasing "closeness of supervision" due to conformity to minimum subunit norms. Structure, then, may not be an ill itself, but often is the nutrient for the growth of ills.

Another variation is the perception of a dilemma, and resulting dialectic, between Structure and creative initiative. Blau and Scott (1962) argue that organizations need both the coordination, regularity and discipline, and central planning fostered by Structure, and the general problem-solving communication, professional orientations, and individual initiative that are stifled by Structure. Blau and Scott argue that effective organizations undergo a sort of dialectic of change, pendulating (as with the negotiated order theory) between innovation or conflict and systematization, but learning and improving through the experience. Here Structure, while dysfunctional, is a necessary and contributory moment of development.

STRUCTURE AS RESISTED, EVADED, OR IGNORED

Naturally, a class dominated or harmed by Structure has reason to oppose the control exercised through organizational Structure. And the working class has done so, according to the Marxian analysis. Braverman, for instance, has been criticized repeatedly for neglecting the active resistance of the working class to the successive forms of capitalist organization, especially through the labor movement (Edwards, 1979). But this argument joins a broader theme that analyzes the almost omnipresent failings of Structure to secure conformity from members of organizations.

This theme is also an old one: Organizational theorists as early as Taylor (1903) decried "systematic soldiering" or restriction of output by workers. But workers also ignore or break a variety of rules—they exchange jobs; attribute more authority to some managers than to those managers' bosses; alter work processes; communicate when, where, and what they should not; circumvent key employees in a bureaucratic chain of work—all against regulations. A number of alternative explanations for this phenomenon exist. Most interestingly, violations of Structure may actually be useful to the organization, accomplishing work more efficiently (Gross, 1953). But most violations seem organizationally dysfunctional, including stealing (Mars, 1982) and other worker self-interested acts, conformity to deviant social norms such as output restrictions, and oppositional union activity.

Deviations from Structure-derived predictions about behavior have fascinated students of communication, who have explored the growth of informal deviations from rules (Roy, 1960) and suggested that some deviations may be the result of ambiguous communication—orders interpreted as suggestions and the like (Burns, 1954).

STRUCTURE AS ENACTED/ACCOMPLISHED

This final theme derives from an important insight: Rules of any sort do not simply apply themselves. They always require some degree of creativity and judgment, at its highest in such formalized arenas as the legal system. But the process of adaptation or accomplishment is not the same as negotiation—it resolves not discrepant member interests, but an uncertainty that is present in all human action. Organizational Structure is a clear case in which this insight itself applies.

One school of thought that has developed this theme is ethnomethodology. Ethnomethodologists argue that our sense of the "everydayness" of life is actively *accomplished* by people, not a natural state of affairs. In organizations, people can and do "follow a routine" but only by being more creative than standard organizational theories ever imply. For instance, Zimmerman (1970) studied a clinic in which a receptionist was supposed to assign patients to various physicians by writing their names on one or another physician's list. But some physicians were delayed by difficult cases; to prevent inordinately long waits, especially for seriously ill patients, the receptionist sometimes juggled the lists, more or less radically, depending on her judgment. Even that simple rule had to be adapted to a variety of exceptional circumstances, an adaptation best regarded as "common sense," not an underlying, more complex decision rule.

Another influential and related development of this theme relates to the concept of "organizing" initially developed by Weick (1969, 1979). For Weick, our Structure is retained in the multitude of possible organizational memory banks; as such, it is limited by many kinds of phenomena such as assimilation to prior memory organization, memory deterioration or forgetting, and problems and costs of recall. Moreover, Structure is not simply recalled and conformed to. Its application is part of a process whereby the organization's environment is engaged or "enacted," and features from the equivocal whole are "selected" or interpreted in an organizational response that is itself retained as a gloss on Structure. Enactment, retention, and especially selection are all social processes, so once again communication determines the practical implications of Structure.

REPRISE

All these themes allow and deserve much more discussion than I have given them here; all have their weaknesses that have been criticized, and their answers to critiques. I think of them as theoretic "molecules" or "words" that can be connected in many different developments of thought about organizations. I have separated them to allow re-mention in what follows, and to make several general points. First, in many of these themes, Structure has consequences that are undesirable from many points of view. Indeed, only the theme of Structure as information processing or coordination mechanism describes it as clearly and generally useful. This negative tone recalls the views of Argyris and Kanter, mentioned above, and is in line with a long-term revelatory and critical current in social science that organizational communication theorists, until recently, have tended to ignore. Its opposition to the rational, scientific efforts of organizational designers remind one of the Romantic classic *Frankenstein:* Are organizations the social-scientific equivalent of the monster? I mean this question (perhaps it should be phrased a bit less emotionally) seriously—Is Structure, in principle, an ill? Even in its identity as coordination mechanism? And what are the implications of this question for the study of organizational communication?

The rest of this chapter will fall into three sections. In the first, I will discuss some peculiarly communicational implications of Structure. Then I will introduce the theory of structuration, a perspective that will, in the third part, facilitate an enriched account of organizational Structure integrating many of the themes just discussed.

THE NATURE OF STRUCTURE

In the introductory section of the chapter, defining qualities of organizational Structure were stipulated. Here I want to emphasize the qualities of Structure that are related to the way it is communicated or established. The very existence of Structure is dependent on its communication in a formal, explicit, authoritative way, often in writing, in a *document* that has recognized status (though often limited circulation) in the organization. Also, with accompanying changes in Structure there is sometimes a ritual of announcement, of public proclamation of an employee's promotion, a new department, or a new system. Although Structure has effects on behavior, it *is not* fundamentally a behavior pattern— we would operationalize Structure, not by observing behavior (which is often informal deviation or resistance), but rather finding and reading an authoritative pronouncement (and making sure, by asking an authority, that it still reigns). Structure is fundamentally communicational, then. Of course, in observing Structure we should not stop with document-reading. On the contrary, an advantage of this view of Structure is that it forces us to view, as a system, three aspects in a balanced way: the process of design (that is, writing the documents), the process of communication, and the process of response (interpreting and responding to the documents over time). The design and response aspects have been studied repeatedly, but the central aspect, communication, has often been treated simply as a matter of implementation. I want to give more theoretical attention to this central aspect, actually a distinct subsystem of organizational communication with its own distinctive type of sublanguage. Two features of the communication of Structure (called "Structure-communication" below) will be emphasized in this section.

STRUCTURE-COMMUNICATION
IS INDIRECT COMMUNICATION

First, we should recognize some intended results of establishing an organizational Structure. If someone is given a formal supervisory position, some fairly common arguments in work settings are thereby, in theory, resolved. There is to be no more arguing about "who gives orders to whom," or when and what the workers are supposed to do. If there is disagreement about a decision, the supervisor need not spend time persuading the others that his/her decision is the best—at some point the person uses his/her authority to get work started again, and that is that. (A manager reading this will moan, "If only it were that easy!") Similarly, employees are trained, and standard operating procedures are established, so that when certain situations arise, the employees know what to do—they do not have to ask somebody and wait for a decision, or argue about it among themselves. Structure as an information-processing mechanism works just so: If General Motors, starting to build a new car, gathered all its employees together and asked, "OK, what sort of car should we build and how shall we do it?" discussion might go on forever. In a small group, or even a body such as Congress, that is often how things proceed. But the formal Structure of GM, which prevents that result, is a substitute (Kerr, 1977) for the communication—makes it *indirect*, through rules, hierarchy, the division of labor, and so forth, rather than a direct social dialogue.

What are the implications of this indirect communication in Structure? First, it deprives the employee of "voice" (Hirschman, 1970). The employee's interests, as an "honest workman," as a craftsman, as occupant of a role that is an element of the overall system of work, are rarely represented during the design of Structure. Instead, he or she must either comply with or leave the organization. For instance, if a company installs new work procedures, they are almost always articulated from above. The employee is not able to engage the industrial engineer in creative dialogue or participate in an exchange of rationales; at most, employees' critical reactions or occasional suggestions may lead to change if they translate persuasively into the industrial engineer's language. Relevant examples reflecting the lack of direct communication are "whistle-blowing" and the lengths to which managers will go to avoid hearing about (assuming responsibility for) grievous company errors (Congressional Subcommittee on Economy in Government, 1982). A further consequence is the typical situation of an employee—his or her "appropriate information environment" often lacks information about the company in general or any matters that are not perceived, from above, to be immediately relevant to work decisions.[1]

A second implication is the inevitable communicative distortion due to indirectness. This takes many guises. One is intentional distortion by senders who try to please or conform to expectations of their formal superiors. Another is Simon's information absorption—information is not just collapsed as it is passed up the line, but, often, rationale and context are shorn from facts (as are orders, down the line), which are twisted to fit pre-established information system categories. Moreover, as Ruesch and Bateson (1968: 280-281) note, it is common for sources to try to escape responsibility for messages in the system, by blaming "the system" or representing themselves as mere conduits, doing their jobs. All this makes it unsurprising that some chief executives systematically visit the line workers to get a "feel" for the work they cannot get through Structural channels. Almost by definition, the "substitute" communication channel of Structure is distorted in Habermas's sense—inappropriate, inauthentic—simply because it is indirect. (See the discussion in Habermas, 1984, especially pp. 339ff).

But we must acknowledge more pleasing consequences, too. Most obviously, indirect communication can be relatively efficient, avoiding the arguments and concerns that overwhelm people's "bounded rationality." Contingency theory and research indicate persuasively that relatively centralized Structures are appropriate in certain situations, and that people appreciate the centralization in those situations (Palumbo, 1969). Indeed, one benefit of indirect relations, via Structure, with others in the organization is that employees enjoy freedom from the constraints of direct relationships—creative autonomy on the job, protection from particularism, and academic freedom are among the benefits of Structure (as are civil rights in society at large) (Perrow, 1979).

STRUCTURE-COMMUNICATION IS EXPLICIT, AUTHORITATIVE METACOMMUNICATION

A second feature of the communication of Structure is revealed by the very fact that it is formal. Look at the language of a job position description: "The Director, Traffic Office, is responsible to the Vice President—Purchasing for recommending major Company traffic and transportation policies, plans, and objectives; developing and administering programs designed to maintain and further business relationships between the Company and its transportation services suppliers; coordinating . . . ," and so on, with 128 words in the sentence. This is not ordinary language; how is it distinct?

For one thing, it is *about* the discourse of the organization, self-consciously defining its terms and charting its course. In that way, it is *metacommunication*, communication about the process of communication (Watzlavick et al., 1967). Typically, metacommunication is thought of as the relationship-defining element of any message—for instance, the style of a put-down comment, which tells the receiver it is intended as an affiliation-expressing joke, not as a divisive insult. Such metacommunicative elements are generally on a different, higher level from, and more powerful than, ordinary communication; but they are also typically thought of as implicit, a tacit self-referential modification of the surface content of a message. So the communication of Structure is an odd sort of metacommunication—it is explicit and openly authoritative. It is also unusual in that it is not unambiguously the highest controlling level of communication, as it is in everyday discourse: It must be adapted/accomplished using ordinary language, the "last metalanguage" (Habermas, 1980).[2]

There are several natural implications of this view of Structure-communication. First, because it is explicitly on a separate, commanding level of discourse, it has been able to develop as a technology. Or, rather, a series of technologies have become specialized professions with numerous subspecialties, each with a technical vocabulary, perspective, and standard modes for interpreting and attacking problems. Examples of these include: bookkeeping, accounting, and finance; industrial engineering; organizational development and human resources accounting; strategic planning; and management information and control systems. Each makes claim to apply to various kinds of work—to R and D and education, as well as to assembly-line operations. And these Structure-creating occupations work most naturally in a *command* capacity, except perhaps for organizational development as their practitioners lose efficiency, and often patience, if they have to engage in power-equalized dialogue about what they are doing.

A second implication: The metacommunication of Structure is partially formalized, which creates the possibility of an almost mechanical process of control over organizational operations. For instance, it is very difficult to evaluate the work of a craftsman on *its own* terms—by definition, the work has involved creativity, so an appropriate reaction to it can only be that of educated judgment, to which evaluations are liable to be tentative, multifaceted, and dynamic. But if we dictate terms to the craftsman—make so many pieces, so large, in such-and-such a time, evaluation becomes easy—we simply count and measure pieces and minutes. That dictation is the communication of Structure. And the highly mechanical, unrelenting counting—disregarding circumstantial excuses—is the ultimate cybernetic control mechanism that is possible in organizations.

The key word here is "possible." Of course, not all, or perhaps even most, organizational evaluation works this way. But it is generally taken by organization members to be typical and unassailable; so it hangs as a threat, a spectre, over the heads of organization members. (I write as one who has just sweated out the possibility of "publication counting" in a tenure decision.)

One last implication, linked to the preceding ones: The formal and technical metacommunication of Structure allows for a number of crucial ties between the organization and its environment. Since this metalanguage is on a distinct level from, more general than, and in control of, the language of the organization's specific work content, the metalanguage tends to be shared by environmental actors. For instance, the language of accounting and finance is used to represent the organization to the Internal Revenue Service and to the financial markets where capital can be raised. More generally, the documents recording Structure have legal status, giving the State a "handle" for dealing with and controlling the organization as a legal entity. And, of course, the language of job titles and responsibilities is used by employees to define themselves to other organizations with which their own organization is dealing, or to explain their qualifications for other jobs.

So Structure is stated, recorded, and constituted in a peculiar sort of communicative practice: It is indirect relative to the natural coordinative dialogue that would normally accompany work processes, and it is explicit, authoritative metacommunication, in relation to the range of actually occurring organizational communication. That is my theme in this essay; to elaborate it I turn to a perspective in general social theory for a relevant and fertile vocabulary.

THE THEORY OF STRUCTURATION

The specific approach to Structure and communication in organizations that I shall develop rests on the theory of structuration, which has been explained at length in several other essays (McPhee and Poole, 1981; Poole and McPhee, 1983; see Poole, this volume; Giddens, 1981, 1984. In structurational theory, social life is seen as a system of structured practices. Here *Structure* is the matrix of rules and resources that people draw on to enable (but also constrain) action. We can find structure by looking for the regularities that make interaction meaningful and consequential. For instance, in speech we would no doubt find syntactic, semantic, and pragmatic rules, but we would also find that we regularly break linguistic rules in conversation (implicature), in "baby talk," in poetry, and the like; such regular aberrations are part of the structure of language—of its rules and nature as a social resource. Across social classes and ethnic groups, language skills are regularly differentiated: Groups have unique vocabularies, speech styles of varying "correctness," unique forms of word play. Such differences help groups separate members from outsiders and help some groups dominate others. In other words, the structure of language use involves power relations—it is a structure of domination. The various practices and groups using language are themselves linked by it—they may be seen as an interdependent social *system*.[3]

Structuration's major argument is that every action bears a *dual* relation to structure: It both *produces* and *reproduces* structure and the related social system. In our example, "production" means that speech *as such* embodies structure—makes it meaningful, consequential human action rather than motion. "Reproduction" means that every speech episode contributes to the continuity and dissolution of more general social structures, such as "language" or "class domination." In research, we may focus on production (often in "analysis of strategic conduct") or reproduced forms (often in "institutional analysis"), but we must seek and create mutual reference and consistency in these research approaches. In the next few sections, some structurational subconcepts of special relevance to our topic are highlighted.

MODALITIES

Giddens argues that every instance of the "production of interaction has three fundamental elements: its constitution as 'meaningful'; its constitution as a moral order; and its constitution as the operation of relations of power" (1976: 104). He seems to have derived this distinction from linguists' view that any competent speaker of a language must be able to engage in three sorts of activities—to understand sentences, to recognize acceptable and inadequate sentences, and to produce sentences appropriately and purposefully (1977: 129). This is an analytic distinction, and the three elements are compounded in every social act—thus it is hard to consider moral norms without considering their interpretation—a matter of meaning—and the process by which they are "made to count"—a matter of power.

The interesting matter is how this distinction intersects the duality of structure. Giddens (1976) uses the following grid:

Interaction	communication	power	morality
(Modality)	interpretative scheme	facility	norm
Structure	signification	domination	legitimation

The middle row, the modalities, "refer to the mediation of interaction and structure in processes of social reproduction" (p. 122) and Giddens explicitly holds that the general link between structure and interactive reproduction holds in the case of these three elements. So, for instance, all social acts involve power—the capacity to alter a course of events by intervening, where "the course of events" may include the activities of others. By the very nature of action, then, the above scheme implies that a peculiar type of institution—an order of domination—exists and is reproduced. All actions, embodying meaning, imply and reproduce an "order of signification"—an institutionalized communication structure. And all acts, involving normative judgments, imply and reproduce an order of legitimation—an institutional dimension that itself implies general, basic, and valid social value judgments.

DISTANCIATION

One of Giddens's most important recent concepts concerns space and time as social phenomena of equal importance with structure:

> The problem of order in social theory is how *form* occurs in social relations, or (put in another fashion) how social systems "bind" space and time. All social activity is formed in three conjoined moments of difference: temporally, structurally (in the language of semiotics, paradigmatically), and spatially; the conjunction of these express the *situated* character of social practices. The structuration of all social systems occurs in time-space, but also "brackets" time-space relations; every social system in some way "stretches" across time and space. Time-space distanciation refers to the modes in which such stretching takes place or, to shift the metaphor slightly, how social systems are "embedded" in time and space [Giddens, 1981: 4-5, 30].

Space and time are not just dimensions of separation—they are "bound" by practices, to which they give character and form. For instance, Lawrence and Lorsch's (1967) concept of differentiation is crucially different from distanciation. Differentiation holds organizational departments *apart*, in need of integration; distanciation describes them as held *in place*, part of a whole (which may not work together as a whole very efficiently, to be sure).

Giddens (1981: 30, 4-5) notes that primitive societies are not "stretched" very far in space: interdependent actors are almost always present or easily accessible to one another, and coordination in primitive social orders depends on this "high presence-availability." Without writing, only human memory could "bind" time and space in religious and kinship traditions. The invention of writing was an alternate and very powerful source of social "storage capacity," allowing for much larger social systems with much more frequent indirect interaction. The effects of this greater capacity on social systems are sometimes understated, Giddens argues. For instance, writing makes possible records that live longer and travel wider than their contexts, creating the problems of differing interpretations motivating hermeneutics (1981: 150). More pertinent to our topic, writing increased the importance of authoritative resources in societies: It began in, and allows, records of expected and actual behavior and events that underlie the use of authoritative control, in the practices of *surveillance*. " 'Surveillance' involves two things: the collation of information relevant to state control of the conduct of its subject population, and the direct supervision of that conduct" (Giddens, 1981: 5). Giddens notes that surveillance also allowed the extension of management control into the workplace; ease of surveillance was a major reason for the rise of the giant modern corporation. In this case, as in the case of the growth of cities, distanciation leads to less direct control but allows the generation of enormous power through coordination and concentration of control.

Another consequence of distanciation is a change in the processes leading to system unity or cohesion. Giddens (1979: 76-77) alters the usual distinction between two such processes, saying that *social integration* yields "*systemness on the level of face-to-face interaction*," and *system integration* yields "*systemness on the level of relations between social systems or collectivities . . .*" "The systemness of social integration is *fundamental to the systemness of society as a whole*. System integration cannot be adequately conceptualized via the modalities of social integration; nonetheless, the latter is always the chief prop of the former, *via the reproduction of institutions in the duality of structure.*" In a social system involving lots of "stretch" in space and time between interdependent agents, the process of social integration is weakened; system integration must substitute for it, yet is itself weakened because it too is dependent on social integration. This is the modern "legitimation crisis" of cultural heterogeneity.

REFLEXIVITY/RATIONALIZATION

As Cicourel (1978) has noted, Giddens emphasizes the reflexive monitoring of conduct and links it to the rationalization of action. Agents plan and monitor their conduct, and its context and results, in an ongoing process; they thereby make it "fit in" with standard social practices in that they make it meaningful and able to be accountable or rationalized. This reflexivity and rationalization of action is directly linked to the duality of structure: agents "draw on" structure strategically in acting, and the meaningful accountability of their conduct means that social structure is reproduced in the conduct. Of course, accountability involves three senses that are aligned with the three modalities: An account can tell us what someone's action means, how they describe what they were doing. It can also relate the action to relevant norms and values, as good or appropriate conduct. Finally, it can shed light on the agent's power over and responsibility for outcomes—are they intended, or did the agent have insufficient resources to achieve his or her goal, or did he or she lose command of the flow of action, and so on. Also power-revealing, accounts can show the kinds of reasons that do "count" in the social system: "The reflexive elaboration of frames of meaning is characteristically imbalanced in relation to the possession of power, whether this be a result of the superior linguistic or dialectical skills of one person in conversation with another; the possession of relevant types of 'technical knowledge'; the mobilization or authority or 'force,' etc." (Giddens, 1976: 113).

Giddens's approach to reflexivity/rationalization is distinctive primarily because he expands this "explanation-giving" sense of the concepts, relating them to large-scale social process and institutions, and distinguishing various forms of them. For one thing, he notes that the "explanation" level is important primarily at the face-to-face level of social integration. But descriptive accounts, in a medium that binds time-space, can extend beyond immediate interaction to relations among social subsystems. Giddens (1979: 78) argues that system integration can occur at three cybernetic levels: The first is purely causal at the system level, involving homeostatic causal loops—the unintended causal consequences of actions. Second is the level of self-regulation through feedback, involving especially a "receptor, control apparatus, and effector." Giddens (1976: 121) notes that this level is often assimilated to homeostasis, but is different in three crucial ways: It involves a distinct control apparatus; it can result in structural transformation, not just system equilibrium or disintegration; and it rests on a time-space patterning of interdependence that expresses social power. But there is a third level of system integration, "reflexive self-regulation," which involves purposeful social action on the social system itself, grounded in "self-knowledge and in knowledge of the social and material worlds which are the environment of the acting self" (1976: 85). In such grounding, action is rationalized and expresses a rationality. In an organization, surveillance supplies the knowledge that underlies the creation and implementation of Structure as reflexive self-regulation.

THE DIALECTIC OF CONTROL

The growth of system integration and the power of system-level reflexive self-regulation may seem to forecast the emergence of complete control over individuals in a "one-dimensional" society. But Giddens (1982) notes a countervailing process, the dialectic of control. Basically, he argues that agents, even those with very little power, retain a capacity to resist if they retain any action capacities at all. This capacity to resist gives them "some degree of control over the conditions of reproduction of the system. In all social systems there is a dialectic of control, such that there are normally continually shifting balances of resources, altering the overall distribution of power" (p. 32).

Giddens introduces this concept as an antidote to Weber's picture of completely rationalized control of individuals in bureaucracies. Several variants of the dialectic of control exist in organizations. First, greater interdependence and spatial separation of offices allow employees many opportunities for creating bargaining power relative to the organization and a "space of control" over their own activities—a "back region" in Goffman's sense, involving the strategic countermanipulation of the media of surveillance. Power of lower participants is supported by the capitalist "free labor market" (employees are free to quit; their skills and knowledge thus give them bargaining power). Second, the dialectic operates on two sites—in firms, as stated above, and in the public sphere as the labor movement takes political action affecting the work place. Third, subordinated employees develop insight or "penetration" of the system. This may be inside knowledge of system workings, superior even to that of powerful agents. Often it involves humor and irony, similar to Goffman's "role distance." And such orientations may deceive, seeming to express practical acceptance of control while actually nourishing a search for opportunities for countermeasures and a growing shared opposition.

But we should recognize the common limitations of the dialectic of control. It is extended in time, and depends for practical importance on the existence and knowledge of available alternatives to present arrangements. Without "conception of how things could be otherwise" (Giddens, 1981: 149), the dialectic may actually reinforce control, as when a wife has greater knowledge of her husband than he of her, but uses it primarily to adjust to his wishes and fashion a life that avoids conflict with them.

This ends our overview of the structurational perspective. Its application to organizational Structure has clearly already begun, and continues below.

THE STRUCTURAL ANALYSIS OF STRUCTURE

I have already described Structure as articulated in explicit, authoritative metacommunication and as being a medium of indirect communication. That description partly neglects the relations of such communication to the social system in which it occurs, and to the range of other organizational communication (after all, the communication of Structure is much less frequent than formal work-oriented communication or informal communication). These relationships are especially important because they help explain how Structure-communication achieves and maintains its metacommunicative status and how it can substitute for more direct modes. In this section we shall explore the implications of the structurational concepts introduced above for Structure-communication. My thesis is a fairly simple one: Time-space distanciation in

	No Structure-Oriented Conflict	Structure-Oriented Conflict
No Promulgation of Structure	*Work operations:* Labor force members (and others) develop work routines and experience, "informal organization."	*Implicitly Structural conflict:* Labor force members (and others) resist, strike tacit bargains to violate existing Structural provisions.
Promulgation of Structure	*Design of Structure:* Technically trained staff creates and proposes original versions of or changes in hierarchy, rules, systems.	*Conflict over Structural design:* Powerful members dispute, negotiate about, officially authorize Structural changes.

Figure 6.1   The Four Sectors

organizations, the meta-level on which Structure-communication occurs, and its indirectness as organizational communication mediate and mutually support each other. Yet the "weaving dance" of these phenomena has varying and often novel results.

In organizations, distanciation has several forms. Organizations' physical sites may be widely scattered or transient; inside a single site, members may be divided or fasciculated by physical or status forces; the division of labor, separating employees' work and rendering it autonomous or interdependent, "binds" possible employee interaction. We will deemphasize these axes of distanciation, looking instead at four "sectors" of organizational activity that differ in their relation to Structure-communication. These sectors *may* overlap physically; they vary greatly in size; their borders are indistinct and frequently crossed by employees, decisions, memos, and the like. Yet distanciation among these sectors, I argue, grounds the peculiar properties and power of Structure-communication in modern organizations.

The four sectors are separated along two dimensions, as indicated in Figure 6.1: whether a sector's occupants promulgate Structure, and whether the sector typically involves Structure-oriented conflict. (Conflict is "Structure-oriented" when at least one party to conflict, consciously or not, moves to change the explicit content *or practical implications* of Structure for organizational work.) Despite the possibility of overlap, I will argue that these sectors are usually quite different in physical location, roster of participants, and style of interaction. Such differences allow Structure-communication to be indirect and meta-communicative in the ways described above.

WORK OPERATIONS

This sector contains people doing organizational work where prescriptions of Structure result in no Structure-directed conflict. Opinions vary about the frequency of this state in capitalist organizations, with Marxists asserting that, examined historically, conflict is endemic; still, this sector seems worth examining, if only as an abstract, transient moment in societal evolution. For instance, it is probably the most commonly accepted goal state for those who directly manage, or reflexively control, organizational operations.

In organizational processes occurring in this sector, a number of phenomena of interest even to Marxists must be recognized. For one thing, work processes are experienced and relevant Structure is accomplished/adapted to. In addition to the problematic nature of this accomplishment mentioned above, adaptation does not usually represent blind conformity—some Structural provisions are treated as live and authoritative, while others are evaded or ignored. Such evasions do not represent conflict here: For many Structural provisions, *nobody* expects conformity, and they are ignored with the explicit (and presumptively authoritative) consent of superiors. As employees experience work processes, they concurrently build a joint awareness of problems with work arrangements and a consequent solidarity. As Sayles noted, factors like similarity of experience and perspective are the foundation for future problems that will "resonate" among workers to trigger resistance (Chapple and Sayles, 1961). This joint, crystallized experience is one element in the dialectic of control, which works even in this sector. Even the most mechanical work processes allow employees some margin of choice; this readily becomes a "space of action," perhaps to be defended or expanded (if the situation slides into the next sector; to be discussed below).

As part of this sort of process, interdependent workers build the usual "informal organization" or "culture." This involves not just ordinary interpersonal affiliations, but also distinctive work practices, with the three modalities of structure described by Giddens. For instance, workers develop a jargon and communicative practices nicely molded to the problems and constraints of work (Meissner, 1969, 1976). They also develop characteristic time perspectives matched to work and informal routines (Roy, 1960; Lawrence and Lorsch, 1967; Zerubavel, 1979). Often, employees themselves recognize, in so many words, the interpretive, normative, and empowering implications of this informally generated structure (Riley, 1983).

The consequences of this kind of social integration are variable. In almost every case, we might describe them in terms of *autonomy*, as Katz (1968) aptly observed. For some work groups, autonomy is merely a right to import elements of external subcultures—to create a friendly, more tolerable existence (see Roy, 1960). The group merely becomes interpretively impenetrable, not easily understood by outsiders—not a particularly effective defense against domination by outsiders. For other groups, autonomy is a source of further power, of domination over other organizational groups (Crozier, 1964; Chapple and Sayles, 1961), as we will discuss further below. Finally, for professional, staff, and managerial groups, the group's autonomy—including its characteristic vocabulary, self-scheduling, and so forth—is often centered on work-relevant decisions. In this case, the logic and language of the group's work may necessarily merge with that of local or general organizational Structure— dividing labor, planning, and the like, become as much technical problems as

Structural problems. For instance, a group of engineers, in designing a new instrument, will use the initial plan of the instrument to determine subgroups of specialists who must work together, a schedule of deadlines, a budget of resource needs, and the like. Again, implications of this phenomenon are discussed further in the next section, but here we should note that the matter is not merely one of the variable "task complexity" having a high value. Structural mediations in technical decisions are also a result of strategic action by professional employees for whom expert knowledge is a power resource; they also follow from general organizational strategy in "technological capitalism" (Karpik, 1978), as the organization decides to compete by overwhelming rivals with innovative product introductions, thereby empowering and burdening the individuals responsible for innovation.

IMPLICITLY STRUCTURAL CONFLICT

Into this sector—very difficult to tell from the first and fourth—falls organizational interaction, which involves structure-relevant conflict, but which is not carried on specifically as a debate about proposed Structural change. Actually, there are two sorts of cases within this general category. First is the kind of conflict that is never brought into the open, based on fait accompli and gamesmanship, included as negotiation by the negotiated-order theorists. Here, members are aware of their differences, but maneuver so that their differences can remain submerged. Second, many conflicts centered on particular issues are actually about the interpretation and implementation of Structual provisions. Examples of research describing both cases are Strauss's description of the hospital's negotiated order, interdepartmental relations—especially involving line and staff units (Tuggle, 1978)—and Goldner's (1970) account of how industrial relations specialists use their expert knowledge of labor agreements, practices in other plants, and wider possible consequences of single issues to control line managers and protect their own influence rights. Another set of examples involves the struggles of work groups against revisions of work rates (for example, the imposition of work restrictions and manipulation of reported output figures described in Roethlisberger and Dickson, 1939).

Notice that conflicts such as this do not necessarily involve "lower participants" pitted against management—they can involve lateral relations at any level of the organization. Moreover, such conflicts do not necessarily pit informal arrangements against Structure—generally, social-psychological processes carried by Structure are responsible, and, in the case of labor grievances, one Structural provision (the grievance proceeding) is often pitted against another. Nonetheless, it is reasonable to regard these disputes as moves in the dialectic of control, as the struggle for influence and autonomy is directed variously against perceived unjust restraints from any source.

Such conflicts are characterized primarily by their variety. Their processes can include all the happenings found in any other sort of political struggle. But two very typical phenomena in this sector are worth discussing. First, in this kind of conflict, bargains or resolutions are very often localized—described as exceptional and subordinate to the general regularities of the organization. Structure remains unchallenged reality (a "deep structural" matter in Clegg's [1975] terms—see Conrad and Ryan, this volume) as is also shown by the tactics employed in conflict. For instance, a supervisor announcing an unpleasant decision will often blame higher-ups for it, assuming with his or her audience that disobedience or resistance is not a live option (Hunt and Lichtman, 1969). The less powerful have persuasive resources, too—such as attention and immediate presence at the scene—but these are weak as support for generalized Structure-level changes. For example, the creation of "back regions" shielded from the purview of management, and the manipulation of control systems, depend on the ability of employees to "get around" Structure, not to change it or challenge it on its own terms. Indeed, resistance strategies like these often eventuate in reactive Structural changes, possibly triggering the dysfunctional cycles of bureaucracy reviewed above.

A second matter worthy of note is that even conflicts at this level involve differences, not just in interests and purposes, but also in frames of reference. Especially in the case in which conflict involves different units, its participants differ in their situational interpretations, and thus also in their views about the legitimacy of claims and pressure strategies, and in their capacities for such strategies. Moreover, each side's perspective is mediated in such conflicts in three ways: in the practical issues in dispute, in the history or tradition in which the particular dispute is embedded, and in the images held by other participants. Such mediations can have important consequences: for instance, a professional group may come to be identified with a stand on a minor or dead issue that is unimportant in terms of its value scheme, but that it cannot abandon without losing face, that it can never win, and that renders it energyless to pursue more important issues (Pettigrew, 1973).

As we mentioned above, actual cases that seem to fall into the first sector really belong in the second—conflict may be temporarily quiescent, or stifled from above. There seems to be little distance between these two sectors; the main difference seems to be one of strategic consciousness, as employees in the second quadrant are aware, or made aware, of the conflict implications of every relevant act. In a number of ways, it is difficult to return from the second sector to the first—a resolution of conflict must be very thorough to remove it from the reproduced structures of the participating groups. Very often a Structural change is necessary, though not always sufficient. But conflict resolution via informal arrangements, I contend, is typically widely separated from conflict issuing in Structural change. There is a fairly clear dividing line in most organizations dividing units and processes that deal in Structure from other units. This line may follow the divisions of supervision from management, or middle management from upper management, or line from staff. But the line commonly signals a climatic shift in the organization, often separating units in which organizational politics seems exceptional and irrelevant from those where it seems omnipresent (Riley, 1983).

THE DESIGN OF STRUCTURE

This sector involves operations that create or change the organization's Structure, in their ordinary work procedures, without the direct intrusion of conflicting interests. In this sector, organizational hierarchies and work flows are designed, job position descriptions are devised, strategic plans are elaborated, manuals of forms and procedures are written, piece-work rates and salary structures are decided. Of course typical managers or even employees sometimes do parts of this work, but it is generally the domain of technologists of structure—the personnel specialists, accountants, industrial engineers, and the like. As organizations develop a certain sophistication of Structure, people like these are hired and split in separate units, and the job of Structure-communication is assigned to them. This work is purposefully aimed, by the designers of design units, at system integration; it involves designed reflexivity/rationalization. These aims are reflected in the training and ideologies of "design staff" members—they speak, and conceive their work, in terms of the Structure as a coordination mechanism or as the form of a cybernetic system.

Structure designers vary widely in authority relative to other parts of the organization. Sometimes they are clearly superior to the parts of the organization they Structurally redesign—industrial engineers changing work-flow pattern or systems analysts studying information flow in the organization to design control systems, for instance. On other occasions, their autonomy and authority are lower and more negotiable. For example, Structure-designing staff members may approach line units as internal consultants to clients—their entry into project work, as well as the implementation of the suggested Structural change, will depend on the more or less free choice of the line unit, subject to persuasion by the staff members. Another case might be the staff member who is assigned to research and report on proposed Structural change (see Cyert et al., 1956). This member's activity may simply be a phase in an extensive decision process, although that depends in part on the political status of the proposal and the nature of the report produced.

The design of Structure does not proceed in isolation, of course. Very often, facts and opinions from the Work Operations and Implicit Conflict sectors are collected—but they are used in two main ways. First, they are treated as *data*, abstracted from context and processed, not as messages to be understood and responded to. Second, the informal arrangements from the second sector, as well as the decisions in the fourth, may command respect, and be treated as boundaries or constraints to whatever Structural changes are proposed, and thus to the autonomous professional decisions of the design staff. Such constraints, of course, bring the dialectic of control into play, as the staff tries to maximize its own "space" of action. Staff strategies in this dialectic include professionalization and expertise, mystification via an overly complex "scientific" description, and treatment of proposed changes as general or universal (overriding local constraints). Where participation is sought from employees whose primary work is in other sectors, it is usually contrived in terms of some controlled participation technology—nominal groups, quality circles, and so forth. Probably the most effective strategy, though, is a distancing achieved by treating the client group "as an object," as a source of data, as the topic of metacommunication. This distancing is justified moralistically as objectivity and removal from bias; it is supported by the training and technical expertise of the design staff. A separation is also supported by the differentiated perspective of those who have a part in designing organizational Structure. As mentioned above, such work is often organized as projects, with time frames quite different from those found in, for example, the Work Operations sector.

CONFLICT OVER STRUCTURAL DESIGN

This final sector includes decision processes about Structural issues at various levels of significance, from a promotion and title change for an employee to dissolution of the organization. Naturally, such decisions may proceed very smoothly, as is often the case when made by a single person or committee with sufficient authority. But typically, Structural decisions involve commitments of resources that must be approved at a variety of levels, where it is possible for them to become objects of politics. Typical decision processes of this sort do not follow clear preformalized plans; they resemble creative problem solving with an incremental logic much more than rationalized action or debating societies (see March and Olsen, 1976; Mintzberg et al., 1976; Quinn, 1980).

For our purposes, only a few points about this sector need to be raised. First, occupants of the other sectors, even the third, are typically not present in these decisions forums. Workers are sometimes represented, by a union official who is correspondingly distanciated from his/her membership. A staff member who designed a proposed change may be present at certain forums to make a presentation, but often has no direct voice after that. The level of discussion in such forums varies, in line with such factors as degree of intelligibility of the proposal and relevance to interests of powerful parties. What discussion does occur is singularly alive to the political implications of Structure as a power object and resource, if not always aware of the technical meaning of the proposal. It is certainly metacommunication, although it may not be at the level of technicality attained in the previous sector.

Our point can perhaps best be illustrated through an example, amalgamated from several sources and my own knowledge (Simon, Cyert, and Trow, 1956; Pettigrew, 1973). A company (that is, sector 4) decides to introduce computerized word processing. In an initial step, it sends around a staff-designed (sector 3) questionnaire about line department processing needs (sector 1). (Answers to the questions, as well as the disposition of processor use, become matters for implicit conflict on the line—sector 2.) Based on this and other information, a staff member (or team or multiple individuals—sector 3) explores the range of available hardware and software choices, making a report perhaps including recommendations. The report becomes the basis of considerable conflict in several executive committees (sector 4), with one side having an advantage due to a near monopoly of information and the technicality of comparisons between products; but finally a decision on a specific purchase is made. Staff experts (sector 3) devise a training program for line operatives (sector 1) who will use the equipment.

Notice the shifts in levels of discourse and decision loci. Line department typing routines are only tenuously related to choice among word processing products, through the channels of staff data processing and reporting, and executive discussion. There is usually considerable slippage between dimensions used by typists to describe their requirements, and the choice dimensions along which product options are compared by technical staff. In such ways, the language in which decisions are analyzed and made is distinguished and elevated from the language of work. Of course there is great variation across organizations regarding this distinction, probably related to the variation among types of organizations mentioned at the beginning of the chapter.

How is this different from the commonplace position that the top of the organization controls the bottom? The easiest answer is that I have distinguished three meanings of "control" or differences between the top and the bottom. Hierarchy as indirect communication: people at the bottom are managed, controlled, through the avoidance of direct voice or communication. As explicit, authoritative metacommunication: people at the bottom are *unable* to speak, illiterate in the technical language in which Structural decisions might be debated. As distanciation: people at the bottom see Structure as "someone else's job" and responsibility, just like another part of the division of labor. In all three senses Structure seems to be an unquestionable reality.

CONCLUSION

My general theme in this article—that there is a close relationship between the communication style used to produce statements of Structure in organizations, and the distanciation of organizational sectors that are related to Structural pronouncements in different ways—has forebears. There is a parallel between the analysis of Structure-communication, for instance, and the analysis of communication by various critical theorists (for example, Habermas, 1984). But there are equally relevant parallels between the argument that certain Structural responsibilities and social processes are localized in organizational sectors, and the contingency perspective of Henry Mintzberg (1979, 1983). The parallel to critical theory should lead us to be a little less surprised by answer of this essay to a central question posed earlier: Structure does tend, in typical modern organizations, toward undesirable consequences. The process of deciding on and elaborating Structure is separate from and dominating over work processes, with consequent deprivation of voice and distortion of communication inside the organization. There is some ambivalent evidence that unusually egalitarian participative management designs may slow or even reverse this tendency (Miles, 1980: chap. 12, on Sweden and Israel).

In anthropology, a debate about Samoan culture between Margaret Mead and Lincoln Freeman has been attributed to the fact that they were differently located in Samoan social structure, with informants who differed systematically by status and gender. A tacit argument of this chapter has been that the various themes outlined at the beginning are separated by a rather similar consideration: They each describe as basic and general a phenomenon that is localized and has a main specific role—perhaps as technique, or ideology, or unintended consequence—in some particular sector. Each is thus a partial view. But more importantly, they cannot simply be "added up" or arrayed as in a textbook or the first part of this chapter, to give a valid view of organizational communication. Communication must be viewed as an emergent "field" in organizations, constituted in the relations of many different sorts of processes; so it cannot be captured without discussing both the processes and the relations among them.

This chapter, then, has implications on two levels. The "empirical" implications are fairly obvious. If the argument sketched out above is true, interviews should reveal systematic differences among employees in their knowledge of and attitudes about Structure, their formal power and autonomy, their articulation of its jargon and rationales, and their participation in its creation and change, as we go, say, up and down the hierarchy, or among different line and staff functions. But apart from the truth of this particular implication, my argument implies that the study of organizational communication necessarily involves and invites multiplicity. I have tried to develop several relatively new themes and array them with the old in a new pattern. But I expect that the pattern, and the themes themselves, will require many reconstructions in a context of new studies and historical change in organizations themselves. Such reconstructions and repatternings are usual in intellectual discourse (McKeon, 1967), but they are especially suitable in the social science of differentiated, reflexive, society-embedded, and formalized organizations.

NOTES

1. The description of indirectness, like the description of metacommunication and of distanciation, is couched at the level of general theory. It is definitely true that many organizations make special provisions to allow "voice" to their employees, through participative management, quality circles, and the like (but see my reference to these devices later in the chapter). But even in such organizations, the effect of Structure is to make communication generally indirect, and participative devices can only be occasional or limited therapy for the general disability.

2. An argument similar in its general point to this subsection, and to this chapter in general, is that of Hummel (1982), and I did not realize the resemblance till my essay was almost complete. Hummel's book draws on critical theory to criticize bureaucratic processes, and is definitely worthy of study, despite occasional sensationalism, but seems

to differ from my position in several ways. First, his general focus is on human service agencies dealing with clients, and he assimilates communication among organization members to agent-client communication, whereas I try to isolate distinctive traits of one subset of intermember communication. Second, his approach is almost totally negative—he seems not to make an effort to provide a balanced description of communication in bureaucracies, or consider nonbureaucratic interaction in the organization, or analyze the benefits of Structure. Thus he describes communication as unidirectional, not indirect, thereby (a) ignoring the prevalence of upward and horizontal communication, as well as noncommunicative phenomena that have the same substitutive function, and (b) neglecting the coordination function of communication to pay attention to control. Third, he sets forth a number of features of "life in bureaucracy" without connecting them systematically, whereas the connections among three such features are of central interest in this chapter. His argument is too complex to be reviewed fully here, but deserves consideration at more length.

3. An elementary note: "reproduction" can, indeed must, involve change—it is not a static process of conformity. The concept involves the simple assumption that action is and must be in a situation—we never act after "wiping the slate clean"—and so our acts and their outcomes embody, in a sense, the initial situation. But they can embody it and still change it radically.

Chapter 7

COMMUNICATION AND UNOBTRUSIVE CONTROL IN CONTEMPORARY ORGANIZATIONS

Phillip K. Tompkins and George Cheney

As St. Bernard of Clairvaux wrote perceptively to the Pope in 1150: "Your power is not in possessions, but in the hearts of men" [Curran, 1982: 204].

Much that happens to a professional forester in the Forest Service thus tends to tighten the links binding him to the organization. . . . whatever the purposes, one outcome of [such experiences] is that field officers (among others) make their administrative decisions in terms of the consequences for the Forest Service, and in terms of criteria the leaders of the Forest Service wish them to employ [Kaufman, 1960: 197].

It's surprising how little is said about the shaping of values in current management theories. . . . The estimate of 3M quoted [earlier]—"The brainwashed members of an extremist political sect are no more conformist in their central beliefs"— remember, is the same 3M that's not known for its rigidity but for its unbridled entrepreneurship [Peters and Waterman, 1982: 103].

To say that we must recognize the dilemmas of organization society is not to be inconsistent with the hopeful premise that organization society can be as compatible for the individual as any previous society. We are not hopeless beings caught in the grip of forces we can do little about, and wholesale damnations of our society lend a further mystique to organization. Organization has been made by man, it can be changed for man [Whyte, 1956: 13].

In his review of the established paradigm (that is, tradition) in organizational theory, Benson (1977) found that power had been relegated to the status of just another variable, one among many variables determining the regularities of organizational behavior. Commonsense and casual observation would suggest otherwise; that power may be *the* overarching factor in determining such regularities. Benson called this the power critique of the established paradigm, and in his review of theory and research in organizational communication,

AUTHOR'S NOTE: This chapter was originally presented at the Second International Communication Association/Speech Communication Association jointly sponsored Conference on Interpretive Approaches to Organizational Communication, Alta, Utah, August 1982. A second draft was presented at the Speech Communication Association Annual Meeting, Louisville, Kentucky, November 1982.

Tompkins (1984: 706) concluded that "the *power* critique is devastatingly applicable to research on organizational communication. *Rarely is power mentioned* even as a variable in organizational life." The purpose of this chapter is to link the concept of power with other core concepts toward the goal of limning the profile, if not all details, of a communication-centered and rhetorically informed theory of organization that is explained within a historical context. We shall proceed by first analyzing power and control; second, decision making; third, a revised theory of the enthymeme; fourth, the premise of identification; and fifth, communication. Throughout, the role of unobtrusive control in contemporary organizations will be stressed.

POWER, CONTROL, AND ORGANIZATIONAL HISTORY

We find it useful to distinguish between power and control. We define the noun *power* as an ability or capacity to achieve some goal even against the resistance of others; we define the verb *control* as the exercise or act of achieving a goal; we define the direct object of control as those members who can provide services essential to organizational goal attainment.

Organizational power then is the ability or capacity of a person or persons to control the contributions of others toward a goal. Much existing theory has failed to see the relationships among these grammatical elements. For example, power is rarely mentioned by positivistic social scientists because it is not palpable, directly observable, or easily measured (by contrast, social actors often treat power with misplaced concreteness—for example, a reification of power). Control, on the other hand, can sometimes be directly observed, but it may be oversimplified in isolation if the act of controlling is not linked to the "invisible" nouns of ability or capacity; to complicate matters further, control today is increasingly exercised in unobtrusive ways.

Because the social locus of power has shifted significantly in the past five centuries or so, and because there has also been a change in the methods of organizational control, this section of the chapter will be historical in method. We shall give special attention to the rise of "juristic persons" in their most common manifestation—the modern corporation. We shall also examine how the strategies of controlling behavior in organizations have changed in this century, resulting in a trend that we expect to continue.

In the hope that neither minors nor mental incompetents are included among us, the writers and readers of this paper are what the law calls "natural persons." "Juristic persons," by contrast, are such entities as corporations, churches, trade associations, and towns.

We live in an age in which power is separated from its source. Natural persons, including owners and agents, are now men and women marginal to the corporation and are easily replaced. The sum total of power held by natural persons has decreased while the sum total of power held by juristic persons has increased. Thus the dilemma faced at incorporation—that to gain the advantages of organization natural persons must give power to the corporate actor—has tilted in favor of the juristic person. Even Ford has now wrested power away from the family that gave the corporation its name. Natural persons, says Coleman, will continue to suffer the psychic consequences of this shifting of power: alienation and powerlessness.

And organizations will continue to enjoy the benefits of their "person-status." As Burke (1973: 275) notes in his brilliant essay, "The Rhetorical Situation," tracking down the actions of corporations in their roles as persons opens a "whole new set of persuasive marvels." Tompkins and Lampert (1980) highlight one example of the power of the person metaphor in that a single corporation is exempt from conspiracy law; that is, a "person" cannot conspire with itself. It would be interesting indeed to explore the relations among the terms corporation, corporate, corporeal, and corpus, suggesting the reification of organization as an "extension" of body.

From sketching the growth of the juristic person, we now turn to an examination of the corporation's base for power and mechanisms of control. In an analysis not inconsistent with Coleman's, Galbraith (1979: 61) traces the shift of power in Western societies in the following way: "As before with land and later with capital, power goes with what is difficult, costly and uncertain of procurement. So it is with organization—organized competence—that the power now lies." The locus of power *within* the corporation, he continues,

> embraces all who bring specialized knowledge, talent or experience to group decision-making. This, not the narrow management group, is the guiding intelligence—the brain—of the enterprise. There is no name for all who participate in group decision-making or the organization they form. I propose to call this organization the Technostructure [Galbraith, 1979: 74].

Given this view of the concentration of societal power in the corporation and corporate power in the Technostructure, how is this power exercised in the internal management of the corporation? The answer to this question requires another historical analysis, this time not of power, but of the organization's exercise of *control* over its own members.

According to Edwards (1981), a system of organizational control must contain three (inescapably communicative) processes: (1) the direction of work tasks; (2) the evaluation of the work done; and (3) the rewarding and disciplining of the workers. Edwards also sees three historically important and essentially different strategies of organizing these communicative processes:

> The first is what I term "simple control"; capitalists exercise power openly, arbitrarily, and personally (or through hired bosses who act in much the same way). Simple control formed the organizational basis of 19th century firms and continues today in the small enterprises of the more competitive industries. The second is "technical control": the control mechanism is embedded in the physical technology of the firm, designed into the very machines and other physical apparatus of the workplace. The third is "bureaucratic control": control becomes embedded in the social organization of the enterprise, in the contrived social relations of production at the point of production [Edwards, 1981: 161].

These strategies or methods of control represent both the pattern of historical evolution and the array of methods available to contemporary managers. Development has been uneven, of course, from economic sector to sector, and all three types appear in the contemporary economy. For example, simple control was the rule in 19th century businesses (for example, the "mom-and-pop" shop) and survives today in small businesses, though it is not the principal organizing strategy of today's large corporations. And technical control has been a hallmark of the mass-production industrial age, but worker resistance and apathy, as well as unfolding economic realities, are leading gradually to its replacement by bureaucratic means. Let us examine these transformations more closely.

In the late 19th century the increased concentration of capital engendered the growth of organizations; as the number of workers increased so did the layers of supervisors. Tyrannical hired bosses who had the power to hire, set work rates, assign tasks, discipline, and even fire workers, began to use this power for their own rather than the owner's interests. This "uncoupling" of the organization plus the obtrusive, often abusive, supervision that provoked labor unrest made simple control inefficient in large organizations. Owners and managers pursued two solutions to the problems experienced with simple control: technical control of the blue collar workers and bureaucratic control of white collar employees. These latter two strategies of control were found to be more impersonal and predictable than the simple control. Technical control, according to Edwards (1981: 166), is more than mere machine pacing; technical control

> only emerges when the entire production process of the plant, or large segments of the plant, are based on a technology which paces and directs the labor process. In this case, the pacing and direction of work transcend the particular workplace and are thus beyond the power of even the immediate boss.

This kind of technical control went well beyond the principles of "Taylorism." Scientific management was limited to rather small segments of work and still relied on direct supervision, albeit of the functional variety. Around the turn of the century, one of the earliest industries to approach complete technical control through continuous-flow production was meat packing (in this case, a *dis*assembly production line). Another was textiles. The apotheosis of technical control was achieved with the "endless conveyor" of Ford's Highland Park plant. As Edwards (1981: 168-169) puts it:

> The line eliminated "obtrusive foremanship," that is, close supervision in which the foreman simultaneously directed production, inspected and approved work, and disciplined workers. In its place, the line created a situation in which the foreman was relieved of responsibility for the first element of the control system. This change marked an important first step away from the simple control model which granted the foreman all the prerequisites of an "entrepreneur" within his own shop.

In 1914, at the Ford plant the ratio of foremen (all ranks) to workers was an amazing 1 to 58, in violation of the classical principle of span of control, proof that the work was directed by the *line*, not by the foreman. Some supervisors were still needed, however, for the second and third elements of control—evaluation of work, and dispensation of rewards and punishment.

Like simple control, complete technical control reached a limit of efficiency when workers realized that a small group could stop all work by shutting down part of the line; all other workers necessarily joined the strike. Resentment of complete technical control on the part of workers was manifested in the sit-down strikes and the organizing success of the CIO in the 1930s. Worker resistance motivated other large corporations to seek a less obtrusive method of control, sometimes combined with the other strategies and sometimes implemented in a relatively pure form: bureaucratic control. The rule of law—the law as handed down by the corporation to its members—replaced the rule of the supervisor's command. "Work activities became defined and directed by a set of work criteria: the rules, procedures, and expectations governing particular jobs" (Edwards, 1981: 172). The supervisor now had little to do by way of directing work; even the evaluation of the job was done by criteria specified above and known to the employee. Edwards provides an extended case study of such strategies as utilized by Polaroid. The worker or employee is rated on a seven-point scale in four categories; one category deals with the worker's competence, another with the quantity of work done, leaving two to cover the worker's compliance with rules; this implies that the firm values *compliance with rules* at least as highly as productivity.

In motivating workers, bureaucratic firms have chosen to emphasize the positive incentives of rewarding cooperation and reliability rather than the negative sanctions of docking and sacking. "The positive incentives, relief from capricious supervision, the right to appeal grievances and bid for jobs, the additional job security from seniority—all these make the day-to-day worklife of Polaroid's workers more pleasant" (Edwards, 1981: 178). Good jobs up the hierarchical ladder become available to workers loyal to the firm; the firm uses its policy of promotion from within as one conscious strategy of identification. Polaroid

> thus provides tremendous rewards—higher pay, more rights, greater job security—to workers who accept the system and seek by individual effort, to improve their lot within it. Moreover, the considerable rewards to workers who stay long periods at Polaroid insure that this identification will be a long-term affair. Organizing efforts to build a union at Polaroid have failed due in large measure to this structure [Edwards, 1981: 177-178].

If it appears that bureaucracy has solved the problems that plagued simple and technical control, some think this an illusion. Bureaucratic control, says Edwards, is building up discontent, boredom, frustration, and dissatisfaction among workers; and to the degree that workers enjoy job security so will they strive for a greater degree of industrial democracy, a goal that can be threatening to those who now have power and exercise control over others.

In recognition of recent economic and social developments, we add a fourth category of control to Edwards's list: "concertive." With apologies for the introduction of a neologism, we mean to account for the emergence of a new and postbureaucratic type of control—one that stresses teamwork and coordination at all stages of production (see, for example, Reich, 1983), flexibility and innovation (see, for example, Reich, 1983), "flat" hierarchy (see, for example, Mintzberg, 1979), blurring of line and staff distinctions (see, for example, Mintzberg, 1979), intense face-to-face interaction concerning nonroutine decisions (see, for example, Peters and Waterman, 1982), and relative value consensus (see, for example, Ouchi, 1980; Peters and Waterman, 1982). In the concertive organization, the explicit written rules and regulations are largely replaced by the common understanding of values, objectives, and means of achievement, along with a deep appreciation for the organization's "mission." This we call—to modify a phrase in current use—the "soul of the new organization." Concertive organizations display simultaneous "loose" and "tight" properties (Peters and Waterman, 1982) because members can be depended upon to act within a range of alternatives tied to implicit but highly motivating core values. Further, we speculate that the multilateral nature of control in concertive organizations might actually increase the *total amount of control* in the system.

Of course, organization of this type is not entirely new; research and development labs have consistently displayed the characteristics mentioned above, thus coming into conflict with the bureaucratic organizations of which many are part. However, today we see the spread of concertive organization in a variety of forms. Most notable are the small and moderately sized high-technology work units of the Silicon Valley. Such organizations and their characteristic processes illustrate what Reich (1983: 47) means by "flexible systems of production": "they all depend on the sophisticated skills of their employees, skills that are often developed within teams. And they all require that traditionally separate business functions (design, engineering, purchasing, manufacturing, distribution, marketing, sales) be merged into a system that can respond quickly to new opportunities." Their products that demand such innovative organization are precision manufactured, custom tailored, and technology driven. Interestingly, some large and traditionally bureaucratic corporations are also beginning to display shades of the concertive form of organization. In the enormously successful French multinational Schlumberger, for example, the emphasis is on creating coexistent feelings of belonging and autonomy (Auletta, 1983). In other words, employees, particularly managers, are allowed a great deal of decision-making freedom while they adhere tenaciously to a set of core values; they communicate directly with one another in order to handle novel cases or the challenges of innovation. Consequently, decision makers do not get a sense that they are working for a giant impersonal company (even though Schlumberger operates in 92 countries), but can earnestly say, as does one unit manager: "I have the impression that I'm running my own company" (p. 107). Thus it is not surprising that Schlumberger is one of the select few corporations exalted in the recently popular *In Search of Excellence* (Peters and Waterman, 1982).

To summarize this section, we have seen a historical trend in which power has been transferred from natural persons to juristic ones, from land and capital to organized competence. Power has been exercised in four different control modes: simple, technical, bureaucratic, and concertive. These control strategies represent an evolutionary process, yet all exist today, and often in various combinations rather than in pure forms or "ideal types." The trend is away from obtrusive control by owners, their agents, and the assembly line to the unobtrusive control of workers by shared premises—both explicit and implicit, from negative sanctions that instill fear to the positive incentives of security, identification, and common mission; from personal, localized, and capricious control to the nonpersonal, pervasive and predictable. Here, of course, we have operated from the organization's "perspective," illustrating trends in the acquisition of power and use of control. Here we consider the bureaucratic and concertive forms as contexts where unobtrusive control predominates.

DECISION MAKING AND DECISIONAL PREMISES

As if in anticipation of Edwards's evolutionary analysis of organizational control strategies, Simon (1976) set out several decades ago what Perrow (1979) has called a theory of *unobtrusive* control. Although presented in the first edition of his *Administrative Behavior* (published in 1947, parts of which were written eight years earlier), Simon's theory has, if anything, increased in relevance as our society has become more organizationally complex. Written as it was from the disciplinary perspective of public administration, a subfield of political science, the theory was not intended to apply to small firms and primitive factory conditions, and for that reason we place it in the larger context of this quadripartite theory of control.

In his search for the appropriate unit of analysis for the study of human behavior, Simon (1976: xii) rejected the concept of role as too imprecise and the concept of act as too gross, settling instead on the decisional *premise*. Choice, or decision, is "the process of 'drawing conclusions from premises.' It is therefore the *premise* (and a large number of these are combined in most decisions) rather than the whole *decision* that serves as the smallest unit of analysis." Organizational behavior is oriented toward goals or objectives. In general, these objectives provide the ethical or value premises of organizational decisions; means are associated with factual premises believed to be true or probably true even when not empirically established. A hierarchical means-ends chain connects (however imperfectly) the overarching objectives of an organization with the smallest of instrumental tasks.

Organizations (that is, managers) control the behavior of their members, according to Simon, by controlling their decisions. In echoing Barnard (1968: 152), who argued that the "inculcation of motives" is the most powerful and subtle means of organizational persuasion, Simon explains that members are impressed with the decisional premises, value and factual, from which their decisions are to be drawn. "Given a complete set of value and factual premises," holds Simon (1976: 223), "there is only one decision which is consistent with rationality." (Or, as we find more typically, a decision maker is directed toward a range of decisions that are consistent with the premises deemed relevant to the particular situation.) And, "the behavior of a rational person can be controlled, therefore, if the value and factual premises upon which he bases his decision are specified for him. This control can be complete or partial" (Simon, 1976: 223).

The methods by which the organization influences decisional premises of its members (in effect, asking employees to apply *its* premises on *the* premises) include the criterion of efficiency and organizational identification, which have an internal locus; and authority, training, and communication (the latter Simon treats in a circumscribed manner), which have an external locus (Simon, 1976). To the list we add the screening of decisional premises during recruitment and selection of new members; this helps shape the ongoing decision processes of the organization.

Thus using Simon's theory along with concepts and principles to be discussed later, we answer in organizational terms what Lukes (1974) called for—a three-dimensional view of the exercise of power. While a one-dimensional view focuses on observable decision-making and influence behavior concerning *public* issues, a two-dimensional view admits the ways in which potential issues and related viewpoints are denied access to the public arena through "non-decisions" which explicitly disallow them.[1] But a three-dimensional view, says Lukes, is more encompassing because it stresses the (1) institutional forces and social arrangements that (2) subtly and often unapparently act to (3) create an image of consensus. And we witness this in organizations, "industries," institutions, sectors, and societies. Clegg (1979), who on a number of other issues disagrees sharply with Lukes (for example, the influence of economic order), makes a parallel point about the structure of control, "which maintains its effectiveness not so much through overt action, as through its ability to appear to be *the* natural convention" (p. 147). Burke's and Gramsci's (1971) independent formulations of "hegemony" (see the discussion of both in Tompkins, 1985) and Marcuse's (1964) critique of one-dimensional society display a similar thrust, arguing that the forms and values of control become commonsensical in such a way that opposition and even reflection are automatically suppressed. With these ideas about power and control in mind, let us continue to explain the workings of communication and unobtrusive control in organizations.

Even when the process of controlling decisional premises is subtle or unobtrusive, why would an individual member or employee accept the organization's decisional premises as controlling his or her decisions? First, individuals necessarily sacrifice a degree of autonomy when they participate in organizational life. Second, and more apparent, is the acceptance of decisional premises in exchange for incentives, typically wages and salaries, offered by the organization. Members who feel that their efforts are equitably compensated for by the organization will usually continue to participate and use organizational premises as guides for making work-related choices (Barnard, 1968; March and Simon, 1958; Simon, 1976).[2]

Third, and often overlaying these first two relational dimensions, is the "aura" of authority, or perceived "legitimate" power. Barnard (1968) sees authority as interpreted by the receiver of a directive at the time the directive is issued. Authority, for Barnard, is "the character of a communication (order) in a formal organization by virtue of which it is accepted by a contributor or a 'member' of the organization as governing the action he contributes" (p. 163). And he continues: "If a directive communication is accepted by one to whom it is addressed, its authority for him is confirmed or established" (p. 163). Such authority has two essential aspects for Barnard: the subjective—how it is perceived—and the objective—the identifiable aspect of an "authoritative" message. (In this way Barnard's view is basically compatible with Weber's, 1978, classic formulation, which concerned itself with both the meanings social actors ascribe to authority in everyday life and with the fact of compliance itself.)

Nevertheless, Barnard's (1968) stress is on the *receiver* of a message or directive and his or her interpretations of its authoritativeness. Importantly, Barnard notes that authority is usually stable because (1) certain conditions prevail (that is, *most* directives are seen as being in the organization's and the individual's best interests); (2) a "zone of indifference" exists within which organizational members will not question directives; and (3) most groups and organizations foster an informal norm of conformity.

In sum, the perception of significant authority, along with the necessary sacrifice of autonomy and the appeal of specific incentives serve as compelling reasons for individual cooperation and acceptance of organizational premises as controlling his/her decisions.

But there is much more at work here. These principles do not fully capture the dynamics of the individual-organization relationship. Moreover, while we have omitted numerous details and qualifications in our abstract of Simon's theory, we criticize Simon for not directly addressing the failure of organizations to exercise complete control over their members' decisions.

It is a fact, for example, that employees disobey, engage in whistle blowing, organize unions, strike, and even commit sabotage. A tentative explanation is that individuals bring their personal decisional premises, value and factual, with them to the organization. When the organization's premises are in conflict with these personal ones, the latter may control decisions. Moreover, even when individuals seek to apply the premises of the organization, they often find it necessary or desirable to modify them. In addition, the informal organization as well as the union or the professional association often try to inculcate the individual with premises that are similarly in contradiction to those of the organization. If more successful than the organization in inculcating decisional premises, informal groups and unions will thereby weaken the organization's control.

Thus it is essential that our analysis now shift from a largely organizational (managerial) perspective on control of members to a more individual perspective on participation in organizations. First, we build on, but, to some extent, depart from Simon to explain the enthymemic nature of the decision process and later return to Simon's theory to emphasize the individual or "internal" source of organizational influence—identification.

THE ORGANIZATIONAL ENTHYMEMES

The preceding discussion of decision making as the drawing of conclusions from premises calls to mind at least two long-established forms of thought and expression: the logical syllogism and the rhetorical syllogism. For reasons to be developed later we can disregard the logical syllogism at this point and concentrate instead on the rhetorical form.

The rhetorical syllogism, or what we call enthymeme$_1$, is thought to be one of Aristotle's original discoveries. Even though Aristotle called it the substance of rhetorical persuasion, we have no unambiguous definition of enthymeme$_1$ in his words. After summarizing a variety of conflicting interpretations of enthymeme$_1$, Bitzer (1959: 408) cogently argued that it "succeeds as an instrument of rational persuasion because its premises are always drawn from the audience." The persuader can either express or suppress its parts as taste dictates. Extending this analysis, Delia (1970) showed that enthymeme$_1$ is evaluated by the criteria of logically valid inference only at the risk of committing the "logic fallacy."

Ordinary beliefs, values, opinions, and expectations form the premises of enthymeme$_1$, continued Delia, and the process builds upon the universal psychological process of harmony, equilibrium, or consistency maintenance. Moreover, even if they cannot in fact achieve it, humans prefer to *appear* rational to themselves and others.

It will probably never be known with any degree of certainty whether or not these commentaries are consistent with Aristotle's conception of enthymeme$_1$.[3] Nor will we know with any certainty Aristotle's explanation of how an audience's premises come to be where they are, as they are. However, we can speculate that Aristotle saw little need to account for the sources of premises in a society that was, at least by today's standards, quite homogeneous, even "univocal." Our own society "speaks" through a pluralism of voices, though some are more compelling than others and a few even achieve an occasional or sustained "solo." These reasons and our present purposes require a second conceptualization of the enthymeme.

We shall define enthymeme$_2$ as a syllogistic decision-making process, individual or collective, in which a conclusion is drawn from premises (beliefs, values, expectations) inculcated in the decision maker(s) by the controlling members of the organization. One or more parts of enthymeme$_2$ *may* be suppressed. Organizations offer inducements to the individual in exchange for accepting its decision premises as controlling his or her decisions. Organizationally appropriate decisions, once the premises are inculcated, are motivated by the universal psychological process of consistency maintenance and the individual's desire to "behave organizationally."

We make this distinction for two reasons: (1) the uncertainty and disagreement about what Aristotle *meant* by his invention—enthymeme₁—will probably never be settled, thus giving us additional responsibility for specifying our own intentions with enthymeme₂; (2) the well-known process of socialization (or acculturation) effected in many organizations (that is, of the bureaucratic and concertive types) moves a step beyond Aristotle's assumption that an audience's premises or opinions are "given." Nevertheless, we stress that both forms are structurally the same, must be worked through in some kind of "interaction," and must be audience *focused*. Further, we view the operation of both enthymemes in organizational life as constitutive of secondary socialization or "second culture" in that cultures, like enthymemes, are made of value and factual premises.

We stress that enthymeme₁ and enthymeme₂ are not different processes, and their premises will often overlap. But, they are different ways of treating the sources of major premises. With enthymeme₁, such premises are *assumed* to be in the mind and the messages of the "audience" or organizational member (this is how Aristotle considered the process). Hence a corporate recruit brings a variety of premises to the organization, these being derived from a variety of socializing forces such as family, peer group, education, religion, nation, previous employers, and the like. However, when we can identify the employing organization as an important socializing force *in itself*—that is, when it actively advances a cluster of major premises, seeking to shape employees to fit "the mold"—then it is appropriate to speak of enthymeme₂, a model that highlights the organization as an important premise-source. Some organizations (for example, Mobil, the Roman Catholic Church, the Pentagon) are more active than others in promoting and inculcating major premises, but for most organizations we can identify a ratio or mixture of enthymemes one and two.

Early in 1984 the chief executive officer of General Motors provided us with a good, if hypothetical, example of enthymeme₂. While interviewed on WGN about his corporation's response to competition from the Japanese, he revealed that he had unleashed the corporation's internal media to convince all employees that *quality* was to become the number one priority (decisional premise, in our terms) for all employees. He admitted meeting resistance, even disbelief, but vowed to make it clear even to plant managers that they could "shut down the line" in the interest of quality. This case shows the inculcation of reordered premises (*quality* replaces *quantity*) as well as a minor premise and conclusion supplied by a plant manager to complete the process of enthymeme₂.

It is important to consider which form—the enthymeme or the syllogism of logic— is closer to Simon's theory discussed above. Simon (1976: xxviii) says: "Administrative theory is peculiarly the theory of intended and bounded rationality—of the behavior of human beings who *satisfice* because they have not the wits to *maximize.*" By this very principle one must conclude that "complete control" is not possible; members are directed toward ranges or zones of alternatives. The informal enthymemic process rather than the formal logical process is closer to Simon's rather general remarks.

Other writers have mentioned decisional premises; some have even begun to categorize, if not describe, the decisional processes in which premises are involved. Hickson and McCullough (1980: 52) note that dominant departments within an organization "may have power to shape the premises from which decisions ensue, and the limits of what is considered: they may shape the structure within which the decision is arrived at." Weeks (1980) asserts that premises underlying decision making are maintained by the careful selection of personnel. Thompson (1980: 220) observes that "organizational control need not be exercised anew with regard to each situation and decision; it is pre-established in the premises of decision-making" and calls this "formal rationality." He also observes, following Weber, a "substantive rationality" or "logics-in-use," one such being the "logic of symbolic-appropriateness." Thompson (1980: 221) then provides a starting point for an ideological critique: "It must be emphasized that the social construction of reality in organizations, the process of defining and interpreting what exists, is an ongoing accomplishment. And the rationalities and logics employed are seldom merely technical and neutral; in fact, the very claim to technical neutrality frequently constitutes a value-laden ideology."

Karpik (1978) has offered a concept, "logics of action," which is similar to our "organizational enthymemes." The exact degree of overlap may be impossible to determine because Karpik's concept is expressed in highly abstract terms. He has said that the concept is related to the notion of rationality, but because what characterizes an organization is a chain of ends and means, there can be no one best way. "Hence, there is no one rationality but forms of rationality, which I call *logics of action*" (Karpik, 1978: 46). The concept is an analytic instrument, one constructed by on observer wishing to designate forms of coherence among organizational objectives. The logics can be used equally well as criteria of evaluation by organizations and their subunits, and "which are as valid for decisions and procedures as for individual and collective practices" (Karpik, 1978: 46). As can be seen by these paraphrases and quotations, Karpik's concept is somewhat elusive. More useful are the categories of logics of action he distinguished in a study of the strategies pursued by French corporations. These logics of action include (1) adaptive, (2) prestige, (3) technical, (4) production, (5) profitability, (6) puissance, and (7) innovative logics.

To this list we add a superordinate logic, what Scott and Hart (1979) call the "organizational imperative." Put one way the imperative reads: "*Whatever is good for the individual can only come from the modern organization*" (Scott and Hart, 1979: 43). This master logic undergirds the others and in many instances results in organizational values being accepted "as *given*, beyond reflection and discussion" (Scott and Hart, 1979: 9). In the 1980s, while we witness growing and popular attacks on "big government," we see increasing confidence among many in the ability of "big business" to solve societal problems.

In considering enthymeme₂ and organizational logics of action, we have moved closer to the individual perspective on the intricate process of decision making in organizations. We have shown how individuals become engaged in the process, allowing key premises to be inculcated and then "filling in" minor premises and producing decisions consistent with organizational "logics." However, here we still find the member in a relatively passive role; thus we have not gone far enough. To capture the active nature of individual participation, we must consider both enthymeme₁ and enthymeme₂ and synthesize them with the concept of identification.

ORGANIZATIONAL IDENTIFICATION

The link between organizational identification and decision making is a powerful one.[4] Simon treats identification as central to understanding the ongoing process of decision making in an organization. He explains that the act of identifying leads the decision maker to select a particular alternative, to choose one course of action over another. Simon's (1976: 205) operational definition of identification reflects this decision-making emphasis: "A person identifies with a group when, in making a decision, he evaluates the several alternatives of choice in terms of the consequences for the specified group." Viewed in this sense, organizational identification reduces the range of decision: the decision maker's choice is largely confined to the alternative(s) associated with his or her personal targets of identification.

From an organizational (or managerial) perspective, member identification is beneficial in that it "guarantees" that decisions will be consistent with organizational objectives, even in the absence of external stimuli (Simon, 1976). This is the idea behind an IBM personnel director's comment that the company's policies are aimed at providing employees with "the opportunity to contribute in their own way to the business objectives" (Piersol, 1980: 1). Identification is directed toward the organization, but it must have its "source" within the individual; the employee makes his or her *own* contribution through making decisions in accord with the organization's interests (Cheney, 1983b). In this way, the individual acquires an "organization personality"; he or she finds an area of acceptance within which he or she will assume the "role" of the organization, accepting the value and factual premises of the organization as relevant to on-the-job decisions (Barnard, 1968; Simon, 1976).

But we often find the member surrounded by a myriad of values and goals tied to an array of organizational and extra-organizational targets. It is the process of identification, according to Simon, that focuses the attention of the decision maker on *particular* values and facts—those associated with the most salient organizational targets. In short, identification becomes a necessary cognitive coping mechanism for the individual making decisions in a complex organizational setting; it is a means by which the member constructs the "environment of decision" and effectively contends with the problem of rational choice. Thus through identification, the decision maker's range of "vision" is narrowed "by selecting particular values, particular items of empirical knowledge, and particular behavior alternatives for consideration, to the exclusion of other values, other knowledge, and other possibilities" (Simon, 1976: 210). The organization member "sees" that with which he or she identifies.

The identification itself may be with either a key organizational objective (for example, manufacturing automobiles, making a profit, educating children, serving the public) or with the sheer "conversation" of an organization, aimed at preserving and augmenting an organization's influence in society (Simon, 1976). Note that in both cases the ultimate target can be either the organization as a whole or one of its subunits.

As Simon (1976: 218) explains, there is an "undesirable" effect of identification in that "it prevents the organized individual from making (organizationally) correct decisions in cases where the restricted area of values with which he identifies himself must be weighed against other values outside that area." In all cases, the decision maker is biased toward alternatives tied to his/her targets of identification—these alternatives are not always in the entire organization's interests. Such is the case when a decision maker's identification with a subunit overshadows his/her identification with the larger organization.

A crucial concern for the organization then becomes how to ensure that decision-making members will be attracted to alternatives that are consonant with organizational values and goals. Upper management may view part of its job as the "managing" of identifications. Following Simon's advice, the manager or administrator should be aware of "competing" targets of identification that can command their own allegiance and the allegiances of other organization members. Moreover, from the organization's perspective, decisions should be "allocated" to positions where efforts directed at corporate goals will be maximized. As Simon (1976: 215) states, "Each decision should be located at a point where it will be of necessity approached as a question of efficiency [the degree to which goals are reached relative to the available resources] rather than a question of adequacy [the degree to which certain goals are reached]." For Simon, the individual *seeks to supply* the efficiency premise, but must have favorable circumstances to use the criterion effectively.

Thus the manager with the criterion of adequacy in mind may view the success of his/her department only in terms of the gross output of goods or services, with little or no thought to weighing the production of the department in terms of broader organizational concerns. Simon (1976) suggests that such a parochial outlook can often be traced to narrow identification with department goals and the preservation and growth of that subunit of the organization. Hence the authority to measure a department's success should, according to Simon, reside with a decision maker one level above, one who can evaluate the contributions of a number of departments relative to the organizationwide criterion of efficiency.

Of course, the allocation of the decision-making function is equally important, if not more so, to the organization member: Individuals frequently experience tension when they must weigh the relative merits of alternatives tied to more than one salient target of identification. As Simon (1976: 215-216) notes, "The administrator who is faced with a choice between social [i.e., extra-organizational] and organizational values usually feels a twinge of conscience, stronger or weaker, when he puts organizational objectives before broader social ones." While Simon acknowledges that organizations cannot totally free the decision maker of such conflicts (especially those involving extra-organizational targets), he maintains that they can and should reduce the tensions between opposing identification targets within the organization. Through the careful *allocation of the decision-making function*, organization members will less often find themselves in approach-approach conflicts where two alternatives are associated with equally attractive targets of identification. (Of course, Simon approaches this subject in terms of what is best for the organization.)

Interestingly, individual decision makers often do not weigh the values of one organizational unit against those of another, even when they identify with both units and both sets of the relevant goals. Empirical evidence to this effect led Tompkins and Cheney (1983) to refine Simon's theory of decision making and identification. They use the concept of *role*—a sociological notion discarded by Simon as too rigid and constraining—to explain the anomaly. Specifically, the researchers (Cheney, 1982; Tompkins and Cheney, 1983) found that identifications seen as relevant to one role are not always viewed as relevant by the same organization member in another role. That is, a member who clearly identifies with an organizational target may not consider the consequences of his/her actions for that target *if* the individual does not view the target (and the target's values and goals) as relevant to a particular sphere or scene of activity. Consistent with this interpretation, Tompkins and Cheney (1983: 144) offer a restatement of the relationship between organizational identification and decision making: "A person identifies with a unit when, in making a decision, the person in one or more of his/her organizational roles perceives that unit's values or interests as relevant in evaluating the alternatives of choice." The researchers' confidence in this reformulation is bolstered by a personal communication from Simon to the senior author. Simon (1981) acknowledges that "a person may simultaneously hold several identifications, each being invoked in turn when he finds himself in a different role."

In another study of the relationship between identification and decision making, Cheney (1983a) found that some employees of a corporation acted on certain organizationally held premises without identifying very strongly with their employer. That is, some members had interests that *coincided* with those of the organization; they did not, however, truly "share" the premises of the organization or value those premises *because* the organization did. In this way, a design engineer can be concerned with safety as a value premise—one that is frequently voiced by the organization—yet not identify with the organization.

For this reason, Cheney (1983a: 353; emphasis deleted) added special emphasis to part of the operational definition: "A person identifies with a unit when, in making a decision, the person in one or more of his/her organizational roles perceives that unit's interests—*as* that unit's interests—to be relevant in evaluating the alternatives of choice." And Cheney explains: "For the identifying employee the fact that his/her organization holds particular premises in high regard makes them more appealing."

We subsequently realized that the administrative bias in Simon's definition—it *assumes* that the consequences for the group will be positive—had crept into our definitions as well. In order, then, to allow for role-relevance, noncoincidental alignment of perceived interests, and selection on the basis of positive consequences, we redefine organizational identification as follows: *A decision maker identifies with an organization when he or she desires to choose the alternative that best promotes the perceived interests of that organization.*

By turning to Burke (1966), we can further elaborate on the connection between organizational identification and decision making. In his novel, *Towards a Better Life*, Burke (1966: 215) writes that "if decision were a choice between alternatives, decisions would come easy. Decision is the selection and formulation of alternatives." It seems likely that an individual's identifications come into play in this preliminary stage of the decision-making process, as well as in the actual choosing from among alternative. The organization member is limited at the outset to alternatives tied to his/her identifications; other options will simply not come into view, and therefore will not be considered. Thus identification can be used to explain how alternatives are recognized as such by the organization member.

This amplifies Simon's point about the necessity and utility of identification. Our identifications focus our attention in two ways: (1) by guiding us to "see" certain "problems" and alternatives, and (2) by biasing our choices toward alternatives tied to the most salient identifications. At both stages, identifying operates to narrow the decision maker's span of attention. As a result, the process of intentionally rational choice becomes greatly simplified. In the same communication mentioned above, Simon (1981) accepts this interpretation: "I agree strongly with your view that the most important impact of identifications upon decisions may be through the determination of which decision alternatives will be considered."

In sum, organizational identification guides the individual member in supplying premises for participation in the organization. It plays a subtle and powerful role in this process because as Burke (1937: 140) writes, "In America, it is *natural* for a [person] to identify [him- or herself] with the business corporation [he or she] serves." Identification acts in concert with both enthymeme₁ and enthymeme₂. For example, an individual may wish to identify with a large corporation even prior to entry, thus seeking out the organization's major premises during the hiring process, orientation, and the first days on the job. Also, identification may accompany the acquisition of premises during organizational socialization for that individual or for another who did not hold identification as an original aim. When the organization takes members as "givens," making only a minimal effort to modify decisional premises (a rare occurrence indeed given our society's heterogeneity), the decision process will most closely parallel the traditional notion of the enthymeme, what we call enthymeme$_1$. When the organization acts to inculcate major premises (i.e., its overarching goals and objectives) in members, hoping that members will see extensions to minor premises that point them to specific decisions consistent with organizational "logics," this we call enthymeme$_2$. In sum, while enthymeme$_1$ is an adaptation *to* the "audience," enthymeme$_2$ is an adaptation *of* the "audience." But in each case the member is arriving at conclusions drawn from organizationally preferred premises.[5]

THE ROLE OF COMMUNICATION

We regard identification and the enthymeme as inherently communicative. However, we must now add details about the process of communication. To begin at the beginning, it seems obvious that for power to be effective, its holders must communicate their wishes, orders, and requests—even though subordinates often try mightily to anticipate the desires of the powerful. Communication manifests itself in interacts and double interacts, the latter having been variously described by Weick as the "substance of organizing" (1979: 4), "organization acts" (1979: 34), the organizational "unit of analysis" (1979: 89), and the "elements of organization" (1979: 118). We see a particular double interact as more basic and elemental than others: the *double interact of control*. Supervisor A gives *directions* to subordinate B; subordinate B complies (or fails to comply) and the "messages" concerning compliance and goal attainment are *monitored* through feedback loops leading back to A; supervisor A assesses the results of B's performance and accordingly dispenses *rewards* and *punishments* to B. This double interact of control—directing, monitoring, and rewarding/punishing—simultaneously provides us with the basic act of organizing and demonstrates why communicating and organizing are nearly synonymous.[6] Simple control is the paradigm case of the double interact of control: In superior-subordinate communication, we have the one giving directives to the other, monitoring the result, and communicating rewards and punishments. The last three strategies of control (technical, bureaucratic, and concertive) substitute the line, the rules, and the premises for the command; even here, however, the superior must teach the subordinate how to adjust to the line, must teach the subordinate the rules to be followed and the premises to be applied. Monitoring and dispensation must, in any case, still be effected via communication, albeit nonverbal in nature much of the time.

The transition from *one* form of control to another seems to have had a crucial impact on the informal communication practices of the workers. Edwards (1981: 167) has noted how the change from simple control to technical control limited the opportunity for workers to support one another:

With each worker fixed to a physical location in the production process, contact between and among workers nearly ceased. Whereas before workers had made the workday pass more quickly by talking, reading to each other, etc., now each worker simply tended his or her machine. Of particular interest to their employers was the fact that workers had little opportunity to discuss common grievances, compare foremen, exchange views on pay rates or job conditions, etc. Thus, despite their physical proximity, workers had little chance to communicate.

In the bureaucratic and concertive conditions, control becomes "invisible," submerged in the structure of the firm. Moreover, in the bureaucratic mode, highly differentiated job descriptions and finer status distinctions among workers eroded the basis for the workers' identification with one another. Instead, the worker faced the impersonal organization alone. These conditions, of course, are less conducive to union organizing and solidarity, and coupled with the policy of promotion from within add up to a powerful inducement to identify with the formal organization or at least with some large subunit thereof (for example, a division). These circumstances are conducive to the operation of enthymeme$_1$.

It is the case of unobtrusive control on which we wish to concentrate our remaining remarks about communication. In regard to enthymeme$_2$, an organization must communicate decisional premises, value and factual, to its members. When the member perceives a discrepancy between an existing and desired state of affairs, he or she may draw a conclusion from the inculcated premises and act individually. He or she may, however, communicate the discrepancy to other interested parties for a collective decision. The collective formulation of alternatives will necessarily involve communication, as will the search for additional alternatives and evidence of expected consequences. Once a decision has been reached, it must be communicated; otherwise it could not be implemented. In addition, a high-level decision can become a premise for lower-level decisions, as when it is decided by administrators that publication is to be more valued than teaching in university tenure decisions to be made at the department level.

Communication is also required in the act of dissenting from organizationally preferred premises, as well as in the modifying of them. Communication is required when organizations attempt to get actors in their external environment to accept their decisional premises. We believe that much of the communication in this entire process is tacit; that is, there are many kinds of suppressed premises, and this is what makes the organizational enthymemic process so elusive, subtle, pervasive, and, from the organization's standpoint, effective. Organizational members often "fill in" premises while nearly always accepting the "master premise" of putting the organization first. Even whistle blowers nearly always act in ways indicating they have accepted this master premise (Perrucci et al., 1980).

In his classic study of the U.S. Forest Service, Kaufman (1960) has shown how this communication process operates. Although Kaufman's analysis is of a unique kind of public agency, as opposed to a large bureaucratic corporation (our primary object of analysis), his description and interpretation point us to something of an "ideal type" of unobtrusive organizational control. As Kaufman explains, the Forest Service achieved a high degree of integration, despite powerful tendencies toward fragmentation. Through such techniques as authorizations, directions, prohibitions, clearances, and financial allotments the leaders of the agency communicated "preformed decisions," or what we would call enthymemic premises, to the Rangers dispersed in the field throughout the country. Not content to communicate such premises of preformed decisions, the leaders tightened the invisible loop by adding an upward communication system with which to detect and discourage deviation. As Kaufman (1960: 159) put it:

> To resort to an analogy currently in fashion, the Forest Service may be described as a system that has been "programmed" and equipped with a built-in "feedback loop." The program is the set of instructions, the series of sequential steps embodied in the preformed decisions, prescribing the behavior of the members of the organization. The feedback mechanism consists of all the modes of scanning actual behavior in the field and detecting departures from the program; this information flows back to the leaders of the agency, who, if the very fact of detection does not result in corrective action by the personnel involved, then apply sanctions to induce them to conform.

Admitting that the machine metaphor may be misleading because the human range of response is infinitely more complex than mechanical or electrical contrivances, Kaufman (1960: 159) does think it illuminates the great problem of organizational leaders, "the lack of uniformity and predictability in the elements of the system whose operations the leaders seek to control." The analogy also illuminates the impersonal, bureaucratic control mechanism by which the leaders monitor the actual decisions triggered by their enthymemic premises or preformed decisions.

We must emphasize that this job is made easier by the extremely high degree to which Rangers identify themselves with the Forest Service. Would-be Rangers select the Service as a career to be sought early in life. Applicants who probably lack the predisposition to conform to organizational premises or preformed decisions are winnowed out. Postentry training, placement, transfer, and promotion policies broaden their competence and develop the will and capacity to conform. The premises become internalized and adherence to them comes from *inside* the Rangers. Homogeneity of values, the use of agency uniform and badge as symbols, participation in public relations, attention to upward communication, all of these contribute to a deep identification with and commitment to the organization. "Rangers handle most situations precisely as their superiors would direct them to if their superiors stood looking over their shoulders, supervising every detail," wrote Kaufman (1960: 222), in a description of near-perfect unobtrusive control. Kaufman does recognize that this represents a threat to human dignity, a point we cannot stress enough. We would also emphasize an apparent and important irony in the fact that the Rangers consider themselves free, autonomous, independent actors even though they do conform tightly to the organization's decisional premises.

Communication, in our judgment, plays an important, perhaps its most powerful, role in the period temporally prior to decision; that is, in the *process of inculcating enthymemic premises* of the organization. To the extent that enthymemic processes are unobtrusive and the receivers are predisposed to identify with the organization, it may be *dangerous*. We could just as well label the process of premise setting "as indoctrination, brainwashing, manipulation, and false consciousness" (Perrow, 1979: 152). It could even be called "consciousness raising."

As this theory of communication and unobtrusive control has been articulated over a period of several years, a number of researchers at Purdue University and elsewhere have made substantial contributions with seminar and convention papers, articles and book chapters, theses and dissertations. Cheney (1983b) developed a set of categories for analyzing appeals used by major corporations in their house organs to foster identification with the firm on the part of their employees. Following Burke, his coding system revealed appeals to common ground, identification by antithesis, the assumed "we," and the use of unifying symbols.

Tompkins and Cheney (1983), as mentioned above, adapted account analysis, combining it with a questionnaire tapping organizational identification (OIQ), in a study of decision making within the Department of Communication at Purdue University. This led them to a reformulation of Simon's definition of identification as presented above. This study also provided glimpses of the *process* of identification, both the *coming to* and the *resisting of* the organization's attempts to foster identification.

Cheney (1983a) conducted a similar study in one of the 100 largest of the list of *Fortune* 500 corporations. Again triangulating the phenomenon of identification by means of account analysis and the OIQ, Cheney was able to provide insight into, among other things, the process of transferring identifications; that is, the firm studied had been a locally owned tool and gear company before being acquired by a corporate giant. Moreover, Cheney was able to describe the individual members' efforts either to identify or to resist identification.

A study conducted at the University of Arkansas (Laird and Hemphill, 1983) tested three hypotheses drawn from a synthesis by Tompkins and Cheney (1983) of identification and the rules theory of Pearce and Cronen (1980). The research was conducted by means of interviews and questionnaires in two *Fortune* 500 companies. The three hypotheses were: identification varies contextually; identification is positively related to evaluations of communication competence and productivity; and identification is negatively related to the range of acceptable alternative actions that an individual is able to conceive in a given interaction (Laird and Hemphill, 1983: 6). They concluded: "All three hypotheses were supported by results. Multivariate regression demonstrates identification as the strongest of a number of dependent variables influencing evaluation of productivity and communication competence" (Laird and Hemphill, 1983: 1).

Even though Laird and Hemphill measured identification in a way different from our own, we are encouraged by the conclusion that their data support our theoretical position; we are particularly encouraged by their confirmation that identification restricts the range of alternative actions that an individual is able to conceive.

In a dissertation at Purdue University, Bullis (1984) conducted a follow-up of Kaufman's classic study of the U.S. Forest Service. By employing, in addition to the OIQ, a questionnaire developed by Hall et al. (1970) not long after Kaufman's study (1970) for use in the Forest Service, Bullis was able to compare the state of identification at two points in time. She found that the level or state of identification with the organization had dropped significantly (Bullis, 1984). Older members of the organization expressed regret over the change and nostalgia for the "good old days." A host of reasons for this change were advanced, including an influx of specialists (such as wildlife biologists) who maintain an extra-organizational identification with an "invisible college" of like-minded specialists. Bullis also found that organizational control, perhaps as a concomitant to decreasing levels of identification, had become more *obtrusive* since the time of Kaufman's study.

In another dissertation done at Purdue, Cox (1983) pursued the relationship between organizational and extra-organizational identifications held by the same individuals. He selected a racial group as his extra-organizational target of identification and began by developing a Black Identification Questionnaire (BIQ) by the methods used to develop the OIQ. He administered the two instruments to faculty and staff members of three midwestern universities. Not surprisingly, the black staff produced lower organizational identification scores than did the whites. What was surprising is the finding that those black staff members who did identify most highly with the organization also tended to produce the highest black identification scores. In short, blacks who identified highly with their university of employment were not "Uncle Toms." To the contrary, they also tended to identify with their black "brothers and sisters" within and outside the organization.

These results also raise some serious questions for future research. Are some individuals more strongly predisposed to identify with organizational and extraorganizational targets? And if, as it appears, the answer to that question is yes, what factors affect that predisposition? What appeals and inducements offered by an organization cause individuals to come to, or resist, identification? Cox is correct in concluding that his provocative findings have practical applications of considerable potential.

Four seminar papers written at Purdue University in the spring of 1982 became a panel entitled "Communication, Decision Making, and Identification in Organizations" at the Eastern Communication Annual Convention in April 1983. The first, by Mills and Applegate (1983), found evidence of the enthymemic processes described above in a simulated organization created in an undergraduate course in organizational communication. Specifically, they showed that some decisional premises can be verbalized and that such identifiable premises are easily adapted to syllogistic form. Following McGuire (1968, 1981), they attempted a definition of decisional premise as

> a verbalizable object of thought placed upon a dimension of judgment. By a verbalizable object of thought it is meant that a person can describe a nominally categorized stimulus situation, either simple or complex, and make some discriminating response (e.g., regarding its truth or falsity, probability of occurrence, or desirability of occurrence) [Mills and Applegate, 1983: 17].

In the second paper, Gahris (1983) conducted a natural field experiment, including discourse analysis, of enthymemic processes. Students in an introductory course on communication at Purdue University were divided into groups with the assigned task of preparing and executing a fifty-minute presentation to their entire class. The three groups were asked to record all of their planning discussions. They were assured that the tapes would not be transcribed until after the presentations had been graded and that nothing said during the taped discussions could affect their overall grade. The objectives of and the criteria for grading the assignment (value premises) were printed in the class workbook and were highlighted orally by the instructor. The recorded planning discussions were held a week later and the tapes of two groups were transcribed for analysis.

Group decision episodes were isolated and the decisional premises were discovered in the lines of argument leading up to group decisions. In some cases the members were observed to express and discard premises of *personal* preference in favor of the decisional premises inculcated by the workbook and the instructor's oral assignment. The conclusion: "It seems clear . . . the enthymeme$_2$ reasoning process does exist and is operative in the idea that personal premises are supplanted by organizational ones if the inducements for doing so are great enough" (Gahris, 1983: 34).

In the third paper, Geist and Chandler (1983) also employed a form of discourse analysis, this time in a "real-world" organization. Working with transcriptions of weekly staff meetings of a health-care team in a children's psychiatric hospital, the researchers retested the claims made for account analysis by Tompkins and Cheney (1983). The discussions centered on decisions concerning the treatment regimens of patients. "The methods of account analysis," concluded the researchers, "provides an understanding of the broader organizational influence. Accounts, as stated, negotiated, and questioned in small group interaction, provide information about the decisional premises and identifications of the individual members" (Geist and Chandler, 1983: 76).

In the fourth paper, Dionisopoulos and Samter (1983) administered questionnaires to 112 police officers in four departments located in the eastern and midwestern regions of the United States. In addition, Dionisopoulos engaged in research "conversations," some carried out during "ride alongs" with officers on duty. The questionnaire was the OIQ supplemented by similar Likert scales measuring "first impressions," job-related talk, and social interaction within subunits of the departments studied.

The researchers divided the officers into groups of high (N = 30), medium (N = 49), and low (N = 29) identification with the organization after tabulating the 108 usable questionnaires. Although officers at all levels of identification agreed they learned more from fellow officers on the job than in their formal training, there were significant differences in their perceptions of the way in which a new member was welcomed into a section. The questionnaire item, "when I was first assigned to this section, the other officers suggested ways to help me adjust," elicited responses that showed a strong rising monotonic effect across identification levels. This supports the commonsense observation that the identification process is at a pivotal point when a new member first reports to a work group. The kind and amount of verbal support given the new member determines, in part, the degree of bonding that will develop subsequently.

All the other items measuring job-related talk exhibited similar significant trends. High and medium identifiers reported that their work groups engaged in more talk about police-related matters than did low identifiers. The researchers also concluded that "the policeman's professional world is dichotomized into 'us' and 'them.' 'Them' is a very large group, consisting not only of the criminal element, but also honest citizens . . . and even with administrative elements of the department" (Dionisopoulos and Samter, 1983: 27).

In a related vein, Sampugnaro's (1984) master's thesis used network message content as a predictor of organizational commitment, a concept close to organizational identification. The study replicated and extended the work of Eisenberg et al. (1983), which investigated the relationships among network involvement, job involvement, and organizational commitment. Sampugnaro's study stresses that the *content* of messages exchanged in a network is important. In the investigation of a branch of a nationwide computer software firm it was found that (1) job involvement accounts for a significant amount of the variance in organizational commitment ($r = .36$); (2) there is no significant relationship between network involvement and organizational commitment; (3) both message effect (the way employees feel about the organization after communicating with others) and message content are predictive of organizational commitment (r's of .31 and .29, respectively), with those employees who *send positive messages* about the organization being the most committed ($r = .36$).

In an outward-looking study, Paonessa (1983) attempted to link organizational identification, internal organizational communication, and external public relations (or corporate advocacy) in a division of General Motors. She tracked the internal dissemination of the corporation's position on various public issues (such as foreign competition and air bags). Questionnaires were analyzed from 417 employees, measuring the extent to which the employees were targets of advocacy messages, the degree to which employees identified with the organization, and the degree to which the employees relayed the corporation's advocacy positions to people outside the corporation.

The results showed that employees are targets of advocacy messages. The messages originated at the corporate level via such house organs as *Issue Update* containing excerpts from speeches given by GM executives on various public issues. The messages were also carried by another corporate organ and several divisional ones. Paonessa found that most employees received the messages via these publications on all four issues. Supervisors were relied on no more heavily than coworkers and the union, a finding disappointing to the corporation. Paonessa also found correlations ranging as high as .36 between degree of organizational identification and self-reports of advocacy outside the corporation (for example, with friends and relatives). In short, messages about GMs stands on public issues are sent to GM employees and are received by the employees who in turn relay the messages to receivers outside the corporation; those who identify highly with the organization are more likely than others to engage in this boundary-role activity. Although the relationship between identification and external advocacy may be somewhat tautological, it is important to have confirmation that employees do "act out" their identification in communicative action and that in such circumstances the "two voices" are speaking in unison. Paonessa (1983: 70) saw an ethical issue in this situation: "A democracy requires public deliberation, debate and dialogue about political issues. By means of its great size and resources, GM can deliver a ... monologue, even a lecture, to large captive audiences of individuals economically dependent on it."

In another master's thesis conducted at Purdue, Jensen (1983), born and educated in Japan, and as a result fluent in the Japanese language, derived a "popular model" of decision making in Japanese organizations. It was summarized as follows:

> First, a section develops a proposal for implementation in the organization. The proposal is discussed among the subordinates in the department and then moves to other sections of the organization horizontally and upwardly. Having reached either general consensus or disagreement, a meeting is held in which the proposal is discussed formally. If the proposal is accepted, a formal draft is written up, passed up to the relevant parts of the organization and finally approved by the executive. At times it is not necessary to have a conference and a ringisho [i.e., circulated decision document] is written up immediately after nemawashi [i.e., a kind of lobbying] [Jensen, 1983: 21].

By applying a decision-making schema (Ference, 1971) inspired by Simon and his colleagues to 35 books and 46 journal articles reporting data and observations of Japanese organizations, Jensen found the popular model deficient in several respects. First, it is skewed toward the later stages of decision, omitting any discussion of how problems come to be identified. Second, the popular model does not address the decisional premises that affect the outcomes. Third, the model concentrates on nonprogrammed decisions at the expense of the routine or programmed decisions.

When viewed through the template synthesized from the work of Simon, Ference, and Tompkins and Cheney, Japanese organizational decision making is not so different from American practices. Japanese organizations do stress the value premises of long-term growth and market share more than most U. S. concerns. But, the value homophily of Japanese society, including business organizations, makes the characterization of "bottom-up" decisional processes somewhat misleading in that organizations do more by way of reinforcing than inculcating the value premises of decision. Second, communicative practices within Japanese and U. S. companies are strikingly similar. Some differences do appear to exist, however, and Jensen (1983: 4) has characterized Japanese organizational communication by four factors that decrease the "boundedness" of rationality in the decisional process:

(1) An aggressive information-acquisition style. Vogel (1979) observed that the key to the Japanese success lay in their aggressiveness that is group directed. Since a group can attend to more information in the environment and the collective retention power is greater, the boundaries of rationality are broadened.

(2) An extensive four-way stretch within the organization that allows otherwise inaccessible information to come to the attention of the decision-making unit.

(3) A high degree of face-to-face interaction as the primary mode of communication, thus allowing for more effective transfer of relevant information.

(4) A retention system that resides in the collective and individual memory of members who remain in the organization for a long period of time. Successful solutions are stored in the collective memory, which combined with a high degree of face-to-face interaction, are readily accessible to the decision-making unit. The memory capacity and power to retain information is thus enhanced.

The distinction between programmed and nonprogrammed decisions was taken into consideration in a subsequent study of a high-tech firm also exalted in Peters and Waterman's *In Search of Excellence* (1982). Mills (1984) employed a combination of account analysis, OIQ, and a questionnaire about the modes and media by which the organization inculcated the premises of enthymeme$_2$ in its employees. Although the analysis had not been completed at the time of this writing, it appears that the highest identifiers with the firm received decisional premises via oral, face-to-face discussions with coworkers and superiors. The lowest identifiers, by contrast, relied more on print media, consistent with the concept of the highly identified member as an active and involved participant, bonded more tightly by orality with others in the organization, while low identifiers are more passive and detached from colleagues, tied mainly to the organization by means of the impersonal print media.

To summarize this program of research we can claim tentatively that, in addition to other correlations cited above, organizational identification is a dynamic phenomenon that varies contextually, changes over time, and is even capable of transference from one organizational entity to another; it is directly related to members' evaluations of competence and productivity and is inversely related to the range of conceivable alternatives. Extraorganizational identification by members does not necessarily negate organizational identification, though such loyalties often come into conflict. A person's organizational identification is strongly affected by the informal communication in the work group at the moment of the newcomer's entry. High identifiers seem to engage more often in oral communication (or at least perceive more) than low identifiers. Organizational identification provides the energy and motivation for informal boundary-role communication, that is, the energy and motivation for converting internal communication to external corporate advocacy. Organizational identification is somewhat more difficult to foster in relatively heterogeneous societies (for example, the United States) than in radically homogeneous ones (for example, Japan).

In regard to enthymemic processes, it appears that decisional premises can be verbalized and adapted to enthymemic forms. Decisional premises can be identified in discourse leading to agreement; organizational premises can be shown to "drive out" personal premises in decision-making discourse. Discourse analysis by means of account analysis reveals organizationally preferred decision premises and the targets of identification.

CONCLUSION

We have integrated a variety of theories and concepts in laying a foundation for a theory of contemporary organizations. Throughout our analysis we have featured the role of unobtrusive control for the organizations of an emerging postindustrial society. In turn we have highlighted: power and control; decision making and the enthymeme; identification; and of course, communication.

The implications of this evolving theory for research are many. Allow us in closing to discuss three. First, we recommend the four types—simple, technical, bureaucratic, and concertive—as "frames" for examining such microphenomena as superior-subordinate communication in larger contexts.[7] Along the same lines, we believe that communication networks in organizations can be profitably analyzed with respect to the patterns of control. In both cases, we expect to find differences in both the qualities and quantity of communication.

Second, one could extend and elaborate our arguments and develop a communication-centered *model* of contemporary organizations. In what Galbraith (1979: 138) calls the "most famous definition of an organization," Barnard described the formal organization as "a system of consciously coordinated activities or forces of two or more persons" (Barnard, 1968: 81). In addition, Barnard emphasized both the structural and dynamic aspects of this system. He viewed the organization as having both relatively constant elements and shifting, evolving processes. But he featured the symbolic aspect of organizing: "In an extensive theory of organization, communication would occupy a central place, because the structure, extensiveness, and scope of organization are almost entirely determined by communication techniques" (Barnard, 1968: 91).

In an analysis consistent with Barnard's, Welck (1979) conceptualizes organizations as "loosely coupled systems" in which organizational units, processes and products are not *tightly* interwoven, but linked indirectly and through symbolic mediation. The process of organizing is both complex and subtle as members adapt to environmental constraints, enact and select much of their social reality, and retain patterns of behavior for future use.

Barnard's definition and Weick's model can be further elaborated with our notions of unobtrusive control. In many large contemporary organizations coordination is possible and "loose coupling" allowable because of the subtle and powerful processes of unobtrusive control. What holds such organizations "together" is the achievement of indirect influence over members and the relative predictability this brings to decision making.

This process is greatly facilitated when professionals, such as accountants and engineers, present themselves to the organization with some of the socialization process having already taken place; they offer constellations of premises that are "exchanged" in decision making for monetary and other inducements. Both public and private institutions prepare professionals in this manner. Some social critics would argue that this "premise-packaging" is more evident today in American society than ever before (see, for example, Galbraith, 1979).

A third, and perhaps more important, implication is that the emphasis on unobtrusive control provides a springboard for developing a critical approach to the study of organizations. Habermas (1979) maintains that a comprehensive analysis of social phenomena should be at once empirically oriented, interpretive, and aimed at the critique of ideology (systematic distortion in communication that allows for and maintains situations of unwarranted power in society). In summarizing Habermas's hope for the social sciences, McCarthy explains that "an adequate social methodology would have to integrate interpretive understanding and critique of ideology with an historically-oriented analysis of social systems" (in Habermas, 1979: xii).

Built into the theory of unobtrusive control is a recognition of objective historical-material constraints that have affected the development of modern organizations. Even more important, we place a strong emphasis on *Verstehen,* the researcher's understanding of the subjective meanings of organizational actors who bring their personal premises to organizations, make sense of organizational "logics," participate in the ongoing process of decision, and account for these experiences to us, the researchers.

Finally, following Galbraith (1979), we express concern about the *apparent* merger of individual and organizational goals in the emerging postindustrial society. Galbraith sees identification and a complementary process, the adaptation of organizational goals, as key bases of motivation in today's large corporations. And he scolds economists and organizational analysts for not recognizing this and the resulting subordination of "traditional" (more individual) values to those of the corporation. (Ironically, of course, much of this symbolic maneuvering goes on under the rubric of "individualism.")

Of course, a complete exploration of these ideas would require another lengthy essay. Nevertheless, we may observe that the processes of unobtrusive control are more effective in fostering the acceptance of administrative, organizational, and corporate premises than were the more direct means of the past. Further, while certain aspects of the individual's acceptance of organizational goals are quite rational (for example, the process of narrowing one's span of attention through identification), others are subject to ideological critique (for example, the unqualified portrayal of a corporation's interests as representing the interests of the individual). Wherever we find organizations restricting the flow of communication that reflectively examines the nature and aims of the individual-organization relationship, there is room for the social-rhetorical critic. And the critic-as-advocate is charged with bringing about (or at least encouraging) an *awareness* of the possibilities of freer dialogue within and among organizations.[8]

NOTES

1. "Nondecision making" is important for organizational researchers on at least two levels. First, there is a kind of individual nondecision (or "negative" decision) referred to by Barnard (1968). For Barnard, this decision "not to decide" is "a more frequent decision, and from some points of view probably the most important" (p. 193). Further, he ascribes a critical role to this kind of action by managers when he writes: "The fine art of executive decisions consists in not deciding questions that are not now pertinent, in not deciding prematurely, in not making decisions that cannot be made effective, and in not making decisions that others should make" (p. 194, emphasis deleted). This conception seems to fit Luke's "two-dimensional view" of power, which highlights how certain issues and positions are denied entry into the decision-making process through rather observable responses to their suggestion (for example, delaying "action," procrastination, "passing the buck," and the like).

On another, but more systemic level, nondecision is far more difficult to track. Lukes, in outlining his "three-dimensional view" of power, mentions the case where collective action is taken to set an agenda, and neither the decision (a choice among alternatives) nor the nondecision (the suppression or exclusion of concerns that challenge the prevailing interests) can be attributed to particular individuals. Lukes includes also under this head the phenomenon of system- or organizationwide "mobilization of bias," where certain issues and positions are removed from view through the very form and nature of organization.

As will be demonstrated in this chapter, our conception of "unobtrusive control" spans both levels of nondecision making. First, it can be used to explain why particular decision makers exclude or fail to consider some potential issues and positions when engaged in the process and decision. Here the "range of vision" for the decision maker is limited by an interaction of individual preference and organizational bias. Second, on a systemwide basis, values, and choices persist and challenges often fail to emerge. For a study which, according to Lukes (1974), typifies the three-dimensional view of power, see Crenson (1971).

2. Here we find reference to Burawoy's (1979) interesting study of conflict and consent (or consensus) in industry to be useful. Burawoy approaches his detailed, longitudinal case study with an eye for the means by which workers in capitalist firms routinely *consent* to their own exploitation. In his analysis of changes in labor organization in a British factory, Burawoy concentrates on the often unapparent ways in which workers are led to cooperate for the pursuit of profit. Central to his discussion are explanations of how surplus value is simultaneously obscured and secured, how the labor process is constituted as a game, how workers are constituted as individuals rather than as members of a class, and how conflict and competition are redistributed.

While we neither embrace nor reject Burawoy's (1979) explicitly Marxist analysis, we would like to take one of his theses for moving the discussion of workplace consensus and conflict to a higher level of abstraction. We find especially appealing Burawoy's (1979: 12) proposition that "conflict and consent are not primordial conditions but products of the particular organization of work." Like Burawoy, we seek to be free of the misplaced emphasis inherent in both "consensus theories" and "conflict theories." The theory of unobtrusive control is shaped by such an objective: it is designed to account for the simultaneous existences—of cooperation, value consensus, and communion on one hand, and conflict, disagreement, and alienation on the other.

Like Burawoy's (1979) framework, the theory of communication and unobtrusive control is historically-based, yet it is not intended as a critique of capitalism. We draw heavily from businesses as examples because those are the organizations that dominate contemporary Western society. However, the forms and principles of control we outline are applicable to many other kinds of organizations. Thus we seek to explicate basic processes of *organizing* that can be seen across historical periods and in many different contexts, albeit in varying proportions.

3. While completing the final draft of this chapter, we examined a recent study (Conley, 1984) of commentary on the enthymeme before, by, and after Aristotle and we see no reason to change our conclusion. As our previous discussion should indicate, we are in agreement with Conley's statement of consensus about the enthymeme: It is a deductive argument, is not a formalist conception, and is not a truncated syllogism; its premises are probabilities, although they may enjoy certainties; if there are missing premises they are supplied by the audience to fill out the argument; the premises may reflect statements of values as well as fact; the enthymeme functions not just as logos but involves ethos and pathos as well; finally, the invention and comprehensive exposition of the invention is Aristotle's. We differ not so much with Conley's expression of consensus as we do with Conley's (1984: 40) personal opinion: "My own inclination is to accept the argument from example, or analogy, or even metaphor as the critical paradigm." We also think we have in this chapter corrected half of the deficiency seen by Conley in traditional or mainstream rhetorical theory; that is, that current theory "has been almost completely unable to assimilate the contributions of the most important modern writers on the subject of rhetoric, Perelman and Burke" (Conley, 1984: 35). For studies concentrating on Aristotle's theory of the enthymeme we are most closely in agreement with Grimaldi (1972: 16), who writes: "The enthymeme as "the main instrument of rhetorical argument incorporates reason and emotion in discourse." We should also mention our awareness of the enthymeme as both an *artifact* to be discovered in discourse and a *process* of communication.

4. The concept of identification has a long history of speculation and investigation in the social sciences, beginning with Freud's (1922: 60) Oedipally grounded consideration of it as "the earliest expression of an emotional tie with another person." Other theorists, mainly psychologists, who have explicitly considered identification—either as a product or as a process—include Bronfenbrenner (1969), Erikson (1963, 1968), Foote (1951), Kagan (1958), Kelman (1958), Lasswell (1965), Lazowick (1955), Mowrer (1950), Parsons and Bales (1955), Sanford (1955), Sears (1957), Sherif and Cantril (1947), Stoke (1950), Stotland and Dunn (1962), Stotland and Hillmer (1962), Stotland and Patchen (1961), Tolman (1943), Winch (1962), and Zander et al. (1960). For our purposes, the most relevant treatment of identification here listed is Foote's (1951: 17): "We mean by *identification* appropriation of and commitment to a particular identity or series of identities. As a process, it proceeds by *naming*; its products are ever-evolving self-conceptions—with an emphasis on the *con-*, that is, upon ratification by significant

others." Relevant also is the fact that Foote credits both Mead's (1934) work on the self and Burke's (1950, 1969) writings on motives and identification for inspiration.

The use of identification (and the related concepts of commitment, loyalty, attachment, and so on) in organizational identification (considered broadly) is presumed related to a variety of organizational outcomes such as goal achievement, quality of performance, and job satisfaction (Likert, 1967; McGregor, 1967). In a widely cited article, Katz (1964) isolates the "internalization of group objects" as one important pattern of motivation in organizations. Two major typological works consider identification as the key motivator in certain kinds of organization (Blau and Scott, 1962; Etzioni, 1975). Galbraith (1979) also links identification and motivation, arguing that it has succeeded compulsion and pecuniary reward as the most important employee motivator. French and Raven (1968) consider identification as the basis of an important type of power—"referent"—in groups and organizations. The most significant classic theoretical pieces for purposes of our work are Simon's (1976) and March and Simon's (1958) considerations of the relationship of identification to decision making. March and Simon, for example, offer a fairly developed model, which treats group (or organizational) identification as a function of (1) perceived prestige of a group, (2) perceptions of shared goals, (3) frequency of interaction, (4) individual need satisfaction, and (5) amount of competition among members. Simon's (1976) framework we consider in the text of this chapter.

While a few empirical research efforts have recognized the *process* aspects of organizational identification (for example, Rotondi, 1975b; Tompkins et al., 1975), most have operationalized the construct as a product or state, usually measuring identification with single- or multi-item questionnaires. See, for example, Brown (1969); Greene (1978); Hall and Schneider (1972); Hall et al. (1970); Lee (1969, 1971); Long (1978); Patchen (1970); Rotondi (1975a, 1975b, 1976); Schneider et al. (1971); and Tompkins et al. (1975). Such investigations have found support for links between identification and motivation to work (Brown, 1969), and high degrees of interaction (Patchen, 1970; Tompkins et al., 1975). Attempts to establish a positive relationship between length of employment and identification have found mixed results (Hall and Schneider, 1972; Hall et al., 1970; Schneider et al., 1971).

A number of research efforts have focused on tensions between organizational and professional identifications, often using the experience of industrial scientists as exemplary (see, for example, Becker and Carper, 1956; Bennis et al., 1958; Glaser, 1964; Gouldner, 1957, 1958; Korhauser, 1962; McKelvey, 1969; Miller and Wager, 1971; Pelz and Andrews, 1976). While these researchers draw varying conclusions about the effects of multiple identifications, at least one (Rotondi, 1975b) finds evidence to suggest that behaviors related to organizational identification may often be quite dysfunctional by stunting creativity and decreasing effectiveness.

Organizational identification and related phenomena have been linked to other processes. They have been associated with interorganizational personnel flow in that high identifiers are difficult to recruit away from their employers (Horovitz, 1981); they have been tied to organizational boundary-spanning in that the actual and perceived loyalties of boundary role persons affect their credibility, freedom, and effectiveness (Adams, 1976); and they have been found to be somewhat negatively related to turnover (Mobley et al., 1979).

A number of researchers have treated organizational commitment, a construct closely related to identification, as one outcome of formal and informal organizational socialization (see, for example, Buchanan, 1974; Schein, 1968; Van Maanen, 1975). Personnel policies such as selection, training, promotion, and transfer have also been associated with organizational identification. For example, Byrne (1971) suggests that recruiters hire persons similar to themselves, those who are likely to accept organizational goals and values, if they do not already at the time of entry. Other organizational policies and activities that can help to foster identification include participative decision-making (Likert, 1961) and internal corporate communications such as house organs (Cheney, 1983b).

For our present purposes, the most thorough and interesting study of organizational identification is Kaufman's (1960) case analysis of the U.S. Forest Service. Kaufman found that the rangers were characterized by an extremely high identification; that many policies of the service served intentionally or unintentionally to foster this identification; and that this identification was enhanced through public relations and advocacy activities of rangers. Through assuming a process-oriented perspective on identification, Kaufman highlights the important linkages among identification, communication, and decision making. He explains to some extent why and how rangers "make their decisions in terms of the consequences for the Forest Service, and in terms of criteria the leaders of the Forest Service wish them to employ" (p. 197). Kaufman's study is an inspirational model for the present line of research.

We conclude this lengthy footnote by addressing briefly the issue of conceptual and construct related distinctiveness. Our survey of organizational literature reveals that conceptualizations of identification and commitment overlap to a significant extent; further, we observe the closely related concepts of organizational loyalty (Lewis, 1967; Bennis et al., 1958), job involvement (Gorn and Kanungo, 1980; Saleh and Hosek, 1976; Lodahl and Kejner, 1965), job attachment (Koch and Steers, 1978), central life interest (Dubin, 1956; Dubin et al. 1975) and reciprocation (Levinson, 1965).

Rather than become trapped in a theoretical mire, we will acknowledge that some organizational commitment researchers are in fact considering aspects of organizational identification. However, in a manner consistent with Burkean and Simonian theories from which we draw, we contend that the term "identification" is more descriptive and embracing than "commitment," which for us suggests the notion of a pledge or a promise (see dictionary definitions of commitment). Identification is the more descriptive term, we maintain, because (1) it suggests the relevance of "identity" and "self," and (2) it is used in everyday language with such richness of meaning. We find "identification" to be more embracing than "commitment" because it can be applied more readily to process *and* product aspects than the latter. Nevertheless, we find great value in studying organizational commitment along with identification in that they fit together as do form and substance, respectively (see the extended discussion of this relationship in Cheney and Tompkins, 1984a).

For theoretical and empirical treatments of organizational commitment, see, for example, Angle and Perry (1981); Bartol (1979); Becker (1960); Buchanan (1975); Gordon et al. (1980); H. P. Gouldner (1960); Grusky (1966); Hall and Schneider (1973); Hrebiniak and Alutto (1972); Kanter (1968); Knocke (1981); Kidron (1978); London and Howat (1978); Morris and Sherman (1981); Morris and Steers (1980); Morrow (1983); Mowday et al. (1979); O'Reilly and Caldwell (1981); Porter, Steers, Mowday, and Boullan (1974); Ritzer and Trice (1969); Salancik (1977); Steers (1977); and Wiener and Wardi (1980). For a thorough treatment of commitment as a general social phenomenon, see Kiesler (1971).

5. Although identification is important—and certainly quite apparent—it should not be stressed to the point of committing a fallacy of emphasis. Thus we propose as a future research direction the simultaneous investigation of *alienation* as the counterpart and limiting factor of identification. The subject of alienation will be treated from a Burkean

perspective in our forthcoming work. For a perspective on the ethics of identification, which will be elaborated later, see Cheney and Tompkins (1984b).

6. Note that here we substitute the word "monitoring" for Edwards's term "evaluation" because readers of an earlier draft of this paper were misled into thinking that evaluation was a message sent from superior to subordinate rather than the value judgment reached by the superior after surveying a subordinate's performance of a task. We also want to stress that the monitoring feedback loops may vary greatly in form, length, and complexity, including such techniques as direct observation of the performance of a task, quality and quantity figures looped back by a third party, and of course the subordinate's own verbal reports about the task.

7. For a thorough review of the literature on superior-subordinate communication, see Jablin (1979). It should be profitable to reanalyze the studies surveyed by Jablin with our typology of control in mind.

8. Of course, as researchers we must also be aware of the ideological assumptions that often limit our views of organizations—in terms of theory, method, and analysis. See, for example, the criteria by Redding (1979).

Chapter 8

LEARNING TO PORTRAY INSTITUTIONAL POWER
The Socialization of Creators in Mass Media Organizations

Joseph Turow

CREATING MATERIAL FOR the mass media typically involves telling stories. The chief difference between news stories and entertainment stories is that news is constrained by "the facts" and entertainment is not. A nonfiction writer or photographer will generally avoid making up incidents. On the other hand, a fiction writer or imaginative photographer will feel free to bend happenings and characterizations in ways that do not match up with specific facts "out there." Note, however, that news, like entertainment, involves selection and exclusion: Even though journalists cannot make up tales, they must choose their stories from many possible stories and their facts from a multitude of impressions.

Whether the subject is news or entertainment, the product is the result of a regularized, collaborative effort. Media personnel work together on the selection and creation of material in an organizational setting that exists within an industrial environment that, in turn, exists within a larger society. The most important considerations about this process converge on its relationship to power and hierarchy in the society. Starting with the basic premise that "every society works to reproduce itself" (Gitlin, 1979: 264), many contemporary mass communication scholars from a variety of backgrounds agree that the portrayals of the most widespread media—television, newspapers, magazines, radio, film, and popular books—both reflect that activity and play a part in it. Gaye Tuchman (1978: 210), for example, argues that "news both draws upon and reproduces institutional structure." Phillip Tichenor et al. (1980: 224) observe that "where there is diversity in social power, media tend to reflect the orientations of those segments that are higher up on the power scale." And George Gerbner (1972: 153) describes entertainment as "the celebration of conventional morality" and dubs media producers "the cultural arms of the industrial order from which they spring."

Reflecting social power, celebrating conventional morality, and acting as cultural arms of the industrial order can collectively be taken broadly to mean legitimating—that is, upholding the authority of—the established economic, political, educational, cultural, religious, and military institutions of the society. Taking this position does not mean believing that mass media material is unquestioning and bland. Certainly, commercial TV often carries reports of arguments on various political issues, popular magazines and newspapers often describe social injustices, and popular films often depict social problems. Moreover, intellectual and material fashions change, social divisions and ideological contradictions occur, and these and other tensions find their way into the media. It seems clear, too, that facets of media material often displease members of the elite (for example, business leaders) as well as other portions of the public.

But recognizing that media materials often reflect social tensions and conflicts does not sweep away the argument that the most widespread mass media content tends to legitimize the establishment. Despite depictions of social problems, these media rarely use their portrayals as platforms to challenge explicitly the fundamental legitimacy of the nation's dominant institutions and to raise realistic alternatives. Rarely, for example, do U.S. television programs hold extended discussions about solving the nation's problems by doing away with the capitalist system, about reducing the nation's armament problems by completely dismantling the military establishment, or about reducing personal monetary difficulties by stealing and then flouting the police. On the contrary, in every society except those undergoing violent upheaval the essentially legitimate entrenchment of the establishment and its values is an implicit theme weaving through the most popular mass media material.

That much is accepted to a greater or lesser degree by a broad spectrum of contemporary mass media researchers. Saying it, however, does not detail how people in media production firms go about generating and continually reproducing patterned portrayals that legitimize the social structure. Nor does saying it detail systematically whether and when a greater or lesser range of institutional criticisms will be the norm within the media organization, or when any policy that repudiates certain institutions might be tenable. Filling in the details is particularly difficult in a society such as the United States, where political and economic governance is under mixed private and public control and where mass media are neither agencies of the state nor responsible to centralized private interests. In such societies, people who create mass media material are not indoctrinated explicitly with principles that lay out the normative relationship between their symbolic creators and institutional power. In fact, many who produce entertainment would prefer to echo Sam Goldwyn's remarks about the social import of mass entertainment: "If you want to send a message, call Western Union!"

The question, then, boils down to this: In the absence of direct coordination by government or the private sector, what are the ways in which people in mass media organizations come to portray the legitimacy of institutional power in the material they create? In this chapter, I will tackle this question in two steps. First, I will argue that the two major streams of research on mass media industries—research taking a Marxist view and research taking an "industrial" view—have both been contributing important studies that can illuminate this question. However, they have not set forth conceptual schemes that will systematically explain different ideological latitudes across media industries or that will point to multileveled schemes for exploring media organizations to understand the way creators learn to portray social power. Then I will argue that a "resource dependence" perspective on organizations and their environments provides a promising way to merge findings from both approaches to form the basis for a textured understanding of the process and point toward further relevant research.

TWO RESEARCH STREAMS

The emergence of mass market journalism in the United States and parts of Europe in the nineteenth century brought many analysts of the social scene to comment upon its role and power in society. Perhaps the most influential commentator was Karl Marx. A journalist by trade (he wrote for the *New York Tribune,* among other newspapers), Marx was keenly concerned with the relationship between material production and symbolic production. He stated his position concisely in one of his early works, *The German Ideology* (Marx and Engels, 1974: 64-65):

> The class that has the means of material production at its disposal has control at the same time over the means of mental production. . . . Insofar as they rule as a class and determine the extent and compass of an epoch, they do this in its whole range, hence among other things [they] also regulate the production and distribution of the ideas of their age: thus their ideas are the ruling ideas of the epoch.

Precisely what were the organizational mechanisms through which this "regulation" of ideas took place? Marx did not explore this subject in detail, but in at least one long example—an analysis of the factors that led British newspapers to support the American South during the Civil War—he placed strong emphasis on the direct involvement by specific members of the nation's elite with the ownership and editorial guidance of Britain's newspapers. However, Marx never relied solely on this "instrumental action" type of analysis. Alongside the ideas of elite control Marx developed a structural approach. This view focused not on the interests and activities of particular capitalists, but on the way the capitalist economy was structured so as to narrow the options of activity in the society (Murdock, 1982: 118-150).

Marx's ideas have ignited a wide spectrum of approaches that aim to understand the relationships between "the structure of capital" in society and its mass media content. Broadly speaking, most researchers have set out to accomplish one of two tasks through their work: (1) mapping out the institutional factors that guide and constrain the production of certain ideologies in mass media or (2) teasing out the ideological implications of mass media materials and in doing so, inferring organizational activities that guide those ideologies. Only recently—and in much smaller numbers—have researchers begun to connect institutional lines of power and patterns of content to the regular process of learning and working that takes place *within* mass media firms.

Results of the first task can be seen clearly in the work of scholars who follow what is perhaps the most fundamentalist Marxist direction, the political economy of media institutions. Graham Murdock (1982: 118-150), reviewing the literature of this area, notes that contemporary researchers have pursued both Marx's "action" and "structure" strands of analysis. Much output in the action tradition tries to follow the lines of power that connect media companies to one another. Writers in this area see interlocking boards of directors, strong individual stock controllers, and the growth of media conglomerates as powerful evidence that the capitalist class works to legitimate its ideology regularly, though often quite subtly. Some writers argue that boards of directors set overall policies for the production of media material and that therefore "their ideological interests are guaranteed by the implicit understandings governing production." Others contend that positing such near-conspiratorial understandings may not be necessary, since simply guiding the organization toward making money will ensure ideological output compatible with capitalist class interests.

Writers picking up the structure strand, by contrast, concentrate on ways in which the logic of the capitalist system rather than the motivations of class-based actors guide legitimation in mass media material. For example, they note that escalating costs of entering major mass media markets means that these markets are really open only to entrepreneurs with substantial capital. As a result, they conclude, enterprises that survive will "largely belong to those least likely to criticize the prevailing distribution of wealth and power," and "those most likely to challenge these arrangements" will be "unable to command the resources necessary for effective communication to a broad audience" (Murdock and Golding, 1977: 37). Similarly, these writers point to the advertising industry's important subsidizing role in much of the mass media and try to determine the consequence that role has for the spectrum of ideological choice that those media present (for example, see Curran, 1978; Tuchman, 1974).

Discussing the political economy approaches, Graham Murdock (1982: 125) says that a "a full analysis of control . . . needs to look at the complex interplay between intentional action and structural constraint *at every level of the production processes.*" In actuality, however, political economists' general preoccupation with institutional and interorganizational levels of analysis has meant that they have typically neglected to track the way institutional and interorganizational lines of power into media organizations are translated into legitimating portrayals of social power. James Curran et al. (1982: 18), in a concise review of political economy writings, point to this problem quite directly:

The precise mechanisms and processes whereby ownership of the media or control of their economics are translated into controls over the message are, according to proponents of this approach, rather complex and often problematic. . . . The workings of these controls are not easy to demonstrate—or to examine empirically. The evidence quite often is circumstantial and is derived from the "fit" between the ideology implicit in the message and the interests of those in control.

Curran et al. (1982: 18) suggest that "the links between the economic determinants of the media on the one hand and the contents of the media of the other" ought to be pursued by studying how both relate to the work practices and professional ideologies of media professionals. It is an important suggestion, but one that has not been followed in a sustained manner by Marxist analysts. The great proportion of their work connecting the social structure and media firms' processes has really come from examining media content. So, for example, when Stuart Hall (1982: 65-88) asks, "How does the ideological process work and what are its mechanisms?" his review of the relevant literature is mostly an analysis of the symbolic and linguistic character of ideological discourse—"the politics of signification" and "the class struggle organizational activities that guide the processing of reality." Hall does note his strong interest in demonstrating "how institutions could be articulated [that is, connected] to the production and reproduction of dominant ideologies, while at the same time being 'free' of direct compulsion." However, his conclusions on this topic derive from analyses of the way media newspapers and television bespeak the legitimacy of "the ruling class" and from anecdotes about high-level decision making in the British Broadcasting Corporation and the British press. The ideas that Hall and others infer from such explorations are valuably suggestive toward understanding how creators learn to portray social power. However, they provide no substitute for careful organizational and interorganizational analysis, guided by a solid organizational scheme.

During the past decade or so, a small number of researchers with neo-Marxist orientations have recognized this omission and begun to do something about it. Gaye Tuchman (1978), Todd Gitlin (1983), Harvey Molotch and Marilyn Lester (1973), and a few others have begun to describe the complex ways that creative activities in mass media organizations relate to economic forces. Their work has focused almost exclusively on two media sectors: television and newspaper journalism, and television entertainment. Insisting that the organizations they study be placed firmly in the context of their industries and the larger society as a whole, these researchers see routine activities of newsworkers and TV entertainment personnel as accomplishing two critical purposes. First, the routines help the creators get their jobs done on time, on budget, and in ways that will be lauded by management and colleagues. Second, the routines embody perspectives on the world that guide creators toward framing their stories about the world in ways that support the values of liberal capitalism or, at the very least, insist that no viable alternatives exist.

Writers in this vein have paid particular attention to U.S. journalism's venerable notion of "objectivity," showing how both its historical origin and its contemporary application feed the needs of established economic power. Gitlin (1979, 1983), extending and modifying notions about ideological hegemony by Antonio Gramsci, has been particularly active in carrying this approach beyond journalism into TV entertainment. His general point is that when TV program creators apply certain expected features to prime-time entertainment—for example, time-tested formulas, settings, and plot solutions—they are not simply doing their jobs with the aim of attracting audiences and advertisers. Whether they know it or not, they are perpetuating forms that derive from and reflect "the dominant system of discourse and the prevailing structures of labor, consumptions, and politics."

The writings by Marxist sociologists on mass media organizations form an important perspective for trying to understand how media creators learn to portray social power. At the same time, however, their work falls short of pointing the way toward a textured, many-leveled analysis of the way in which and the extent to which this processing of institutional legitimacy takes place. One limitation—though it is not an inherent one—is that the frameworks they use are individual and social, not organizational. For example, the concepts of hegemony, power, and frame analysis that Gitlin and Tuchman blend in their works do serve the writers well as take-off points for astute observation and analysis of individuals within organizations. They do not in themselves, however, hold provocative propositions or intriguing observations about *organizational* dynamics that other researchers might follow up to pursue new avenues of research on mass media. And, after all, mass media materials are not created by individuals, but by individuals in organizations that operate as parts of large-scale industries.

Another problem with this Marxist stream of work as it has developed is its failure to investigate creators' relationships to social power in a broad range of mass media organizations. During the past few decades many writings by Marxist social and political philosophers have argued the "relatively auto-nomous" position of ideology with respect to the society's economic base (see, for example, Bennett, et al., 1981; Williams, 1973; Hall, 1982). Rather than reducing all cultural products to a simple reflection of society's economic base, they have pointed to institutional and interinstitutional conflicts that shape sometimes contradictory images within complex, dominant cultures. In the general sociology of art area, these writings have received a good deal of attention (see Wolff, 1983). Marxist researchers who study mass media organizations, however, have not integrated these ideas into their analyses of process and output. For one thing, they have maintained a near-exclusive focus on popular journalism and network TV entertainment that has stifled an awareness of the way some sectors of media industries—scholarly books, for example—allow far broader latitudes in portraying social legitimacy than do others. For another, they have only rarely traced the way complex institutional conflicts and their underlying economic and political dimensions make their way into even mainstream material.[1]

A different range of formulations regarding mass processes and content is characteristic of the second major stream on mass media industries. The stream—which might be called "industrial" for lack of a better term—goes back at least as far as Max Weber's (1976) systematic research program on the organization of the press in 1910. Basic to this thrust is the idea that media output is not best explained by invoking bottom-line issues of ownership of capital in society. Rather, this approach starts implicitly with a model that sees media power as diffused pluralistically (though perhaps unequally) into the hands of many parties, organizational and individual. It holds that the production of mass media material is best explained through intensive scrutiny of two areas: (1) the nature and variety of competition between organizations in the marketplace, and (2) the activities of production organizations and the people who work there.

Each of the two areas has received its share of special attention. Researchers who have emphasized the marketplace have set forth models about the way interacting organizations influence the production of mass media material, and they have explored the consequences that interacting organizations hold for media material. So, for example, Paul Hirsch (1972) has urged a broad "organization set analysis" to explain the production and distribution of "cultural items," and Paul DiMaggio (1977) has suggested specifically that the number of production firms in a media industry determines the "degree of innovation and diversity of popular culture products." In a more investigatory vein, Peterson and Berger (1975) have explored the impact of a rising and falling number of production firms on innovation in the record industry, and Barnouw has argued that the television sponsorship system most incisively explains the contemporary state of TV programming.

Studies that look predominantly at the internal activities of production organizations are numerous. They range from case studies of local television networks to large-scale studies of the characteristics of American journalists.[2] Many researchers in this area focus on the ways in which and extent to which individuals and organizations outside the creators' home bases influence them. Thus Muriel Cantor's (1971) classic study of the Hollywood television producer examined the goal conflicts that certain types of TV producers feel when they compare their creative needs with their expectations of what network officials want. And Hortense Powdermaker's (1950) memorable look at the Hollywood "dream factory" in the late 1940s linked the output of the movie industry to the lifestyles and interpersonal power relationships that she saw in the world's great film colony.

This work on the "production of culture" by mass media industries has accumulated a tremendous amount of rich material at several levels of analysis. It has integrated theoretical concerns about the sociology of occupations and organizations with solid observational and interview work to present a picture of the widely varied yet conceptually related forces that guide the production and distribution of messages. At the same time, though, what Richard Peterson

(1979: 152) has noted as the pragmatic focus of this research line—ignoring the slippery relationship of media material to "society" and emphasizing instead a concern with directly observable aspects of production—has vitiated interest by many industrially oriented writers in the links of media organizations to centers of societal power. So, for example, Horace Newcomb and Paul Hirsch (1983) admit in passing that network TV's variety "works for the most part within the limits of American monopoly capitalism and within the range of American pluralism," but they are not interested in precisely how those limits come to influence the material. In fact, the great number of writers on media organizations barely mention the social power/media content link. Systematic questions about legitimacy simply have not been the dominant concern of this research stream.

And yet, the textured studies of media production can be a tremendous help in trying to tease out these links. The main theme of this chapter is that the strong points of both Marxist analysis and industrial analysis both ought to be considered in trying to move toward a solid organizational analysis of the institutional connections to media content. In the following pages, I argue that a most fruitful way to do that is to adopt an approach that has been gaining popularity among industrial sociologists, the "resource dependence" perspective. Then, drawing upon previous research, I sketch in a preliminary manner some basic mechanisms by which creators in different media industries learn to portray institutional power. The discussion raises some important questions and points toward a number of lines for future research.

MASS COMMUNICATION, RESOURCES, AND POWER

Developing the resource dependence framework and its relevance first requires confronting some basic terms. Mass communication can be defined as the industrialized ("mass") production, reproduction, and multiple distribution of messages through technological devices (Turow, 1984: 4). The word "industrialized" means that the process is carried out by a mass media complex or industry—that is, by a conglomeration of organizations that interact regularly in the process of producing and distributing messages. "Industrialized" also implies the use of technology for production and distribution. It is a use that provides production organizations with the potential for reaching large, separated, diverse groups of people.

Howard Aldrich's (1979: 4) definition of organizations is helpful here: "Organizations are goal directed, boundary maintaining activity systems." "Goal directed" means that members of the organizations behave *as if* the organizations have goals. "This is not the same as asserting that organizations *do* have goals but only that much of the activity we observe appears directed toward some common purpose," as opposed to being purely friendly interaction. In fact, notes Aldrich, participants in organizations engage in "activity systems,"that is, in interdependent behaviors (roles) revolving around particular technologies for accomplishing work.

Aldrich's (1979: 5) definition of an organization highlights its essentially social nature; as he says, organizations are "products of, and constraints upon," social relations. The definition also points to the importance of an organization's *environment* in keeping the organization going. The environment comprises every person not admitted to participation in the organization (that is, everyone outside its boundaries) and everything not already a part of, or a product of, the activity systems of organizational personnel. Clearly, it is the environment toward which the organization directs the productions of its activities. At the same time, it is the environment that provides people for recruitment into the organization; supplies used in the performance of organizational activities; required information, permission, and services to help the acceptability, or permissibility, of its activities in that environment; and money to pay for it all.

People, supplies, permission, information, services, money—very broadly defined, they represent the material and symbolic resources that must continually infuse an organization if it is to survive. Organizations are continually in competition with other organizations for resources, especially because resources are not distributed randomly throughout the environment. Rather, they are concentrated in various areas of the environment and are often under the control of other organizations. Awareness that the consequences of this situation are quite broad is what Aldrich (1979: 4) calls the "resource dependence perspective:

> The resource dependence perspective . . . goes beyond the idea of simple exchange in arguing that one consequence of competition and sharing of scarce resources is the development of dependencies of some organizations on others. . . . The implicit assumption made regarding managerial and administrative behavior is that major goals of organizational leaders are avoiding dependence on others and making others dependent on one's own organization. The general picture is one of the decision-makers attempting to manage their environments as well as their organizations.

Here, then, we arrive at the concept of power in interorganizational relations, given that, as Richard Emerson (1967: 900) notes, an organization's power resides in another organization's dependence. Power in this framework is the capacity of one organization to control resources so as to restrict the options available to another organization in such a way that the latter takes actions consistent with the former's vested interests.

The point applies clearly to mass communication. A mass media production organization cannot possibly generate internally all the resources it requires to ensure the viability of its creative and administrative activities. For example, money must be found; talent has to be hired; machines, videotape, or other exhaustible materials have to be bought; the distribution and exhibition services of other organizations have to be contracted; the favorable services of law firms and regulations of government agencies have to be ensured; the *in*activity of some pressure groups might have to be ascertained or negotiated; and information about available talent, activities of competitors, and the potential of the public's interest in the planned products has to be presented and evaluated. In other words, the production firm has to rely on entities in the environment for resources, and those entities might demand substantial recompense for their help.

THE ARRANGEMENT OF POWER
IN A MASS MEDIA INDUSTRY

It stands to reason from what has been said that some organizations in the environment of production firms have greater power over the ongoing stream of production activities than do others. A large and still-growing body of literature suggests that governments, investors, and organizations that support the distribution of particular products (*patrons*, such as advertisers) constitute the most important forces guiding a media production firm toward certain approaches to content as opposed to others. The literature also suggests that within any particular society the major authority, investor, and patron power roles tend to have converging, if not congruent, interests. Moreover, those interests ultimately reflect the overall power relations of the society in which the media industry emerges and develops (see Turow, 1984: 37-48). In the United States, for example, the primacy of liberal capitalism is a consideration that underlies the activities of federal, state, and local agencies that regulate various mass media, the banks and investment syndicates that fuel the work of major media production companies, and the advertisers and other corporations (such as stores and movie distribution firms) that act as major patrons.

Within this broad economic frame, established and alternative institutions vie for consideration and favorable images in the mass media. The resource dependence perspective at this level points to the notion that certain kinds of mass media firms are more likely than others to please the establishment. Production firms that rely on getting a great many of their most important resources (money, authority, personnel, services, and the like) from the mainstream of society (government, giant advertisers, powerful advocacy organizations, necessarily huge audiences) will likely arrange their activities so as to offend as few of these entities as possible. Conversely, production firms that can rely on resources from areas of society that are outside the mainstream (for example, nongovernmental bodies, atypical advertisers, specialty distributors and exhibitors, rather homogeneous audiences) might not hesitate to attack the mainstream. The difference is between what we will call "mainstream" and "peripheral" media output. So, for example, in the United States it is possible to produce novels extolling communist ideologies as a solution to social problems; the First Amendment to the United States Constitution prohibits government interference. However, it is extremely doubtful that such peripheral material would be highlighted on network television or considered attractive by major movie studios.

ORGANIZING CREATIVE WORK BY COPING WITH RISK

How are lines of interorganizational influence tied to the arrangement of creative activities within the production firm? How do media executives come to signal the latitude they and other creators have in portraying the legitimacy of certain institutions? And in mainstream media, where latitude is narrowest, how do creators go about portraying power in a patterned manner while keeping the feeling of autonomy that is often considered requisite in some media professions, notably, journalism? The task is to explore how "structural constraint and discretionary decision-making interface" at different levels of resource exchange (Glasberg and Schwartz, 1979: 326).

One approach to this explanation lies in Jeffrey Pfeffer and Gerald Salancik's (1978) argument that the arrangement of key organizational activities represents attempts by the organization's leaders to cope with risks they perceive in exchanging their products for environmental resources. Pfeffer and Salancik (1978: 229) diagram "the mechanisms by which organizational environments may affect organizations" in the following way:

Environment
(source of uncertainty, constraint, contingency)
↓
Distribution of Power and Control
Within Organization
↓
Selection and Removal of Executives
↓
Organizational Actions and Structures

A way to understand this process in the context of the present discussion is to conceive of the relationships between a mass media production firm and organizations in its environment as communication systems that involve leaders of the production firms and members of the other organizations constituting the media industry. The purpose of such a system for each organization in the relationship can be specified by recalling Howard Aldrich's proposition that "major goals of organizational leaders are avoiding dependence on other [organizations for resources] and making others dependent on one's own organization." The communication system allows production firm leaders and their boundary personnel to keep in touch with changing environmental circumstances so that they can make adjustments in creative policy, personnel, and structure that meet those exigencies. Executives whose creative expertise relates to those areas of the environment that organizational leaders have chosen to exploit would potentially have much power within the organization. If those executives did not succeed in convincing top management and the owners that their approaches to creative activities are the most profitable (monetarily and/or politically), they would be removed; other executives with other approaches to creative activities would then take the helm.

In general, the task of creative leaders in a mass media production organization is to ensure that the organization's activities are oriented toward continually varying its cultural products successfully and efficiently. Those products must be different from one another in order to keep attracting the interests of the same distributors, exhibitors, and audiences. So, every new book a publishing firm releases must be different from other books that have come out. Every day's newspaper must have stories different from those of the day before. And every episode of a television series must be recognizably different from other episodes of the series.

Yet, there's a key rub. While the search for novelty is a necessity for the creators, it also poses for them a gamut of individual and collective difficulties and possibilities for failure. Three sets of broad problems come to mind. One relates to the need to satisfy forces in the environment that are crucial to getting material out to the public. Exhibitors, distributors, patrons, investors, and pressure groups might have welcomed the firm's previous creations, but that alone is no assurance that they will feel the same way about the new products. The second set of problems relates to pleasing the targeted audience. Simply put, there is no guarantee the audience will respond to new products as it responded to the old ones. And third, there are potential problems that relate to the functioning of the organization itself. Production personnel must carry out their activities in a space of time that both satisfies the needs of the environment and maximizes the production firm's efficiency. That can be hard to do when novelty becomes an important part of the equation. New ideas might bombard selectors from all sides; new ways of doing work might constantly pop into creators' minds; and new perspectives on the creative process might enter the minds of the people involved. Creators facing time constraints must be able to control these possibilities in such a way that the material they release is both novel and efficient—and ultimately successful.

All three sets of difficulties boil down to a kind of balancing act between the need of creators to search continually for novelty and their need to limit that search in the interests of predictability and efficiency. Using journalism as her example, Gaye Tuchman (1972) points out that the major way mass media creators organize to cope with risks of failure when they search for novelty is to control that search by using routines. Routines are patterned activities that people learn to use in carrying out certain tasks. As Tuchman notes, the control of work has been a dominant theme in the sociology of organizations. Writers in this area have stressed that individuals in organizations learn to routinize their tasks if possible because using routines makes predictability and control over work possible.

The implication, then, is that production executives will implement organizational approaches to coping with environmental risks that involve routines. Taking a cue from Pfeffer and Salancik, we can suggest that the kind of routines a production firm's creative leaders encourage will depend on the nature and degree of economic and political risk those leaders perceive in their organization's relationship with its environment. Potential for economic loss can be considered low when the amount of cash needed to generate an individual product is relatively small. The potential for political loss is relatively low when the product is not likely to fall under the critical scrutiny of governmental organizations or powerful social pressure groups. Potential for relatively high economic and political loss—and thus for high risk—can be found in situations in which product development costs and public concerns are high. Contrasting the creation of prime-time network TV programs (high political and economic risk) with the creation of scholarly monographs (relatively low risk on both counts) will illustrate these points.

We can go further and suggest that the greater the risk involved, the greater the chance that a production firm's executives will both (1) orient their company's creative activities toward highly predictable, highly patterned mass media content and (2) orient their routines toward certain "administrative" techniques of coping, techniques that, while not stressing patterned content, do nevertheless add an important layer of predictability to the material. When environmental risks are not deemed as great, the executives will tend to orient their routines toward *only* administrative coping techniques. The nature of the political or economic risks will influence the specific elements of the routines. Most relevant here is how emphasizing one or the other set of routines for coping serves, often implicitly, to mark off for creative personnel the boundaries of their company's approach to institutional legitimacy.

EMPHASIZING ADMINISTRATIVE TECHNIQUES

Administrative techniques of coping are routines designed to help creators in executive roles seek out information or personnel that will maximize the chance of a particular product's success. Two broad forms of these techniques stand out—the use of *track-record talent* and the use of *market research*. A track-record talent is a creator who has a list of proven successes and a strong reputation in his or her field. Sometimes a track-record creator is the primary star of a particular endeavor. At other times, the track-record talent works behind the main creator, is less well known, but still has the reputation for bringing the magic of success to the project.

The second broad administrative technique that production executives use—market research—involves a very different approach to the problem of risk. While use of track record talents relies on the ability of people who had previous success in the marketplace to try to repeat their success, market research aims to probe the market itself in attempts to ensure the salability of the organization's creative output. We can speak of two kinds of market research—research to get ideas for the creation of a new product and research to evaluate and alter a product that already exists or is under development. Both types can involve surveying a broad range of forces in the organization's environment, including patrons (for example, advertisers), investors (for example, banks), exhibitors (for example, movie theaters), powerful authorities (for example, the Federal Communications Commission), pressure groups (for example, the Gay Task Force), and audiences.

Whether production executives know it or not, choosing creators with a reputation for delivering the right kind of material profitably often goes beyond helping personnel manage the creation of novelty efficiently. Because the creators have generated acceptable works previously, hiring them again tends implicitly to ensure that novelty will rarely run counter to the industry sector's fundamental perspective on the legitimacy of certain dominant institutions. Certainly, tendencies are not guarantees; artists can change perspectives and become unacceptably controversial. Still, in many cases, a person's track record is quiet assurance that the creator's ideology will fall within the limits of that organization's approaches to social power.

A more explicit recognition by production executives of ideological limits sometimes comes through market research. In the magazine industry, for example, executives thinking of releasing a new consumer periodical or changing the direction of one that already exists are likely to solicit information from members of the advertising industry about the utility advertisers see in the magazine; from members of the investment community about their feelings regarding the wisdom of the production firm's plans; from magazine distributors about their willingness to carry the periodical to stores; and from potential audience members about their desire to buy it. The aim of this information gathering will be to chart the magazine's overall chances in the marketplace as well as to garner support and advice. Generally, if the magazine looks useful from a marketing standpoint, executives from the production organization and from key firms in its environment will give the magazine the green light to test its fate among the public (Mogel, 1979; Click and Baird, 1979).

In rare instances, however, the editorial thrust of a magazine targeting an audience useful to advertisers will portend consistent institutional criticism. When that happens, opinions expressed by representatives of powerful organizations in the production firm's environment are likely to imply policy boundaries for the handling of social controversy. To most executives, these limits will relate to the problems the magazine's articles may create for advertisers. Producers, investors, and distributors realize that advertisers show reluctance to patronize material in any medium that does not create a good selling aura for their products, even if the viewpoints expressed have no direct bearing on the advertisements. Editorial environments that consistently challenge or offend established societal values and "commonsense" beliefs are eschewed regularly by the most powerful corporate sponsors in the United States. As the advertising director for General Motors put it in 1981, "When it comes down to it [advertising executives] have to look through the eyes of what we think is General Motors or Proctor & Gamble and what we stand for" (Margulies, 1981, A-29). Speaking specifically about *Penthouse* magazine in 1981, an unnamed advertising agency official noted frankly: "Many agencies and corporations consider it an endorsement of an editorial point of view if you advertise in a magazine"(Advertising Age, October 19, 1981: 28). He added that many of the companies find *Penthouse*'s morality offensive and its photography too sexually explicit for their tastes.

Of course, executives in some magazine companies will choose to alienate certain advertisers in order to maintain a certain viewpoint and readership for their periodicals; the same is true for other media. The cheaper the production costs for a medium and the greater and more varied the possible distribution methods, the more likely such "peripheral" media are to exist. Newspapers and magazines are relatively cheap to make and easy to circulate and thus logical vehicles for companies with ideological axes to grind. Movies, by contrast, are more expensive, harder to circulate, and so not likely to encourage a steady, organized stream of "alternative" productions. For executives not committed to nonmainstream perspectives, however, continually offending social and political values in even minor ways may eventually be considered a nuisance to be abandoned if possible in favor of more advertising profits and distribution clout. To do that, they might institute organizational policies that attempt to bring their products more in line with the mainstream without driving away the specialized audience they have chosen to attract. So, for example, while *Penthouse* did proclaim to the trade in 1981 that it was "provocative and proud of it," its associate editor admitted by the end of the year that the magazine's leadership had instituted "subtle evolutionary changes" to mollify advertisers and attract more of them to *Penthouse* (Advertising Age, October 19, 1981: 28).

To what extent do perspectives by members of the audience on the production firm's approach to institutional legitimacy inform executives' activities? Only weakly and indirectly, since production executives necessarily derive images of their target audience through means that often mix the needs of patron, distribution, and other organizations in the environment together with needs of the public that attends to the messages. Beyond checking past sales records, audience research is likely to be quite expensive and out of the question for many media products. For example, book publishing executives could not afford to test every new title they intend to release (Coser et al., 1982); nor could even a wealthy TV production company afford to test audience reaction to every episode of a series before its airing (though executives might well test a "pilot" program of the series before its airing). Consequently, in many cases the organization's tradition, the track record of creators, and the demands of patron, distribution, and exhibition forces in the environment become guiding forces toward inferring the interests of the targeted audience. Notions about the audience based on people's choice of products from within the established spectrum of marketplace choice are interpreted by executives in the production firm and by executives from firms in their company's environment.

A broad assumption that most production executives seem to hold is that if people buy or attend to media material, it means they enjoy it. Moreover, the executives usually consider this gauge of popularity the best gauge of interest; to them, phone calls and letters from audience members are often unrepresentative (Turow, 1984: 84-89). As a result, their notions about primary audience concerns come from near-term market observations: picking up on the subjects, characters, and prices from the current spectrum of choice that are likely to keep the audience acting favorably toward them in the marketplace. It is through such short term concerns and narrow vistas that executives who care about their audience's changing perspectives on institutional legitimacy must most often make their inferences.

More systematic forms of audience research are likely to be considered by production executives when political or economic costs of a new venture promise to be high. There are many ways of testing audience reaction to a new concept or a nearly completed product. The techniques range from in-depth interviews of a few people to superficial surveys of large numbers of people. Note, however, that it is the production executives, not the consumers, who set the objectives of the research and guide its question-and-answer agenda. Note, too, that it is in the executives' best interests to keep the advice they get from ultimate consumers confined to a limited range of workable choices. After all, production leaders are trying to lower the risks of their activity from all sides. If they invite (or pursue) consumer notions that will challenge the legitimacy of their sector's organizational supporters (investors, authorities, patrons, pressure groups, and the like), that can place them in uncomfortable position with their counterparts in those organizations. Moreover, it might force them to rethink drastically their ideas regarding the kinds of environmental resources to pursue, including the kinds of creative track records that are relevant. While such drastic breaks with organizational tradition have been known to happen, they are typically not instigated unless the production firm's overall resource situation is quite insecure. Typically, audience research involves testing material with perspectives on institutional legitimacy that are considered unproblematic by those carrying out the audience research.

EMPHASIZING CONTENT-RELATED TECHNIQUES

One particularly useful aspect of the administrative routines production executives implement to cope with risks is that the techniques often allow quite a bit of leeway for creators of the content. The reasons leeway is useful is that in some sectors of the mass media "quality" is identified with material that reflects the voice of an individual and that emphasizes "artistic" approaches to the world. Using track record talent and audience research, creators can lessen their risk in responding to this kind of environment while still fulfilling its demands— including, we have seen, its implicit and explicit demands regarding the portrayal of institutional legitimacy.

So, for example, editors in a trade book publishing firm can confidently contract with a John Updike, Norman Mailer, John Irving, or James Michener to write novels, fully expecting that the book will get substantial serious critical attention in addition to earning money in advance of release through sale of paperback rights. Too, having reviewed research on the kinds of nonfiction books chain stores expect will become popular, the editors might persuade well-known personalities with expertise in those areas to write books on those subjects. The result will be sold to critics and the public as the writer's individual accomplishment. The editors, for their part, will breathe much easier through the whole process than if the books had been written by the people whose acceptance in the marketplace had not been tested (Whiteside, 1981).

There are, however, areas of the mass media where executive creators do not expect that forces in the environment require them to speak through an invididual voice or emphasize unusual approaches to the world. High risk products tend overwhelmingly to fit this description. The reason seems to be that patron organizations contributing a lot of money or political capital to the creation of a product are likely to be more interested in ensuring that the product fills their monetary or political objectives than in advancing the cause of art. Network television programs and Hollywood movies fall into this class. At the same time, areas of the mass media do exist where product costs are low and individual artistry still is not emphasized. Paperback romances, pornographic novels, and pornographic films fit this category. We can suggest, then, that in most high-risk situations and in some low ones, creators find it possible to routinely generate highly patterned, predictable mass media material that itself has a record of success. In these situations, administrative techniques become only first steps in trying to reduce the risk of a particular item's failure in the marketplace. Risk reduction through previously tested formulas plays an important role as well.

A formula, John Cawelti (1975: 29) states, is a "conventional system for structuring cultural products. It can be distinguished from invented structures, which are new ways of organizing art." Formulas represent widely recognized principles for selecting and organizing material. In nonfiction, a formula is characterized by the subject, the point of view, and the sequence in which the argument is developed (Turow, 1984: 162-163). In fiction, which is the area Cawelti discusses, formulas consist of certain plots, characters, and settings. Every fiction formula implies an array of plot types, character types, and locales. Combining these in different ways can yield a multitude of stories. Combining elements from two or more formulas can yield new formulas that may appear more creative and sophisticated than traditional ones.

To John Cawelti (1975: 32), a formula "is a culture's way" of reaffirming its values as well as "simultaneously entertaining itself and . . . creating an acceptable pattern of temporary escape from the serious restrictions and limitations of human life." In fact, a growing number of research has, over the past decade, been explicating how the routine approaches that creators in certain media industries use implicitly structure the symbolic world so as to protect national institutions from fundamental public disillusionment. While some of this literature deals with entertainment, by far the greatest amount of research focuses on that special form of nonfiction: news. Some writers have traced the history of mainstream news routines to understand the way contemporary journalists come to have certain ideologies embedded in their very activities of news work (Schudson, 1978; Schiller, 1981). Other writers (for example, Tuchman, 1978; Fishman, 1980) have tracked how in contemporary society the subject, point of view, and presentation sequence of normative journalistic activity (embedded most strongly in the routines that news workers collectively call "objective") serve to frame the major agencies of U.S. society as, at best, crucial and, at worst, correctable, and anyway having no viable alternatives.

Understanding that entertainment and news formulas came to embody certain perspectives on society and its institutions through their historical development in the society is crucial to understanding the way they can embody patterned reflections on the legitimacy of institutions without executive creators often even realizing that. Editors can talk about the tradition of journalistic independence in the United States, not realizing that the very activities of journalism bring them to frame the world in certain ways. Similarly, producers can talk of pulp westerns and TV cop shows as "mere entertainment," ignoring that presentations of the society's institutions have developed historically as part of those formulas.

All they need to know to arrange their company's creative activities is that certain formulas will work in their marketplace. Yet, as Robert Sklar (1981) points out, that is often enough to protect them even in the face of environmental turmoil. Sklar's example comes from the early history of the movie industry. After World War I, the nascent industry became the target of assaults by pressure groups in the society that feared that movies were against them in a battle they were waging over values in American life. To simplify for the purpose of this brief discussion, their aim was to maintain a conservative, "small-town" perspective in the face of an increasingly urban, industrial, and ethnically diverse society. They saw American movies, with their vivid portrayals of crime and salacious behavior, as standing in direct opposition to this goal. To those spokespersons for the traditional middle and upper classes, the direction of the movies was particularly worrisome because power over the photoplay rested largely in the hands of foreign-born Jewish producers who, they felt, could not be trusted to promote traditional American values.

The producers' response, Sklar (1981: 91) says, was to steer a middle course through the warring factions in American society with the help of content-based routines. The film executives did present new lifestyles on the screen, but in such a way as to "clearly avoid breaking away from the fundamentalist economic and social mold." A major way they protected themselves, notes Sklar, was to base their films on time-tested formulas, varied in style and minor detail to suit the period:

> Faced with an audience more divided, more defensive, and yet increasingly avid for visions of alternative styles and behavior, moviemakers not unnaturally sought the subjects and treatments that pleased the most and alienated the fewest. The noisy and well-organized opposition and their own settled beliefs and filmmaking practice kept them from straying too far beyond the remaining stereotypes and formulas of the middle-class order. What they became adept at was reformulating

older conventions; only when the need was obvious and overwhelming did they dare to generate a new formula. The results were not so different from traditional culture as reformists and censors sometimes made it appear.

SOCIALIZING ARTISTS THROUGH RECRUITMENT

The foregoing discussion suggests that the ways production executives cope with risks lead them to organize creative tasks so that the output is implicitly in harmony with accepted approaches to the legitimacy of society's institutions. The discussion does not, however, bring us to the level of people who work for those executives and actually create the material. These "artists" must learn the norms of work, whether executives want them to adapt formulas or allow them more individual creative freedom. Given organizational arrangements that dictate certain approaches to coping with interorganizational demands, how do people who actually work on the material learn acceptable approaches and the way they should be applied?

Part of the answer surely lies in growing up in the society with certain approaches to life and certain experiences with media. Studies of the people who join mainstream United States media production firms to help create material suggest that many of them accept the values that underlie their production activities. Studies of journalists consistently reflect what John W.C. Johnstone et al. (1976: 26) have called "the fact that in virtually any society those in charge of mass communication tend to come from the same social strata as those in control of the economic and political systems," the upper-middle and upper classes. The same tendency seems to hold true with regard to nonnews in the United States. Moreover, hiring throughout the mainstream mass media has tended to reflect sexual, racial, and class dominance patterns in U.S. society as a whole.

Reflecting on the mainstream characteristics that describe mass media creators, some researchers have been tempted to suggest that the individuals involved perpetuate the theme of institutional legitimacy primarily through the imposition of their personal values—what Herbert Gans (1979: 213) calls their "lay values"—on the content. Gans, however, reaches more to the heart of the matter when he states that neither the lay values nor the upper-middle-class status of most journalists really explains the establishment-oriented nature of news work (p. 210). Surely, some personal likes and dislikes influence what appears in print or on the home screen. But, barring major societal changes, Gans asserts, the "basic shape of news" would not be different if a journalist came, for example, from a working class home. The reason, as we have seen, is that mainstream perspectives guiding news work are built into the news work activities. Working-class people, Gans suggests, would have a tough time filling the employment prerequisites for news work. Even when they could, to act as journalists they "would likely have to shed their working class values and reality judgments." Having a background that reflects dominant values, then, helps a recruit adapt to mainstream media work more easily than people without that background.

RECRUITMENT AND SOCIALIZATION

The process of recruitment holds important consequences for the portrayal of institutional legitimacy. We can distinguish two ways that executives recruit artists as resources for production firms. Sometimes, they take what Arthur Stinchcombe (1959) calls a "bureaucratic" approach. That is, they hire artists mainly on a long-term, full-time basis; newspaper executives typically take this approach to reporters. Other times, though, executives hire artists in a "craft" fashion: They contribute material for a specific project and are let go when they finish. Film writers, film directors, and freelance journalists are examples.

Each type of recruitment implies a different locus of organizational socialization. Socialization is viewed here as an active, creative process in which "people learn to use . . . norms or rules as a resource for the construction of meaning" (Tuchman, 1978: 206). The idea is that as people move through social situations, including organizations, they become involved in activities. Through these activities, they and the people they work with negotiate rules explicitly and implicitly about their interdependent behaviors (their roles). It is an idea that applies to both craft or bureaucratic recruitment styles. However, socialization does take place differently if an artist is a full-time, long-term member of a particular production firm than if he or she works freelance, getting recruited stop-and-go by various organizations.

A key difference between craft and bureaucratic artists is the major site of their competition with other artists for privilege and prestige. For bureaucratic artists, that site is the "home" organization, the firm in which they work. Daily, the continuation of their employment and their promotability are judged primarily by people within that firm. Freelance artists, on the other hand, must not only convince the companies they work for at any point in time to hire them again, they must also cultivate bases outside those companies to continue to generate more work in other places. Doing that effectively generally requires admission to a community of similar artists. It is a community in which a complex hierarchy, an elaborate system of contacts, and an often ritually prescribed gamut of competition strongly influence the artists' ability to enter production organizations, as well as the artists' market value.

In both recruitment forms, socialization operates to lead artists toward continuing the implicit and explicit norms of the production organization in which they work. In the craft case, the members of artistic communities make it their business to discern the needs of recruiters in various production firms, and the pressures on them. The need for new talent differs across media industries and across sectors of those industries. Similarly, the nature and level of cautions that selectors follow in hiring artists varies. (The editor of a "little magazine" might be willing to take a chance on a writer who has never published a story before, but the editor of a large circulation magazine might not.) Established artists and agents in an artistic community assimilate these critical elements and approach new artists with them in mind. As Robert Faulkner (1972) suggests, the members of an artistic community's inner circle are likely to feel ambivalent about suggesting new names. On the other hand, recruiters want to learn about new faces, and they are likely to be grateful to artists who can help them in their search. On the other hand, suggesting artists who fail can be worse than not suggesting anyone at all. Note, too, that established artists and agents see newcomers partly as threats. Artists might feel that too many people are reaching for their jobs. Agents might feel that newcomers not affiliated with them may take jobs from current clients (see Faulkner, 1972; Stebbins, 1972; Peterson and White, 1981).

Fear of competition, then, combined with an awareness of the needs and cautions that recruiters face in their production organizations, leads the various inner circles of many an artistic community to coordinate an artist sponsorship system that both minimizes threats to established artists and protects artist-sponsors and agents from recruiters' wrath. A common way to do that is to promote the idea that artists should not be suggested to recruiters unless they have "paid their dues" in related endeavors and begun to establish track records. This approach ensures that a relatively small number of newcomers will move through the recruitment gauntlet, thereby protecting most members of the inner circles. More important for our purpose, however, the approach also tends to weed out artists who might disrupt the chain of a production firm's typical activities and profits. Newcomers who want to move upward must prove themselves reliable to their artistic community. Doing that means performing activities in such a way as fundamentally not to rock the boat. Too, it means that the artist must negotiate a creative approach and image that resonates with the approach and image that at least one of the community's inner circles holds of itself. It means, in short, becoming part of that community's establishment.

A good way to illustrate this mechanism is to sketch the position black writers find themselves in when they want to help create those most mainstream of mass media materials, network television programs. According to several industry sources, a large number of black writers have been interested in applying their skills to this lucrative field, but their efforts have been stymied. In 1980, only 15 of 2,746 members of the Writers Guild, West, who found TV work in the previous two years were black (Riley, 1980: 34). As Len Riley (1980) found when he investigated the subject for *Emmy Magazine,* an important contributor to this situation is the craft system of recruitment with its key requirements of connections, paying dues, and track record. Inexperienced black writers find it harder to develop the trusting, helpful contacts they need in the overwhelmingly white TV community. As Riley (1980: 39) notes, the doors to employment may be declared open to minorities, but "the buddy system transforms them into revolving doors."

The few writers who do make it through the doors to write for TV pose no threat to the United States economic or political system, the U.S. TV system, or its time-tested formulas. Comparing black and white writers, Riley (1980: 54) found that "the two groups have similar educations, speak the same language with the same idioms, swing in the same economic and social mainstream . . . [and are] all products of the television generation." Still, even these people cannot get the widespread work they want because production firm recruiters associate them from the start with writing only about the black experience. Literary agent Rick Ray's solution (in Riley, 1980: 54) to this problem is straightforward:

> A dramatic writer is a dramatic writer and it doesn't matter if he's green. If I were to encourage a new black writer, I'd say, "Sit down and write a good script that doesn't have a single black man in the damn thing. Make it a totally non-color oriented experience.

It turns out that in the early 1980s the Writers Guild did set up a program with this approach. It gave a minority writer a chance to work with an established writer who had been recommended by a producer "as someone in tune with that producer's series" (Riley, 1980: 56). According to a Writers Guild executive, the program allowed an inexperienced writer to be "shepherded through the system—from initial story conference through finished script—while deriving inside knowledge about the particular show" (Riley, 1980: 56). Clearly, such a program is designed to help new writers with talent find jobs by plugging them into the inner circles and operations of the artistic community. Clearly, too, the program is not designed to bring out any new perspectives about life that minority writers might be able to contribute to the artistic community. Rather, it is set up to help them shed from their work any ethnic background that might fundamentally change formulas and activities that people in the industry share as standard. Certainly, this kind of education system ends up ensuring the usefulness of those writers to production organizations. It also makes it quite unlikely that writers will generate stories that expose unexposable tensions in society and seriously challenge the right of society's establishment to rule.

The same statement could be made about writers recruited to a bureaucratic style of work in a mainstream media firm, though the process by which their socialization takes place is likely to be different from the one craft writers follow. It is possible to exaggerate the difference. Bureaucratically employed artists— for example, permanently employed magazine writers, public relations practitioners, and journalists—are by no means hermits confined to firms. Many of them become actively involved with counterparts from outside their organizations. And, from the standpoint of occupational socialization these involvements influence their work in ways that parallel the influences that communities of craft artists exert on their members.

We can identify four particularly important avenues of socialization outside the firm that bureaucratically employed artists might move through: (1) school training; (2) job mobility; (3) on-the-job contacts outside the home organization; and (4) participation in professional associations and subscriptions to professional media. Not every avenue holds equal importance in every media industry or every industry sector. In mainstream U.S. journalism, for example, school training has only been a significant factor since after World War II (Johnstone et al., 1976: 176). On the other hand, on-the-job contacts have always been important. Journalists from different papers meet one another often in the course of assignments. They file similar stories after viewing the same events, speaking to the same sources, reading the same press releases, and sharing ideas about how to "objectively" report it all. The phenomenon has been called "pack journalism," and it has been cited (Crouse, 1972) as a key reason for the similar subjects and angles that the many reporters covering the same event tend to use. Often, too, reporters receive ideas of what is important and how to report it by reading the same elite newspapers and turning to the same wire services (see MacNeil, 1968: 30).

It warrants emphasizing, though, that while these and other forms of contact with the field help reinforce work routines, the primary training group for reporters—in fact, the primary training ground for all bureaucratically employed artists—is the organization in which they work. Organizational resources serve as incentives. Superiors control resources—permissions, salary increases, company perquisites, authority to make decisions independently—which they can release to artists carrying out "good" work. Colleagues, too, control resources. They are likely to be more friendly and helpful to artists who do good work than to those who do not. An artist learns that good work means activities that fit nicely with superiors' policies regarding what the organization should create and how it should create it.[2] As we have noted, the approaches that flow from these policies necessarily embody perspectives on the domains of legitimate social power, authority, and justice—and on the limits artists have in questioning them. By extension, then, an artist who does good work at the same time perpetuates those perspectives at the core of his or her material.

CONCLUSION

The purpose of this chapter has been to use a resource dependence perspective on interorganizational relations as a basis for understanding how executives and artists of mass media organizations come to portray the legitimacy of their society's institutions in a patterned manner. Coming at the media's portrayal of institutional legitimacy with this framework points to ways of integrating findings from both Marxist and "industrial" research so as to track the relationship among social power, industrial and organizational exigencies, and the mass media content that creators produce. The resource dependence perspective also serves to suggest the circumstances under which repudiations and alternatives to various established institutions and institutional values might be attempted consistently by production organizations. In fact, one theme running quietly through this chapter is the value of comparing and contrasting the way creators come to portray power across a variety of media industries and industry sectors. Such a comparative approach would be a substantial departure for research on media organizations, which has tended to focus on individual industries, and on the most visible and controversial of them—TV and newspapers.

Careful comparative research on the way creators "learn to portray social power" in a wide range of mass media organizations—from broadcast TV firms to billboard companies, from newspaper companies to direct mail setups—would bring much needed texture to our understanding of how the "consciousness industries" operate in U.S. society. As this exposition has indicated, the research can take place at many levels of the organization, and of the organization's interactions with other organizations. Certainly, the framework proposed here is very preliminary; much work needs to be done to pin down and operationalize some key terms (such as legitimation) in the context of specific comparative research problems. In addition, researchers should consider linking analyses of organizational and interorganizational activities with analyses of the depiction of certain institutions in the material the focal production organizations release. There is much to understand and do. The research dependence perspective can provide a useful entry into some of the most important though unexplored areas relating to mass media organizations.

NOTES

1. An important exception is the study by Gitlin (1979), which focuses on the way the commercial U.S. television networks covered Students for a Democratic Society (SDS) during the Vietnam war era.

2. The classic study of the process in journalism is Warren Breed (1972); see also Gans (1979) and Cantor (1971). All three writers also deal with the questions of value conflicts among creators in mass media organizations, an area too broad to add here. For additional comments on this subject, see Turow (1984: 142-145).

Chapter 9

POWER, PRAXIS, AND SELF IN ORGANIZATIONAL COMMUNICATION THEORY

Charles Conrad and Mary Ryan

NO CONCEPT IN sociological and organizational theory is more ubiquitous and perplexing than "power." Sometimes the focus of research, often an implicit dimension of other constructs, power and power relationships long have captured the attention of researcher-theorists perplexed by the actions of the people who comprise social collectives. Although existing models of social and organizational power often have included communication as a dimension of power relationships, the role that symbolic action plays in the creation, maintenance, and modification of organizational power relationships rarely has been the focus of attention. Recently two changes in perspective have led to a more central role for communication in theories of organizational power. First, during the past two decades depictions of organizations as socially and thus communicatively constructed realities have occupied a progressively more important place in social and organizational theory (Pfeffer, 1982; *Administrative Science Quarterly*, 1983). Second, during the same era, organizational communication theorists have started to define their field of inquiry in far more comprehensive terms. Although information flow and networks of message exchange continue to be important elements of definitions of "organizational communication," the phrase now seems also to encompass a variety of forms of symbolic action that long have been considered by rhetorical and literary theorists but largely have been overlooked in organizational communication research (for example, stories, rituals, myths, and metaphors).[1]

As theoretical perspectives have become more diverse and complex, and as definitions of organizations, communication, and power have become more abstract and comprehensive, the relevant literature has grown rapidly in scope and depth. Our objective in this essay is to survey contemporary perspectives on social and organizational power and power relationships. First, we shall suggest that existing models of organizational power can be viewed productively as forming clusters of points arrayed along a continuum defined by the differing assumptions implicit in the models. Second, we shall argue that the most recent and least extensively developed of these models—a cluster that we will label "radical-critical" perspectives—provides distinctive opportunities for organizational communication theorists to contribute to our understanding of organizational power relationships.

MODELS OF SOCIAL AND ORGANIZATIONAL POWER

Existing models of power relationships can be defined and compared in terms of what they presume about three key issues. The first and most basic of these involves the nature of the construct itself. Each model presumes or assumes that "power" has a particular definition and form. These definitions differ from one another in three ways: (1) the degree of abstractness of the construct, including the relationship between the construct and the communicative action (language-in-use) of members of organizations, (2) the "level" of analysis from which the construct is viewed, and (3) the significance of the role of reification in the definition.

The second differentiating issue involves assumptions about the degree to which power relationships and the societal and organizational structures that accompany them are stable. All three groups examine two factors that contribute to the stability (or instability) of social structures—the incentives to cooperate and/or compete, which are believed to exist within the social structures, and the place and functions of contradictions within those structures. However, the models differ in substantive ways in their assumptions about the role these forces play in "normal" social structures. At one pole are models that suggest that social structures continue to exist because incentives to cooperate are greater than incentives to compete, at least over the long term. These models also assume that there is normally a congruence among the needs of the larger society, the needs, identities, values, beliefs, and frames of reference of members of the society, and their everyday activities. There are, of course, instances in which competitive incentives are temporarily dominant or when incongruities arise within the social structure and instability is created. But these instances are deviations from the norm and are the products of errors in judgment or breakdowns in communication. At the other pole are models that assume competition and conflict are inherent in social life and that contradictions among the identities of workers, their activities, and their social structures are not only normal, but are the constant, defining condition of organizational life.

The third issue involves the relationship between power and communication. In some models, communication is a means through which power is defined and exercised. They are both conceptually and functionally discrete constructs. In others, the two constructs are interrelated. And in still others, the locus of power is in symbolic action; power and communication are essentially identical processes.

The final differentiating issue involves questions about the critical "distance" that exists between a researcher-theorist and his or her topic, and the function that research plays in the creation and modification of organizational and societal power relationships (Pacanowsky and Strine, 1985). In the following section of this chapter we shall describe three clusters of models of organizational power that differ from one another in terms of these three focal issues. Because the range of models we will consider is so broad, the picture we paint of each model will be formed only of very broad strokes. As a result, nuances of differences among the perspectives may be obscured in the process.

TRADITIONAL MODELS OF POWER

Initially, research on organizational power took one of two directions. One strain sought to determine the attributes of employees and/or their organizational roles, which were related to their ability to achieve their objectives, overcome resistance to their efforts or influence events and outcomes (Raven and Kruglanski, 1970; March, 1958; Conrad, 1983). The second strain attempted to determine the relationship between various distributions of perceived power and job satisfaction and organizational performance (Tannenbaum, 1968; Lawrence and Lorsch, 1967). As power is defined in traditional models the construct has three characteristics:

(1) It is an abstraction, located in the minds of employees and/or researchers, and is a product of language-in-use but has an identity and function that is independent of symbolic action.

(2) It is examined primarily at an individual or work-group level of analysis. Power is viewed as an attribute of individual employees and/or units of organizations. Although organizational or societal factors may influence either an individual employee's (or unit's) ability to obtain or control bases of power or the relative salience of the different bases to particular organizational situations, power is something that individuals or groups of individuals possess. For example, although the nature of the environment an organization faces and the types of uncertainties the environment-organization interface imposes on an organization's decision makers may mean some employees/units are more strategically located than others, it is their capacity to exploit their organizational roles that determines their power in their organization (Butler et al., 1977; Pettigrew, 1972).[2] Similarly, while broad social and cultural factors may influence the relative importance of task, expertise, charisma, control over financial rewards, and so on, it is the individual's capacity to obtain and display salient attributes that create power.

(3) Power may be reified; that is, it is an abstract concept that researcher-theorists sometimes may treat as if it is concrete and has causal force. Although all three perspectives are concerned with the reification of power, they treat reification in very different ways. In traditional models, reification is an

epistemological and/or methodological *problem*. If "power" actually exists in organizations—if it is a concrete attribute of individuals, units or organizational roles—then it can be discerned, measured, linked to other concrete variables, and incorporated into social scientific theories. But, if it is an illusion, a symbolic construct that employees use to explain, justify, or rationalize their actions or a theoretical construct that researchers impose on their observations in order to unify discrete items of data, including it in social scientific theories (particularly "positivistic" theories) would render them suspect at best. In traditional models, the potential for the reification of power presents methodological and epistemological problems.

In contrast, in symbological models the reification of power is *problematic*. "Power" is an abstraction of concrete attributes created by employees themselves. The symbolic, communicative, and cognitive processes through which employees reify power and in turn employ the reified construct in their day-by-day actions is a central focus of symbolical models. In them, reification is of *substantive* rather than merely methodological interest. The radical-critical perspective extends the problematic element of reified conceptions of power even further. In it, reification of power is treated as a recurring, essential aspect of social structures. Throughout social history, abstract conceptions of power have been built into the very fabric of societies and their institutions, providing individuals with preconscious parameters for action. These parameters, and the processes of reification that support them, support the alienation of workers from themselves and their peers and perpetuate internally contradictory social structures.[3] But, in traditional models reification is, at most, an element of the epistemic situation within which research is conducted and theories constructed. It is not a focal point for research and theory; not a substantive element of the model itself. It may raise questions about the legitimacy of models that collapse widely varying features of individuals, organizational roles, and societal values into a single construct and may suggest that there are limitations to the viability of neo-positivist social scientific methods in research on power relationships. But in traditional models, reification is a *problem* requiring researchers to constrain and condition their interpretations of their data; it is not *problematic*.

The second distinction among models of organizational power relationships involves their treatment of stability, conflict, and contradiction. In traditional models of power, organizations are viewed as essentially stable structures; as enterprises composed of interdependent individuals whose incentives to cooperate with one another are at least sufficient to keep their behavior from being dominated by their incentives to compete. Although the power possessed by various individuals may change as they obtain control over key organizational resources, use or abuse the power they have, or attempt to deal with environmental changes that alter their importance to the uncertainty-reducing processes of their organizations, the structure of organizations and organizational power relationships remains relatively stable. Although contradictions may arise within power relationships or between structures of power and other dimensions of an organization's structure or operation, they will eventually be overcome by natural adaptive processes that reestablish equilibrium within the organization and between it and its environment.[4] The processes through which power equilibrium is maintained are at most secondary topics of analysis. More often these processes are presumed to be theoretically uninteresting.[5] Thus organizational power relationships can be characterized as stability in temporary flux. Although particular power relationships may be changing constantly in minor ways, the construct is sufficiently stable to allow it to be linked with other constructs as either a dependent or an independent variable. In the most extreme of the traditional models, contradictions within and among power relationships are treated as error variance. In none of the traditional models is contradiction and its management the focus of analysis.

The third differentiating factor is the way in which the models treat the relationships between power and communication. In traditional models, power and communication are related only indirectly to each other. In some models, communication provides the raw material from which individuals can build expertise and thus gain power (Pettigrew, 1972; Butler et al., 1977). In others communicative processes create, perpetuate and disseminate information about individual members' reputations for having or not having influence (Kipnis, 1976). In others, power is a constraint that limits communication to certain topics and forms and/or guides communication in certain directions (Bacharach and Baratz, 1962; Baratz, 1970). But, in each traditional model, communication is viewed as an entity whose identity is relatively independent of the entity power. Because communicative processes are (at most) either the means through which individuals obtain and control bases of power or one of the effects of power relationships, the two constructs are only indirectly related to each other.

Finally, in traditional models of power the researcher is viewed as a relatively independent, autonomous, and objective observer of his or her object of study. Her or his function is to discover and clarify the dimensions of power and relationships to other variables that are operating in an organization or type of organization. Although the results of his or her research may be employed in ways that maintain or alter existing societal and organizational power relationships, neither the assumptions underlying the research nor the activity of performing research are viewed as part of organizational power dynamics. Of course, many traditional models do confront the considerations regarding the subject-object relationship that underlie contemporary reevaluations of positivist social science, but these considerations are part of the epistemic context that surrounds the act of theorizing rather than a focal point for research and theory (Abell, 1975; Bacharach and Lawler, 1981).

In an important way, traditional models of organizational power provide a touchstone from which more abstract perspectives can be examined and understood. Grounded in the assumption that organizations are the planned creations of rational individuals whose goals can be met only through collaborative action, developed within the epistemic framework implicit in traditional neopositivist social science and oriented toward enhancing the stability, attractiveness, and productivity of formal organizations, traditional models have provided both clear evidence that organizational power relationships are exceptionally complex constructs and the impetus for the development of perspectives that incorporate very different assumptions and methods. Traditional perspectives form one pole on our continuum of models of organizational power relationships (see Figure 9.1). Their (1) definition of power, (2) assumption that organizational structures are relatively stable, (3) lack of emphasis on communicative processes, and (4) presumptions that researchers are objective and distant from their subjects differentiate them from more contemporary models.

SYMBOLOGICAL MODELS OF POWER

In some senses traditional and symbological models of organizational power are mirror images of one another. Both clusters deal with the same issues and concerns, but from very different perspectives. The focal points of traditional models provide the conceptual backdrop for symbological models. In Gestaltist terms, the concepts that form the "figures" of one model form the "ground" for the other framework. The conceptual problems that traditional models manage either by presuming the legitimacy of a particular set of solutions or defining them as "theoretically uninteresting," "beyond the scope of analysis," or "products of error variance" are the central concerns of the symbological perspective. The topics that are central to traditional models—the bases of power, optimal distribution of perceived power, and relationships among roles, environments, uncertainties, and power—largely are treated as subsidiary or subordinate concerns in symbological models. The most important conceptual differences between the two perspectives involve (1) definitions of the construct "power" and the place occupied by communication in those definitions, and (2) the nature and degree of stability of power structures.

COMMUNICATION AND
DEFINITIONS OF POWER

Both traditional and symbological models view power as a multifaceted, multidimensional construct. The differences between the two definitions involve the interrelationships among these dimensions and the place that processes of reification occupy within the construct. In traditional models, personal attributes and the characteristics of organizational roles are conjoined. For instance, an employee whose formal position allows her or him to control the distribution of rewards or resources, or an employee who occupies a central niche in communication networks is provided with an opportunity to obtain and use organizational power. But this potential power will be transformed into actual power only if the employee is able to capitalize on the opportunities provided by his or her role. Conversely, a highly expert individual will gain power from this personal attribute only if provided opportunities to publicly use that expertise to solve significant organizational problems (Kanter, 1977).

Because the potential power implicit in organizational roles and individual attributes are interrelated, treating them as distinct constructs is questionable. Because potential power and power-in-use are conceptually distinct, integrating constructs like "possesses technical competence" and "strategically controls information flow" is difficult, at best.

In traditional models, problems synthesizing role characteristics and individual attributes typically are treated as statistical or measurement-related difficulties if they are treated at all (Raven and Kruglanski, 1970). The processes through which potential power is actualized generally are either excluded from analysis or assumed to be sufficiently simple and invariant that researchers can focus on the outcomes of the processes (perceived power relationships) without systematically examining the processes themselves (Bacharach and Lawler, 1980).

In contrast, symbological models presume that theories of power should focus on and must be able to explain (1) the processes through which role characteristics and individual attributes coalesce and divide in employees' perceptions to form power relationships, and (2) how potential and enacted power mutually influence each other. For example, the threat/promise potential, which is part of an employee's organizational role, is inextricably linked to other employees' perceptions of his or her capacity and propensity to use that potential in attempts to influence their actions (Schelling, 1960, 1978; Tedeschi, 1970). While traditional models might collapse these considerations into a variable labeled "perceived reward or coercive power," symbological models would focus on patterns of threatening and promising in an organization, and the ways in which these processes influence and are influenced by perceptions of threat/promise potential.

Implicit in this example is a second distinction between traditional and symbological definitions of power. In traditional models, the synthesis of dimensions of power (and its associated difficulties) are viewed as researcher-theorists' problems. In symbological models, synthesizing the multiple dimensions of power is viewed as a complex process that is carried out by members of organizations and societies as well as by researchers. In order to make sense of their situations, symbological models assume, organizational actors construct integrated and comprehensive views of the amount and type of influence possessed by each member of their organization at a given point in time and around a given issue. Power therefore has a history and is influenced by expectations of its future use. These constructs are formed, shared, validated, and sustained through communication. The central problem facing symbological theories of power is to describe employee-actors' constructs and explain how they function for the actors themselves (Weber, 1947, 1964; Gadamer, 1975).

As suggested earlier in this chapter, symbological and traditional definitions of power also differ in their views of the significance of processes of reification. In traditional models, the reified nature of the concept of power is a methodological or epistemological problem that stems from traditional social scientific methods rather than from the definition of power itself. In symbological models, processes of reification provide a significant focus for analysis at two different levels. The first level involves processes through which employees reify (concretize the abstract concept) power. In all organizations, this perspective argues, members develop a language of power that both articulates the dimensions of the construct that actors have developed and validated intersubjectively, and gives the construct a concrete linguistic referent. Persons are defined as powerful or powerless, actions are viewed as power plays, domination or submission; inaction is defined as acquiescence. The actors' reified conception of power provides the parameters within which they define their situations and choose from among a repertoire of response strategies, and provides them with an explanation of their actions or inaction. In a complex cycle,[7] acting generates perceptions of power and labeling transforms actions into examples of symbolic categories (expertise, ignorance, power, vulnerability, and so on), which guide choices and interpretations of action. The first task of researchers operating from a symbological perspective is to understand the meaning that this cycle has for the actors themselves. The researcher's second task—and the second level at which reification is a substantive focus of analysis—is to explain the implications that actors' symbolic actions hold for power relationships in their organizations and in general. However, this task involves the researcher in a second cycle that reifies power. She or he proceeds by observing employees' actions, interpreting the meaning their actions hold for them, observing her or his own interpretive acts, examining the impact and implications of her or his interpretations, reinterpreting actors' actions and interpretations, and so on. The presence and function of this second interpretive circle implies both that processes of reification (actors' and researchers') must be a focal point of attempts to develop theories of power and that the theorizing process is reflexive in the fullest sense of that term (Hawes, 1978).

ASSUMPTIONS ABOUT THE STABILITY OF POWER AND SOCIAL STRUCTURE

The second major difference between symbological and traditional models of power involves their assumptions about the stability of organizational power relationships and organizational structures. In traditional models, both constructs are assumed to be relatively stable. Although key events may temporarily upset these stable patterns of action, equilibrium will eventually return to the system because stability is an essential attribute of power (at least as it is defined within the traditional framework). Symbological models posit a more complex view of organizational structures and power relationships. Typically, these models explain the stability and change of organizational structures through some form of a "grammatical analog," a depiction of power relationships that is analogous to the transformational views of grammar popularized by Noam Chomsky and his successors (Conrad, 1983; Clegg, 1979; Giddens, 1976, 1983; Poole et al., 1982; Poole and McPhee, 1983; Ranson et al., 1980). Deep structures are preconscious guidelines and constraints whose appropriateness as ways of interpreting and responding to organizational situations is taken for granted by members of an organization. They are normal—with the term meaning both "typical," with its overtones of "sameness," and "proper," with all the moral implications that term entails—and flexible and adaptive. In a sense, deep structures tell employees who they are—what their role in their organization is and where they "fit" in the formal and informal hierarchies that constitute the organization. Only during those relatively rare cases in which an employee acts in ways that violate the deep structure do members become consciously aware of its existence, character, and function as a set of parameters for their actions. It is through these preconscious parameters of action that power normally is exercised in organizations. Employees choose to act in certain ways, not because of overt threats or promises, but because doing so is consistent with their taken-for-granted assumptions about their identities and organizational roles, and about what actions constitute natural, appropriate adaptations to the actions of others (Clegg, 1979). Deep structures of power are located in the patterns of action that recur in an organization and in members' language use, particularly those linguistic forms that have long been recognized to express the preconscious parameters that guide the actions of a culture—myth and metaphor (Conrad, 1983; Lakoff and Johnson, 1980; Meyer and Rowan, 1977).

A second dimension of organizational power relationships is their surface structure. Power is exercised overtly through four symbolic forms: justifying, rationalizing, threatening, and promising. Organizational actors do openly argue in favor of or against particular courses of action and they do openly discuss possible rationalizations for actions that have already been taken or decisions that have already been made. They also do overtly threaten to withhold resources or rewards or promise to grant requests or favors in order to influence the choices made by others. The specific character of their overt communicative displays is influenced by the features of the organizational situation that they face—the issue, perceptions of the other participants and their relationships, precedents, norms, and so on. Overt displays of power constitute a second dimension of organizational power relationships.

The final dimension of the grammatical analogue involves processes of interpenetration, ways in which the deep and surface structures influence each other. Through recurring patterns of communicative displays, employees produce deep structures of power. Through guiding and constraining actors' choices, these preconscious patterns of action influence what is communicated overtly and how it is communicated, thereby perpetuating the deep structure. The two dimensions of action interpenetrate each other; their relationship is a dual, recursive one. The interrelationship between preconscious parameters and overt, communicative action is often revealed by organizational rituals because it is in ritual that preconscious guidelines are articulated in concrete situations.[8]

At times elements of the deep and surface structures may become inconsistent with each other. Individual actors may communicate in unexpected, "abnormal," or "irrational" ways. Their overt displays may contradict taken-for-granted parameters of action in their organization. In some cases their aberrant behavior may generate changes in the deep structure. In some cases these changes may occur without the members consciously recognizing what has happened. One employee acts in unexpected, but somehow fulfilling ways, and other employees mirror his or her action, thus creating a new pattern of action. In other cases the transformation may be quite conscious. One actor may act in ways that lead to overt, open consideration of the appropriateness or relevance of an element of the deep structure. Taken-for-granted assumptions are no longer taken for granted. Even if the ensuing discussion does not lead to a rejection of the element, the act of discussing it will influence its constraining power. Because deep and surface structures are intersubjectively validated symbolic creations, they are constantly revealed by language use.[9] Although deep structures are *relatively* more stable than surface structures, both dimensions of power relationship are constantly being formed, re-formed, and transformed through language. Normally, deep and surface structures are consistent with and supportive of each other. Contradictions occur, are experienced, and are managed symbolically. They are recurring but temporary aberrations, and as such are an important topic for analysis. But contradictions are neither the substance of power and power relationships nor the central focus of symbological models of organizational power.

SUMMARY: TRADITIONAL AND SYMBOLOGICAL MODELS OF POWER

Traditional and symbological perspectives toward organizational power relationships differ from each other in two fundamental ways. First, while traditional models view communication as a means through which power is obtained, managed, and publicized, symbological models view communicative processes as the substance of power relationships. In the former perspective, power and communication can be separated analytically and their interrelationships examined statistically. In the latter framework, power relationships inhere in language-in-use and are contained in the dominant myths, metaphors, rituals, and arguments expressed by organizational actors.[10] Second, while traditional models view power relationships as stable elements of stable organizational structures, symbological models assume that power relationships involve a number of subsidiary structures that mutually influence—stabilize and upset—each other. In the former framework, contradictions within power relationships are defined (or operationalized) out of existence, or treated as temporary and theoretically uninteresting moments in equilibrium-maintaining processes. In the latter perspective, contradictions within and among structures of power and the communicative processes through which those contradictions are managed are among the most central foci of research and theory.

Although these distinctions suggest that analysis of communicative processes plays a more important role in research conducted from a symbological framework, they do not indicate that organizational communication research cannot make important contributions to traditional perspectives of organizational power. For instance, major surveys of traditional research conducted more than a decade apart both concluded that a number of important

(1) How do individual employees' values and beliefs influence
   (a) their choices of communicative strategies to employ in order to exercise the various bases of power?
   (b) their responses to various strategies used to exercise the different bases of power?
(2) How do communicative processes influence the relative salience of different beliefs and values in employees' choices and responses to different bases of power?
(3) How does the exercise of one base of power alter perceptions of, reliance on, and responses to other bases (for example, how does coercion alter "referent power" within superior-subordinate relationships)?
(4) How do the norms, precedents, values, and so on (that is, the "culture") of an organization
   (a) guide and/or constrain the exercise of different bases of power?
   (b) become salient during the exercise of different bases of power?
(5) How do various interactions between bases of power and communicative strategies (especially the ways in which threats and promises are proposed) influence processes of escalation during organizational conflicts?
(6) Through what communicative processes and forms are perceived power relationships formed and maintained?
(7) In what ways does centrality or peripherality in communication networks influence employees' access to different sources of power and/or their ability to exercise their power?

NOTE: Many of these topics are treated in detail in Raven and Kruglanski (1970) and Bacharach and Lawler (1981).

Figure 9.1 Organizational Communication Research and Traditional Models of Power

communication-related questions still confront traditional models of organizational power (see Figure 9.1) (Raven and Kruglanski, 1970; Bacharach and Lawler, 1981).

Symbological models both encompass these questions and offer an expanded definition of symbolic action. Of course, these broadened definitions generate a different set of research hypotheses about the interrelationships between communication and power. Questions about the constraining force of information flow, social norms, and individual values that are crucial to traditional models are transformed into questions about the symbolic processes through which organizational myths and rituals lead employees to define themselves, their actions, and their organizations in particular ways. Issues about the relationships between potential power and power-in-use are submerged in the view that the locus of power is in symbolic process (rather than *in* individuals or roles). Because the social, organizational, and communicative theories that underlie symbological models of power rest on the concept that organizational realities are created intersubjectively, rather than the traditional view that the realities of organizational life are discovered through communication, symbolic action broadly defined plays a more central role in power research and theory.

RADICAL-CRITICAL MODELS OF SOCIAL
AND ORGANIZATIONAL POWER

Grounded in recent reinterpretations of the seminal works of Max Weber and the young Karl Marx, radical-critical perspectives extend further the trend away from traditional assumptions that was initiated by symbological theorists. Long an important part of sociological perspectives on organizations, radical-critical views have only recently captured the attention of organizational theorists and have yet to occupy even a marginal place in organizational communication theory and research.[11] This situation is not surprising given the assumptions and research methods that traditionally have characterized the latter areas of thought. However, it is unfortunate because, as we shall argue in the remainder of this chapter, symbolic/communicative processes are central elements of radical-critical perspectives. Consequently, organizational communication reseachers can provide important and distinctive contributions to this perspective on social and organizational power, and radical-critical models of power can enhance our understanding of the symbolic acts of employees.

Radical-critical models parallel symbological perspectives in two respects. First, they generally accept some version of the assumption that "power" has multiple "faces" or "levels" that are both revealed in and obscured by various forms of symbolic action. Second, they usually offer some version of the argument that communicative action both constitutes and is constituted by deep structures of power.

But radical-critical and symbological models differ in three equally important ways. First, the two perspectives treat the concepts of inconsistencies and contradictions in fundamentally different ways. Both perspectives do discuss the inconsistencies that arise between structures (general patterns of action) and particular symbolic acts. But, symbological models tend to view the various levels of action as normally being congruent with each other. Those instances in which contradictions do occur are revealed through communication and are either confronted through argument or manipulated through myth and ritual. Through these symbolic processes, deep structures are modified so that they become more internally consistent and more congruent with surface structures. In radical-critical models contradictions, both within structures and between deep and surface structures, are seen as the norm rather than the exception (Coward and Ellis, 1977). Symbolic action either obscures or redefines contradictions, thus perpetuating internally inconsistent power relationships. Only in very rare cases of major organizational or cultural upheaval are contradictions confronted or structures of power modified (Tucker, 1977; Heydebrand, 1977; Benson, 1977).[12]

The second difference involves the more detailed treatment of deep structures of power that is typical of radical-critical models. Indeed, concepts of "hegemony"—the processes through which taken-for-granted assumptions about how reality should be interpreted and how choices regarding how to act should be made are formed, serve as constraints on action and are maintained and revised—form the core of radical-critical views (Gramsci, 1971; Bourdieu, 1977). Although symbological models include some concept of hegemony, the construct functions more as a single component of a larger model or as the context within which other components are examined than as the focus of analysis.

The final distinction involves the scope of analysis adopted by symbological and radical-critical theories. The latter group of models explicitly examine the ways in which features of a culture (particularly its socioeconomic structures and institutions) coalesce with organization-specific structures to solidify power relations. Of course, both perspectives assume that the structures of power that exist within an organization reflect the structures of the broader culture. But, where symbological models tend to focus on organizational power relationships, using them as symbols of the structures of domination present in the culture, radical-critical models focus on cultural structures as the only context within which organizational power relationships can be understood. The scope of the two groups of models differs in a second way. Radical-critical perspectives assume that the meaning of workers' actions, both for them and for researchers, evolves from a complicated interrelationship between their physical, productive activities and their communicative acts. This distinction does not imply either that material, physical acts are devoid of symbolic dimensions or that the creation of communicative acts is substantively different than the creation of more tangible products. It does suggest that the identities of employees are influenced in fundamental ways by the meanings they attribute to all their productive activities. Power relationships evolve out of the matrix of meanings formed by the processes of material and communicative action, individual definitions of self and hegemonic domination. Power is exercised through the symbolic and technical manipulations of that matrix.

Of course, these paragraphs have provided only a skeletal introduction to radical-critical models and the role that communication plays in them. The objective of the final sections of this chapter is to begin to flesh out that framework and suggest some of the contributions that organizational communication research can make to the development of radical-critical perspectives on organizational power relationships.[13]

RADICAL CRITICAL PERSPECTIVES AND ORGANIZATIONAL COMMUNICATION RESEARCH

The central concern of radical-critical frameworks is the concept of hegemony and the communicative processes through which it is formed and maintained. Deep structures support hierarchical power relationships through two interrelated symbolic processes: (1) the manipulation of identity, and (2) the rationalization of action.

POWER AND THE MANAGEMENT OF IDENTITY

Perhaps the most important element of Marxian ontology is the assumption that humans have the unique capacity to transform nature through their own actions (Marx and Engels, 1974: 232). In doing so, humans separate themselves from the nonhuman elements of creation. Through creating lasting material products (including progeny and instruments with which additional products can be created), humans begin to realize that they can master the temporal and spatial limits that dominate the rest of creation. And, through material acts, humans encounter other humans and create the social dimension of their identities: "Language is as old as consciousness [identity], language is practical consciousness *that exists also for other men, and for that reason alone it really exists for me* as well; language like consciousness, only arises from the need, *the necessity,* of intercourse with other men" (Marx and Engels, 1974: 230; also see Brown, 1982). Individual identities and ontological awareness are bound together by and in practical linguistic acts. Humankind's capacity to act freely, to dominate nature, provides it with its potency and its solidarity as a species. If any factors interfere with the self-constituting processes through which these meanings are attached to action, humankind's power is reduced. If some persons can manipulate the meaning of action, they can manipulate the identities of other humans. If they can manipulate identities, they can control the power and solidarity of others.

Marxist theory suggests that in capitalist socioeconomic systems, organizations manipulate worker identities in (at least) two ways. First, they control the items of value that workers associate with their activities. If the outcome of their labor is commodities or substitutes for commodities (wages in capitalist economies) instead of products, workers' power is reduced. No longer can they define themselves as beings who are capable of transforming nature. As important, their identities begin to depend on their relationship to their employers rather than their relationship to the products of their labor or to other human beings. This seemingly subtle distinction is crucial. When identity is linked to commodities provided by others, workers depend on their employers for both the means of their survival and the substance of their existence, for their identities. When workers are separated from the products of their labor, they are denied the ability to regain their potency as individuals and maintain their solidarity with others.[14] Organizational power is grounded in the employer's ability to threaten the selves of their employees. Hierarchical power relationships support and are supported by control of the outcomes of labor.

Employees' identities are also manipulated through symbolic processes that lead workers to define themselves in individualistic terms.[15] Individualism can be perpetuated through strategies that are as overt as piece-work reward systems, union contracts that provide separate reward structures for full- versus part-time workers and senior versus junior employees, and policies favoring "promotion from within." Individuality can also be maintained through processes as subtle as the implementation of systems of "power-sharing" or participatory decision making.[16] Two frequently offered criticisms of power-sharing strategies are that (1) they are often resisted by both labor and management and (2) even when employed in supportive contexts, they often fail to affect fundamental changes in organizational power relationships.[17] Radical-critical perspectives suggest that participatory systems inevitably solidify hierarchical power relationships because of the impact they have on workers' identities. Participatory decision making involves workers in actions that define them as managers; they produce decisions, not lasting products. This change in actions and self-definition seems to be the basis of resistance by both high and low power employees.[18] Often, resistance eventually leads firms to abandon the programs or to take steps to redefine workers as managers (for example, by shifting some of them to salaried from hourly reward systems). Workers' practical acts and processes that exchange their labor for commodities separate them from their identities and from their peers, thus reducing their perceived potency. Conversely, the right to participate in decision making depends on the bequest of management, not from the power implicit in material action. Workers become progressively more dependent on management for their definitions of self, a dependency that progressively reduces their relative power.

POWER, PRAXIS, SELF, AND
ORGANIZATIONAL COMMUNICATION RESEARCH

Unfortunately, the complex interrelationships among action, self, and dominance that are so central to modern radical-critical theory have played only a minor role in related research.[19] This gap seems to be the result of three factors. First, the "rediscovery" of Marx's ontological theory has been relatively recent and research tends to lag behind changes in theoretical perspective (Kuhn, 1970). Second, radical-critical theorists have concentrated on macroscopic relationships between sociopolitical factors and processes of organizational control, deemphasizing the more microscopic factors through which workers' identities are influenced by structural and symbolic processes (Silverman and Jones, 1976). Third, Marx's ontology has served as an assumption from which radical-critical frameworks have been developed and has been treated as that—a taken-for-granted premise on which analyses are based rather than as a focus for research.

As a result of these assumptions, radical-critical theorists have paid relatively little attention to communicative processes and the implications they hold for societal and organizational power relationships. When communication has been examined it is usually in response to the charge that Marx inadequately examined language and communication. Often these responses merely assert that communicative processes are neither necessary nor central to Marxist thought (Baran and Sweezy, 1966). However, a number of radical-critical theorists recently have started to examine the complex interrelationships among social structures, symbolic action, worker identities, and power relationships. Three specific lines of thought seem to be emerging from communication-centered radical-critical research.

The first strain examines workers' communication as collections of symbols that reveal their identities (self-definitions), especially in terms of the link between identity and the roles played in hierarchical social structures. For instance, Michael Burawoy's analysis of industrial conflicts in Zambian mining firms (1974) suggests that (1) communiques issued by union leaders during strikes indicate the leaders perceived themselves as part of the self-disciplined (white), ruling elite rather than the undisciplined (black) miners, a self-definition that supported their implicit collusion with mine owners in perpetuating oppressive labor-management relationships, and (2) that workers were able to persuade foremen to violate social and organizational norms that sanction punitive treatment of miners by manipulating their self-definitions as "civilized" (that is, self-disciplined and humane) and "superior" persons (also see Burawoy, 1979). By focusing on employee communication, Burawoy examined both the processes through which workers' identities sustain power relationships and the ways in which those structures are manipulated through symbolic action.

The second strain of communication-centered research views speech (language-in-use) as a process that "contains" social and organizational power relationships. In this perspective, speech *is* community and community *is*, at least in part, the enactment of individual identities and hierarchical power relationships. Silverman and Jones's (1976) analyses of selection, training, evaluation, and promotion activities in a public organization demonstrate the ways in which communication functions to maintain self-images and thereby perpetuate patterns of dominance and submission in organizational decision making.

The third strain of research focuses on the processes through which speech and symbolic forms allow contradictions among self, action, and power to be maintained. For example, Clegg's (1975) detailed study of tape-recorded conversations and interviews at a construction site focuses on the ways in which breakdowns in everyday practice are managed symbolically.[20] Typical of his analysis is the episode he labels the "Joiners' Tale." Three themes emerged from workers' conversations about their perception that they spend a great deal of time pretending to be busy: (1) something is amiss here, (2) because proscribed behaviors are tolerated by managers, (3) which demonstrates the inferiority of this organization compared to another (idealized) one. As the conversation progresses, the idealized organization begins to function as an icon around which the employees create verbal pictures of their organization. These images locate the responsibility for their action in the behavior of others (managers), absolve them of responsibility for their actions, and thereby perpetuate their self-definitions as relatively powerless pawns.

In all three lines of research, communicative processes serve as both the substance of research and a central element of the researchers' model of societal and organizational power relationships.[21] Fortunately, a variety of perspectives currently popular among communication theorists can readily be modified and employed to examine interrelationships among power, speech, and identity management.[22] Because it is through communication that self emerges, develops, and guides and constrains action, communication scholars are uniquely equipped to examine these complex interrelationships (see Figure 9.2).

POWER AND THE RATIONALIZATION OF ACTION

The term "rationalization" long has been one of the most enigmatic constructs in social and organizational theory. It has been defined by radical-critical theorists both as (1) processes through which material relationships are transformed into abstract constructs, thus separating employees' definitions of

(1) How do workers at different levels, in different sectors, and with different kinds of tasks define themselves
    (a) vis-à-vis their work activities?
    (b) vis-à-vis other employees?
(2) Through what symbolic processes are worker self-definitions shared? Does convergence of identities occur, and if so in what ways (for example, for newly-hired employees)?
(3) How are worker self-definitions related to job satisfaction and alienation?
(4) What levels and kinds of threat potentials do workers perceive that they have? That their supervisors have? In what ways are these forms salient to them, and especially to their identities?
(5) What means of control do workers perceive are used in their organization or unit? How are these perceptions related to the nature of task structure (as in Offe and Edwards) in their units?
(6) How do perceived self-definitions and threat potentials change with the advent of systems of participatory decision making or worker ownership? Are these changes (if they do occur) related to attitudes about and/or opposition to the power-sharing strategies?
(7) Who do workers define as "others" or "enemies"
    (a) in day-to-day activities?
    (b) during "crises" (for example, contract negotiations or organizational conflicts)
(8) How are processes of self-definition related to interactional "rules"?

Figure 9.2 Power, Self, and Organizational Communication Research

themselves from their work, and obscuring the contradiction that exists between their potency as human beings and the powerlessness of their social and economic roles (see Coward and Ellis, 1977: 67-68; Althusser, 1971: 155), (2) processes through which the political-economic and legal structures of a society and its dominant ideology reciprocally justify the continuation of hierarchical power relationships.[23] Organizational theorists generally have used the term to refer either to processes through which managers construct and articulate logical justifications for decisions they already have made on nonrational grounds, or to the broad symbolic processes through which decision makers perpetuate the myth that they make decisions on the basis of objective, careful, information-based considerations of all available options.

At first glance these varied uses of the term "rationalization" may seem to be inconsistent with each other. But, if viewed through the perspective provided by contemporary models of organizational power, a synthesis is possible. By separating identity from practical action, rationalization establishes criteria for evaluating the correctness (or naturalness or rightness) of employees' actions in abstract, symbolic terms rather than in terms of the effects or practical outcomes of their activities. Not only does this process reduce workers' potency, it also establishes a setting within which the other rationalizing processes can have their greatest impact. Organizational decision making is legitimized as a wholly abstract activity and thus can be evaluated only in terms of its success in the manipulation of abstract symbols. The right and power to make decisions stems from managers' capacity to "correctly" manipulate symbols, a capacity that is disproportionately located in their hands for three reasons: (1) their formal organizational roles provide them with superior access to information and almost complete control of the dissemination of decision-relevant information, (2) their training and experience provide them with superior verbal skills, and (3) their ability to control workers' access to information that would undermine the myths of rational decision making and thus perpetuate the image that their analytical and verbal skills legitimize their superior organizational roles. Incongruities between nonrational, organizational decision processes and socially sanctioned myths of individual and corporate rationality create pressures to rationalize decisions, that is, to give an abstract accounting for nonrational decisions that is independent of the decision making or the decision. By rationalizing nonrationality, the organizational hierarchy and its control systems can be maintained. Powerful individuals can continue to be defined in terms of culturally legitimized, ontological superiority—their expertise and communicative or argumentative skills, superior access to information, broader "organizationwide" perspective, and so on. Less powerful individuals can acquiesce to nonrational decisions without feeling dissonance and save face by defining themselves as possessing less information, a narrow perspective, limited cognitive skills, or inadequate training or experience. Face is saved, self is maintained, and hierarchical power relationships are supported.[24]

The interrelationships among the rationalization of action, the rationalization of decision making, and organizational power relationships are complicated and supported further by the impact of societal institutions and ideologies that naturalize processes of rationalization. To the extent that ideology and superstructures perpetuate the myths that rational-symbolic activity is the essential feature of humankind (and therefore the factor that elevates us above the rest of creation and some of us above the remainder) and that organizational competence is related directly to capacities for "rational adaptation to organizational contingencies," existing structures of domination can be maintained. Four institutions—schools, churches, the state, and popular art—inculcate a definition of self that centers on the concept of rationality. This definition creates the conviction that decisions can and should be made through discursive communication and that the test of one employee's right to exercise power over others is his or her rationality which depends on his or her ability to discursively convince others in ambiguous situations. Value claims are to be resolved through "substantial arguments," which logically connect particular problems to abstract conceptions of value and power. Rules of procedure regarding organizational action and communication serve as the legitimizing premises for socioeconomic power relationships. The exercise of dominance need not be legitimized because it symbolizes the actors' identities as human beings and absorbs the uncertainties they face (Habermas, 1970: 43-107). Hierarchical power relationships are legitimized not only from within through the rationalization of work and decision making but also from without, through intersubjectively validated definitions of self created in right, reasoned discourse (Clegg, 1979). Arbitrary socioeconomic relationships are made to seem natural and proper through argument.[25] Changes in existing power relationships can be made only if the rationalizing matrix is overcome, only when powerless employees exercise the "power to disbelieve, the first power of the weak (which) begins . . . with the refusal to accept the definition of oneself that is put forward by the powerful" (Janeway, 1981: 167).

Like all perspectives, radical-critical views of organizational power render some research questions appropriate, others important, and others trivial. Our goal in the preceding section of this chapter has been to suggest that contemporary radical-critical theories provide researchers who are interested in organizational communication with important opportunities to increase our understanding of social and organizational power relationships. The processes through which employees' identities are manipulated, the actions of members of organizations are rationalized, and structures of dominance are exercised and maintained are communicative-symbolic processes. Their complex inter-relationships and their impact on the actions of people at work can be evaluated most productively through the frames of reference provided by contemporary organizational communication theory. Our goal in these sections has not been to develop explicitly any particular program of organizational communication research designed to confront the implications of radical-critical views of power. Our objective has been to suggest that developing and implementing such a program would be both valuable and justifiable.

CONCLUSION

Concepts of power and powerlessness have long played a central role in social and organizational theory. At times the construct has been defined so broadly and its relationships to action so overdetermined and obscured that its usefulness as an explanatory construct has been minimized (March, 1958). Recently, as perspectives toward organizations have become more eclectic and definitions of organizational communication more comprehensive, the function of symbolic forms and processes in the construction and modification of power relationships has been viewed as an important potential focus for research. Our objective in this essay has been to summarize extant perspectives on organizational power relationships and suggest preliminary directions for systematic research on the complex interrelationships among power, action, and communication. We hope, recalling Raven and Kruglanski's refrain, that we have raised far more questions than we have answered.

NOTES

1. Illustrative of this broadened definition are the essays in Putnam and Pacanowsky, (1983).
2. We will define this term in detail as the chapter progresses. Although our definition in some ways parallels Burrell and Morgan's distinction between "radical-humanist" and "radical-structuralist" paradigms (1979), it is important to not impose their dichotomy on the analysis that we will present. For a critique and synthesis of their perspectives see Putnam in Putnam and Pacanowsky (1983).

3. This line of thought is summarized and critiqued in Stuart Clegg (1975, 1979).

4. The concept of response to environmental uncertainty is summarized in Howard Aldrich (1979) and Alan Meyer (1982). Interrelationships among dimensions of organizational structure are considered at length by Anthony Giddens (1979, 1981).

5. For critiques of these assumptions see Steven Lukes (1974), Clegg (1975, 1979), and the essays in Tom Burns et al. (1979).

6. The term "symbology" is used to mean, roughly, a structured discussion of symbols (in this case of organizational power). Detailed definitions are available in Kenneth Burke's *A Rhetoric of Motives* (Berkeley: University of California Press, 1969) and the *The Rhetoric of Religion* (Berkeley: University of California Press, 1970).

7. Or, to be more precise, "circle," since symbological models of power borrow this concept directly from contemporary hermeneutics. See David Hoy (1981), Hans George Gadamer (1975), and Roy Howard (1979).

8. Perhaps a Biblical parallel would clarify this point. The Abrahamaic covenant articulated the deep structure that defined the Hebrew people. "I will be your God and you my people" expressed both the identity (self) of the Hebrews, the hierarchical relationship among them and between them and Jehovah, and a "rational" set of patterns of action. Only when the preconscious parameters implicit in the covenant started to break down was an overt statement of what constituted proper behavior and an open expression of threat and promise (the Commandments and Wilderness experience) necessary. In the interim, the deep structure *was* the operant power relationship. Once articulated, the Commandments—symbolized tangibly by the Ark and ritualistically by a number of activities—continually reaffirmed the constraints implicit in the Covenant.

9. Purists among symbological theorists would argue that the structures *are* symbols; that there is no structure independent of language-in-use. See the discussion of language and structure in Stanley Deetz and Astrid Kersten (1983).

10. For an expanded discussion of these relationships, see Conrad (1983); also see Burke (1969a, 1969b).

11. Exceptions are provided by Deetz and Kersten (1983), Richard Harvey Brown (1977, 1978), and Kenneth Benson (1977).

12. Most readings of Marx would use the term "proletariat" where we use the term worker. We have chosen not to use the more common term because Marx's early work used "proletariat" to refer to a diverse group of people who fully understood the relationships between material production and human ontology. This "class," and an opposing "evil" class, did not then exist, but needed to be created through careful, strategic symbolic action (Karl Marx, *"Critique of Hegel's Philosophy of the Right"*). Unless otherwise noted, all citations to Marx's work are taken from Robert Tucker (1972).

13. Because of the complexity of Marx's thought we will not attempt to provide a summary here. For fine summaries see Tucker (1977) and the essay by Phillip Tompkins in this volume. Because of the wide variety of ways in which key Marxian terms have been used, we shall avoid using Marxist terminology except when absolutely necessary.

14. Marx discusses three processes of "alienation": (1) the separation of workers from the products of their material acts (see especially "The Manuscripts of 1844," pp. 40-50), (2) the definition of workers' identities in terms of the commodities exchanged for their labor ("The Manuscripts of 1844" and "The German Ideology," pp. 120-132), and (3) alienation from other workers because of the loss of the material identities that bind them together as members of the same species ("The Manuscripts of 1844," pp. 52-65). The functions of individualistic identities in the processes of alienation are discussed by Marx in "Marx on the History of His Opinions," especially p. 10 and by Coward and Ellis (1977: 75), Louis Althusser (1971: 166) and Goff (1980: 67).

In order to maintain their dominance in the face of worker alienation and opposition, employers must develop effective means of control. One means is simple—the overt exercise of threats of dismissal (or of punishments like suspension, which depend on the implied threat to fire). "Simple control" depends on the visible presence of a reserve army of unemployed workers waiting to take the jobs of dismissed employees and the absence of adequate governmental support for the unemployed. Although still typical in small firms (Edwards, 1978), simple control has been supplemented by more subtle strategies.

Structural control relies on employers' ability to manipulate the pace and direction of work activities and to control the labor market. A large proportion of recent Marxist thought has focused on the first form of alienation and task-completing processes (Henry Braverman, 1965; Edwards, 1978). The general argument is that division of labor and mechanization combine to reduce the complexity, challenge, and meaningfulness of work. As tasks are rationalized—segmented, reduced, and routinized—workers are progressively more alienated, both in the sense of "angered" and in the Marxist sense of being separated from the products of their creative activity. In addition, task rationalization enhances management's power in a number of ways: it places workers in physical arrangements where it is difficult for them to communicate with one another, reducing their ability to engage in collective action (for an intriguing analysis of the communicative processes that workers use to offset this process, see Pandawa and Simusokwe, 1971); it forces them to adapt to the pace of work established by machinery and it initiates cycles of wage increases and capital expenditures that also reduce their power. Alienation is "bought off" through increased wages and fringe benefits, thus making rationalized jobs attractive to unemployed and underemployed persons, thereby increasing management's threat potential. It also makes it difficult for workers to leave the firms without making major sacrifices in their standard of living, thus decreasing their threat potential. Finally, it leads them to define themselves in monetary terms, further reducing the potency that comes from productive action (see Goldthorpe et al., 1967).

In other firms, control is bureaucratic. Seemingly objective rules, operating procedures, and task assignments further isolate workers from one another and lead them to define themselves in terms of their organizational roles rather than their solidarity with other workers. Less alienating tasks are given only to supervisors, and when combined with policies of "promoting from within," create internal "reserve armies" of underemployed persons (Edwards, 1978; also see Claus Offe, 1973). Thus various forms of organizational control differ along two dimensions of communication. In traditional modes of control, subtle restrictions on worker communication and interaction reduce their solidarity with one another. Less traditional forms of control rely more heavily on subtle symbolic processes to obscure threat potentials and increase the significance of worker identification with their organizational roles as the source of their identities.

15. Marx ("History," p. 10; "German," pp. 143-160). These processes are solidified in an additional way by the effects of more general societal factors (Althusser, 1969; Habermas, 1970, 1976).

16. This interpretation seems to be supported by the observations of participatory decision making reported to Mauk Mulder (1971), Abraham Zaleznik (1970), and Richard Edwards (1978). Deetz and Kersten (1983) provide a related analysis of systems of participatory decision making and Elizabeth Janeway (1981) discusses processes through which workers are alienated from one another in her analysis of "horizontal hostility." Barbara Garson (1977) provides vivid examples of these processes and they are linked to radical-critical theory by Paul Goldman and Donald van Houten (1977: 108-125), and examined in more general terms by H. P. Dachler and F. Wilpert (1978).

17. See Charles Conrad (1985), especially chapter 5, for a summary of this research. Unfortunately, many treatments of participatory systems obscure the complex patterns of response that have been observed when power-sharing strategies have been implemented. Power-sharing strategies tend to be abandoned at predictable points in their development, each of which follows characteristic forms of opposition. The first decision point seems to come soon after the systems are implemented. At this point the apparent cost inefficiencies of the programs (participatory systems usually have high initial training and start-up costs and low short-term benefits from improved efficiency and morale), opposition from threatened managers or the effects of inadequate preparation and training of employees lead firms to abandon the projects (Pateman, 1979; Ronald Mason, 1982).

The second transition point comes much later, after systems that are retained start to be highly profitable and traditional power relationships have begun to be meaningfully changed. Actual decisions to terminate the programs often follow highly visible successes of the programs. Two cases in point are experiments at Polaroid and at General Foods. Polaroid is a company that is generally regarded as a progressive firm. Employees form ad hoc committees that deal with special problems and there is a general perception that top management is responsive to employees. During the 1960s a group of 120 workers was assigned to a special project that called for them to spend an appreciable amount of time training other employees and learning to coordinate work activities in addition to operating the machinery. The experiment was a thorough success. The group exceeded performance expectations and even met a pressing deadline that many managers felt could not have been met under standard operating procedures. Despite (or perhaps because of) these accomplishments, the program was soon abandoned. As Ray Ferris, the Polaroid training director, said, "It was too successful. What were we going to do with the supervisors? We didn't need them anymore. Management decided it just didn't want operators (to be) that qualified" (cited in David Jenkins, 1973: 314).

Another participatory program that was dismantled after what appeared to have been a success was at the Topeka plant of General Foods. Although costs were reduced and annual savings progressively increased, the program was abandoned when managers saw their roles being filled by the rank-and-file (Espinosa and Zimbalist, 1978). Participatory systems begin when management decides to grant workers power within a narrowly circumscribed sphere of responsibility. When workers become sufficiently capable, they begin to press against those boundaries. At that point, the organizational roles, and thus the power and identities of supervisors, are threatened and the programs are abandoned. For additional examples, see Samuel Bowles and Herbert Gintes (1975) and Richard Edwards et al. (1972). For a discussion of the different experiences of European experiments, see David Garson (1977) and Burns et al. (1979).

18. Attempts to implement power sharing also seem to be influenced by another factor. Implicit in the idea of power is the concept of responsibility (Goldner, 1970). When definitions of self are particular and individual, conceptions of potency are also particular and individual (Goffman, 1961). Participatory strategies promise to expand both an individual's range of power and his or her zone of responsibility. For high-power individuals, participatory strategies promise to either reduce their power and their responsibility or reduce their power while maintaining or increasing their responsibility. For low-power individuals, participation promises increased power in the long term and increased responsibility immediately. Thus for both groups participatory systems may threaten their individualized selves (Kanter, 1977; Burns et al., 1979), generating employee resistance to participatory decision making.

19. An exception to this generalization is Goldthorpe et al. (1967).

20. The theoretical base for his analysis is Heidegger's (1962) metaphor of "instruments being broken."

21. Theoretical discussions of these interrelationships are available in Habermas (1970) and Clegg and Dunkerley (1979).

22. For example, the research paradigms typically labeled "constructivism," "rules theory," "phenomenology," and "pragmatics" provide appropriate starting points. See the essays by Dance, Cronen et al., and Delia et al. in Dance (1982).

23. Althusser refers to the former as superstructures and the latter as ideologies and discusses their impact in (1971), pp. 129-130. Our interpretation is based on Althusser's reading of Marx. Although Marxist scholars have taken issue with him on a number of counts, his analysis of Marx's view of the "levels of society" seems to be rather widely accepted.

24. Rationalizing nonrationality has a number of additional stabilizing effects: it allows actors to act, thereby managing (though not necessarily reducing) ambiguity and perpetuates nonrational policies and procedures that serve as overt constraints on action.

25. Radical-critical theorists argue that educational institutions play an important role in perpetuating definitions of humankind that rest on notions of rationality and thus solidify hierarchical power relationships (Bowles and Gintes, 1976). Organizational theorists, and by implication organizational communication theorists, have been mentioned as directly responsible for these processes. First, by assuming that rational adaptation to organizational contingencies should be the goal of research, theory, and education, organizational scholars place the dialectic of self, power, and rationality beyond the scope of analysis. Organizational analysis becomes, to use Benson's phrase, "someone's tool!" and the "someone" is the powerful (1977: 35; also see Janeway's [1981] critique of Janis and Mann). Second, by treating these constructs as reified (rationalized) attributes of persons, organizational theory perpetuates the matrix of rationalization:

> [Organizational theorists'] abstractions correspond closely to the conventional administrative view and function as an ideology justifying, rationalizing administrative actions as well as a normative model or goal of administrative actions. That the model corresponds to our experience and seems reasonable is an indicator of our indoctrination within the administrative perspective and the success of administrators in constructing a world in this image. The history of organizational theory may be seen, in part, as a process in which a series of "nonrational" factors have been conjured up only to be subdued by the rationalizing core [Benson, 1977: 10].

In the memorable phrase of a nonradical-critical, nonorganizational theorist, "We have met the enemy and he is us" (from the comic strip *Pogo*, 1967; also see Marx and Engels, 1974: 43).

REFERENCES

ABELL, P. (1975) Organizations as Bargaining and Influence Systems. London: Heinemann.

ADAMS, J. (1976) "The structure and dynamics of behavior in organizational boundary roles," M. D. Dunnette (ed.) Handbook of Industrial and Organizational Psychology. Chicago: Rand McNally.

Administrative Science Quarterly (1983) 28: 331-502.

Advertising Age (1981) October 19: S-28.

ALBRECHT, T. (1979) "The role of communication in perceptions of organizational climate," in D. Nimmo (ed.) Communication Yearbook 3. New Brunswick, NJ: Transaction.

ALBROW, M. (1970) Bureaucracy. London: Pall Mall.

ALDERFER, C. (1972) Human Needs in Organizational Settings. New York: Free Press.

ALDRICH, H. (1979) Organizations and Environments. Englewood Cliffs, NJ: Prentice-Hall.

ALEXANDER, T. (1982) "Teaching computers and the art of reason." Fortune (May 17): 82-84.

ALLEN, R. and C. KRAFT (1982) The Organizational Unconscious. Englewood Cliffs, NJ: Prentice-Hall.

ALLEN, R. W., D. L. MADISON, L. W. PORTER, P. A. RENWICK, and B. T. MAYES (1979) "Organizational politics: tactics and characteristics of its actors." California Management Review 22: 77-83.

ALLEN, T. and S. COHEN (1969) "Information flow in research and development laboratories." Administrative Science Quarterly 14: 12-20.

ALLISON, G. (1971) Essence of Decision: Explaining the Cuban Missile Crisis. Boston: Little, Brown.

ALTHUSSER, L. (1969) For Marx. London: Penguin.

———(1971) Lenin and Philosophy and Other Essays. London: New Left.

ANGLE, H. and J. PERRY (1981) "An empirical assessment of organizational commitment and organizational effectiveness." Administrative Science Quarterly 26: 1-14.

ANGRIST, A. W. (1953) "A study of the communications of executives in business and industry." Speech Monographs 20: 277-285.

ARENSBERG, C. and D. McGREGOR (1942) "Determination of morale in an industrial company." Applied Anthropology 1: 12-34.

ARGYRIS, C. (1964) Integrating the Individual and the Organization. New York: John Wiley.

———(1957) Personality and Organization. New York: Harper & Row.

ASTLEY, W. and P. SACHDEVA (1984) "Structural sources of intraorganizational power: a theoretical synthesis." Academy of Management Review 9: 104-113.

AULETTA, K. (1983) "Profiles: a certain poetry—I." New Yorker (June 6): 46ff.

BACHARACH, P. and M. BARATZ (1962) "Two faces of power." American Political Science Review 56: 947-952.

BACHARACH, S. and M. AIKEN (1977) "Communication in administrative bureaucracies." Academy of Management Journal 20: 365-377.

BACHARACH, S. and E. LAWLER (1980) Power and Politics in Organizations. San Francisco: Jossey-Bass.

BAIRD, J. (1973) "An analytical field study of 'open communication' as perceived by superiors, subordinates, and peers." Ph.D. dissertation, Purdue University.

BAKER, H. (1948) Company-Wide Understanding of Industrial Relations Policies: A Study in Communication. Princeton, NJ: Princeton University, Industrial Relations Section.

———J. BALLANTINE, and J. TRUE (1949) Transmitting Information Through Management and Union Channels. Princeton, NJ: Princeton University, Industrial Relations Section.

BAKKE, E. W. (1950) Bonds of Organization: An Appraisal of Corporate Human Relations. New York: Harper & Row.

———(1959) "Concept of the social organization," pp. 16-75 in M. Haire (ed.) Modern Organization Theory. New York: John Wiley.

BARAN, P. and P. SWEEZY (1966) Monopoly Capital. New York: Monthly Review Press.

BARATZ, M. (1970) Power and Poverty. New York: Oxford University Press.

BARITZ, L. (1960) The Servants of Power. Middletown, CT: Wesleyan University Press.

BARKER, R. G. (1963) "On the nature of the environment." Journal of Social Issues 19: 17-38.

BARLEY, S. (1983) "Semiotics and the study of occupational and organizational cultures." Administrative Science Quarterly 28: 393-413.

BARNARD, C. (1968) The Functions of the Executive. Cambridge, MA: Harvard University Press. (Originally published 1938)

BARNLUND, D. C. (1955) "Experiments in leadership training for decision-making discussion groups." Speech Monographs 22: 1-14.

———and C. HORLAND (1963) "Propinquity and prestige as determinants of communication networks." Sociometry 26: 467-479.

BARTELL, T. (1976) "The human relations ideology: an analysis of the social origins of a belief system." Human Relations 29: 737-749.

BARTHES, R. (1971) S/Z. Paris: Seuil.

BARTOL, K. (1979) "Professions as a predictor of organizational commitment, role stress, and turnover: a multidimensional approach." Academy of Management Journal 22: 815-821.

BATESON, G. (1958) Naven. Stanford, CA: Stanford University Press.

BAVELAS, A. (1950) "Communication patterns in task oriented groups." Journal of the American Acoustical Society 22: 725-730.

———and M. BARRETT (1951) "An experimental approach to organizational communication." Personnel 27: 366-377.

BECKER, H. (1960) "Notes on the concept of commitment." American Journal of Sociology 66: 32-40.

———and J. CARPER (1956) "The elements of identification with an occupation." American Sociological Review 21: 341-348.

BEDNAR, D. and W. CURINGTON (1983) "Interaction analysis: a tool for understanding negotiations." Industrial and Labor Relations Review 36: 389-401.

BEDNAR, D. and M. GLAUSNER (1981) "Interaction analysis of collective bargaining: the Barrington Oil Company case," in K. Chung (ed.) Academy of Management Proceedings '81. Mississippi State, MS: Academy of Management Association.

BEISECKER, T. (1970) "Verbal persuasive strategies in mixed motive interactions." Quarterly Journal of Speech 56: 149-160.

BELL, D. (1979) "Communication technology—for better or for worse." Harvard Business Review 57: 20-42.

BENNETT, T., G. MARTIN, C. MERCER, and J. WOOLACOTT [eds.] (1981) Social Process. London: Open University.

BENNIS, W. G., N. BERKOWITZ, M. AFFINITO, and M. MALONE (1958) "Reference groups and loyalties in the out-patient department." Administrative Science Quarterly 2: 481-500.

BENSON, K. (1977) "Organizations: a dialectical view." Administrative Science Quarterly 22: 1-21.

BERCOVITCH, J. (1983) "Problems and approaches in the study of bargaining and negotiation." Department of Political Science, University of Canterbury, Christchurch, New Zealand. (unpublished)

BERLINSKI, D. (1976) On Systems Analysis: An Essay Concerning the Limitations of Some Mathematical Methods in the Social, Political, and Biological Sciences. Cambridge: MIT Press.

BERNARD, H. and P. KILLWORTH (1977) "Informant accuracy in social network data II." Human Communication Research 4: 3-18.

———(1978) "Informant accuracy in social network data IV." Presented at the Fifth Annual Colloquium on Social Networks, Social Sciences and Linguistics Institute, University of Hawaii at Manoa.

———and L. SAILER (1980) "Informant accuracy in social network data IV: a comparison of clique-level structure in behavioral and cognitive network data." Social Networks 2: 191-218.

BERTALANFFY, L. (1968) General Systems Theory. New York: George Braziller.

BEYER, J. (1982) "Ideologies, values, and decision making in organizations," in P. Nystrom and W. Starbuck (eds.) Handbook of Organizational Design, Vol. 1. London: Oxford University Press.

BITZER, L. F. (1959) "Aristotle's enthymeme revisited." Quarterly Journal of Speech 45: 399-408.

BLACKBURN, R. (1981) "Lower participant power: toward a conceptual integration." Academy of Management Review 6: 127-131.

BLAU, P. (1963) The Dynamics of Bureaucracy. Chicago: University of Chicago Press.

———and R. ALBA (1982) "Empowering nets of participation." Administrative Science Quarterly 27: 363-379.

BLAU, P. and R. SCHOENHERR (1971) The Structure of Organizations. New York: Basic Books.

BLAU, P. and W. SCOTT (1962) Formal Organizations. San Francisco: Chandler.

BONOMA, T. V. and J. TEDESCHI (1974) "The relative efficacies of escalation and deescalation for compliance-gaining in two party conflicts." Social Behavior and Personality 37: 251-261.

BORDEN, R. (1935) Public Speaking—As Listeners Like It! New York: Harper & Row.

BOURDIEU, P. (1977) Outline of a Theory of Practice. Cambridge: Cambridge University Press.

BOWLES, S. and H. GINTES (1975) "Class power and alienated labor." Monthly Review 26: 9-25.

———(1976) Schooling in Capitalist America: Educational Reform and the Contradictions of Economic Life. New York: Basic Books.

BRADLEY, P. (1978) "Status and upward communication in small decision-making groups." Communication Monographs 45.

BRAVERMAN, H. (1965) Labor and Monopoly Capital. New York: Monthly Review Press.

BREED, W. (1972) "Social control in the newsroom," in W. Schramm (ed.) Mass Communications. Urbana: University of Illinois Press.

BREWER, F. (1971) "Flow of communication, expert qualifications, and organizational authority structure." American Sociological Review 36: 475-484.

BRONFENBRENNER, V. (1969) "Freudian theories of identification and their derivatives." Child Development 31: 15-40.

BROWN, M. (1969) "Identification and some conditions of organizational involvement." Administrative Science Quarterly 14: 346-355.

BROWN, R. (1977) A Poetic for Sociology. Cambridge: Cambridge University Press.

———(1978) "Bureaucracy as praxis." Administrative Science Quarterly 23: 365-380.

BROWNE, C. and E. NEITZEL (1952) "Communication, supervision, and morale." Journal of Applied Psychology 36: 86-91.

BROWNELL, J. (1978) "Elwood Murray: a case study in educational integration and innovation." Ph.D. dissertation, Syracuse University.

———(1983) "Elwood Murray's interdisciplinary view: expanding the boundaries of the speech field." Western Journal of Speech Communication: 244-252.

BUCHANAN, B. (1974) "Building organizational commitment: the socialization of managers in work organizations." Administrative Science Quarterly 19: 533-546.

———(1975) "To walk an extra mile: the whats, whens, and whys of organizational commitment." Organizational Dynamics 3: 67-80.

BULLIS, C. (1984) "The forest ranger revisited." Ph.D. dissertation, Purdue University.

BURAWOY, M. (1974) Constraint and Manipulation in Industrial Conflict. Lusaka, Zambia: Institute for African Studies.

———(1979) Manufacturing Consent. Chicago: University of Chicago Press.

BURKE, K. (1937) Attitudes Toward History, Vol. 2. New York: New Republic.

———(1966) Toward a Better Life. Berkeley: University of California Press.

———(1969a) A Grammar of Motives. Berkeley: University of California Press.

———(1969b) A Rhetoric of Motives. Berkeley: University of California Press.

———(1970) The Rhetoric of Religion. Berkeley: University of California Press.

———(1973) "The rhetorical situation," pp. 263-275 in L. Thayer (ed.) Communication: Ethical and Moral Issues. London: Gordon & Breach.

BURLINGAME, J. (1961) "Information technology and decentralization." Harvard Business Review 39: 121-126.

BURNS, T. (1954) "The directions of activity and communication in a departmental executive group." Human Relations 7: 73-97.

BURNS, T. and G. STALKER (1966) The Management of Innovation. London.

———L. KARLSSON, and V. RUS [eds.] (1979) Work and Power. Beverly Hills, CA: Sage.

BURRELL, G. and G. MORGAN (1979) Sociological Paradigms and Organizational Analysis. London: Heinemann Educational.

BURT, R. (1980) "Cooptive corporate director networks: a reconsideration of interlocking directorates involving American manufacturing." Administrative Science Quarterly 25: 557-581.

BUSS, B .M., E. R. VALENZI, D. L. FARROW, and R. J. SOLOMON (1957) "Management styles associated with organizational, task, personal and interpersonal contingencies." Journal of Applied Psychology 60: 720-729.

BUTLER, R., D. HICKSON, D. WILSON, and J. AXELSSON (1977) "Organizational power." Organization and Administration Sciences 8: 45-59.

BYRNE, D. (1971) The Attraction Paradigm. New York: Academic.

CAMPBELL, J., M. DUNNETTE, E. E. LAWLER, and K. WEICK (1970) Managerial Behavior, Performance, and Effectiveness. New York: McGraw-Hill.

CANTOR, M. (1971) The Hollywood TV Producer. New York: Basic.

CARLSON, S. (1951) Executive Behavior. Stockholm: Stromborgs.

CARLUCCI, C. and W.J.E. CRISSY (1951) "The readability of employee handbooks." Personnel Psychology 4: 383-395.

CARNEGIE, D. (1936) How to Win Friends and Influence People. New York: Simon & Schuster.

CARTWRIGHT, D. and A. ZANDER (1953) Group Dynamics: Research and Theory. Evanston, IL: Row, Peterson.

CASS, E. L. and F. G. ZIMMER [eds.] (1975) Man and Work in Society. New York: Van Nostrand Reinhold.

CAWELTI, J. (1975) The Six Gun Mystique. Bowling Green, OH: Popular Press.

CEDERBLOM, D. (1982) "The performance appraisal interview: a review, implications, and suggestions." Academy of Management Review 7: 219-227.

CHAPPLE, E. and L. SAYLES (1961) The Measure of Management. New York: Macmillan.

CHASE, S. (1945) Men at Work: Some Democratic Methods for the Power Age. New York: Harcourt Brace Jovanovich.

————(1948) The Proper Study of Mankind: An Inquiry into the Science of Human Relations. New York: Harper & Row.

CHENEY, G. (1982) "Identification as process and product: a field study." Master's thesis, Purdue University.

————(1983a) "On the various and changing meanings of organizational membership: a field study of organizational identification." Communication Monographs 50: 343-363.

————(1983b) "The rhetoric of identification and the study of organizational communication." Quarterly Journal of Speech 69: 143-158.

————and P. TOMPKINS (1984a) "Coming to terms with organizational identification and commitment." Presented at the annual convention of the Speech Communication Association, Chicago.

————(1984b) "Toward an ethic of identification." Presented at a conference by and for Kenneth Burke, Philadelphia.

CHERTKOFF, J. and M. CONLEY (1967) "Opening offer and frequency of concession as bargaining strategies." Journal of Personality and Social Psychology 7: 181-185.

CHILD, J. and T. ELLIS (1973) "Predictors of variation in managerial roles." Human Relations 26: 227-250.

CLEGG, S. (1975) Power, Rule, and Domination. London: Routledge & Kegan Paul.

————(1979) The Theory of Power and Organization. London: Routledge & Kegan Paul.

————and D. DUNKERLEY [eds.] (1979) Critical Issues in Organizations. London: Routledge & Kegan Paul.

CLICK, J. and R. BAIRD (1979) Magazine Editing and Production. Dubuque, IA: William C. Brown.

COCH, L. and J. FRENCH (1948) "Overcoming resistance to change." Human Relations 1: 512-532.

COHEN, A. (1958) "Upward communication in experimentally created hierarchies." Human Relations 11: 41-53.

COHEN, M. and J. MARCH (1974) Leadership and Ambiguity: The American College President. New York: McGraw-Hill.

————and J. OLSEN (1972) "A garbage can model of organizational choice." Administrative Science Quarterly 17: 1-25.

COLEMAN, J. (1974) Power and the Structure of Society. New York: Norton.

————E. KATZ, and H. MENZEL (1966) Medical Innovation: A Diffusion Study. Indianapolis: Bobbs-Merrill.

COLLINS, G. R. (1924) "Public speaking in colleges of business administration and United Y.M.C.A. Schools." Quarterly Journal of Speech Education 10: 374-379.

Congressional Subcommittee on Economy in Government (1982) "Air Force A-7D brake problem," in P. Frost et al. (eds.) Organizational Reality: Reports from the Firing Line. Glenview, IL: Scott, Foresman.

CONLEY, T. (1984) "The enthymeme in perspective." Quarterly Journal of Speech 70: 168-187.

CONNOLLY, T. (1977) "Information processing and decision making in organizations," in B. Staw and G. Salancik (eds.) New Directions in Organizational Behavior. Chicago: St. Clair.

CONQUERGOOD, D. (1984) "Drama, cosmology, and culture in organizations." Presented at the annual convention of the Speech Communication Association, Chicago.

CONRAD, C. (1983) "Organizational power: faces and symbolic forms," in L. Putnam and M. Pacanowsky (eds.) Communication and Organizations: An Interpretive Approach. Beverly Hills, CA: Sage.

————(1985) Strategic Organizational Communication. New York: Holt, Rinehart & Winston.

COOK, P. H. (1951) "An examination of the notion of communication in industry." Occupational Psychology 25: 1-14.

CORSON, J. J. (1946) "Management: tongue-tied, deaf and blind?" Advanced Management 11 (September): 101-104.

COSER, L., C. KADUSHIN, and W. POWELL (1982) Books: The Culture and Commerce of Publishing. New York: Basic Books.

COWARD, R. and J. ELLIS (1977) Language and Materialism. London: Routledge & Kegan Paul.

COX, M. (1983) "The effectiveness of black identification and organizational identification on communication supportiveness." Ph.D. dissertation, Purdue University.

CRENSON, M. (1971) The Un-Politics of Air Pollution: A Study of Non-Decision Making in the Cities. Baltimore: Johns Hopkins University Press.

CROSS, J. G. (1977) "Negotiations as a learning process." Journal of Conflict Resolution 21: 581-606.

CROUSE, T. (1972) The Boys on the Bus. New York: Random House.

CROZIER, M. (1964) The Bureaucratic Phenomenon. Chicago: University of Chicago Press.

CUMMINGS, L. and D. HARNETT (1969) "Bargaining behavior in a symmetric bargaining triad: the impact of risk-taking propensity, information, communication, and the terminal bid." Review of Economic Studies 36: 485-501.

CURRAN, J. (1978) "Advertising and the press," in J. Curran (ed.) The British Press: A Manifesto. London: Macmillan.

———M. GUREVITCH, and J. WOOLACOTT (1982) "Communication, power, and social order," in M. Gurevitch et al. (eds.) Culture, Society, and the Media. London: Methuen.

CYERT, R. and J. MARCH (1963) A Behavioral Theory of the Firm. Englewood, Cliffs, NJ: Prentice-Hall.

CYERT, R., H. SIMON, and D. TROW (1956) "Observation of a business decision." Journal of Business 29: 237-248.

DACHLER, H. and F. WILPERT (1978) "Conceptual dimensions and boundaries of participation in organizations: a critical evaluation." A 23: 1-39.

DAHL, R. (1957) "The concept of power." Behavioral Science 2: 201-215.

DAHLE, T. (1954) "An objective and comparative study of five methods of transmitting information to business and industrial employees." Speech Monographs 21: 21-28.

DANCE, F. [ed.] (1982) Human Communication Theory. New York: Harper & Row.

DANDRIDGE, T. C., I. MITROFF, and W. F. JOYCE (1980) "Organizational symbolism: a topic to expand organizational analysis." Academy of Management Review 5: 77-82.

DAVIDSON, C. (1945) "A college administrator looks at the teaching of communication." Quarterly Journal of Speech 31: 143-144.

DAVIS, J. (1967) "Clustering and structural balance in graphs." Human Relations 20: 181-187.

DAVIS, K. (1952) "Channels of personnel communication within the management group." Ph.D. dissertation, Ohio State University.

———(1953) "Management communication and the grapevine." Harvard Business Review 31: 43-49.

———(1957) Human Relations in Business. New York: McGraw-Hill.

———and J. HOPKINS (1950) "Readability of employee handbooks." Personnel Psychology 3: 317-326.

DAY, R. and J. DAY (1977) "A review of the current state of negotiated order theory: an appreciation and a critique." Sociological Quarterly 18: 126-142.

DEAL, T. and A. KENNEDY (1982) Corporate Cultures: The Rites and Rituals of Corporate Life. Reading, MA: Addison-Wesley.

DEE, J. F. (1957) "An analysis of the formal channels of communication in an industrial union local." Ph.D. dissertation, Ohio State University.

———(1959) "Written communications in the trade union local." Journal of Communication 9: 99-109.

———(1961) "Oral communication in the trade union local." Journal of Communication 11: 77-87.

———(1962a) "Channels of talk in the trade union local." Today's Speech 10: 7-8, 23.

———(1962b) "Speech training in worker education: a survey and report." Speech Teacher 11: 55-57.

DEETZ, S. A. and A. KERSTEN (1983) "Critical models of interpretive research," in L. Putnam and M. Pacanowsky (eds.) Communication and Organizations: An Interpretive Approach. Beverly Hills, CA: Sage.

DEITERLY, D. and B. SCHNEIDER (1974) "The effects of organizational environment on perceived power and climate: a laboratory study." Organizational Behavior and Human Peformance 11: 316-337.

DELIA, J. (1970) "The logic fallacy, cognitive theory, and the enthymeme: a search for the foundations of reasoned discourse." Quarterly Journal of Speech 56: 140-148.

DE NISI, A., W. RANDOLPH, and A. BLENCOE (1982) "Level and source of feedback as determinants of feedback effectiveness." Proceedings of the Academy of Management 42: 172-179.

DENNIS, H. S., III (1974) "A theoretical and empirical study of managerial communication climate in complex organizations." Ph.D. dissertation, Purdue University.

DENZIN, N. K. (1970) The Research Act. Chicago: Aldine.

DERRIDA, J. (1976) Of Grammatology (G. Spivak, trans.). Baltimore: Johns Hopkins University Press.

DEUTSCH, M. (1973) The Resolution of Conflict. New Haven: Yale University Press.

———and R. KRAUSS (1960) "The effect of threat on interpersonal bargaining." Journal of Abnormal and Social Psychology 61: 181-189.

DICKENS, M. (1945) "Discussion method in war industry." Quarterly Journal of Speech 31: 144-150.

DiMAGGIO, P. (1977) "Market structure, the creative process, and popular culture." Journal of Popular Culture 11 (Fall): 436-452.

DIONISOPOULOS, G. and W. SAMTER (1983) "Identification by antithesis: an analysis of the 'us versus them' orientation of police." Presented at the annual convention of the Eastern Communication Association, Ocean City, MD.

DOISE, W. (1977) Groups and Individuals: Explanations in Social Psychology. Cambridge: Cambridge University Press.

DONOHUE, W. (1978) "An empirical framework for examining negotiation processes and outcomes." Communication Monographs 45: 247-257.

———(1981a) "Analyzing negotiation tactics: development of a negotiation interact system." Human Communication Research 7: 273-287.

———(1981b) "Development of a model of rule use in negotiation interaction." Communication Monographs 48: 106-120.

———and M. DIEZ (1983) "Information management in negotiation." Presented at the annual convention of the International Communication Association, Dallas.

———and M. HAMILTON (1984) "Coding naturalistic negotiation interaction." Human Communication Research 10: 403-425.

DONOHUE, W., M. DIEZ, and R. STAHLE (1983) "New directions in negotiation research," in R. Bostrom (ed.) Communication Yearbook 7. Beverly Hills, CA: Sage.

DONOHUE, W., M. DIEZ, and D. WEIDER-HATFIELD (1984) "A valence theory of mediator competence," in R. Bostrom (ed.) Communication Competence. Beverly Hills, CA: Sage.

DOOHER, M. J. and V. MARQUIS [eds.] (1956) Effective Communication on the Job. New York: American Management Association.

DOUGLAS, A. (1957) "The peaceful settlement of industrial and inter-group disputes." Journal of Conflict Resolution 1: 69-81.

———(1962) Industrial Peacemaking. New York: Columbia University Press.

DOUGLAS, M. (1982a) Natural Symbols: Explorations in Cosmology. New York: Pantheon.

————(1982b) In the Active Voice. London: Routledge & Kegan Paul.

DOVER, C. (1959) "The three eras of management communication." Journal of Communication 9: 168-172.

DREXLER, J. A. (1977) "Organizational climate: its homogeneity within organizations." Journal of Applied Psychology 62: 38-42.

DRUCKER, P. F. (1973) Management: Tasks, Responsibilities, Practices. New York: Harper & Row.

DUBIN, R. (1956) "Industrial workers' worlds: a study of the central life interests of industrial workers." Social Problems 3: 131-142.

————(1962) "Business behavior behaviorally viewed," in G. Strother (ed.) Social Science Approaches to Business Behavior. Homewood, IL: Dorsey.

————J. CHAMPOUX, and L. PORTER (1975) "Central life interests and organizational commitment of blue-collar and clerical workers." Administrative Science Quarterly 20: 411-421.

DUBIN, R. and S. SPRAY (1964) "Executive behavior and interaction." Industrial Relations 3: 99-108.

DUNCAN, R. (1972) "Characteristics of organizational environments and perceived environmental uncertainty." Administrative Science Quarterly 17: 313-327.

Editors of Time-Life Books (1969) This Fabulous Century: 1930-1940. New York: Time-Life Books.

EDWARDS, R. (1978) Contested Terrain. New York: Basic Books.

————(1981) "The social relations of production at the point of production," in M. Zey-Ferrell and M. Aiken (eds.) Complex Organizations: Critical Perspectives. Glenview, IL: Scott, Foresman.

————M. REICH, and T. WEISSKOPF [eds.] (1972) The Capitalist System. Englewood Cliffs, NJ: Prentice-Hall.

EISENBERG, E., P. MONGE, and K. MILLER (1983) "Involvement in communication networks as a predictor of organizational commitment." Human Communication Research 10: 179-202.

ELLIS, D. (1979) "Relational control in two group systems." Communication Monographs 46: 153-166.

EMERSON, R. (1967) "Power-dependence relations." American Sociological Review 32.

EMERY, F. and E. TRIST (1965) "Socio-technical systems," pp. 83-97 in C. Churchman and M. Verhulst (eds.) Management Science: Models and Techniques, Vol. 2. Oxford: Pergamon.

ERICKSON, E. (1963) Childhood and Society. New York: Norton.

————(1968) Identity: Youth and Crisis. New York: Norton.

ESPINOSA, J. and A. ZIMBALIST (1978) Economic Democracy. New York: Academic.

ESTES, C. T. (1946) "Speech and human relations." Quarterly Journal of Speech 32: 160-169.

ETZIONI, A. (1975) A Comparative Analysis of Complex Organizations. New York: Free Press.

EWING, D. W. (1977) Freedom Inside the Organization. New York: Dutton.

EXTON, W. (1950) "Semantics of industrial relations." Personnel 26: 418-423.

FARRELL, D. and J. PETERSON (1982) "Patterns of political behavior in organizations." Academy of Management Review 7: 403-412.

FAULKNER, R. (1972) "Hollywood studio musicians: making it in the Los Angeles film and recording industry," in C. Nanry (ed.) American Music: From Storyville to Woodstock. New Brunswick, NJ: Transaction.

FERENCE, T. (1971) "Organizational communication systems and the decision process." Management Science 17: B83-B96.

FESTINGER, L. (1957) A Theory of Cognitive Dissonance. Evanston, IL: Row, Peterson.

FISHMAN, M. (1980) Manufacturing the News. Austin, TX: University of Texas Press.

FLEISHMAN, E. A. (1951) Leadership Climate and Supervisory Behavior. Columbus: Ohio State University, Personnel Research Board.

————(1953) "Leadership climate, human relations training, and supervisory behavior." Personnel Psychology 6: 205-222.

————E. HARRIS, and H. BURTT (1955) Leadership and Supervision in Industry. Columbus: Ohio State University, Bureau of Educational Research.

FOLGER, J. P. and M. S. POOLE (1984) Working Through Conflict. Glenview, IL: Scott, Foresman.

FOLLETT, M. (1924) Creative Experience. New York: Longmans, Green.

FOMBRUN, C. (1978) Network Methodologies: Problems and Prospects. New York: Columbia University Graduate School of Business.

————(1983) "Attributions of power across a social network." Human Relations 36: 493-508.

FOOTE, N. (1951) "Identification as the basis for a theory of motivation." American Sociological Review 16: 14-22.

Foundation for Research on Human Behavior (1959) Communication in Organizations. Ann Arbor: University of Michigan.

FREDERIKSEN, N., O. JENSEN, and A. E. BEATON (1972) Prediction of Organizational Behavior. New York: Pergamon.

FRENCH, J. and B. RAVEN (1968) "The bases of social power," in D. Cartwright and A. Zander (eds.) Group Dynamics. New York: Harper & Row.

FRENCH, J.R.P., I. C. ROSS, S. KIRBY, J. R. NELSON, and P. SMYTH (1958) "Employee participation in a program of industrial change." Personnel 35: 16-29.

FRESHLEY, D. (1955) "A study of the attitudes of industrial management personnel toward communication." Ph.D. dissertation, Ohio State University.

FREUD, S. (1922) Group Psychology and the Analysis of the Ego. New York: Boni & Liveright.

FRIEDMAN, A. (1977) Industry and Labour. London: Macmillan.

FUNK, F. (1956) "Communication attitudes of industrial foremen as related to their rated productivity." Ph.D. dissertation, Purdue University.

FUNK, H. and R. BECKER (1952) "Measuring the effectiveness of industrial communications." Personnel 29: 237-240.

GADAMER, H. G. (1975) Truth and Method (G. Barden and J. Cumming, trans.). New York: Seabury.

GAHRIS, P. (1983) "Organizational premises, modes of influence, and enthymeme$_2$ in decision making: a discourse analysis approach." Presented at the annual convention of the Eastern Communication Association, Ocean City, MD.

GALBRAITH, J. K. (1967) The New Industrial State. New York: Signet.

————(1973) Designing Complex Organizations. Reading, MA: Addison-Wesley.

GANS, H. (1979) Deciding What's News. New York: Vintage.

GARDNER, B. (1945) Human Relations in Industry. Chicago: Irwin.

————and W. F. WHYTE (1945) "The man in the middle: position and problems of the foreman." Applied Anthropology [Special issue] 4 (Spring).

GARFINKEL, H. (1967) Studies in Ethnomethodology. Englewood Cliffs, NJ: Prentice-Hall.

GARRETT, M. (1940) European History: 1500-1815. New York: American Book.

GARSON, B. (1977) All the Livelong Day. London: Penguin.

GARSON, D. [ed.] (1977) Worker Self-Management in Industry. New York: Praeger.

GEERTZ, C. (1973) The Interpretation of Cultures. New York: Basic.

GEIST, P. and T. CHANDLER (1983) "Organizational influence in group decision making: an account analysis." Presented at the annual convention of the Eastern Communication Association, Ocean City, MD.

General Electric Company (1952) "Employee communication—executive summary." (Booklet issued by the Employee and Plant Community Relations Staff, General Electric Company, New York)

GEORGE, J. and L. BISHOP (1971) "Relationship of organizational structure and teacher personality characteristics to organizational climate." Administrative Science Quarterly 16: 467-475.

GERBNER, G. (1972) "Communication and social environment." Scientific American pp. 227-153.

GERGEN, K. (1969) The Psychology of Behavior Exchange. Reading, MA: Addison-Wesley.

GIBB, J. (1961a) "Defensive communication." Journal of Communication 11: 141-148.

———(1961b) "Defense level and influence in small groups," in L. Petrullo and B. Bass (eds.) Leadership and Interpersonal Behavior. New York: Holt, Rinehart & Winston.

GIBSON, J., J. IVANCEVICH, and J. DONNELLY (1982) Organizations: Behavior, Structure, Processes. Plano, TX: Business Publications.

GIDDENS, A. (1971) The Class Structure of the Advanced Societies. New York: Harper & Row.

———(1976) New Rules of Sociological Method. New York: Basic Books.

———(1977) Studies in Social and Political Theory. New York: Basic Books.

———(1979) Central Problems in Social Theory. Berkeley: University of California Press.

———(1981) A Contemporary Critique of Historical Materialism. Berkeley: University of California Press.

———(1982) "Power, the dialectic of control, and class structuration," in A. Giddens and G. Mackenzie (eds.) Social Class and the Division of Labor. New York: Cambridge University Press.

———(1983) Profiles and Critiques in Social Theory. Berkeley: University of California Press.

GINTES, H. (1972) "Alienation in capitalist society," in R. Edwards et al. (eds.) The Capitalist System. Englewood Cliffs, NJ: Prentice-Hall.

GITLIN, T. (1978) The Whole World Is Watching. Berkeley: University of Calfornia Press.

———(1979) "Prime time ideology." Social Problems 26: 264.

———(1983) Inside Prime Time. New York: Pantheon.

GLASBERG, D. and M. SCHWARTZ (1979) "Corporate power," pp. 311-331 in A. Inkeles (ed.) Annual Review of Sociology, Vol. 5. Palo Alto, CA: Annual Reviews.

GLASER, B. (1964) Organizational Scientists. Indianapolis: Bobbs-Merrill.

GOETZINGER, C. S., Jr. (1954) "An analysis of irritating factors in initial employment interviews of male college graduates." Ph.D. dissertation, Purdue University.

GOFF, T. (1980) Marx and Mead. London: Routledge & Kegan Paul.

GOFFMAN, E. (1961) Asylums. Garden City, NY: Doubleday.

GOLDFIELD, R. (1983) "Future phones." Working Woman (May): 66-70.

GOLDMAN, P. and D. VAN HOUTEN (1977) "Managerial strategies and the worker." Sociological Quarterly 18: 108-125.

GOTTMAN, J. M. (1979) Marital Interaction: Experimental Investigations. New York: Academic.

GOLDNER, F. (1970) "The division of labor: process and power," in M. Zald (ed.) Power in Organizations. Nashville: Vanderbilt University Press.

GOLDTHORPE, J.D., J. LOCKWOOD, G. BEECHOFFER, and H. PLATT (1967) "The affluent worker and the thesis of embourgeoisement." Sociology 1: 11-32.

Goodyear Tire and Rubber Co. (1953) Goodyear Supervisional Training, 1952-53 Sessions: Communications. Akron, OH: Author.

GORDON, M., J. PHILPOT, R. BURT, C. THOMPSON, and W. SPILLER (1980) "Commitment to the union: development of a measure and an examination of its correlates." Journal of Applied Psychology Monographs 65: 479-499.

GORN, G. and R. KANUNGO (1980) "Job involvement and motivation: are intrinsically motivated managers more job involved?" Organizational Behavior and Human Performance 26: 265-277.

GOULDNER, A. (1954) Patterns of Industrial Bureaucracy. New York: Free Press.

———(1957) "Cosmopolitans and locals: toward an analysis of latent social roles—I." Administrative Science Quarterly 2: 281-306.

———(1958) "Cosmopolitans and locals: toward an analysis of latent social roles—II." Administrative Science Quarterly 2: 444-480.

GOULDNER, H. (1960) "Dimensions of organizational commitment." Administrative Science Quarterly 4: 468-487.

GRAMSCI, A. (1971) Selections from the Prison Notebook (Q. Hoare and P. Nowell-Smith, eds. and trans.). London: Lawrence & Wishart.

GRANOVETER, M. (1973) "The strength of weak ties." American Journal of Sociology 68: 1360-1380.

GREENBAUM, H. H. and R. L. FALCIONE (1975) Organizational Communication Abstracts 1974. Urbana: American Business Communication Association.

GREENE, C. (1978) "Identification modes of professionals: relationship with formalization, role strain, and alienation." Academy of Management Journal 21: 486-492.

GREENLEAF, W. (1948) "Preface," in K. Sward (ed.) The Legend of Henry Ford. New York: Atheneum.

GREENWOOD, J. (1974) "Opportunity to communicate and social orientation in imaginary-reward bargaining." Speech Monographs 41: 49-81.

GRIMALDI, W. (1972) Studies in the Philosophy of Aristotle's Rhetoric. Wiesbaden: Frans Steiner Verlag GMBH.

GRONER, A. (1972) The American Heritage History of American Business and Industry. New York: American Heritage.

GROSS, E. (1953) "Some functional consequences of primary controls in formal work organizations." American Sociological Review 18: 368-373.

GRUSKY, O. (1966) "Career mobility and organizational commitment." Administrative Science Quarterly 10: 488-503.

GUETZKOW, H. (1965) "Communications in organizations," pp. 534-573 in J. G. March (ed.) Handbook of Organizations. Chicago: Rand McNally.

GUION, R. (1973) "A note on organizational climate." Organizational Behavior and Human Performance 9: 120-125.

GULLIVER, P. (1979) Disputes and Negotiations: A Cross-Cultural Perspective. New York: Academic.

HABBE, S. (1952) Communicating with Employees. New York: National Industrial Conference Board.

HABERMAS, J. (1970) Legitimation Crisis. Boston: Beacon.

———(1976) "Problems of legitimation in late capitalism," in P. Connerton (ed.) Critical Sociology. New York: Penguin.

———(1979) Communication and the Evolution of Society (T. McCarthy, trans.). Boston: Beacon.

———(1980) "The hermeneutic claim to universality," in J. Bleicher, Contemporary Hermeneutics. London: Routledge & Kegan Paul.

———(1984) The Theory of Communicative Action, Vol. 1: Reason and the Rationalization of Society. Boston: Beacon.

HACKMAN, J. and E. LAWLER (1971) "Employee reactions to job characteristics." Journal of Applied Psychology 55: 259-286.

HAGE, J. (1974) Communication and Organizational Control. New York: John Wiley.

———and M. AIKEN (1966) "Program change and organizational properties." American Journal of Sociology 72: 503-519.

———(1969) "Routine technology, social structure, and organizational goals." Administrative Science Quarterly 17: 366-376.

HAIRE, M. and F. MORRISON (1957) "School children's perceptions of labor and management." Journal of Social Psychology 46: 179-197.

HALL, D. and B. SCHNEIDER (1972) "Correlates of organizational identification as a function of career path and organization type." Administrative Science Quarterly 17: 340-350.

———(1973) Organizational Climates and Careers: The Work Lives of Priests. New York: Seminar.

———and H. NYGREN (1970) "Personal factors in organizational identification." Administrative Science Quarterly 15: 176-190.

HALL, S. (1981) "Cultural studies: two paradigms," in T. Bennett et al. (eds.) Culture, Ideology, and Social Processes. London: Open University.

———(1982) "The rediscovery of 'ideology': return of the repressed in media studies," in M. Gurevitch et al. (eds.) Culture, Society, and the Media. London: Methuen.

HALPIN, A. and D. CROFTS (1963) "The organizational climate of schools." Administrator's Notebook 11.

HANEY, W. V. (1960) Communication: Patterns and Incidents. Homewood, IL: Dorsey.

HARRIS, L. and V. CRONEN (1979) "A rules-based model for the analysis and evaluation of organizational communication." Communication Quarterly 27: 12-28.

HARTNETT, D. and L. CUMMINGS (1971) "Bargaining behavior in an asymmetric triad," in B. Lieberman (ed.) Social Choice. New York: Gordon & Breach.

HAWES, L. (1978) "The reflexivity of communication research." Western Journal of Speech Communication 42: 12-20.

———and D. SMITH (1973) "A critique of assumptions underlying the study of communication in conflict." Quarterly Journal of Speech 59: 423-435.

HAY, R. (1974) "A brief history of internal organization communication through the 1940s." Journal of Business Communication 11 (Summer): 6-11.

HEIDEGGER, M. (1962) Being and Time (J. Macquiarie and E. Robinson, trans.). London: SCM.

HEIDER, F. (1958) The Psychology of Interpersonal Relations. New York: John Wiley.

HELLREIGEL, D. and J. SLOCUM (1974) "Organizational climate: measures, research, and contingencies." Academy of Management Journal 17: 255-280.

HELMER, J., K. MARTIN, and M. S. POOLE (1984) "A new conceptualization of organizational climate." Presented at the annual convention of the Speech Communication Association, Chicago.

HERON, A. (1942) Sharing Information with Employees. Palo Alto, CA: Stanford University Press.

HEYDEBRAND, W. (1977) "Organizational contradictions in public bureaucracies." Sociological Quarterly 18: 83-107.

HEYEL, C. (1939) Human-Relations Manual for Executives. New York: McGraw-Hill.

HICKS, M. (1955) "Speech training in business and industry." Journal of Communication 5: 161-168.

HICKSON, D. and A. McCULLOUGH (1980) "Power in organizations," in G. Salaman and K. Thompson (eds.) Control and Ideology in Organizations. Cambridge: MIT Press.

HICKSON, D., W. ASTLEY, R. BUTLER, and D. WILSON (1981) "Organization as power," in B. Staw and L. Cummings (eds.) Research in Organizational Behavior. Greenwich, CT: JAI.

HICKSON, D., C. HININGS, C. LEE, R. SCHNECK, and J. PENNINGS (1971) "A strategic contingencies theory of intraorganizational power." Administrative Science Quarterly 16: 216-229.

HINDS, G. L. (1954) "The new frontier: speech education in industry." Speech Teacher 3: 26-28.

———(1955) "Developing industrial conference leaders." Speech Teacher 4: 266-269.

HIRSCH, P. (1972) "Processing fads and fashions." American Journal of Sociology 77: 639-659.

HOLLAND, P. and S. LEINHARDT (1975) "The statistical analysis of local structure in social networks," in D. Heise (ed.) Sociological Methodology 1975. San Francisco: Jossey-Bass.

HOMAN, W. (1923) Public Speaking for Businessmen. New York: McGraw-Hill.

HOROVITZ, B. (1981) "Where headhunters hunt." Industry Week, February 9: 43-47.

HOUSE, R. (1971) "A path-goal theory of leader effectiveness." Administrative Science Quarterly 16: 321-338.

——— and J. RIZZO (1972) "Toward the measurement of organizational practices: scale development and validation." Journal of Applied Psychology 56: 388-396.

HOWARD, R. (1979) Three Faces of Hermeneutics. Berkeley: University of California Press.

HOWE, J. (1977) "Group climate: an exploration of construct validity." Organizational Behavior and Human Performance 19: 106-125.

HOY, D. (1981) The Critical Circle. Berkeley: University of California Press.

HREBINIAK, L. and J. ALUTTO (1972) "Personal and role-related factors in the development of organizational commitment." Administrative Science Quarterly 17: 555-573.

HUMMEL, R. (1982) The Bureaucratic Experience. New York: St. Martin's.

HUNT, R. and C. LICHTMAN (1969) "Role clarity, communication, and conflict." Management of Personnel Quarterly 9: 26-36.

HUSTON, A. and R. SANDBERG (1943) Everyday Business Speech. Englewood Cliffs, NJ: Prentice-Hall.

INDIK, B. (1965) "Organizational size and member participation: some empirical tests of alternative explanations." Human Relations 18: 339-350.

INGHAM, G. (1970) Size of Industrial Organization and Worker Behavior. Cambridge: Cambridge University Press.

INKSON, J., D. PUGH, and D. HICKSON (1970) "Organization context and structure: an abbreviated replication." Administrative Science Quarterly 15: 318-329.

INKSON, J., J. SCHWITTER, D. PHEYSEY, and D. HICKSON (1971) "A comparison of organizational structure and managerial roles in Ohio , U.S.A., and the Midlands, England." Journal of Management Studies 7: 347-363.

IVANCEVICH, J. (1982) "Subordinates' reactions to performance appraisal interview: a test of feedback and goal setting techniques." Journal of Applied Psychology 67: 581-587.

———and J. McMAHON (1982) "The effects of goal setting, external feedback, and self-generated feedback on outcome variables: a field experiment." Academy of Management Journal 25: 359-372.

JABLIN, F. (1979) "Superior-Subordinate communication: the state of the art." Psychological Bulletin 86: 1201-1222.

———(1980) "Organizational communication theory and research: an overview of communication climate and network research," in D. Nimmo (ed.) Communication Yearbook 4. New Brunswick, NJ: Transaction.

———(1982) "Formal structural characteristics of organizations and superior/subordinate communication." Human Communication Research 8: 338-347.

JACKSON, S. and S. JACOBS (1980) "Structure of conversational argument: pragmatic bases for the enthymeme." Quarterly Journal of Speech 66: 251-265.

JACOBSON, E. and S. SEASHORE (1951) "Communication practices in complex organizations." Journal of Social Issues 7: 28-40.

JAMES, L. and A. JONES (1974) "Organizational climate: a review of theory and research." Psychological Bulletin 81: 1096-1112.

JANEWAY, E. (1981) Powers of the Weak. New York: Random House.

JANIS, J. H. (1958) Business Communication Reader. New York: Harper & Row.

JENKIN, D. (1973) Job Power. Garden City, NY: Doubleday.

JENSEN, S. (1983) "Decisionmaking in Japanese organizations: a proposed temple of understanding." Master's thesis, Purdue University.

JOHANNESON, R. (1973) "Some problems in the measurement of organizational climate." Organizational Behavior and Human Performance 10: 95-103.

JOHNSON, D. (1967) "Use of role reversal in intergroup conflict." Journal of Personality and Social Psychology 7: 135-141.

———(1974) "Communication and the inducement of cooperative behavior in conflicts: a critical review." Speech Monographs 41: 64-78.

———H. McCARTHY, and K. ALLEN (1976) "Congruent and contradictory verbal and nonverbal communication of cooperativeness and competitiveness in negotiations." Communication Research 3: 275-292.

JOHNSTON, H. (1976) "A new conceptualization of source of organizational climate." Administrative Science Quarterly 21: 95-103.

JOHNSTONE, J., E. SLAWSKI, and W. BOWMAN (1976) The News People. Urbana: University of Illinois Press.

JONES, A. and L. JAMES (1979) "Psychological climate: dimensions and relationships of individual and aggregated work environment perceptions." Organizational Behavior and Human Performance 23: 201-250.

JONES, E. and H. GERARD (1967) Foundations of Social Psychology. New York: John Wiley.

JONES, E., K. GERGEN, and R. JONES (1963) "Tactics of ingratiation among leaders and subordinates in a status hierarchy." Psychological Monographs 77 (Whole No. 521).

KAGAN, J. (1958) "The concept of identification." Psychological Review 65: 296-305.

KAHN, R., D. WOLFE, R. QUINN, J. SNOEK, and R. ROSENTHAL (1964) Organizational Stress. New York: John Wiley.

KAHNEMANN, D. and A. TVERSKY (1973) "On the psychology of prediction." Psychlogical Review 80: 237-251.

KANTER, R. (1968) "Commitment and social organization: a study of commitment mechanisms in utopian communities." American Sociological Review 33: 499-551.

———(1977) Men and Women of the Corporation. New York: Basic Books.

———(1983) The Change Masters. New York: Simon & Schuster.

KARPIK, L. (1978) "Organizations, institutions, and history," in L. Karpik (ed.) Organization and Environment: Theory, Issues, and Reality. Beverly Hills, CA: Sage.

KATZ, D. (1964) "The motivational basis of organizational behavior." Behavioral Science 9: 131-146.

———and R. KAHN (1965) The Social Psychology of Organizations. New York: John Wiley.

———(1978) The Social Psychology of Organizations (2nd ed.). New York: John Wiley.

KATZ, D., N. MACCOBY, and N. MORSE (1950) Productivity, Supervision, and Morale in an Office Situation: Part I. Ann Arbor: University of Michigan, Institute for Social Research.

KATZ, D., N. MACCOBY, G. GURIN, and L. FLOOR (1951) Productivity, Supervision, and Morale Among Railroad Workers. Ann Arbor: University of Michigan, Institute for Social Research.

KATZ, F. (1968) Autonomy and Organization. New York: Random House.

KAUFMAN, H. (1960) The Forest Ranger: A Study in Administrative Behavior. Baltimore: Johns Hopkins University Press.

KEEN, P. (1981) "Communication in the 21st century: telecommunications and business policy." Organizational Dynamics 10: 54-67.

KEIDEL, R. (1984) "Baseball, football, and basketball: models for business." Organizational Dynamics 16: 5-18.

KELLEY, H. (1951) "Communication in experimentally created hierarchies." Human Relations 4: 39-55.

KELLEY, J. (1964) "The study of executive behavior by activity sampling." Human Relations 17: 277-287.

KELMAN, H. (1958) "Compliance, identification, and internalization: three processes of attitude change." Journal of Conflict Resolution 2: 57-60.

KELTNER, J. (1965) "Communication and the labor-management mediation process: Some aspects and hypotheses." Journal of Communication 2: 64-80.

KENNEDY, D. (1980) Over Here: The First World War and American Society. New York: Oxford University Press.

KEOGH, C. (1983) "Bargaining communication and arbitration arguments: an analysis of the collective bargaining between the Teaching Assistants' Association and the University of Wisconsin—Madison." Master's thesis, Purdue University.

———(1983) "Bargaining communication and arbitration arguments: an analysis of collective bargaining system: a case study of Teaching Assistants' Association and the University of Wisconsin—Madison." Presented at the annual convention of the International Communication Association, San Francisco, May.

KIDRON, A. (1978) "Work values and organizational commitment." Academy of Management Journal 21: 239-247.

KIESLER, C. (1971) The Psychology of Commitment. New York: Academic.

KILLWORTH, P. and R. BERNARD (1976) "Informant accuracy in social network data." Human Organization 35: 269-286.

———(1979) "Informant accuracy in social network data III." Social Networks 2: 19-46.

KIPNIS, D. (1976) The Powerholders. Chicago: University of Chicago Press.

KNAPP, M. and J. McCROSKEY (1968) "Communication research and the American labor union." Journal of Communication 18: 160-172.

KNOCKE, D. (1981) "Commitment and detachment in voluntary associations." American Sociological Review 46: 141-158.

KOCH, J. and R. STEERS (1978) "Job attachment, satisfaction, and turnover among public sector employees." Journal of Vocational Behavior 12: 119-128.

KOCHAN, T. (1975) "Determinants of the power of boundary units in an interorganizational bargaining relation." Administrative Science Quarterly 20: 434-452.

———(1980) "Collective bargaining and organizational behavior," in B. Staw and L. Cummings (eds.) Research in Organizational Behavior, Vol. 2. Greenwich, CT: JAI.

KOMORITA, S. and J. ESSER (1975) "Frequency of reciprocated concessions in bargaining." Journal of Personality and Social Psychology 32: 699-705.

KORDA, M. (1975) Power. New York: Ballantine.

KORNHAUSER, W. (1962) Scientists in Industry: Conflict and Accommodation. Berkeley: University of California Press.

KUHN, T. (1970) The Structure of Scientific Revolutions. Chicago: University of Chicago Press.

LAFOLLETTE, W. and H. SIMS (1975) "Is satisfaction redundant with organizational climate?" Organizational Behavior and Human Performance 13: 257-278.

LAING, R., H. PHILLIPSON, and A. LEE. (1966) Interpersonal Perception: A Theory and a Method of Research. New York: Harper & Row.

LAIRD, A. and M. HEMPHILL (1983) "The relationship between identification and evaluation in organizational decisionmaking." Presented at the annual convention of the Speech Communication Association, Washington, D.C.

LAKOFF, G. and M. JOHNSON (1980) Metaphors We Live By. Chicago: University of Chicago Press.

LAMM, H. and ROSCH, E. (1972) "Information and the competitiveness of incentive structures as factors in two person negotiation." European Journal of Social Psychology 2: 459-462.

LANDSBERGER, H. (1955) "Interaction process analysis of the mediation of labor-management disputes." Journal of Abnormal and Social Psychology 51: 552-558.

LA PORTE, T., E. ROSENTHAL, and K. LEE (1977) Interactions of Technology and Society: Impacts of Improved Air Transport. NASA Contractors Report CR-2871. Washington, DC: NASA.

LARSON, C. and J. MOCK (1939) "The four minute men." Quarterly Journal of Speech 25: 97-112.

LASSWELL, H. (1965) World Politics and Personal Insecurity. New York: Free Press.

LAWLER, E., D. HALL, and G. OLDHAM (1974) "Organizational climate: relationship to organizational structure, process, and performance." Organizational Behavior and Human Performance 11: 139-155.

LAWLER, E., L. PORTER, and A. TANNENBAUM (1968) "Managers' attitude toward interaction episodes." Journal of Applied Psychology 52: 432-439.

LAWRENCE, P. (1958) The Changing of Organizational Behavior Patterns: A Case Study of Decentralization. Boston: Graduate School of Business Administration, Harvard University.

————and J. LORSCH (1967) Organization and Environment. Boston: Graduate School of Business Administration, Harvard University.

LAWSHE, C. and R. GUION (1951) "A comparison of labor-management attitudes toward grievance procedures." Personnel Psychology 4: 3-17.

LAWSHE, C. and R. GUION (1951) "A comparison of labor-management attitudes toward grievance procedures." Personnel Psychology 4: 3-17.

LAZOWICK, L. (1955) "On the nature of identification." Journal of Abnormal and Social Psychology 51: 175-183.

LEAVITT, H. J. and R. MUELLER (1951) "Some effects of feedback on communication." Human Relations 4: 401-410.

LEE, I. J. (1952) How to Talk with People. New York: Harper & Row.

————(1954) Customs and Crises in Communication. New York: Harper & Row.

————and L. L. LEE (1956) Handling Barriers in Communication: Lecture-Discussions and Conferee's Handbook. New York: Harper & Row.

LEE, S. (1969) "Organizational identification of scientists." Academy of Management Journal 12: 327-337.

————(1971) "An empirical analysis of organizational identification." Academy of Management Journal 14: 213-226.

LEVEL, D. (1959) "A case study of human communication in an urban bank." Ph.D. dissertation, Purdue University.

LEVINE, J. and J. BUTLER (1952) "Lecture versus group discussion in changing behavior." Journal of Applied Psychology 36: 29-33.

LEVINSON, H. (1965) "Reciprocation: the relationship between man and organization." Administrative Science Quarterly 9: 370-390.

LEWIN, K. (1943) "Forces behind food habits and methods of change." Bulletin of the National Research Council 108: 35-65.

————R. LIPPITT, and R. WHITE (1939) "Patterns of aggressive behavior in experimentally-created 'social climates.' " Journal of Social Psychology 10: 271-299.

LEWIS, I. (1954) "A survey of management's attitudes regarding oral communication needs and practices in large industries of Los Angeles County." Ph.D. dissertation, University of Southern California.

LEWIS, L. (1967) "On prestige and loyalty of university faculty." Administrative Science Quarterly 11: 629-642.

LIKERT, R. (1955) Developing Patterns in Management. General Management Series No. 178. New York: American Management Association.

————(1958) "Measuring organizational performance." Harvard Business Review 36 (March/April): 41-50.

————(1961a) New Patterns of Management. New York: McGraw-Hill.

————(1961b) "Patterns in management," pp. 338-355 in E. A. Fleishman (ed.) Studies in Personnel and Industrial Psychology. Homewood, IL: Dorsey.

————(1967) The Human Organization. New York: McGraw-Hill.

———— and J. M. WILLITS (1940) Morale and Agency Management. Hartford, CT: Life Insurance Agency Management Association.

LILLIENFELD, R. (1978) The Rise of Systems Theory: An Ideological Analysis. New York: John Wiley.

LINDBLOM, C. (1959) "The science of 'muddling through.' " Public Administration Review 19: 79-88.

————(1979) "Still muddling, not yet through." Public Administration Review 39: 517-526.

LITWIN, G. and R. STRINGER (1968) Motivation and Organizational Climate. Cambridge, MA: Harvard University Press.

LODAHL, T. and M. KEJNER (1965) "The definition and measurement of job involvement." Journal of Applied Psychology 48: 24-33.

LOMBARD, G. (1955) Behavior in a Selling Group: A Case Study of Interpersonal Relations in a Department Store. Boston: Division of Research, Graduate School of Business Administration, Harvard University.

LONDON, M. and G. HOWAT (1978) "The relationship between employee commitment and conflict resolution behavior." Journal of Vocational Behavior 13: 1-14.

LONG, R. (1978) "The effects of employee ownership on organizational identification, employee job attitudes, and organizational performance: a tentative framework and empirical findings." Human Relations 31: 29-48.

LORENZ, K. (1952) King Solomon's Ring. London: Methuen.

LUKACS, G. (1968) History and Class Consciousness. Cambridge, MA: MIT Press.

LUKES, S. (1974) Power: A Radical View. London: Macmillan.

LULL, P. (1953) "Communications in business and industry." Presented at a meeting of the Directors of the Indiana Manufacturers Association, Purdue University, West Lafayette, IN, July 27.

————F. FUNK, and D. PIERSOL (1954) Business and Industrial Communication from the Viewpoint of the Corporation President. West Lafayette, IN: Purdue University.

MacDONALD, D. (1976) "Communication roles and communication networks in a formal organization." Human Communication Research 2: 365-376.

MacNEIL, R. (1968) The People Machine: The Influence of Television on American Politics. New York: Harper & Row.

McCALL, G. and J. SIMMONS (1978) Identities and Interactions. New York: Free Press.

McGREGOR, D. (1944) "Conditions of effective leadership in the industrial organization." Journal of Consulting Psychology 8: 55-63.

————(1960) The Human Side of Enterprise. New York: McGraw-Hill.

————(1967) The Professional Manager. New York: McGraw-Hill.

McGUIRE, W. (1968) "Theory of the structure of human thought," in R. Abelson et al. (eds.) Theories of Cognitive Consistency: A Sourcebook. Chicago: Rand McNally.

————(1981) "The probabilogical model of cognitive structure and attitude change," in R. Petty et al.(eds.) Cognitive Responses in Persuasion. Hillsdale, NJ: Erlbaum.

McKELVEY, B. (1969) "Expectational noncomplementarity and style of interaction between professional and organization." Administrative Science Quarterly 16: 151-163.

————(1982) Organizational Systematics. Berkeley: University of California Press.

McKEON, R. (1967) "Discourse, demonstration, verification, and justification," in Demonstration, Verification, Justification: Entretiens de L'Institut International de Philosophie. Louvain, Netherlands: Editions Nauwelaerts.

McPHEE, R. (1981) "An ideal-type theory of organizational politics." Presented at the Alta Conference on Interpretive Approaches to Organizational Communication, Alta, UT.

————(1983) "Organizational communication: toward central concepts and phenomena." Presented at the annual convention of the International Communication Association, Dallas.

————and M. S. POOLE (1981) "The theory of structuration as a metatheory for human communication research." (unpublished)

MAIER, N.R.F. (1952) Principles of Human Relations. New York: John Wiley.

————(1958) The Appraisal Interview. New York: John Wiley.

————L. R. HOFFMAN, J. J. HOOVEN, and W. H. READ (1961) Superior-Subordinate Communication in Management. New York: American Management Association.

MAINES, D. (1977) "Social organization and social structure in symbolic interactionist thought," in A. Inkeles et al. (eds.) Annual Review of Sociology, Vol. 3. Palo Alto, CA: Annual Reviews.

MANN, F. and H. BAUMGARTEL (1952) Absences and Employee Attitudes in an Electric Power Company. Ann Arbor: University of Michigan, Survey Research Center, Institute for Social Research.

MANN, M. (1973) Consciousness and Action among the Western Working Class. London: Macmillan.

MANZ, C. and D. GIOLA (1983) "The interrelationship of power and control." Human Relations 36: 459-476.

MARCH, J. G. (1958) "The power of power," in D. Easton (ed.) Varieties of Political Theory. Englewood Cliffs, NJ: Prentice-Hall.

————[ed.] (1965) Handbook of Organizations. Chicago: Rand McNally.

————and J. OLSEN (1976) Ambiguity and Choice in Organizations. Bergen: Universitetsforlaget.

MARCH, J. and H. SIMON (1958) Organizations. New York: John Wiley.

MARCUSE, H. (1964) One-Dimensional Man. Boston: Beacon.

MARGULIES, E. (1981) "Proliferation of pressure groups in prime time symposium." Emmy: The Magazine of Television Arts and Sciences (Summer): A-29.

MARROW, A. J. (1969) The Practical Theorist: The Life and Works of Kurt Lewin. New York: Basic Books.

————and J.R.P. FRENCH (1945) "Changing a stereotype in industry." Journal of Social Issues 1: 33-37.

MARS, G. (1982) Cheats at Work. London: Unwin.

MARTIN, N. (1959) "The levels of management and their mental demands," in W. Warner and N. Martin (eds.) Industrial Man. New York: Harper & Row.

MASON, R. (1982) Participatory and Workplace Democracy. Carbondale, IL: Southern Illinois University Press.

MAYO, E. (1933) The Human Problems of an Industrial Civilization. Cambridge, MA: Harvard University Press.

————(1945) The Social Problems of an Industrial Civilization. Cambridge, MA: Harvard Graduate School of Business Administration.

————and G. F. F. LOMBARD (1944) Teamwork and Labor Turnover in the Aircraft Industry of Southern California. Cambridge, MA: Harvard University, Graduate School of Business Administration.

MEAD, G. H. (1934) Mind, Self, and Society, Chicago: University of Chicago Press.

MECHANIC, D. (1962) "Sources of power of lower level participants in complex organizations." Administrative Science Quarterly 7: 349-364.

MEISSNER, M. (1969) Technology and the Worker. San Francisco: Chandler.

————(1976) "The language of work," in R. Dubin (ed.) Handbook of Work, Organization, and Society. Chicago: Rand McNally.

MELLINGER, G. D. (1956) "Interpersonal trust as a factor in communication." Journal of Abnormal and Social Psychology 52: 304-309.

MEYER, A. (1982) "Adapting to environmental jolts." Administrative Science Quarterly 27: 515-537.

MEYER, J. and B. ROWAN (1977) "Institutionalized organizations: formal structure as myth and ceremony." American Journal of Sociology 83: 340-363.

MILES, R. E. (1965) "Human relations or human resources?" Harvard Business Review 43 (July/August): 148-163.

MILES, R. H. (1980) Macro-Organizational Behavior. Santa Monica, CA: Goodyear.

MILLER, F. and H. REMMERS (1950) "Studies in industrial empathy." Personnel Psychology 3: 33-40.

MILLER, G. and L. WAGER (1971) "Adult socialization, organizational structure, and role orientations." Administrative Science Quarterly 16: 151-163.

MILLS, J. (1984) "Unobtrusive control and communication in complex organizations: a field study." Purdue University. (unpublished)

———— and J. APPLEGATE (1983) "Unobtrusive control in organizations: an analysis of decision making premises." Presented at the annual convention of the Eastern Communication Association, Ocean City, MD.

MINTER, M. (1970) "An analytical study of communication-related themes in the GE-IUE NLRB case." Master's thesis, Purdue University.

MINTZBERG, H. (1975) "The manager's job: folklore and fact." Harvard Business Review 53: 49-61.

————(1979) The Structuring of Organizations. Englewood Cliffs, NJ: Prentice-Hall.

————(1983) Power In and Around Organizations. Englewood Cliffs, NJ: Prentice-Hall.

————D. RAISINGHANI, and A. THEORET (1976) "The structure of 'unstructured' decision processes." Administrative Science Quarterly 2: 246-275.

MITCHELL, T. (1983) People in Organizations. New York: McGraw-Hill.

MOBLEY, W., R. GRIFFETH, H. HAND, and B. MEGLINO (1979) "Review and conceptual analysis of the employee turnover process." Psychological Bulletin 86: 493-522.

MOGEL, L. (1979) The Magazine. Englewood Cliffs, NJ: Prentice-Hall.

MOHR, L. (1971) "Organizational technology and organizational structure." Administrative Science Quarterly 16: 444-459.

MOLOTCH, H. and M. LESTER (1973) "Accidents, scandals, and routines: resources for insurgent methodology." Insurgent Sociologist 3: 1-11.

MONGE, P., J. EDWARDS, and K. KIRSTE (1978) "The determinants of communication and communication structure in large organizations: a review of research," in B. Rubin (ed.) Communication Yearbook 2. New Brunswick, NJ: Transaction.

MONGE, P. and G. LINDSEY (1973) "Communication patterns in large organizations." San Jose State University. (unpublished)

MONROE, A. (1935) Principles and Types of Speech. Evanston, IL: Scott, Foresman.

MORGAN, G. [ed.] (1983) Beyond Method. Beverly Hills, CA: Sage.

MORGAN, H. W. (1984) "The gilded age." American Heritage 35, 5: 42-48.

MORRIS, J. and J. SHERMAN (1981) "Generalizability of an organizational commitment model." Academy of Management Journal 24: 512-526.

MORRIS, J. and R. STEERS (1980) "Structural influences on organizational commitment." Journal of Vocational Behavior 17: 50-57.

MORROW, P. (1983) "Concept redundancy in organizational research: the case of work commitment." Academy of Management Review 3: 486-500.

MORSE, N. and E. REIMER (1956) "The experimental change of a major organizational variable." Journal of Abnormal and Social Psychology 52: 120-139.

MOWDAY, R., R. STEERS, and L. PORTER (1979) "The measurement of organizational commitment." Journal of Vocational Behavior 14: 224-247.

MOWRER, O. (1950) Learning Theory and Personality Dynamics. New York: Ronald.

MUCHINSKY, P. (1977) "Organizational communication: relationship to organizational climate and job satisfaction." Academy of Management Journal 20: 592-607.

MULDER, M. (1971) "Power equalization through participation?" Administrative Science Quarterly 16: 31-38.

MURDOCK, G. (1982) "Large corporations and the control of communications industries," in M. Gurevitch et al. (eds.) Culture, Society and the Media. London: Methuen.

———and P. GOLDING (1977) "Captialism, communication, and class relations," in J. Curran et al. (eds.) Mass Communication and Society. London: Edward Arnold.

MURRAY, E. (1952) "Human intercommunication as a unified area of research." Journal of Communication 2: 33-43.

MUSSMAN, W. M. (1947) "Two-way communication within management," pp. 125-130 in National Council of the YMCA, Proceedings of the 29th Silver Bay Industrial Conference. New York: Association Press.

NANCE, J. (1978) "Communication networks in a hospital emergency department." Master's thesis, University of British Columbia.

NEWCOMB, H. and P. HIRSCH (1983) "Television as a culture platform." (unpublished)

NEWMAN, J. (1975) "Understanding the organizational structure-job attitude relationship through perceptions of the work environment." Organizational Behavior and Human Performance 14: 371-397.

NICHOLS, R. (1951) "Development and growth of NSSC." Journal of Communication 1, 1: 1-11.

NILSEN, T. (1953) "The communication survey: a study of communication problems in three office and factory units." Ph.D. dissertation, Northwestern University.

NISBETT, R. and L. ROSS (1980) Human Inference: Strategies and Shortcomings of Social Judgment. Englewood Cliffs, NJ: Prentice-Hall.

NORTHRUP, H. R. (1964) Boulwarism: The Labor Relations Policies of the General Electric Company. Ann Arbor: University of Michigan, Bureau of Industrial Relations, Graduate School of Business Administration.

ODIORNE, G. S. (1954) "An application of the communication audit." Personnel Psychology 7: 235-243.

OFFE, C. (1973) Structural Problems in the Capitalist State. Frankfurt: Suhrkamp.

OLSON, M. (1983) "Towards a mature social science." International Studies Quarterly 27: 29-38.

O'REILLY, C. (1977) "Superiors and peers as information sources, work group supportiveness, and individual decision-making performance." Journal of Applied Psychology 62: 632-635.

———(1978) "The intentional distortion of information in organizational communication: a laboratory and field approach." Human Relations 31: 173-193.

———(1980) "Individuals and information overload in organizations: is more necessarily better?" Academy of Management Journal 23: 684-696.

———and D. CALDWELL (1981) "The commitment and job tenure of new employees: some evidence of post-decisional justification." Administrative Science Quarterly 26: 597-616.

O'REILLY, C. and L. PONDY (1979) Organizational Communication. Columbus, OH: Grid.

O'REILLY, C. and K. ROBERTS (1976) "Relationships among components of credibility and communication behavior in work units." Journal of Applied Psychology 61: 99-102.

———(1977) "Task group structure, communication, and effectiveness in three organizations." Journal of Applied Psychology 62: 674-681.

OUCHI, W. (1978) "The transmission of control through organizational hierarchy." Academy of Management Journal, 20: 559-569.

———(1980) "Markets, bureaucracies, and clans." Administrative Science Quarterly 25: 129-141.

PACANOWSKY, M. and N. O'DONNELL-TRUJILLO (1982a) "Communication and organizational cultures." Western Journal of Speech Communication 46: 115-130.

———(1982b) "Organizational communication as cultural performance." Communication Monographs 50: 126-147.

PACANOWSKY, M. and M. STRINE (1985) "The positionality of the interpretive researcher." Southern Journal of Speech Communication 45.

PALUMBO, D. (1969) "Power and role specificity in organizational theory." Public Administration Review 27: 237-248.

PANDAWA, A. and SIMSUOKWE (1971) Determinants of Work Behaviour—Smelter Observations. Lusaka, Zambia: University of Zambia Sociological Association.

PAOLILLO, J. (1982) "R&D subsystem climate as a function of personal and organizational factors." Journal of Management Studies 19: 327-334.

PAONESSA, K. (1983) "Corporate advocacy and organizational member identification: a base study of General Motors." Master's thesis, Purdue University.

PARSONS, T. (1937) The Structure of Social Action. New York: Free Press.

———and BALES (1955) Family, Socialization, and Interaction Process. New York: Free Press.

PATCHEN, M. (1970) Participation, Achievement, and Involvement on the Job. Englewood Cliffs, NJ: Prentice-Hall.

———(1979) "Models of cooperation and conflict: a critical review." Journal of Conflict Resolution 14: 389-407.

PATEMAN, C. (1970) Participation and Democratic Theory. Cambridge: Cambridge University Press.

PATTERSON, D. and J. JENKINS (1948) "Communication between management and workers." Journal of Applied Psychology 32: 71-80.

PAUL, W. B., F. SORENSEN, and E. MURRAY (1946) "A functional core for the basic communications course." Quarterly Journal of Speech 32: 232-244.

PAYNE, R. and R. MANSFIELD (1973) "Relations of perceptions of organizational climate to organizational structure, context, and hierarchical position." Administrative Science Quarterly 18: 515-526.

PAYNE, R. and D. PUGH (1976) "Organizational structure and climate," in M. Dunnette (ed.) Handbook of Industrial Psychology. Chicago: Rand McNally.

PAYNE, R., S. FINEMAN, and T. WALL (1976) "Organizational climate and job satisfaction: a conceptual synthesis." Organizational Behavior and Human Performance 16: 45-62.

PEARCE, W. B. and V. E. CRONEN (1980) Communication, Action, and Meaning: The Creation of Social Realities. New York: Prager.

PELZ, D. (1952) "Influence: a key to effective leadership in the first-line supervisor." Personnel 29: 209-217.

———and F. ANDREWS (1976) Scientists in Organizations. Ann Arbor, MI: Institute for Social Research.

PERROW, C. (1967) "A framework for the comparative analysis of organizations." American Sociological Review 32: 194-208.

———(1970) Organizational Analysis: A Sociological View. Belmont, CA: Wadsworth.

———(1979) Complex Organizations. New York: Scott, Foresman.

———(1984) Normal Accidents. New York: Basic Books.

PERRUCCI, R., R. ANDERSON, D. SCHENDEL, and L. TRACTMAN (1980) "'Whistle-blowing': professionals' resistance to organizational authority." Social Problems 28: 149-164.

PERRY, D. and T. MAHONEY (1955) "In-plant communications and employee morale." Personnel Psychology 8: 339-353.

PETERS, R. (1950) Communication Within Industry. New York: Harper & Row.

PETERS, T. and R. WATERMAN, Jr. (1982) In Search of Excellence: Lessons from America's Best-Run Companies. New York: Harper & Row.

PETERSON, R. (1976) "The production of culture: a prolegomenon." American Behavioral Scientist 19: 669-684.

———(1979) "Revitalizing the culture concept," pp. 137-166 in A. Inkeles et al. (eds.) Annual Review of Sociology, Vol. 5. Palo Alto, CA: Annual Reviews.

———and C. BERGER (1975) "Cycles in symbol production: the case of popular music." American Sociological Review 40: 158-173.

PETTIGREW, A. (1972) "Information control as a power resource." Sociology 6: 187-204.

———(1973) The Politics of Organizational Decision Making. London: Tavistock.

PFEFFER, J. (1978) Organizational Design. Arlington Heights, IL: AHM.

———(1981) Power in Organizations. Marshfield, MA: Pitman.

———(1982) "Management as symbolic action," in L. Cummings and B. Staw (eds.) Research in Organizational Behavior, Vol. 3. Greenwich, CT: JAI.

———and H. LEBLEBICI (1977) "Information technology and organizational structure." Pacific Sociological Review 20: 241-261.

PFEFFER, J. and G. SALANCIK (1977) "Administrator effectiveness: the effects of advocacy and information on achieving outcomes in an organizational context." Human Relations 30: 641-656.

———(1978) The External Control of Organizations. New York: Harper & Row.

PHEYSEY, D. and R. PAYNE (1970) "The Hemphill group dimensions description questionnaire: a British industrial application." Human Relations 23: 473-497.

PHILLIPS, A. (1908) Effective Speaking. Chicago: Newton.

PHILLIPS, D. C. (1955) Oral Communication in Business. New York: McGraw-Hill.

————(1976) Holistic Thought in Social Science. Stanford, CA: Stanford University Press.

PIERSOL, D. (1980) Personal communication.

————(1955) "A case study of oral communication practices of foremen and assistant foremen in a mid-western corporation." Ph.D. dissertation, Purdue University.

PIGORS, P. (1949) Effective Communication in Industry. New York: National Association of Manufacturers.

PLANTY, E. and W. MACHAVER (1952) "Upward communications: a project in executive development." Personnel 28: 304-318.

POLANYI, M. (1966) The Tacit Dimension. Garden City, NY: Doubleday.

PONDY, L., P. FROST, G. MORGAN, and T. DANDRIDGE. [eds.] (1983) Organizational Symbolism. Greenwich, CT: JAI.

POOLE, M. S. and R. D. McPHEE (1983) "A structurational theory of organizational climate," in L. Putnam and M. Pacanowsky (eds.) Organizational Communication: An Interpretive Approach. Beverly Hills, CA: Sage.

POOLE, M. S., D. SEIBOLD, and R. McPHEE (1982) "A structurational theory of group decision-making." Presented at the Pennsylvania State University Conference on Group Communication Research.

PORTER, L. and E. LAWLER (1965) "Perceptions of organizational structure in relation to job attitudes and job behavior." Psychological Bulletin 64: 23-51.

PORTER, L. and K. ROBERTS (1976) "Communications in organizations," in M. Dunnette (ed.) Handbook of Industrial and Organizational Psychology. Chicago: Rand McNally.

PORTER, L., R. ALLEN, and H. ANGLE (1981) "The politics of upward influence in organizations," in B. Staw and L. Cummings (eds.) Research in Organizational Behavior, Vol. 3. Greenwich, CT: JAI.

PORTER, L., R. STEERS, T. MOWDAY, and P. BOULIAN (1974) "Organizational commitment, job satisfaction, and turnover among psychiatric technicals." Journal of Applied Psychology 59: 603-609.

POWDERMAKER, H. (1950) Hollywood: The Dream Factory. Boston: Little, Brown.

POWELL, G. and D. BUTTERFIELD (1978) "The case for subsystem climates in organizations." Academy of Management Review 3: 151-157.

POWLISON, K. (1947) "Explaining the facts to employees." Harvard Business Review 25 (Winter): 145-157.

PRESTHUS, R. (1960) The Organizational Society. New York: Vintage.

PRITCHARD, R. and B. KARASICK (1973) "The effects of organizational climate on managerial job performance and job satisfaction." Organizational Behavior and Human Performance 9: 126-146.

PROTHRO, J. (1969) The Dollar Decade—Business Ideas in the 1920s. New York: Greenwood Reprint.

PRUITT, D. (1971) "Indirect communication and the search for agreement in negotiation." Journal of Applied Social Psychology 1: 205-239.

————and S. LEWIS (1975) "Development of integrative solutions in bilateral negotiations." Journal of Personality and Social Psychology 31: 621-633.

PUGH, D., D. HICKSON, C. HININGS, and C. TURNER (1968) "The dimensions of organizational structure." Administrative Science Quarterly 13: 65-91.

PUTNAM, L. (1983) "The interpretive perspective: an alternative to functionalism," in L. Putnam and M. Pacanowsky (eds.) Communication and Organizations: An Interpretive Approach. Beverly Hills, CA: Sage.

———(1984) "Bargaining as task and process: multiple functions of interaction sequences," in R. Street and J. Cappella (eds.) Sequence and Pattern in Communicative Behavior. London: Edward Arnold.

———and C. BULLIS (1983) "Order and mystery in negotiation groups." Presented at the annual convention of the Eastern Communication Association, Ocean City, MD.

———(1984) "Intergroup relations and issue redefinition in teachers' bargaining." Presented at the annual convention of the International Communication Association, San Francisco.

PUTNAM, L. and P. GEIST (1985) "Argument in bargaining: an analysis of the reasoning process." Southern Speech Communication Journal 50: 225-245.

PUTNAM, L. and T. JONES (1982a) "Reciprocity in negotiations: an analysis of bargaining interaction." Communication Monographs 49: 171-191.

———(1982b) "The role of communication in bargaining." Human Communication Research 8: 262-280.

PUTNAM, L. and M. PACANOWSKY [eds.] (1983) Communication and Organizations: An Interpretive Approach. Beverly Hills, CA: Sage.

QUINN, J. (1980) Strategies for Change. Homewood, IL: Irwin.

RANSON, S., R. HININGS, and R. GREENWOOD (1980) "The structuring of organizational structures." Administrative Science Quarterly 25: 1-17.

RAPOPORT, A. (1964) Strategy and Conscience. New York: Harper & Row.

RAVEN, B. and A. KRUGLANSKI (1970) "Power and conflict," in P. Swingle (ed.) The Structure of Conflict. New York: Academic.

READ, W. (1962) "Upward communication in industrial hierarchies." Human Relations 15: 3-16.

REDDING, W. C. (1960) "Curricula—trends and unmet needs." Presented at the annual convention of the Central States Speech Association, Chicago.

———(1972) Communication Within the Organization: An Interpretative Review of Theory and Research. New York: Industrial Communication Council.

———(1977) "Business and professional speaking: corpse, ghost, or angel?" Presented at the annual convention of the Speech Communication Association, Washington, D.C.

———(1979) Organizational communication theory and ideology: an overview," in D. Nimmo (ed.) Communication Yearbook 3. New Brunswick, NJ: Transaction.

———(1984) The Corporate Manager's Guide to Better Communication. Glenview, IL: Scott, Foresman.

———and G. SANBORN [eds.] (1964) Business and Industrial Communication: A Source Book. New York: Harper & Row.

REDFIELD, C. (1953) Communication in Management: A Guide to Administrative Communication. Chicago: University of Chicago Press.

———(1958) Communication in Management (rev. ed.). Chicago: University of Chicago Press.

REICH, R. (1983) "The next American frontier." Atlantic Monthly (March): 43-58.

RESNIHOFF, H. (1980) "Information systems theory and research: an overview of the societal significance of information science," in D. Nimmo (ed.) Communication Yearbook 3. New Brunswick, NJ: Transaction.

RHEINGOLD, H. (1983) "Our machine Friday." Psychology Today (December): 33.

RICE, R. and W. RICHARDS (1985) "Network analysis methods," in B. Dervin (ed.) Advances in Communication Research, Vol. 6. Norwood, NJ: Ablex.

RICHARDS, I. A. (1936) The Philosophy of Rhetoric. New York: Oxford University Press.

RICHARDS, W. (1979) "Measurement problems in network analysis: reciprocity and directed relationships." Presented at the annual convention of the International Communication Association, Philadelphia.

RICHETTO, G. M. [ed.] (1967) Conference on Organizational Communication: August 8-11, 1967. Huntsville, AL: NASA.

RILEY, L. (1980) Article in Emmy Magazine (Spring): 34.

RILEY, P. (1983) "A structurationist account of political culture." Administrative Science Quarterly 28: 414-437.

RITZER, G. and H. TRICE (1969) "An empirical test of Howard Becker's side-bet theory." Social Forces 47: 475-478.

ROBERTS, K. and L. GALLOWAY (in press) Managing Organizations. Boston: Pitman.

ROBERTS, K. and W. GLICK (1981) "The job characteristics approach to task design: a critical review." Journal of Applied Psychology 66: 193-217.

ROBERTS, K. and C. O'REILLY (1974) "Measuring organizational communication." Journal of Applied Psychology 59: 321-326.

ROBERTS, K., C. HULIN, and D. ROUSSEAU (1974) "Failures in upward communication: Three possible culprits." Academy of Management Journal 17: 205-215.

ROBERTSON, R. and B. HOLZNER (1979) "Introduction," in R. Robertson and B. Holzner (eds.) Identity and Authority: Exploration in the Theory of Society. New York: St. Martin's.

ROETHLISBERGER, F. J. (1941) Management and Morale. Cambridge, MA: Harvard University Press.

———(1945) "The foreman: master and victim of double talk." Harvard Business Review 23 (Spring): 283-298.

———(1948) "Human relations: rare, medium, or well-done?" Harvard Business Review 26 (January): 89-107.

———(1953) "The administrator's skill: communication." Harvard Business Review 31 November/December): 55-62.

———and W. DICKSON (1939) Management and the Worker. New York: John Wiley.

ROGERS, C. and F. ROETHLISBERGER (1952) "Barriers and gateways to communication." Harvard Business Review 30, 2: 46-52.

ROGERS, E. and L. KINCAID (1982) Communication Networks. New York: Basic Books.

RONKEN, H. and P. LAWRENCE (1952) Administering Changes: A Case Study of Human Relations in a Factory. Boston: Harvard University, Division of Research, Graduate School of Business Administration.

ROOS, L. and R. HALL (1980) "Influence diagrams and organizational power." Administrative Science Quarterly 25: 57-71.

ROSS, R. (1954) "A case study of communication breakdowns in the General Telephone Company of Indiana, Inc." Ph.D. dissertation, Purdue University.

ROTONDI, T., Jr. (1975a) "Organizational identification and group involvement." Academy of Management Journal 18: 892-897.

———(1975b) "Organizational identification: issues and implications." Organizational Behavior and Human Performance 13: 95-109.

———(1976) "Identification, personality needs, and managerial position." Human Relations 29: 507-515.

ROY, D. (1960) " 'Banana time': job satisfaction and informal interaction." Human Organization 18: 158-168.

RUBIN, J. and B. BROWN (1975) The Social Psychology of Bargaining and Negotiation. New York: Academic.

RUESCH, J. and G. BATESON (1968) Communication. New York: Norton.

SAINE, T. (1974) "Perceiving communication conflict." Speech Monographs 41: 49-56.

SALAMAN, G. (1979) Work Organizations: Resistance and Control. London: Longman.

———(1981) Class and the Corporation. Glasgow: Fontana.

SALANCIK, G. (1977) "Commitment and the control of organizational behavior and belief," in B. Staw (ed.) New Directions in Organizational Behavior. Chicago: St. Clair.

SALEH, S. and J. HOSEK (1976) "Job involvement: concepts and measurements." Academy of Management Journal 19: 213-224.

SAMPUGNARO, V. (1984) Network Message Content as a Predictor of Organizational Commitment. Master's thesis, Purdue University.

SANBORN, G. (1964) "Communication in business: an overview," in W. C. Redding and G. Sanborn (eds.) Business and Industrial Communication. New York: Harper & Row.

SANDFORD, W. and W. H. YEAGER (1929) Business and Professional Speaking. New York: McGraw-Hill.

———(1952) Practical Business Speaking. New York: McGraw-Hill.

SANFORD, N. (1955) "The dynamics of identification." Psychological Review 62: 102-118.

SAUNDERS, D. (1981) "Management information systems, communications, and departmental power: an integrative model." Academy of Management Review 6: 431-442.

SAVAGE, G. (1984) "Decision making as negotiation: a comparison of two labor-management committees." Presented at the annual convention of the International Communication Association, San Francisco.

——— and R. ROMANO (1983) "E-quality in the workplace: quality circles or quality of working life programs in the U.S." Presented at the annual convention of the Eastern Communication Association, Ocean City, MD.

SCHEFF, T. (1967) "Toward a sociological model of consensus." American Sociological Review 32: 32-46.

SCHEIN, E. (1968) "Organizational socialization and the profession of management." Industrial Management Review 9: 1-15.

SCHELLING, T. (1960) The Strategy of Conflict. Cambridge: Harvard University Press.

———(1978) Micromotives and Macrobehavior. New York: Norton.

SCHILLER, D. (1981) Objectivity and the News. Philadelphia: University of Pennsylvania Press.

SCHNEIDER, A., W. DONAGHY, and P. NEWMAN (1976) "Communication climate within an organization." Management Controls 23: 159-162.

SCHNEIDER, B. (1975) "Organizational climates: an essay." Personnel Psychology 28: 447-479.

————and C. BARTLETT (1968) "Individual differences and organizational climate, I: the research plan and questionnaire development." *Personnel Psychology* 21: 323-333.

SCHNEIDER, B. and D. HALL (1973) "Toward specifying the concept of work climate: a study of Roman Catholic diocesan priests." *Journal of Applied Psychology* 56: 447-455.

————and H. NYGREN (1971) "Self-image and job characteristics as correlates of changing organizational identification." *Human Relations* 24: 397-416.

SCHNEIDER, B., J. PARKINGTON, and V. BUXTON (1980) "Employee and customer perception of service in banks." *Administrative Science Quarterly* 25: 252-267.

SCHNEIDER, B. and A. REICHERS (1983) "On the etiology of climates." *Personnel Psychology* 36: 19-39.

SCHNEIDER, B. and R. SNYDER (1975) "Some relationships between job satisfaction and organizational climate." *Journal of Applied Psychology* 60: 318-328.

SCHRAGE, M. (1983) "Our phones will soon be more intelligent than us." *Washington Post* (reprinted in Daily Californian, December 15, p. 10).

SCHUDNAR, M. (1978) Discovering the News. New York: Basic Books.

SCHUTTE, W. M. and E. R. STEINBERG (1960) Communication in Business and Industry. New York: Holt, Rinehart & Winston.

SCHWARTZ, D. F. (1968) "Liaison communication roles in a formal organization." Ph.D. dissertation, Michigan State University.

————and E. JACOBSON (1977) "Organizational communication network analysis: the liaison communication role." *Organizational Behavior and Human Performance* 18: 158-174.

SCHWARTZ, M., H. STARK, and H. SCHIFFMAN (1970) "Responses of union and management leaders to emotionally-toned industrial relations terms." *Personnel Psychology* 23: 361-367.

Science Research Associates (1966) S.R.A. Attitude Survey. Chicago: Author.

SCOTT, W. G. and D. HART (1979) Organizational America. Boston: Houghton Mifflin.

SCOTT, W. R. (1981) Organizations: Rational, Natural, and Open Systems. Englewood Cliffs, NJ: Prentice-Hall.

SEARS, R. (1957) "Identification as a form of behavior development," in D. Harris (ed.) The Concept of Development. Minneapolis: University of Minnesota Press.

SELEKMAN, B. M. (1947) Labor Relations and Human Relations. New York: McGraw-Hill.

SELLS, S. (1963) "An interactionist looks at the environment." *American Psychologist* 18: 696-702.

SEXTON, R. and V. STAUDT (1957) "The clinic approach to business communication." *Journal of Psychology* 44: 109-110.

————(1959) "Business communication: a survey of the literature." *Journal of Social Psychology* 50: 101-118.

SHANNON, C. E. and W. WEAVER (1949) Mathematical Theory of Communication. Urbana: University of Illinois Press.

SHAW, M. (1964) "Communication networks," in L. Berkowitz (ed.) Advances in Experimental Social Psychology. Reading, MA: Addison-Wesley.

SHELDON, M. E. (1971) "Investments and involvements as mechanisms producing organizational commitment." *Administrative Science Quarterly* 16: 143-150.

SHERIF, M. and H. CANTRIL (1947) The Psychology of Ego-Involvements. New York: John Wiley.

SILVERMAN, D. and J. JONES (1976) Organizational Work. London: Collier-Macmillan.

SIMON, H. A. (1945a) Administrative Behavior. New York: Free Press.

———(1945b) "The fine art of issuing orders." Public Management 27: 206-208.

———(1976) Administrative Behavior (3rd ed.). New York: Free Press.

———(1977) The New Science of Management Decision. Englewood Cliffs, NJ: Prentice-Hall.

———(1981) Personal communication.

SIMS, H. and W. LAFOLLETTE (1975) "An assessment of the Litwin and Stringer organizational climate questionnaire." Personnel Psychology 28: 19-38.

SINCLAIR, J. (1983) "The hardware of the brain." Psychology Today (December): 80.

SINCOFF, M., J. PACILIO, S. BLATT, G. HUNT, and P. ANTON "Organizational communication: perspectives and prospects." Ohio Speech Journal 13: 3-18.

SKLAR, R. (1981) Media Made America. New York: Random House.

SLOBIN, D., S. MILLER, and L. PORTER (1968) "Forms of address and social relations in a business organization." Journal of Personality and Social Psychology 8: 449-468.

SLOVIC, P., B. FISCHOFF, and S. LICHTENSTEIN (1977) "Behavior decision theory," pp. 1-39 in M. Risenzweig and L. Porter (eds.) Annual Review of Psychology, Vol. 28. Palo Alto, CA: Annual Reviews.

SMELSER, N. (1962) Theory of Collective Behavior. New York: Free Press.

SMITH, D. (1969) "Communication and negotiation outcome." Journal of Communication 19: 248-256.

———(1971) "Communication, minimum disposition, and negotiation," in H. Pepinsky and M. Patton (eds.) The Psychological Experiment: A Practical Accomplishment. New York: Pergamon.

SMITH, P., L. KENDALL, and C. HULIN (1969) The Measurement of Satisfaction in Work and Retirement: A Strategy for the Study of Attitudes. Chicago: Rand McNally.

SOTIRIN, P. (1984) "Organizational culture—a focus on contemporary theory/research in organizational communication." Presented at the annual convention of the Speech Communication Association, Chicago.

STAW, B. and G. OLDHAM (1978) "Reconsidering our dependent variables: a critique and empirical study." Academy of Management Journal 21: 539-559.

STEBBINS, R. (1972) "A theory of jazz community," in C. Nanry (ed.) American Music: From Storyville to Woodstock. East Brunswick, NJ: Transaction.

STEERS, R. (1977) "Antecedents and outcomes of organizational commitment." Administrative Science Quarterly 22: 46-56.

———(1984) Introduction to Organizational Behavior. Glenview, IL: Scott, Foresman.

STEINFATT, T., D. SEIBOLD, and J. FRYE (1974) "Communication in game simulated conflicts: two experiments." Speech Monographs 41: 24-35.

STEPHENSON, G., B. KNIVETON, and I. MORLEY (1977) "An interaction analysis of an industrial wage negotiation." Journal of Occupational Psychology 50: 231-241.

STERN, G. (1970) People in Context: Measuring Person-Environment Congruence in Education and Industry. New York: John Wiley.

STINCHCOMBE, A. (1959) "Bureaucratic and craft administration of production." Administrative Science Quarterly 4: 168-187.

STOHL, C. (1984) "Quality circles and the quality of communication." Transactions, International Association of Quality Circles: 157-162.

STOKE, S. (1950) "An inquiry into the concept of identification." Journal of Genetic Psychology 76: 163-189.

STOREY, J. (1983) Managerial Prerogative and the Question of Control. London: Routledge & Kegan Paul.

STOTLAND, E. and R. DUNN (1962) "Identification, 'oppositeness,' authoritarianism, self-esteem, and birth order." Psychological Monographs 76 (Whole No. 528): 1-21.

STOTLAND, E. and M. HILLMER (1962) "Identification, authoritarian defensiveness, and self-esteem." Journal of Abnormal and Social Psychology 64: 334-342.

STOTLAND, E. and M. PATCHEN (1961) "Identification and changes in prejudice and authoritarianism." Journal of Abnormal and Social Psychology 62: 265-274.

STRAUSS, A. (1978) Negotiations: Varieties, Contexts, Processes, and Social Order. San Francisco: Jossey-Bass.

———L. SCHATZMAN, R. BUCHER, D. EHRLICH, and M. SABSHIN (1964) Psychiatric Ideologies and Institutions. New York: Free Press.

STRAUSS, G. (1977) "The study of conflict: hope for a new synthesis between industrial relations and organizational behavior." Proceedings of the 29th Annual Meeting of the Industrial Relations Research Association.

———(1979) "Can social psychology contribute to industrial relations?" in G. Stephenson and C. Brotherton (eds.) Industrial Relations: A Social Psychological Approach. New York: John Wiley.

———(1982) "Bridging the gap between industrial relations and conflict management: an introduction," in G. Strauss (ed.) Conflict Management and Industrial Relations. Kluwer: Nijhoff.

SUTTON, H. and L. PORTER (1968) "A study of the grapevine in governmental organizations." Personnel Psychology 21: 223-230.

SWANSON, D. and J. DELIA (1976) MODCOM: The Nature of Human Communication. Palo Alto, CA: Science Research Associates.

TAGIURI, R. (1968) "The concept of organizational climate," in R. Taqiuri and G. Litwin (eds.) Organizational Climate: Explorations of a Concept. Cambridge, MA: Harvard Business School, Division of Research.

TAJFEL, H. and J. TURNER (1979) "An integrative theory of intergroup conflict," in W. Austin and S. Worchel (eds.) The Social Psychology of Intergroup Relations. Monterey, CA: Brooks/Cole.

TANNENBAUM, A. (1968) Control and Organizations. New York: McGraw-Hill.

TANNENBAUM, R. and W. H. SCHMIDT (1958) "How to choose a leadership pattern." Harvard Business Review 36 (March/April): 95-101.

TATUM, G. L., Jr. (1954) "Communication in the sales training program of IBM Corporation." Ph.D. dissertation, Northwestern University.

TAYLOR, F. (1903) Shop Management. New York: Harper & Row.

TAYLOR, J. and D. BOWERS (1970) The Survey of Organizations. Ann Arbor, MI: Institute for Social Research.

TEDESCHI, J. (1970) "Threats and promises," in P. Swingle (ed.) The Structure of Conflict. New York: Academic.

THAYER, L. G. (1961) Administrative Communication. Homewood, IL: Irwin.

THIBAUT, J. and H. KELLEY (1959) The Social Psychology of Groups. New York: John Wiley.

THOMPSON, J. (1967) Organization in Action. New York: McGraw-Hill.

THOMPSON, K. (1980) "Organizations as constructors of social reality (I)," in G. Salaman and K. Thompson (eds.) Control and Ideology in Organizations. Cambridge: MIT Press.

TICHENOR, P., G. DONAHUE, and C. OLIEN (1980) Community Conflict and the Press. Beverly Hills, CA: Sage.

TICHY, N., M. TUSHMAN, and C. FOMBRUN (1979) "Social network analysis for organizations." Academy of Management Review 4: 507-519.

TOLMAN, E. (1943) "Identification and the post-war world." Journal of Abnormal and Social Psychology 38: 141-148.

TOMPKINS, P. (1962) "An analysis of communication between headquarters and selected units of a national labor union." Ph.D. dissertation, Purdue University.

————(1965) "General semantics and 'human relations.'" Central States Speech Journal 16: 285-289.

————(1967) "Organizational communication: a state-of-the-art review," pp. 4-26 in G. M. Richetto (ed.) Conference on Organizational Communication, August 8-11, 1967. Huntsville, AL: NASA.

————(1978) "Conceptual issues in organizational communication." Presented at the annual convention of the Speech Communication Association, Minneapolis, MN.

————(1983) "On the desirability of an interpretive science of organizational communication." Presented at the annual convention of the Speech Communication Association, Washington, D.C.

————(1984) "The functions of communication in organizations," in C. Arnold and J. Bowfers (eds.) Handbook of Rhetorical and Communication Theory. New York: Allyn & Bacon.

————(1985) "On hegemony—'He gave it no name'—and critical structuralism in the work of Kenneth Burke." Quarterly Journal of Speech 71: 119-131.

TOMPKINS, P. and G. CHENEY (1982) "Toward a theory of unobtrusive control in contemporary organizations." Presented at the annual convention of the Speech Communication Association, Louisville, KY.

————(1983) "Account analysis of organizations: decision making and identification," in L. Putnam and M. Pacanowsky (eds.) Communication and Organizations: An Interpretive Approach. Beverly Hills, CA: Sage.

TOMPKINS, P. and M. LAMPERT (1980) "Conspiracies, corporations, communication." Presented at the annual convention of the Speech Communication Association, New York.

TOMPKINS, P. and W. C. REDDING (forthcoming) "The study of organizational communication: historical perspectives," in G. Goldhaber (ed.) Handbook of Organizational Communication. Norwood, NJ: Ablex.

TOMPKINS, P., J. FISHER, D. INFANTE, and E. TOMPKINS (1975) "Kenneth Burke and the inherent characteristics of formal organizations: a field study." Speech Monographs 42: 135-142.

TUCHMAN, G. (1972) "Making news by doing work: routinizing the unexpected." American Journal of Sociology 77: 660-679.

————(1974) "Introduction," in G. Tuchman (ed.) The TV Establishment. Englewood Cliffs, NJ: Prentice-Hall.

————(1978) Making News. New York: Free Press.

————(1983) "Consciousness industries and the production of culture." Journal of Communication 33: 330-341.

TUCKER, R. [ed.] (1972) Marx and Engels: A Reader. New York: Norton.
——(1977) The Marxian Revolutionary Idea. New York: Norton.
TUGGLE, F. (1978) Organizational Processes. Arlington Heights, IL: AHM.
TUROW, J. (1984) Media Industries: The Production of News and Entertainment. New York: Longman.
TUSHMAN, M. (1979) "Work characteristics and subunit communication structure: a contingency analysis." Administrative Science Quarterly 24: 82-98.
——and D. NADLER (1978) "Information processing as an integrating concept in organizational design." Academy of Management Review 3: 613-624.
——(1980) "Communication structure and communication roles in R & D laboratories." TIMS Studies in the Management Sciences 15: 91-112.
TUSHMAN, M. and T. SCANLON (1981) "Boundary scanning individuals: their role in information transfer and their antecedents." Academy of Management Journal 24: 289-305.
UDELL, J. (1967) "An empirical test of hypotheses relating to span of control." Administrative Science Quarterly 12: 430-439.
VAN de VEN, A., A. DELBECQ, and R. KOENIG (1976) "Determinants of coordination modes within organizations." Administrative Science Quarterly 41: 322-338.
VAN MAANEN, J. (1975) "Police socialization: a longitudinal examination of job attitudes in an urban police department." Administrative Science Quarterly 20: 207-228.
VON NEUMANN, J. and O. MORGENSTERN (1944) Theory of Games and Economic Behavior. Princeton, NJ: Princeton University Press.
VOOS, H. (1967) Organizational Communication: A Bibliography. New Brunswick, NJ: Rutgers University Press.
VROOM, V. (1964) Motivation and Work Behavior. New York: John Wiley.
WALKER, C. R. and R. H. GUEST (1952) The Man on the Assembly Line. Cambridge, MA: Harvard University Press.
——and A. N. TURNER (1956) The Foreman on the Assembly Line. Cambridge, MA: Harvard University Press.
WALKER, P. (1979) Between Capital and Labor. Boston: South End.
WALL, J. (1981) "Mediations: an analysis, review, and proposed research." Journal of Conflict Resolution 25: 157-180.
WALLACE, M., J. IVANCEVICH, and H. LYON (1975) "Measurement modifications for assessing organizational climate in hospitals." Academy of Management Journal 18: 82-97.
WALTON, R. (1982) "New perspectives on the world of work." Human Relations 35: 1073-1084.
——and R. McKERSIE (1965) A Behavioral Theory of Labor Negotiations. New York: McGraw-Hill.
War Manpower Commission (1945) The Training Within Industry Report. Washington, DC: Government Printing Office.
WARNER, W. L. and J. O. LOW (1947) The Social System of the Modern Factory. New Haven, CT: Yale University Press.
WATSON, D. (1965) "Effects of certain power structures on communication in task oriented groups." Sociometry 28: 322-336.
——and B. BROMBERG (1965) "Power, communication, and position satisfaction in task-oriented groups." Journal of Personality and Social Psychology 2: 859-869.

WATZLAWICK, P., J. BEAVIN, and D. JACKSON (1967) Pragmatics of Human Communication. New York: Norton.

WEAVER, C. (1958) "The quantification of the frame of reference in labor-management communication." Journal of Applied Psychology 42: 1-9.

———(1977) "A history of the International Communication Association," pp. 607-618 in B. D. Ruben (ed.) Communication Yearbook 1. New Brunswick, NJ: Transaction.

WEBER, M. (1947) The Theory of Social and Economic Organization. New York: Free Press.

———(1964) Methodology of the Social Sciences. New York: Free Press.

———(1976) "Towards a sociology of the press." Journal of Communication 26: 96-100. (Originally published in 1910)

———(1978) in G. Roth and K. Wittich (eds.) Economy and Society. Berkeley: University of California Press.

WEEKS, D. (1980) "Organizations and decision making," in G. Salaman and K. Thompson (eds.) Control and Ideology in Organizations. Cambridge: MIT Press.

WEICK, K. (1969) The Social Psychology of Organizing. Reading, MA: Addison-Wesley.

———(1979) The Social Psychology of Organizing (2nd ed.). Reading, MA: Addison-Wesley.

WEINBERG, A., L. ULLMAN, W. RICHARDS, and P. COOPER (1980) "Informal advice and information seeking between physicians." Journal of Medical Education.

WEINER, Y. and Y. WARDI (1980) "Relationships between job, organization, and career commitments and work outcomes—an integrative approach." Organizational Behavior and Human Performance 26: 81-96.

WEISS, R. S. (1956) Processes of Organization. Ann Arbor: University of Michigan, Institute for Social Research.

WEISS, R. W. and E. H. JACOBSON (1955) "Method for the analysis of the structure of complex organizations." American Sociological Review 20: 661-668.

WEXLEY, K. (1982) "The performance appraisal interview." Presented at Johns Hopkins University 4th National Symposium for Educational Research, Performance Appraisal: The State of the Art, Washington, D.C.

WHITESIDE, T. (1981) The Blockbuster Complex. Middletown, CT: Wesleyan University Press.

WHITING, R. (1964) "Historical search in human relations." Academy of Management Journal : 46-53.

WHITNEY, D.C. (1982) "Mass communicator studies: similarity, difference, and level of analysis," in J. Ettema and D. C. Whitney (eds.) Individuals in Mass Media Organizations. Beverly Hills, CA: Sage.

WHYTE, W. F. (1948) Human Relations in the Restaurant Industry. New York: McGraw-Hill.

———(1949) "Semantics and industrial relations." Human Organization 8: 4-10.

———(1961) Men at Work. Homewood, IL: Irwin-Dorsey.

WHYTE, W. H., Jr. [ed.] (1952) Is Anybody Listening? New York: Simon & Schuster.

———(1956) The Organization Man. New York: Simon & Schuster.

WIKSELL, W. (1960) Do They Understand You? A Guide to Effective Oral Communication. New York: Macmillan.

WILLIAMS, R. (1973) "Base and superstructure in Marxist cultural theory." New Left Review 82.

WILLIAMSON, O. (1970) Corporate Control and Business Behavior. Englewood Cliffs, NJ: Prentice-Hall.

WILLIS, P. (1977) Learning to Labor. New York: Columbia University Press.

WILSON, C. (1983) "Organizational decision making: a tactic for socialization." Presented at the annual convention of the Speech Communication Association, Washington, D.C.

WINCH, R. (1962) Identification and Its Familial Determinants. Indianapolis: Bobbs-Merrill.

WITTGENSTEIN, L. (1953) Philosophical Investigations. London: Basil Blackwell.

WOFFORD, J. C., E. A. GERLOFF, and R. C. CUMMINS (1977) Organizational Communication: The Keystone to Managerial Effectiveness. New York: McGraw-Hill.

WOLFF, J. (1983) The Social Production of Art. New York: Columbia University Press.

WOODMAN, R. and D. KING (1978) "Organizational climate: science or folklore?" Academy of Management Review 3: 816-826.

WYLLIE, I. (1954) The Self-Made Man in America. New York: Free Press.

YUKL, G. and K. WEXLEY [eds.] (1971) Readings in Industrial and Organizational Psychology. New York: Oxford University Press.

ZALEZNIK, A. (1970) "Power and politics in organizational life." Harvard Business Review (May/June).

ZANDER, A., E. STOTLAND, and D. WOLFE (1960) "Unity of group, identification with group, and self-esteem of members." Journal of Personality 28: 463-478.

ZEITZ, G. (1983) "Structural and individual determinants of organizational morale and satisfaction." Social Forces 61: 1088-1108.

ZELKO, H. P. (1951) "Adult speech training: challenge to the speech profession." Quarterly Journal of Speech 37: 55-62.

———(1954) "Conference management: beware of the gimmicks." Advanced Management 19: 12-17.

———(1956) "How effective are your company communications?" Advanced Management 21, 2.

———and H. O'BRIEN (1957) Management-Employee Communication in Action. Cleveland: Howard Allen.

ZERUBAVEL, E. (1979) Patterns of Time in Hospital Life: A Sociological Perspective. Chicago: University of Chicago Press.

ZIMMERMAN, D. (1970) "The practicalities of rule use," in J. Douglas (ed.) Understanding Everyday Life. Chicago: Aldine.

ZOHAR, D. (1980) "Safety climate in industrial organizations: theoretical and applied implications." Journal of Applied Psychology 65: 96-102.

ABOUT THE CONTRIBUTORS

REBECCA BLAIR is a doctoral student in organizational behavior and industrial relations at the Graduate School of Business, University of California, Berkeley. She received her Master's degree in business administration from the University of California, Irvine. Her current research interests include communication and information processing, and executive career movement and development. Her work includes a study of women in management, published in the *California Management Review.*

GEORGE CHENEY is Assistant Professor in Speech Communication at the University of Illinois, Urbana-Champaign. He received a B.A. in Psychology from Youngstown State University in 1980, and an M.A. and Ph.D. in Communication from Purdue University in 1982 and 1985, respectively. Cheney is interested in a range of organizational phenomena, particularly how individual action is linked to the larger social order. Along with Phillip Tompkins, Cheney explores rhetorical-critical approaches to communication studies. Cheney has coauthored numerous book chapters, and has published in journals such as the *Quarterly Journal of Speech, Communication Monographs,* the *Central States Speech Journal,* and *Communication Quarterly.*

CHARLES CONRAD is Assistant Professor of Speech Communication at the University of North Carolina, Chapel Hill. His primary research interests involve the interrelations between power and symbolic processes in social collectives. His recently published *Strategic Organizational Communication* draws on rhetorical theory to develop a perspective for understanding organizational culture. He currently is engaged in a long-term study of the communicative processes of religious orders, particularly those involved in political action. He received his doctorate in Speech Communication from Kansas University in 1980.

ROBERT D. McPHEE is Associate Professor of Communication at the University of Wisconsin-Milwaukee. His primary scholarly interests include social and communication theory, communicative conditions of organizational work and formal structure, interaction and decision making in small groups, and research methods. He has authored or coauthored a number of articles published in such journals as *Communication Monographs, Human Communication Research,* the *Quarterly Journal of Speech,* and *Communication Research;* he also coauthored an overview article on mathematical modeling in communication, published in the *Communication Yearbook,* which was recognized in a special convention program of the Information Systems division of the International Communication Association. McPhee also coedited *Message-Attitude-Behavior Relationship: Theory, Methodology, and Applications* (1980). He is currently engaged in a program of research on vertically linked communicative relationships in hierarchies. He received his doctorate in Communication from Michigan State University in 1978.

PAMELA McKECHNIE is a doctoral student in organizational behavior and industrial relations at the Graduate School of Business, University of California, Berkeley. She is currently completing her dissertation on the social psychology of creativity in organizations. Her other research interests include attitude-behavior consistency, personality and perception, and the consequences of dissatisfaction. Her work includes a study of the justification of organizational performance, published in the *Administrative Science Quarterly.*

MARSHALL SCOTT POOLE is Assistant Professor of Speech Communication at the University of Minnesota in Minneapolis. His research interests include group decision making, organizational communication, research methodology, and program planning. He is on the editorial boards of *Human Communication Research* and the *Journal of Applied Communication Research.* His writings have appeared in several journals, including *Communication Monographs, Human Communication Research, Academy of Management Review,* and *Small Group Research.* He is the co-author of a recent book, *Working Through Conflict.*

LINDA L. PUTNAM is Associate Professor of Communication at Purdue University. Her research interests include bargaining and negotiations, conflict management in groups and organizations, and the impact of groups in hierarchical structures. She has published numerous articles in such journals as *Communication Monographs, Human Communication Research,* and *Communication Yearbook.*

W. CHARLES REDDING is Professor Emeritus in the Department of Communication, Purdue University. For about 25 years he supervised the graduate program in organizational communication at Purdue, where he directed more than 40 Ph.D. dissertations between 1959 and 1982. He is a Past President and a Fellow of the International Communication Association, and recipient of the Elizabeth Andersch Award for Distinguished Scholarship and Teaching. His publications include *Communication Within the Organization* (1972).

WILLIAM D. RICHARDS, Jr. is Assistant Professor in the Department of Communication at Simon Fraser University in Vancouver, British Columbia. He received his B.A. from Michigan State and his Master's and Ph.D. in Communication Research from Stanford University. He is a member of the Laboratory for Computer and Communication Research and has been working in the area of communication network analysis since 1970. Dr. Richards has written a computer program, NEGOPY, which is being used in North America and Europe.

KARLENE H. ROBERTS is Professor of Business Administration, and Associate Dean of the Undergraduate School of Business, University of California, Berkeley. She has authored and coauthored numerous articles and book chapters on organizational communication. Dr. Roberts is currently engaged in research on communication and decision making in high-reliability organizations. High-reliability organizations are those in which, although the probability of error is low, the outcomes of error are unacceptable to the organization or to a larger society. Three-Mile Island and Union Carbide's Bhopal plant accident are examples of failures of such systems.

MARY RYAN is an instructor in the Department of Speech Communication at North Carolina State University. She is currently completing work on her Master's thesis on the New Right's ideology of the family. Other research interests include popular social movement and feminist theories of ideology.

PHILLIP K. TOMPKINS is Professor of Communication and Associate Dean of the School of Humanities, Social Science, and Education at Purdue University. He has published articles and essays in *Communication Monographs,* the *James Joyce Quarterly,* the *Purdue Alumnus, Esquire,* the *Quarterly Journal of Speech,* and other journals; his work has been cited in the *Psychological Bulletin,* the *American Historical Review,* and other journals in communication and related fields; his work has been reviewed in *Publizistik,* the *Administrative Science Quarterly,* the *Quarterly Journal of Speech,* and the popular press. He has written numerous book chapters, including the one on organizational communication in the *Handbook of Rhetorical and Communication Theory.* As a student at Purdue (Ph.D., 1962), he received a David Ross Fellowship. Tompkins was chairperson of the Department of Communication at SUNY—Albany, 1971-1980. Since returning to Purdue in 1980, he has directed a research program in organizational identification and decision making that is summarized in the chapter written for this volume with George Cheney. In 1983 he became a Fellow in Purdue's Center for Humanistic Studies. In addition to serving as coeditor of this *Annual Review* issue, he was editor of *Communication Monographs,* and is currently a member of the editorial board of the Purdue University Press. He is the author of *Organizational Communication: A State of the Art Review* (1967-1968), a monograph published by NASA; *Communication Crisis at Kent State: A Case Study* (1971), with Elaine Anderson (Tompkins); and *Communication as Action* (1982).

JOSEPH TUROW is an Associate Professor in the Department of Communication, Purdue University. He has written extensively on issues related to the institutional nature of mass media and is the author of three books, including *Entertainment, Education, and the Hard Sell: Three Decades of Network Television* and *Media Industries: The Production of News and Entertainment.*